Silas H. Durand

Hymn and Tune Book

for use in Old school or Primitive Baptist churches

Silas H. Durand

Hymn and Tune Book

for use in Old school or Primitive Baptist churches

ISBN/EAN: 9783337089924

Printed in Europe, USA, Canada, Australia, Japan

Cover: Foto ©Lupo / pixelio.de

More available books at **www.hansebooks.com**

HYMN AND TUNE BOOK

FOR USE IN

OLD SCHOOL OR PRIMITIVE BAPTIST CHURCHES

COMPILED BY

SILAS H. DURAND

AND

P. G. LESTER

LET THE INHABITANTS OF THE ROCK SING.—Isaiah 42: 11.

PUBLISHED BY

THE D. H. GOBLE PRINTING COMPANY

GREENFIELD, INDIANA

PREFACE.

IN response to many requests we have prepared this book to supply a need long felt in our churches. We hope our principal motive in the work has been a desire for the benefit of the Lord's people, and for his own declarative glory.

We have endeavored to select such hymns and tunes as are most commonly used in churches of our faith and order in all the different sections of the country.

In the selection of hymns our first care has been that every sentiment expressed should be in harmony with the truth of God, believing that "Christians should never sing what they do not believe to be true." We have also chosen those that express the common experience of the saints, and which breathe a spirit of praise and holy devotion to God, rather than such as appeal to the natural sympathies, regarding them as more suitable to the purpose for which this book is designed, which is, to be used in the meetings of the saints, whose only object in singing should be the worship of the true and living God in spirit and in truth.

In the association of hymns and tunes we have in some instances had respect to long use; in others we have determined the arrangement according to our own judgment, and the character of melody preferred in different localities.

Should any fail to find in this book some favorite hymn or tune, as may sometimes be the case, we hope they will find others equally desirable, and will remember the impossibility of an arrangement of so small a number that would contain the favorites of all.

We hope for the favorable consideration of our brethren, and humbly ask and hope that our own imperfect labors may be blessed of the Lord to his dear people.

SILAS H. DURAND.
P. G. LESTER.

Southampton, Bucks Co., Pa.: May, 1886.

Table of Contents.

	HYMNS.		HYMNS.
Perfections of God	1– 22	Humility	251–260
Creation and Providence	23– 30	Resignation	261–269
The Gospel	31– 49	Peace and Joy	270–278
The Incarnation of the Son of God	50– 59	Zeal	279–283
		Trust	284–300
Vital Unity of Christ and the Church	60– 72	Encouragement	301–317
		Preservation of the Saints to Glory	318–324
Election and Decrees of God	73– 84		
Covenant of Grace	85– 87	Rest	325–334
Redemption	88–105	Farewell	335–339
Righteousness	106–110	The Church	340–359
Character and Offices of Christ	111–128	Prayer	360–380
Priesthood of Christ	129–133	Praise	381–396
Revelation	134–136	The Christian	397–411
Government of Christ	137–141	Conflicts and Deliverances	412–436
Sufferings and Death of Christ	142–146	Christian Experience	437–459
Resurrection and Ascension of Christ	147–158	Baptism	460–474
		The Lord's Supper	475–488
Salvation	159–167	Before Preaching	489–494
Grace	168–181	After Preaching	495–501
The Holy Spirit	182–189	Washing the Saints' feet	502–507
Faith	190–201	Time and Eternity	508–516
Conversion	202–205	Death	517–539
Repentance	206–214	Resurrection	540–542
Hope	215–225	Heaven	543–559
Love	226–250	Miscellaneous	560–627

The figures in brackets show the number of the hymn in Beebe's Collection. Under the head of " Miscellaneous " will be found hymns not in that collection.

HYMN AND TUNE BOOK.

Perfections of God.

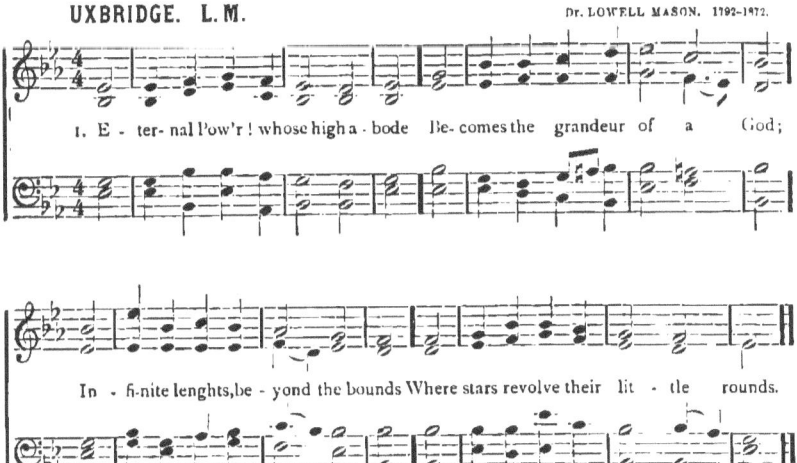

UXBRIDGE. L. M. — Dr. LOWELL MASON. 1792-1872.

1. E-ter-nal Pow'r! whose high a-bode Be-comes the grandeur of a God;
In-fi-nite lenghts, be-yond the bounds Where stars revolve their lit-tle rounds.

1 (1)

1 Eternal Power! whose high abode
Becomes the grandeur of a God;
Infinite lengths, beyond the bounds
Where stars revolve their little rounds.

2 The lowest step around thy seat,
Rises too high for Gabriel's feet;
In vain the favored angel tries
To reach thine height with wond'ring eyes.

3 Lord, what shall earth and ashes do!
We would adore our Maker, too;
From sin and dust to thee we cry,
The Great, the Holy, and the High!

4 Earth from afar has heard thy fame,
And worms have learned to lisp thy name;
But, O! the glories of thy mind
Leave all our soaring thoughts behind.

5 God is in heaven, but man below;
Be short our tunes; our words be few;
A sacred reverence checks our songs,
And praise sits silent on our tongues.

(1) Watts.

PERFECTIONS OF GOD.

LOVING KINDNESS. L. M.   WM. CALDWELL. 1830.

1. Awake, my soul, in joyful lays, And sing thy great Redeemer's praise; He justly claims a song from me! His loving kindness, O how free! His loving kindness, loving kindness, His loving kindness, O how free!

2 (20)

2 He saw me ruin'd in the fall,
Yet lov'd me notwithstanding all ;
He sav'd me from my lost estate ;
His loving kindness, O how great!

3 Though num'rous hosts of mighty foes,
Though earth and hell my way oppose,
He safely leads my soul along ;
His loving kindness, O how strong!

4 When trouble, like a gloomy cloud,
Has gather'd thick and thunder'd loud,
He near my soul has always stood ;
His loving kindness, O how good !

5 Often I feel my sinful heart
Prone from my Jesus to depart ;
But though I have him oft forgot,
His loving kindness changes not.

6 Soon shall I pass the gloomy vale,
Soon all my mortal powers must fail ;
O! may my last expiring breath
His loving kindness sing in death.

7 Then let me mount and soar away
To the bright world of endless day,
And sing, with rapture and surprise,
His loving kindness in the skies.

Medley.

3 (44)   L. M.

1 THE Lord, how wondrous are his ways!
How firm his truth! how large his grace!
He takes his mercy for his throne,
And thence he makes his glories known.

2 Not half so high his power hath spread
The starry heavens above our head,
As his rich love exceeds our praise,
Exceeds the highest hopes we raise.

3 Not half so far hath nature placed
The rising morning from the west,
As his forgiving grace removes
The daily guilt of those he loves.

Watts.

PERFECTIONS OF GOD. 3

SESSIONS. L. M. — L. O. EMERSON.

1. Wait, O my soul, thy Mak-er's will;...... Tumultuous pas-sions, all be still! Nor let a murm'ring tho't a-rise; His ways are just,...... his counsels wise.

By per. O. DITSON & CO.

4 (17)

1 WAIT, O my soul, thy Maker's will;
Tumultuous passions, all be still!
Nor let a murmuring thought arise;
His ways are just, his counsels wise.

2 He in the thickest darkness dwells,
Performs his work, the cause conceals;
But, though his methods are unknown,
Judgment and truth support his throne.

3 In heaven, and earth, and air, and seas
He executes his firm decrees;
And by his saints it stands confest,
That what he does is ever best.

4 Wait then, my soul, submissive wait,
Prostrate before his awful seat;
And, 'midst the terrors of his rod,
Trust in a wise and gracious God.
Beddome

5 (23) L. M.

1 LORD, we are blind, we mortals, blind,
We can't behold thy bright abode;
O 'tis beyond a creature's mind
To glance a thought half way to God.

2 Infinite leagues beyond the sky
The Great Eternal reigns alone,
Where neither wings nor souls can fly,
Nor angels climb the topless throne.

3 The Lord of Glory builds his seat
Of gems incomparably bright,
And lays beneath his sacred feet
Substantial beams of gloomy night.

4 Yet, glorious Lord, thy gracious eyes
Look through, and cheer us from above;
Beyond our praise thy grandeur flies,
Yet we adore, and yet we love.
Watts.

6 (11) L. M.

1 GREAT Former of this various frame,
Our souls adore thine awful name;
And bow and tremble while they praise
The Ancient of eternal days.

2 Thou, Lord, with unsurprised survey,
Saw'st nature rising yesterday;
And, as to-morrow, shall thine eye
See earth and stars in ruin lie.

3 Beyond an angel's vision bright,
Thou dwell'st in self-existent light;
Which shines, with undiminished ray,
While suns and worlds in smoke decay.

4 Our days a transient period run,
And change with every circling sun;
And, in the firmest state we boast,
A moth can crush us into dust.

5 But let the creatures fall around;
Let death consign us to the ground;
Let the last general flame arise,
And melt the arches of the skies:

6 Calm as the summer's ocean, we
Can all the wreck of nature see,
While grace secures us an abode,
Unshaken as the throne of God.
Doddridge.

PERFECTIONS OF GOD.

MELODY. C. M.   A. CHAPIN. 1813.

1. Ho - ly and rev - 'rend is the name Of our e - ter - nal King: Thrice ho - ly, Lord, the an - gels cry; Thrice ho - ly, let us sing.

7 (7)

1 HOLY and reverend is the name
    Of our eternal King:
Thrice holy, Lord, the angels cry;
    Thrice holy, let us sing.

2 Heaven's brightest lamps with him com-
    How mean they look and dim! [pared,
The fairest angels have their spots,
    When once compared with him.

3 Holy is he in all his works,
    And truth is his delight;
But sinners and their wicked ways
    Shall perish from his sight.

4 The deepest reverence of the mind,
    Pay, O my soul, to God;
Lift with thy hands a holy heart
    To his sublime abode.

5 With sacred awe pronounce his name,
    Whom words nor thoughts can reach;
A broken heart shall please him more
    Than the best forms of speech.

6 Thou holy God! preserve my soul
    From all pollution free;
The pure in heart are thy delight,
    And they thy face shall see.
                                   Needham.

8 (15)   C. M.

1 KEEP silence, all created things,
    And wait your Maker's nod!
My soul stands trembling while she sings
    The honors of her God.

2 Life, death, and hell, and worlds un-
    Hang on his firm decree;   [known
He sits on no precarious throne,
    Nor borrows leave *to be*.

3 Chained to his throne, a volume lies,
    With all the fates of men,
With every angel's form and size,
    Drawn by th' Eternal pen.

4 His providence unfolds the book,
    And makes his counsels shine;
Each opening leaf, and every stroke
    Fulfils some deep design.

5 Here he exalts neglected worms
    To sceptres and a crown;
And there the following page he turns,
    And treads the monarch down.

6 Not Gabriel asks the reason why,
    Nor God the reason gives;
Nor dares the favorite angel pry
    Between the folded leaves.

7 My God, I would not long to see
    My fate with curious eyes,
What gloomy lines are writ for me,
    Or what bright scenes may rise;

8 In thy fair book of life and grace,
    O may I find my name
Recorded in some humble place,
    Beneath my Lord the Lamb!
                                   Watts.

PERFECTIONS OF GOD.

ARLINGTON. C. M.
Dr. THOS. ARNE. 1710-1778.

1. Ye humble souls, approach your God With songs of sacred praise, For he is good, immensely good, And kind are all his ways.

9 (18)

1 YE humble souls, approach your God
  With songs of sacred praise,
For he is good, immensely good,
  And kind are all his ways.

2 All nature owns his guardian care,
  In him we live and move;
But nobler benefits declare
  The wonders of his love.

3 He gave his Son, his only Son,
  To ransom rebel worms;
'Tis here he makes his goodness known
  In its diviner forms.

4 To this dear refuge, Lord, we come;
  'Tis here our hope relies;
A safe defense, a peaceful home,
  When storms of trouble rise.

5 Thine eye beholds, with kind regard,
  The souls who trust in thee;
Their humble hope thou wilt reward
  With bliss divinely free.
    Steele.

10 (19) C. M. John 1: 8.

1 AMID the splendors of thy state,
  My God, thy *love* appears
With the soft radiance of the moon
  Among a thousand stars.

2 Nature through all her ample round
  Thy boundless *power* proclaims,
And, in melodious accent, speaks
  The *goodness* of thy names.

3 Thy justice, holiness, and truth,
  Our solemn awe excite;
But the sweet charms of sovereign grace
  O'erwhelm us with delight.

4 Sinai, in clouds, and smoke, and fire,
  Thunders thy dreadful name;
But Sion sings, in melting notes,
  The honors of the Lamb.

5 In all thy doctrine and commands,
  Thy counsels and designs,—
In every work thy hands have framed,
  Thy love supremely shines.

6 Angels and men the news proclaim,
  Through earth and heaven above,
The joyful and transporting news,
  That God the Lord is *Love!*
    Steele.

11 (12) C. M.

1 THY names, how infinite they be!
  Great Everlasting One!
Boundless thy might and majesty,
  And unconfined thy throne.

2 Thy glories shine of wondrous size,
  And wondrous large thy grace;
Immortal day breaks from thine eyes,
  And Gabriel veils his face.

3 Thine essence is a vast abyss
  Which angels cannot sound,
An ocean of infinities
  Where all our thoughts are drowned.
    Watts.

PERFECTIONS OF GOD.

PLENARY. C. M.

1. Sweet is the mem'ry of thy grace, My God, my heav'nly King; Let age to age thy righteousness In
D. S.—Thro' the whole earth his bounty shines, And

songs of glo-ry sing. God reigns on high, but ne'er confines His goodness to the skies;
ev-'ry want sup-plies.

12 (38)

1 SWEET is the memory of thy grace,
  My God, my heavenly King;
Let age to age thy righteousness
  In songs of glory sing.

2 God reigns on high, but ne'er confines
  His goodness to the skies;   [shines
Through the whole earth his bounty
  And every want supplies.

3 With longing eyes thy creatures wait
  On thee for daily food,
Thy liberal hand provides their meat,
  And fills their mouths with good.

4 How kind are thy compassions, Lord!
  How slow thine anger moves!
But soon he sends his pardoning word
  To cheer the souls he loves.

5 Creatures with all their endless race,
  Thy power and praise proclaim;
But saints, that taste thy richer grace,
  Delight to bless thy name.
                                    Watts.

13 (45)   C. M.

1 MY never ceasing song shall show
  The mercies of the Lord,
And make succeeding ages know
  How faithful is his word.

2 The sacred truths his lips pronounce
  Shall firm as heaven endure;
And if he speak a promise once,
  Th' eternal grace is sure.

3 How long the race of David held
  The promised Jewish throne!
But there's a nobler covenant sealed
  To David's greater Son.

4 His seed for ever shall possess
  A throne above the skies;
The meanest subject of his grace
  Shall to that glory rise.

5 Lord God of Hosts, thy wondrous ways
  Are sung by saints above;
And saints on earth their honors raise
  To thine unchanging love.
                                    Watts.

14 (47)   C. M.

1 GREAT is the Lord; his works of might
  Demand our noblest songs;
Let his assembled saints unite
  Their harmony of tongues.

2 Great is the mercy of the Lord,
  He gives his children food;
And ever mindful of his word,
  He makes his promise good.

3 His Son, the great Redeemer, came
  And sealed his covenant sure:
Holy and Reverend is his name,
  His ways are just and pure.

4 They that would grow divinely wise,
  Must with his fear begin;
Our fairest proof of knowledge lies
  In hating every sin.
                                    Watts.

PERFECTIONS OF GOD.

PETERBOROUGH. C. M. R. HARRISON. 1748-1810.

1. A-mong the prin-ces, earth-ly gods, There's none hath pow'r di-vine; Nor is their nat-ure, might-y Lord, Nor are .... their works like thine.

15 (56)

1 AMONG the princes, earthly gods,
There's none hath power divine;
Nor is their nature, mighty Lord,
Nor are their works like thine.

2 The nations thou hast made shall bring
Their offerings round thy throne;
For thou alone dost wondrous things,
For thou art God alone.

3 Lord, I would walk with holy feet:
Teach me thine heavenly ways,
And my poor scattered thoughts unite
In God my Father's praise.

4 Great is thy mercy, and my tongue
Shall those sweet wonders tell,
How by thy grace my sinking soul
Rose from the deeps of hell.
Watts.

16 (58) C. M.

1 GOD shall alone the refuge be,
And comfort of my mind;
Too wise to be mistaken, He,
Too good to be unkind.

2 In all his holy, sovereign will,
He is, I daily find,
Too wise to be mistaken, still,
Too good to be unkind.

3 When I the tempter's rage endure
'Tis God supports my mind;
Too wise to be mistaken, sure,
Too good to be unkind.

4 What though I can't his goings see,
Nor all his footsteps find,
Too wise to be mistaken, He,
Too good to be unkind.
Medley.

17 (25) C. M.

1 GREAT God, how infinite art thou!
What worthless worms are we!
Let the whole race of creatures bow
And pay their praise to thee.

2 Thy throne eternally has stood,
Ere seas or stars were made;
Thou art the ever-living God,
Were all the nations dead.

3 Nature and time quite naked lie
To thine immense survey,
From the formation of the sky
To the great burning day.

4 Eternity, with all its years,
Stands present in thy view;
To thee there's nothing old appears,
Great God, there's nothing new.

5 Our lives thro' various scenes are drawn,
And vexed with trifling cares;
While thine eternal thoughts move on
Thine undisturbed affairs.

6 Great God, how infinite art thou!
What worthless worms are we!
Let the whole race of creatures bow
And pay their praise to thee.
Watts.

PERFECTIONS OF GOD.

ST. THOMAS. S. M.
G. F. HANDEL. 1685-1759.

1. O bless the Lord, my soul; Let all with-in me join, And aid my tongue to bless his name, Whose fa-vors are di-vine.

18 (39)

1 O BLESS the Lord, my soul;
   Let all within me join,
   And aid my tongue to bless his name,
   Whose favors are divine.

2 O bless the Lord, my soul;
   Nor let his mercies lie
   Forgotten in unthankfulness,
   And without praises die.

3 'Tis he forgives thy sins,
   'Tis he relieves thy pain,
   'Tis he that heals thy sicknesses,
   And makes thee young again.

4 He crowns thy life with love,
   When ransomed from the grave;
   He that redeemed my soul from hell,
   Hath sovereign power to save.

5 He fills the poor with good;
   He gives the sufferers rest;
   The Lord hath judgments for the proud,
   And justice for th' oppressed.

6 His wondrous works and ways
   He made by Moses known;
   But sent the world his truth and grace,
   By his beloved Son.
                                    Watts.

19 (43)   S M.

1 My soul, repeat his praise
   Whose mercies are so great;
   Whose anger is so slow to rise,
   So ready to abate.

2 God will not always chide;
   And when his strokes are felt,
   His strokes are fewer than our crimes,
   And lighter than our guilt.

3 High as the heavens are raised
   Above the ground we tread,
   So far the riches of his grace
   Our highest thoughts exceed.

4 His power subdues our sins;
   And his forgiving love,
   Far as the east is from the west,
   Doth all our guilt remove.

5 The pity of the Lord
   To those that fear his name,
   Is such as tender parents feel;
   He knows our humble frame.

6 He knows we are but dust,
   Scattered with every breath;
   His anger, like a rising wind,
   Can send us swift to death.

7 Our days are as the grass,
   Or like the morning flower;
   If one sharp blast sweep o'er the field,
   It withers in an hour.

8 But thy compassions, Lord,
   To endless years endure;
   And children's children ever find
   Thy words of promise sure.   Watts.

PERFECTIONS OF GOD.

SABBATH. S. M.

1. O Lord, our heav'nly King, Thy name is all di-vine; Thy glories round the earth are spread, And o'er the heav'ns they shine, And o'er the heav'ns they shine.

20 (35)

1 O LORD, our heavenly King,
Thy name is all divine;
Thy glories round the earth are spread,
And o'er the heavens they shine.

2 When to thy works on high
I raise my wondering eyes,
And see the moon complete in light
Adorn the darksome skies:

3 When I survey the stars,
And all their shining forms,
Lord, what is man, that worthless thing,
Akin to dust and worms!

4 How rich thy bounties are!
And wondrous are thy ways:
Of dust and worms thy power can frame
A monument of praise.
Watts.

21 (55)   S. M.

1 THE Lord, the sovereign King,
Hath fixed his throne on high;
O'er all the heavenly world he rules,
And all beneath the sky.

2 Ye angels, great in might,
And swift to do his will,
Bless ye the Lord, whose voice ye hear,
Whose pleasure ye fulfil.

3 Let the bright hosts who wait
The orders of their King,
Attend his churches when they pray,
Join in the praise they sing.

4 While all his wondrous works,
Through his vast kingdom show
Their Maker's glory, thou, my soul,
Shall sing his graces, too.
Watts.

22 (61)   S. M.

1 MY soul, with joy attend,
While Jesus silence breaks;
No angel's harp such music yields
As what my Shepherd speaks.

2 "I know my sheep," he cries;
"My soul approves them well;
Vain is the treacherous world's disguise,
And vain the rage of hell.

3 "I freely feed them now
With tokens of my love;
But richer pastures I prepare,
And sweeter streams above.

4 "Unnumbered years of bliss
I to my sheep will give;
And while my throne unshaken stands,
Shall all my chosen live.

5 "This tried Almighty hand
Is raised for their defense:
Where is the power shall reach them there,
Or what shall force them thence?"

6 "Enough, my gracious Lord!"
Let Faith triumphant cry;
"My heart can on this promise live—
Can on this promise die."
Doddridge.

CREATION AND PROVIDENCE.

GRINNELL. L. M.   L. O. EMERSON.

1. Thy ways, O Lord! with wise de-sign, Are fram'd up-on thy throne a-bove;
And ev-'ry dark and bend-ing line Meets in the cen-tre of thy love.

By per. O. DITSON & CO.

23 (65)

1 THY ways, O Lord! with wise design,
Are framed upon thy throne above;
And every dark and bending line
Meets in the center of thy love.

2 With feeble light, and half obscure,
Poor mortals thy arrangements view;
Not knowing that the least are sure,
And the mysterious just and true.

3 Thy flock, thy own peculiar care,
Though now they seem to roam uneyed,
Are led or driven only where
They best and safest may abide.

4 They neither know nor trace the way;
But, trusting to thy piercing eye,
None of their feet to ruin stray,
Nor shall the weakest fail or die.
                     Ambrose Searle.

24 (67)   L. M.

1 THROUGH all the various shifting scene
Of life's mistaken ill or good,
Thy hand, O God! conducts unseen
The beautiful vicissitude.

2 Thou givest with paternal care,
Howe'er unjustly we complain,
To each their necessary share
Of joy and sorrow, health and pain.

3 When lowest sunk with grief and shame,
Filled with affliction's bitter cup,
Lost to relations, friends, and fame,
Thy powerful hand can raise us up.

4 Thy powerful consolations cheer,
Thy smiles suppress the deep-fetched
Thy hand can dry the trickling tear [sigh,
That secret wets the widow's eye.

5 All things in earth and all in heaven,
On thy eternal will depend;
And all for greater good were given,
And all shall in thy glory end.
                     Samuel Collett.

25 (77)   L. M. Ps. 57.

1 My God, in whom are all the springs
Of boundless love, and grace unknown,
Hide me beneath thy spreading wings
Till the dark cloud is overblown.

2 Up to the heavens I send my cry,
The Lord will my desire perform;
He sends his angel from the sky, [storm.
And saves me from the threatening

3 My heart is fixed; my song shall raise
Immortal honors to thy name;
Awake, my tongue, to sound his praise,
My tongue, the glory of his fame.

4 High o'er the earth his mercy reigns,
And reaches to the utmost sky;
His truth to endless years remains,
When lower worlds dissolve and die.

5 Be thou exalted, O my God,
Above the heavens where angels dwell;
Thy power on earth be known abroad,
And land to land thy wonders tell.
                     Watts.

CREATION AND PROVIDENCE.

DUANE STREET. L. M. Rev. G. COLES, 1792-1858.

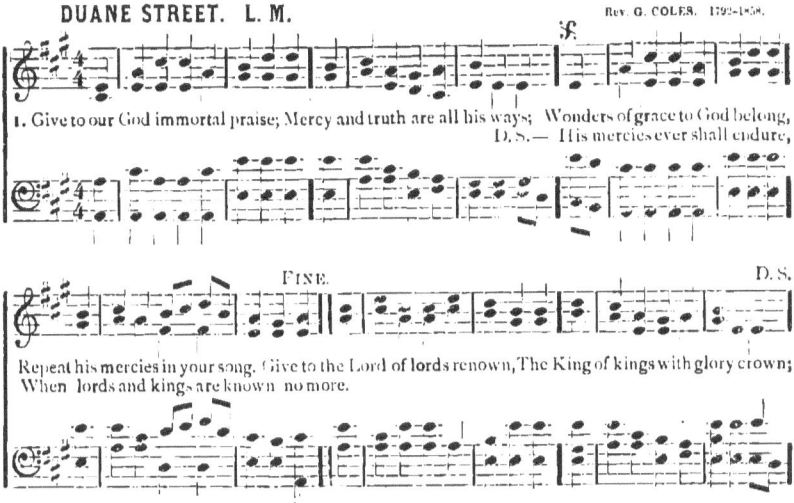

1. Give to our God immortal praise; Mercy and truth are all his ways; Wonders of grace to God belong,
D. S.— His mercies ever shall endure,

Repeat his mercies in your song. Give to the Lord of lords renown, The King of kings with glory crown;
When lords and kings are known no more.

26 (75)

1 GIVE to our God immortal praise;
Mercy and truth are all his ways;
Wonders of grace to God belong;
Repeat his mercies in your song.

2 Give to the Lord of lords renown,
The King of kings with glory crown;
His mercies ever shall endure, [more.
When lords and kings are known no

3 He built the earth, he spread the sky,
And fixed the starry lights on high;
Wonders of grace to God belong;
Repeat his mercies in your song.

4 He fills the sun with morning light;
He bids the moon direct the night;
His mercies ever shall endure, [more
When suns and moons shall shine no

5 The Jews he freed from Pharoah's hand,
And brought them to the promised land;
Wonders of grace to God belong;
Repeat his mercies in your song.

6 He saw his people dead in sin,
But still he loved and pitied them;
His mercies ever shall endure,
When death and sin shall reign no more.

7 He sent his Son with power to save
From guilt, and darkness, and the grave;
Wonders of grace to God belong;
Repeat his mercies in your song.

8 Through this vain world he guides our
And leads us to his heavenly seat; [feet,
His mercies ever shall endure,
When this vain world shall be no more.
Watts

27 (83) L. M.

1 LORD, we adore thy vast designs,
The obscure abyss of providence,
Too deep to sound with mortal lines,
Too deep to view with feeble sense.

2 Now thou arrayest thine awful face
In angry frowns, without a smile;
We through the cloud believe thy grace,
Secure of thy compassion still.

3 Through seas and storms of deep distress
We sail by faith, and not by sight;
Faith guides us in the wilderness
Through all the terrors of the night.

4 Dear Father, if thy lifted rod
Resolve to scourge us here below,
Still let us lean upon our God,
Thine arm shall bear us safely through.
Watts

CREATION AND PROVIDENCE.

EVAN. C. M. — Rev. W. H. HAVERGAL. 1793-1870.

1. God moves in a mysterious way His wonders to perform;
He plants his footsteps in the sea, And rides upon the storm.

28 (68)

1 GOD moves in a mysterious way
 His wonders to perform;
He plants his footsteps in the sea,
 He rides upon the storm.

2 Deep in unfathomable mines
 Of never-failing skill,
He treasures up his bright designs,
 And works his sovereign will.

3 Ye fearful saints, fresh courage take,
 The clouds ye so much dread
Are big with mercy, and shall break
 In blessings on your head.

4 Judge not the Lord by feeble sense,
 But trust him for his grace;
Behind a frowning providence
 He hides a smiling face.

5 His purposes will ripen fast,
 Unfolding every hour;
The bud may have a bitter taste,
 But sweet will be the flower.

6 Blind unbelief is sure to err,
 And scan his work in vain;
God is his own interpreter,
 And he will make it plain.
 Cowper.

29 (69) C. M.

1 GREAT God of providence! thy ways
 Are hid from mortal sight;
Wrapt in impenetrable shades,
 Or clothed with dazzling light.

2 The wondrous methods of thy grace
 Evade the human eye;
The nearer we attempt t' approach,
 The farther off they fly.

3 But in the world of bliss above
 Where thou dost ever reign,
The mysteries shall be all unveiled,
 And not a doubt remain.

4 The Sun of righteousness shall there
 His brightest beams display,
And not a hovering cloud obscure
 That never-ending day.
 Beddome.

30 (78) C. M.

1 LET others boast how strong they be,
 Nor death nor danger fear;
But we'll confess, O Lord, to thee,
 What feeble things we are.

2 Fresh as the grass our bodies stand,
 And flourish bright and gay,
A blasting wind sweeps o'er the land,
 And fades the grass away.

3 Our life contains a thousand springs,
 And dies if one be gone;
Strange! that a harp of thousand strings,
 Should keep in tune so long.

4 But 'tis our God supports our frame,
 The God who built us first;
Salvation to th' Almighty Name
 That reared us from the dust. Watts.

THE GOSPEL.

SELGGUR. C. M. *Arr. by G. P. L.*

1. Blest are the souls that hear and know The gos-pel's joy-ful sound;
Peace shall at-tend the paths they go, And light their steps sur-round.

31 (122)

1 BLEST are the souls that hear and know
The gospel's joyful sound;
Peace shall attend the paths they go,
And light their steps surround.

2 Their joy shall bear their spirits up
Through their Redeemer's name;
His righteousness exalts their hope,
Nor Satan dare condemn.

3 The Lord, our glory and defense,
Strength and salvation gives;
Israel, thy King for ever reigns,
Thy God for ever lives.
Watts.

32 (133) C. M.

1 ON Sion, his most holy mount,
God will a feast prepare,
And Israel's sons and Gentile lands
Shall in the banquet share.

2 Marrow and fatness are the food
His bounteous hand bestows;
Wine on the lees, and well refined,
In rich abundance flows.

3 See to the vilest of the vile
A free acceptance given;
See rebels, by redeeming grace,
Sit with the heirs of heaven!

4 The pained, the sick, the dying, now
To ease and health restored,

With eager appetites partake
The plenties of the board.

5 But O what draughts of bliss unknown,
What dainties shall be given,
When, with the myriads round the throne,
We join the feast of heaven.

6 There joys immeasurably high
Shall overflow the soul,
And springs of life that never dry
In thousand channels roll.
Thomas Gibbons.

33 (125) C. M.

1 CHRIST and his cross are all our theme:
The mysteries that we speak
Are scandal in the Jews' esteem,
And folly to the Greek.

2 But souls enlightened from above
With joy receive the word;
They see what wisdom, power, and love
Shine in their dying Lord.

3 The vital savor of his name
Restores their fainting breath;
But unbelief perverts the same
To guilt, despair, and death.

4 Till God diffuse his graces down,
Like showers of heavenly rain,
In vain Apollos sows the ground,
And Paul may plant in vain. *Watts.*

B

THE GOSPEL.

WELLS. L. M. ISRAEL HOLDROYD. 1710

1. Loud let the tuneful trumpet sound, And spread the joyful tidings round; Let every soul with transport hear, And hail the Lord's accepted year.

34 (135) Psa. 89: 15.

1 LORD let the tuneful trumpet sound,
And spread the joyful tidings round;
Let every soul with transport hear,
And hail the Lord's accepted year.

2 Ye debtors, whom he gives to know
That you ten thousand talents owe,
When humble at his feet you fall,
Your gracious God forgives them all.

3 Slaves, that have borne the heavy chain
Of sin and hell's tyrannic reign,
To liberty assert your claim,
And urge the great Redeemer's name.

4 The rich inheritance of heaven,
Your joy, your boast, is freely given;
Fair Salem your arrival waits,
With golden streets and pearly gates.

5 Her blest inhabitants no more
Bondage and poverty deplore;
No debt, but love immensely great;
Their joy still rises with the debt.

6 O happy souls that know the sound,
Celestial light their steps surround,
And show that jubilee begun,
Which through eternal years shall run.
Doddridge.

35 (136) L. M.

1 How sweetly flowed the gospel sound,
From lips of gentleness and grace,
When listening thousands gathered round,
And joy and reverence filled the place.

2 From heaven he came, of heaven he spoke,
To heaven he led his followers' way;
Dark clouds of gloomy night he broke,
Unveiling an immortal day.

3 Come, children, to your Father's home;
Come, all ye weary ones, and rest;
Yes, sacred Teacher, we will come,
Obey thee, love thee, and be blest.
J. Bowring.

36 (137) L. M.

1 GREAT was the day, the joy was great,
When the divine disciples met;
Whilst on their heads the Spirit came,
And sat like tongues of cloven flame.

2 What gifts, what miracles he gave!
And power to kill, and power to save!
Furnished their tongues with wondrous words,
Instead of shields, and spears, and swords.

3 Thus armed, he sent the champions forth
From east to west, from south to north;
Go, and assert your Saviour's cause,
'Go spread the mystery of his cross.'

4 These weapons of the holy war,
Of what almighty force they are
To make our stubborn passions bow,
And lay the proudest rebel low!

5 Great King of grace, my heart subdue,
I would be led in triumph, too,
A willing captive to my Lord,
And sing the victories of his word.
Watts.

THE GOSPEL. 15

GERAR. S. M. L. MASON.

1. How beauteous are their feet Who stand on Zi-on's hill! Pro-claim sal-va-tion with their tongues, And words of peace re-veal.

37 (130) Isa. 52:7.

2 How charming is their voice!
How sweet the tidings are!
"Zion, behold thy Saviour King,
He reigns and triumphs here."

3 How happy are our ears
That hear this joyful sound
Which kings and prophets waited for,
And sought, but never found!

4 How blessed are our eyes
That see this heavenly light;
Prophets and kings desired it long,
But died without the sight.

5 The watchmen join their voice,
And tuneful notes employ;
Jerusalem breaks forth in songs,
And deserts learn the joy.

6 The Lord makes bare his arm
Through all the earth abroad;
Let every nation now behold
Their Saviour and their God. *Watts.*

38 (117) S. M.

1 THE law by Moses came,
But peace, and truth, and love,
Were brought by Christ, a nobler name,
Descending from above.

2 Amidst the house of God
Their different works were done;
Moses a faithful servant stood,
But Christ a faithful Son.

3 Then to his new commands
Be strict obedience paid;
O'er all his Father's house he stands
The Sovereign and the Head.

4 The man that durst despise
The law that Moses brought,
Behold! how terribly he dies
For his presumptuous fault.

5 But sorer vengeance falls
On that rebellious race,
Who hate to hear when Jesus calls,
And dare resist his grace. *Watts.*

39 (164) S. M.

1 RAISE your triumphant songs
To an immortal tune,
Let the wide earth resound the deeds
Celestial grace has done.

2 Sing how eternal love
Its chief beloved chose,
And bade him raise poor sinners up
From their abyss of woes.

3 His hand no thunder bears,
No terror clothes his brow,
No bolts to drive our guilty souls
To fiercer flames below.

4 'Twas mercy filled the throne,
And wrath stood silent by,
When Christ was sent with mercy down
To rebels doomed to die. *Watts.*

THE GOSPEL.

LENOX. H. M. — LEWIS EDSON. 1748-1820.

40 (134)

1 Blow ye the trumpet, blow
  The gladly solemn sound!
  Let all the nations know,
    To earth's remotest bound,
  The year of Jubilee is come;
  Return, ye ransomed sinners, home.

2 Exalt the Lamb of God,
  The sin-atoning Lamb;
  Redemption by his blood
    Through all the lands proclaim:
  The year of Jubilee is come;
  Return, ye ransomed sinners, home.

3 Ye bankrupt debtors, know
  The sovereign grace of heaven;
  Though sums immense ye owe,
    A free discharge is given:
  The year of Jubilee is come;
  Return, ye ransomed sinners, home.

4 The gospel trumpet hear,
  The news of pardoning grace;
  Ye happy souls, draw near,
    Behold your Saviour's face:
  The year of Jubilee is come;
  Return, ye ransomed sinners, home.

5 Jesus, our great High Priest,
  Has full atonement made;
  Ye weary spirits, rest;

  Ye mournful souls, be glad!
  The year of Jubilee is come;
  Return, ye ransomed sinners, home.
            C. W.   Altered by Toplady.

41 (176) H. M.

1 Awake, awake, arise,
  And hail the glorious morn;
  Hark, how the angels sing,
    "To you a Saviour's born!"
  Now let our hearts in concert move,
  And every tongue be tuned to love.

2 He mortals came to save
  From sin's tyrannic power;
  Come, with the angels sing
    At this auspicious hour;
  Let every heart and tongue combine,
  To praise the love, the grace divine.

3 The prophecies and types
  Are all this day fulfilled;
  With eastern sages join
    To praise this wondrous child:
  God's only Son is come to bless
  The earth with peace and righteousness.

4 Glory to God on high,
  For our Emmanuel's birth;
  To mortal men good will,
    And peace and joy on earth:
  With angels now we will repeat
  Their songs, still new and ever sweet.
                              Anon.

THE GOSPEL.

DUNLAP. C. M. — SAM'L. McFARLAND.

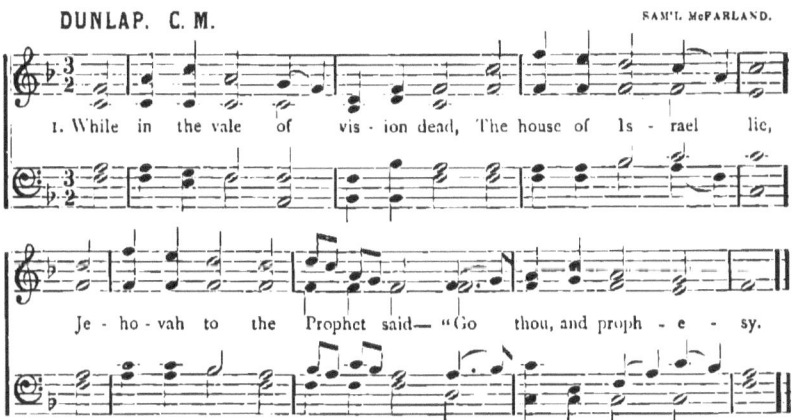

1. While in the vale of vis-ion dead, The house of Is-rael lie, Je-ho-vah to the Prophet said— "Go thou, and proph-e-sy.

42 (139)

2 "Go thou, nor reasoning scruples make,
Because the bones are dry;
My voice shall bid the dead awake;
Go thou, and prophesy.

3 "I'll bid the dying sinner live,
To lift my name on high;
Eternal life 'tis mine to give—
Go thou, and prophesy.

4 " Preach Jesus as he's brought to view,
And thither point their eye;
'Tis I must give to will and do—
Go thou, and prophesy.

5 " From stones, to celebrate my grace,
While mercy's tidings fly,
My arms shall raise a numerous race,—
Go thou, and prophesy."

6 Let Zion's watchmen ne'er refrain
Her silver trump to blow;
For Jesus can, with feeblest strain,
His richest grace bestow.
Kent.

43 (141) C. M.

1 THE glorious gospel of our God,
Is joyful news from heaven—
Salvation free in Jesus' blood,
And life eternal given.

2 'Tis not the gospel's joyful sound,
Nor silver trump we hear,
When Sinai's terrors men confound,
With Zion's beauties fair.

3 He needs no creature power or skill,
His finished work to mend,
But works his own eternal will
As wisdom did intend.

4 When Uzza stretched his puny hand,
Behold his awful fall;
The shaking ark secure shall stand,
When God designs it shall.

5 If 'tis of works, and not of grace,
No crown shall mortals have;
Not all the good of Adam's race,
A single soul can save.

6 To God, the Father's love divine,
The Spirit, and the Son,
Let everlasting honors shine
While years eternal run.
Kent.

44 (147) C. M.

1 FIRM as the earth thy gospel stands,
My Lord, my hope, my trust;
If I am found in Jesus' hands,
My soul can ne'er be lost.

2 His honor is engaged to save
The meanest of his sheep;
All that his heavenly Father gave
His hands securely keep.

3 Nor death, nor hell, shall e'er remove
His favorites from his breast;
In the dear bosom of his love
They must for ever rest.
Watts.

THE GOSPEL.

BARTIMEUS. 8s. & 7s. STEPHEN JENKS. 1800.

1. 'Tis the gos-pel's joy-ful tid-ings, Full sal-va-tion sweet-ly sounds;
Grace, to heal thy foul back-slid-ings, Sin-ner, flows from Je-sus' wounds.

45 (142)

1 'Tis the gospel's joyful tidings,
   Full salvation sweetly sounds;
   Grace, to heal thy foul backslidings,
   Sinner, flows from Jesus' wounds.

2 Are thy sins beyond recounting,
   Like the sand the ocean laves?
   Jesus is of life the fountain—
   He unto the utmost saves.

3 Love's abyss there's no exploring,
   'Tis beyond the seraph's ken;
   Prostrate at thy feet adoring,
   We revere thy love to men.

4 Hail the Lamb who came to save us,
   Hail the love that made him die!
   'Tis the gift that God hath given us,
   We'll proclaim his honors high.

5 When we join the general chorus
   Of the royal blood-bought throng,
   Who to glory went before us,
   Saved from every tribe and tongue;

6 Then we'll make tne blissful regions
   Echo to our Saviour's praise;
   While the bright angelic legions
   Listen to the charming lays.
   Kent

46 (412) 8s. & 7s.

1 HAIL! thou once despised Jesus,
   Hail, thou Galilean King!
   Thou didst suffer to release us;
   Thou didst free salvation bring.

2 Hail, thou agonizing Saviour,
   Bearer of our sin and shame!
   By thy merits we find favor;
   Life is given through thy name.

3 Paschal Lamb, by God appointed,
   All our sins on thee were laid;
   By almighty love anointed,
   Thou hast full atonement made.

4 All thy people are forgiven
   Through the virtue of thy blood;
   Opened is the gate of heaven;
   Peace is made 'twixt us and God.

5 Jesus, hail! enthroned in glory,
   There for ever to abide!
   All the heavenly hosts adore thee,
   Seated at thy Father's side.
   Bakewell.

47 (601) 8s. & 7s.

1 DEAREST Saviour! we adore thee,
   For thy precious life and death;
   Melt each stubborn heart before thee,—
   Give us all the eye of faith:

2 From the law's condemning sentence,
   To thy mercy we appeal;
   Thou alone canst give repentance;
   Thou alone our wounds canst heal.
   Newton.

THE GOSPEL. 19

PORTUGUESE HYMN. 11s. J. READING. 1690-1776.

1. The gos-pel brings tidings to each wounded soul, That Je-sus, the Sav-iour, can make it quite whole; And what makes this gospel most precious to me, It holds forth sal-va-tion so per-fect-ly free! It holds forth sal-va-tion so per-fect-ly free!

48 (146) 1 Tim. 1: 15.

2 The gospel declares that God, sending his Son
To die for poor sinners, gave all things in one;
This, too, makes the gospel most precious to me,
Because 'tis a gospel as full as 'tis free. [

3 Since Jesus has sav'd me, and that freely, too,
I fain would in all things my gratitude show;
But as to man's merit, 'tis hateful to me!
The gospel—I love it; 'tis perfectly free!
                                                     Kent.

49 (21) 11s. Ps. 80: 1.

1 Thy mercy, my God, is the theme of my song, [tongue;
The joy of my heart, and the boast of my
Thy free grace alone, from the first to the last, [fast.
Hath won my affections, and bound my soul

2 Without thy sweet mercy I could not live here,
Sin soon would reduce me to utter despair;
But, through thy free goodness, my spirits revive, [alive.
And he that first made me, still keeps me

3 Thy mercy is more than a match for my heart, [depart;
Which wonders to feel its own hardness
Dissolv'd by thy goodness, I fall to the ground, [found.
And weep to the praise of the mercy I

4 The door of thy mercy stands open all day
To the poor and the needy, who knock by the way;
No sinner shall ever be empty sent back,
Who comes seeking mercy for Jesus' sake.

5 Thy mercy in Jesus exempts me from hell;
Its glories I'll sing, and its wonders I'll tell:
'Twas Jesus my friend, when he hung on the tree,
Who opened the channel of mercy for me.

6 Great Father of mercies! thy goodness I own,
And the covenant love of thy crucified Son:
All praise to the Spirit, whose whisper divine,
Seals mercy and pardon and righteousness mine!
                                                Stocker.

20. THE INCARNATION OF THE SON OF GOD.

JUDKINS. C. M.

1. Shepherds! rejoice, lift up your eyes, And send your fears away; News from the regions of the skies, Salvation's born to-day.

50 (155)

1 SHEPHERDS! rejoice, lift up your eyes,
And send your fears away;
News from the regions of the skies,
Salvation's born to-day.

2 "Jesus, the God whom angels fear,
Comes down to dwell with you;
To-day he makes his entrance here,
But not as monarchs do.

3 "No gold nor purple swaddling bands,
Nor royal shining things;
A manger for his cradle stands,
And holds the King of kings.

4 "Go, shepherds, where the infant lies,
And see his humble throne;
With tears of joy in all your eyes,
Go, shepherds, kiss the Son.

5 "Thus Gabriel sang, and straight a-
The heavenly armies throng, [round
They tune their harps to lofty sound,
And thus conclude the song:

6 "Glory to God that reigns above,
Let peace surround the earth,
Mortals shall know their Maker's love
At their Redeemer's birth."

7 Lord, and shall angels have their songs,
And men no tunes to raise!
O may we lose our useless tongues
When they forget to praise.

8 Glory to God that reigns above,
That pitied us forlorn,
We join to sing our Maker's love,
For there's a Saviour born.

Watts.

51 (169)   C. M.

1 AWAKE, awake the sacred song
To our incarnate Lord;
Let every heart, and every tongue,
Adore th' eternal Word.

2 That awful Word, that sovereign Power
By whom the worlds were made,
(O happy morn, illustrious hour!)
Was once in flesh arrayed!

3 Then shone almighty power and love
In all their glorious forms,
When Jesus left his throne above,
To dwell with sinful worms.

4 To dwell with misery below,
The Saviour left the skies;
And sunk to wretchedness and wo,
That worthless men might rise.

5 Adoring angels tuned their songs
To hail the joyful day;
With rapture then let mortal tongues
Their grateful worship pay.

6 What glory, Lord, to thee is due!
With wonder we adore;
But could we sing as angels do,
Our highest praise were poor.

Mrs. Anne Steele.

THE INCARNATION OF THE SON OF GOD. 21

ANTIOCH. C. M.   G. F. HANDEL, 1685-1759.

1. Joy to the world; the Lord is come; Let earth receive her King; Let ev'ry heart prepare him room, And heav'n and nature sing, And heav'n and nature sing, And heav'n, And heav'n and nature sing.

52 (160)

1 Joy to the world; the Lord is come;
   Let earth receive her King;
  Let every heart prepare him room,
   And heaven and nature sing.

2 Joy to the earth, the Saviour reigns;
   Let men their songs employ;
  While fields and floods, rocks, hills, and plains,
   Repeat the sounding joy.

3 No more let sins and sorrows grow,
   Nor thorns infest the ground;
  He comes to make his blessings flow
   Far as the curse is found.

4 He rules the world with truth and grace,
   And makes the nation prove
  The glories of his righteousness,
   And wonders of his love.
                    Watts.

53 (161)   C. M.

1 Sing to the Lord, ye distant lands,
   Ye tribes of every tongue;
  His new discovered grace demands
   A new and nobler song.

2 Say to the nations, Jesus reigns,
   God's own almighty Son;
  His power the sinking world sustains,
   And grace surrounds his throne.

3 Let heaven proclaim the joyful day,
   Joy through the earth be seen;
  Let cities shine in bright array,
   And fields in cheerful green.

4 Let an unusual joy surprise
   The islands of the sea;
  Ye mountains sink, ye valleys rise,
   Prepare the Lord his way.

5 Behold he comes, he comes to bless
   The nations, as their God;
  To show the world his righteousness,
   And send his truth abroad.

6 But when his voice shall raise the dead,
   And bid the world draw near,
  How will the guilty nations dread
   To see their Judge appear!
                    Watts.

54 (163)   C. M.

1 Come, happy souls, approach your God
   With new melodious songs;
  Come, render to almighty grace
   The tribute of your tongues.

2 So strange, so boundless was the love
   That pitied dying men,
  The Father sent his equal Son
   To give them life again.

3 Thy hands, dear Jesus, were not armed
   With a revenging rod,
  No hard commission to perform
   The vengeance of a God;

4 But all was mercy, all was mild,
   And wrath forsook the throne,
  When Christ on the kind errand came,
   And brought salvation down.
                    Watts.

22. THE INCARNATION OF THE SON OF GOD.

NORTHFIELD. C. M. J. INGALLS. 1764-1828.

55 (172)

1 HARK, the glad sound, the Saviour
　The Saviour promised long! [comes,
　Let every heart prepare a throne,
　And every voice a song.

2 He comes, the prisoners to release,
　In Satan's bondage held;
　The gates of brass before him burst,
　The iron fetters yield.

3 He comes from thickest films of vice
　To clear the mental ray;
　And, on the eyes oppressed with night,
　To pour celestial day.

4 He comes, the broken heart to bind,
　The bleeding soul to cure;
　And, with the treasures of his grace,
　T' enrich the humble poor.

5 Our glad hosannas, Prince of Peace,
　Thy welcome shall proclaim;
　And heaven's eternal arches ring
　With thy beloved name.
　　　　　　　　　　　Doddridge.

56 (177) C. M.

1 Lo! what glorious sight appears,
　To our believing eyes;
　The earth and seas are passed away,
　And the old rolling skies.

2 From the third heaven, where God
　That holy, happy place! [resides,
　The new Jerusalem comes down,
　Adorned with shining grace.

3 The God of glory down to men
　Removes his blest abode;
　His saints the objects of his grace,
　And he their faithful God.

4 His own soft hand shall wipe the tears
　From every weeping eye; [fears,
　And pains, and groans, and griefs, and
　And death itself shall die.
　　　　　　　　　　　Watts.

57 (178) C. M.

1 THE true Messiah now appears,
　The types are all withdrawn;
　So fly the shadows and the stars,
　Before the rising dawn.

2 The smoking sweet, and bleeding lamb,
　The kid and bullock slain,
　And costly spice of every name,
　Would all be burnt in vain.

3 Aaron must lay his robes away,
　His mitre and his vest,
　When Christ the Lord comes down to be
　The offering and the Priest.

4 He took our mortal flesh to show
　The wonders of his love;
　For us he paid his life below,
　And prays for us above.

5 "Father," he cries, "forgive their sins,
　For I myself have died;"
　And then he shows his opened veins,
　And pleads his wounded side.
　　　　　　　　　　　Watts

THE INCARNATION OF THE SON OF GOD. 23

SHERBURNE. C. M. — D. READ.

58 (175)

2 "Fear not," said he, for mighty dread
  Had seized their troubled mind,
 "Glad tidings of great joy I bring
  To you, and all mankind.
3 "To you, in David's town, this day
  Is born, of David's line,
  The Saviour, who is Christ the Lord,
  And this shall be the sign:
4 "The heavenly Babe you there shall
  To human view displayed, [find,

  All meanly wrapt in swathing bands,
  And in a manger laid."
5 Thus spake the seraph, and forthwith
  Appeared a shining throng
  Of angels praising God, and thus
  Addressed their joyful song:
6 "All glory be to God on high,
  And to the earth be peace;
  Good-will henceforth from heaven to men
  Begin and never cease." Tate and Brady.

THE INCARNATION OF THE SON OF GOD.

STAR IN THE EAST. 10s. & 11s.
ENGLISH. 1870.

59 (174)

1 Hail the blest morn! when the great Mediator
Down from the mansions of glory descends;
Shepherds, go worship the babe in the manger,
Lo! for his guard the bright angels attend.

CHORUS.
Brightest and best of the sons of the morning,
Dawn on our darkness, and lend us thine aid;
Star in the east, the horizon adorning,
Guide where our infant Redeemer is laid.

2 Cold on his cradle the dew-drops are shining;
Low lies his head with the beasts of the stall:
Angels adore him, in slumbers reclining;
Wise men and shepherds before him do fall.
Brightest and best, &c.

3 Say, shall we yield him, in costly devotion,
Odors of Edom, and offerings divine,
Gems from the mountains, and pearls from the ocean, [mine?
Myrrh from the forest, and gold from the Brightest and best, &c.

4 Vainly we offer each ample oblation,
Vainly with gifts would his favor secure;
Richer by far is the heart's adoration,
Dearer to God are the prayers of the poor.
Brightest and best, &c.

Heber.

VITAL UNITY OF CHRIST AND THE CHURCH.

HILLSIDE. L. M. L. O. EMERSON.

1. 'Twixt Jesus and the chosen race, Subsists a bond of sovereign grace, That hell, with its infernal train, Shall ne'er dissolve, or rend in twain.

By per. O. DITSON & CO.

60 (183)

1 'TWIXT Jesus and the chosen race,
Subsists a bond of sovereign grace,
That hell, with its infernal train,
Shall ne'er dissolve, or rend in twain.

2 This sacred bond shall never break,
Though earth should to her centre shake;
Rest, doubting saint, assured of this,
For God has pledged his holiness.

3 He swore but once, the deed was done;
'Twas settled by the great Three One;
Christ was appointed to redeem
All that the Father loved in him.

4 Hail sacred union, firm and strong!
How great the grace, how sweet the song!
That worms of earth should ever be
One with incarnate deity!

5 One in the tomb, one when he rose,
One when he triumph'd o'er his foes,
One when in heaven he took his seat,
While seraph's sung all hell's defeat.

6 This sacred tie forbids their fears,
For all he is, or has, is theirs;
With him their head, they stand or fall,
Their life, their surety, and their all.
Kent.

61 (186) L. M.

1 WHY should the saints be filled with
dread,
Or yield their joys to slavish fear?
Heaven can't be full which holds the head,
Till every member's present there.

2 In heaven the head, the members here;
Ten thousand thousand, yet but one!
So far asunder, yet so near! [throne.
Some yet unborn, some round the

3 How bright eternal wisdom shines,
When it displays eternal love;
Instructing by these dazzling lines,
The earth beneath and heaven above.
Swain.

62 (202) L. M.

1 'TWAS with an everlasting love
That God his own elect embraced,
Before he made the worlds above,
Or earth on her huge columns placed.

2 Long ere the sun's refulgent ray
Primeval shades of darkness drove,
They on his sacred bosom lay,
Loved with an everlasting love.

3 Then, in his love and his decrees,
Christ and his bride appeared as one;
Her sin, by imputation, his,
Whilst she in spotless splendor shone.

4 O Love, how high thy glories swell,
How great, immutable, and free!
Ten thousand sins, as black as hell,
Are blotted out, O Love, by thee.

5 Believer, here thy comfort stands,
From first to last, salvation's free;
And everlasting love demands
An everlasting song from thee.
Kent.

26. VITAL UNITY OF CHRIST AND THE CHURCH.

LYRA. C. M. — ROOT.

1. Rejoice, believer, in the Lord, Who makes your cause his own; The hope that's built upon his word Can ne'er be o-ver-thrown.

63 (185) Phil. 3: 3.

1 REJOICE, believer, in the Lord,
Who makes your cause his own ;
The hope that's built upon his word
Can ne'er be overthrown.

2 Though many foes beset your road,
And feeble is your arm,
Your life is hid with Christ in God,
Beyond the reach of harm.

3 Weak as you are, you shall not faint,
Or fainting, shall not die !
Jesus, the strength of every saint,
Will aid you from on high.

4 Though not unseen by outward sense,
Faith sees him always near ;
A guide, a glory, a defense—
Then what have you to fear?

5 As surely as he overcame
And triumphed once for you,
So surely you that love his name,
Shall triumph in him, too.
                        Newton.

64 (191) C. M.

1 COMPARED with Christ, in all beside
No comeliness I see ;
The one thing needful, dearest Lord,
Is to be one with thee.

2 The sense of thy redeeming love
Into my soul convey ;
Thyself bestow ! for thee alone,
My All-in-All I pray.

3 Less than thyself will not suffice
My comfort to restore ;
More than thyself I cannot crave ;
And thou can'st give no more.

4 Loved of my God, for him again,
With love intense, I'd burn ;
Chosen of thee, ere time began,
I'd choose thee in return.

5 Whate'er consists not with thy love,
O teach me to resign ;
I'm rich to all intents of bliss,
If thou, O God, art mine.
                        Toplady.

65 (193) C. M.

1 BLEST be the dear uniting love
That will not let us part :
Our bodies may far off remove,
But we are joined in heart.

2 Joined in one spirit to one Head,
We wait his will to know,
That we in his right steps may tread
And follow him below.

3 O may we ever walk in him,
And nothing know beside ;
Nothing desire, nor aught esteem,
But Jesus crucified.

4 Closer and closer let us cleave,
To his beloved embrace ;
Expect his fulness to receive,
And grace to answer grace.
                        C. Wesley.

VITAL UNITY OF CHRIST AND THE CHURCH.

MERIBAH. 8. 8. 6. Dr. LOWELL MASON. 1792-1872.

1. Hark! how the blood-bought hosts above Conspire to praise redeeming love, In sweet har- -monious strains: { And while they strike the gold en lyres, } That grace tri-umph-ant reigns. { This glo- rious theme each bo- som fires, }

---

66 (199) Rom. 5: 21.

1 HARK! how the blood-bought hosts
Conspire to praise redeeming love, [above
  In sweet harmonious strains;
And while they strike the golden lyres,
This glorious theme each bosom fires,
  That grace triumphant reigns.

2 Join thou, my soul, for thou canst tell
How grace divine broke up thy cell,
  And loosed thy native chains;
And still from that auspicious day,
How oft art thou constrained to say,
  That grace triumphant reigns.

3 Grace, till the tribes redeemed by blood
Are brought to know themselves and God,
  Her empire shall maintain;
To call when he appoints the day,
And from the mighty take the prey,
  Shall grace triumphant reign.

4 When called to meet the king of dread,
Should love compose my dying bed,
  And grace my soul sustain,
Then, ere I quit this mortal clay,
I'll raise my fainting voice, and say,
  Let grace triumphant reign.
                                     Kent.

67 (204) 8. 8. 6.

1 THERE is a friend that sticketh fast,
And keeps his love from first to last,
  And Jesus is his name:
An earthly brother drops his hold,
Is sometimes hot, and sometimes cold,
  But Jesus is the same.

2 He loves his people great and small,
And grasping hard embraceth all,
  Nor with a soul will part:
No tribulations which they feel,
No foes on earth, or fiends of hell,
  Shall tear them from his heart.

3 His love before all time began,
Shall through all time the same remain,
  And evermore endure;   [brought,
Though rods and frowns are sometimes
And man may change, He changeth not,
  His love abideth sure.

4 The law demanded blood for blood,
And out he poured his vital flood
  To pay the mighty debt!   [death,
He toils through life, and pants through
And cries with his expiring breath,
  "'Tis finished," and complete.
                                  Berridge

28 VITAL UNITY OF CHRIST AND THE CHURCH.

NEW HOPE. S. M.
DAVISSON. Arr. by F. L. ARMSTRONG.

1. In union with the Lamb, From condemnation free,
The saints from everlasting were, And shall forever be.

68 (188)

2 In covenant from of old,
  The sons of God they were;
  The feeblest lamb in Jesus' fold
  Was blessed in Jesus there.

3 Its bonds shall never break,
  Though earth's old columns bow;
  The strong, the tempted, and the weak,
  Are one in Jesus now.

4 With joy lift up your heads,
  Ye highly favored few—
  When thro' the earth destruction spreads,
  For what shall injure you?

5 When storms or tempests rise,
  Or sins your peace assail,
  Your hope in Jesus never dies—
  'Tis cast within the veil.

6 Here let the weary rest,
  Who love the Saviour's name;
  Though with no sweet enjoyment blest,
  This covenant stands the same.
                                Kent.

69 (194) S. M. 1 Cor. 6: 17.

1 DEAR Saviour, we are thine,
  By everlasting bands;
  Our names, our hearts, we would resign;
  Our souls are in thy hands.

2 To thee we still would cleave
  With ever-growing zeal;
  If millions tempt us Christ to leave,
  O let them ne'er prevail.

3 Death may our souls divide
  From these abodes of clay;
  But love shall keep us near thy side
  Through all the gloomy way.

4 Since Christ and we are one,
  Why should we doubt or fear?
  If he in heaven hath fixed his throne,
  He'll fix his members there.
                                Doddridge.

70 (214) S. M.

1 As branches from the vine
  Their birth and growth receive,
  And round the stem in friendship twine,
  And by their union live,

2 In Christ so Christians dwell,
  And life from him derive;
  His root makes all the clusters swell,
  And all the branches thrive.

3 In sweetest union joined,
  Immanuel's name they know,
  And veiw the God with man combined,
  And feel his virtue, too.

4 Eternal life is given
  To all his saints below;
  A taste he sends them of his heaven,
  While in the vale of wo.

5 This makes them love their King,
  And lift his name on high!
  And this with ardent praise they sing,
  And shout the victory.
                                Sonnets.

VITAL UNITY OF CHRIST AND THE CHURCH.

DENNIS. S. M. H. G. NAGELI. 1768-1836.

1. What cheering words are these; Their sweetness who can tell? In time and to eternal days, 'Tis with the righteous well.

71 (200) Isa. 3: 10.

1 WHAT cheering words are these;
  Their sweetness who can tell?
In time and to eternal days,
  'Tis with the righteous well.

2 In every state secure,
  Kept as Jehovah's eye,
'Tis well with them while life endure,
  And well when called to die.

3 Well when the gospel yields
  Pure honey, milk and wine;
Well when the soul her leanness feels,
  And all her joys decline.

4 'Tis well when joys arise;
  'Tis well when sorrows flow;
'Tis well when darkness veils the skies,
  And strong temptations blow.

5 'Tis well when at his throne
  They wrestle, weep and pray;
'Tis well when at his feet they groan,
  Yet bring their wants away.

6 'Tis well when they can sing
  As sinners bought with blood;
And when they touch the mournful string,
  And mourn an absent God.

7 'Tis well when on the mount
  They feast on dying love;
And 'tis as well, in God's account,
  When they the furnace prove.

8 'Tis well when Jesus calls,
  " From earth and sin arise,
Join with the host of virgin souls,
  Made to salvation wise."

  Kent.

72 (205) S. M. 1 John 3: 1-3.

1 BEHOLD what wondrous grace
  The Father hath bestowed
On sinners of a mortal race,
  To call them sons of God.

2 'Tis no surprising thing
  That we should be unknown:
The Jewish world knew not their King,—
  God's everlasting Son.

3 Nor doth it yet appear
  How great we must be made;
But when we see our Saviour here
  We shall be like our Head.

4 A hope so much divine,
  May trials well endure;
For we, as sons in Christ, are made
  As pure as he is pure.

5 If in my Father's love
  I share a filial part,
Send down thy Spirit like a dove
  To rest upon my heart.

6 We would no longer lie
  Like slaves before thy throne;
Our faith shall *Abba*, Father, cry,
  And thou the kindred own.

  Watts.

ELECTION AND DECREES OF GOD.

THERON. L. M. — L. O. EMERSON.

1. Who shall the Lord's elect condemn? 'Tis God that justifies their souls,
And mercy like a mighty stream O'er all their sins divinely rolls.

By per. O. DITSON & CO.

73 (224) Rom. 8:33.

1 Who shall the Lord's elect condemn?
'Tis God that justifies their souls;
And mercy like a mighty stream
O'er all their sins divinely rolls.

2 Who shall adjudge the saints to hell?
'Tis Christ that suffered in their stead;
And the salvation to fulfil,
Behold him rising from the dead.

3 He lives, he lives, and sits above,
For ever interceding there;
Who shall divide us from his love?
Or what should tempt us to despair?

4 Shall persecution, or distress,
Famine, or sword, or nakedness?
He that hath loved us bears us thro',[too.
And makes us more than conquerors,

5 Faith hath an overcoming power;
It triumphs in the dying hour;
Christ is our life, our joy, our hope,
Nor can we sink with such a prop.

6 Not all that men or earth can do,
Nor powers on high nor powers below,
Shall cause his mercy to remove, [love.
Or wean our hearts from Christ our
Watts.

74 (228) L. M. 2 Tim. 1:9.

1 Expand, my soul, arise and sing
The matchless grace of Zion's King;
His love, as ancient as his name,
Let all thy powers aloud proclaim.

2 Though sin and guilt infest them here,
In Christ they all complete appear;
The whole that justice e'er demands
Received full payment from his hands.

3 Then let our souls in him rejoice,
As favored objects of his choice;
Redeemed, and saved by grace, we sing
Eternal praise to Christ our King!
Tucker.

75 (229) L. M. Rom. 8:29.

1 Deep in the everlasting mind
The great mysterious purpose lay,
Of choosing some from lost mankind,
Whose sins the Lamb should bear away.

2 Them, loved with an eternal love,
To grace and glory he ordained;
Gave them a throne which cannot move,
And chose them both to ways and end.

3 In them he was resolved to make
The riches of his goodness known;
Them he accepts for Jesus' sake,
And views them righteous in his Son.

4 No goodness God forsaw in his,
But what his grace decreed to give;
No comeliness in them there is
Which they did not from him receive.

5 Faith and repentance he bestows
On such as he designs to save;
From him their souls' obedience flows,
And he shall all the glory have.
Gadsby's Col

ELECTION AND DECREES OF GOD.   31

ROCKINGHAM. L. M.   L. MASON.

1. There is a period known to God When all his sheep, redeem'd by blood, Shall leave the hateful ways of sin, Turn to the fold, and enter in.

76 (240) Rom. 8: 30. John 10: 16.

1 THERE is a period known to God
When all his sheep, redeemed by blood,
Shall leave the hateful ways of sin,
Turn to the fold, and enter in.

2 At peace with hell, with God at war,
In sin's dark maze they wander far,
Indulge their lust, and still go on
As far from God as sheep can run.

3 But see how Heaven's indulgent care
Attends their wanderings here and there:
Still near at hand, where'er they stray,
With pricking thorns to hedge their way.

4 Glory to God, they ne'er shall rove
Beyond the limits of his love:
Fenced with Jehovah's *shalls* and *wills*,
Firm as the everlasting hills.

5 Th' appointed time rolls on apace,
Not to *propose* but *call* by grace;
To change the heart, renew the will,
And turn their feet to Zion's hill.   Kent.

77 (242)   L. M.

1 OF God's great love, ere time began,
His thoughts of peace to rebel man,
Let Zion sing, nor e'er refrain,
To aid the sweet immortal strain.

2 His sons elect, He knows them well,
Nor less beloved when Adam fell;
Bound in life's bundle, called His own,
As sons of peace to Him foreknown.

3 Then, O believer, cease to mourn;
Return, unto thy rest return;
Indulge no more thy grief and wo;
His thoughts of peace eternal flow.

4 When in thy blood He saw thee lie,
He bade thee live, and passed thee by;
Bound up thy wounds, that all might see
His thoughts how peaceful then to thee.

5 Wake then, my soul, thy God to praise,
In all thy sweetest, noblest lays;
No seraph's song should rival thine,
A sinner saved by grace divine.
  Sonnets.

78 (243) L. M. Heb. 6: 17-19.

1 How oft have sin and Satan strove
    To rend my soul from thee, my God,
But everlasting is thy love,
    And Jesus seals it with his blood.

2 The oath and promise of the Lord
    Join to confirm the wondrous grace;
Eternal power performs the word,
    And fills all heaven with endless praise.

3 Amidst temptations sharp and long,
    My soul to this dear refuge flies:
Hope is my anchor firm and strong,
    While tempests blow and billows rise.

4 The gospel bears my spirit up;
    A faithful and unchanging God
Lays the foundation for my hope,
    In oaths, and promises, and blood
  Watts

ELECTION AND DECREES OF GOD.

ZELLA. H. M.   English.

1. O my dis-trust-ful heart, How small thy faith appears! But greater, Lord, thou art Than all my doubts and fears: Did Jesus once upon me shine! Then Jesus is for-ev-er mine.

79 (225) Phil. 1: 6.

2 Unchangeable his will,
  Though dark may be my frame;
His loving heart is still
  Eternally the same:
My soul through many changes goes;
His love no variation knows.

3 The bowels of his grace
  At first did freely move;
I still shall see his face,
  And feel that God is love:
Myself into thy arms I cast,
Lord, save, O save my soul at last!
Hammond.

80 (227) H. M. Eph. 1: 4.

1 ALL the elected train
  Were chosen in their Head,
To all eternal good,
  Before the worlds were made;
Chosen to know the Prince of Peace,
And taste the riches of his grace.

2 Chosen to faith and hope,
  To purity and love,
To all the life of God,
  To all the things above;
Chosen to prove salvation sure;
Chosen to reign for evermore.

3 Nothing but grace appears
  In this eternal choice;
It charms the humble saint,
  And makes the soul rejoice:
Its endless glories shine so bright,
It makes obedience all delight.
Burnham.

81 (273) H. M. Col. 3: 2.

1 COME, raise your thankful voice,
  Ye souls redeemed with blood;
Leave earth and all its joys,
  And triumph in your God.
Dearly we're bought, highly esteemed,
Redeemed, with Jesus' blood redeemed.

2 With heart, and soul, and mind,
  Exalt redeeming love:
Leave worldly cares behind,
  And set your minds above.
Dearly we're bought, highly esteemed,
Redeemed, with Jesus' blood redeemed.
Hart.

ELECTION AND DECREES OF GOD. 33

INVITATION. 8s, 7s, 4s. J. INGALLS. 1805.

1. Sons we are through God's e-lec-tion, Who in Je-sus Christ be-lieve;
D. C.—Lord, thy mer-cy, Lord, thy mer-cy Does both grace and glo-ry give.
By e-ter-nal des-ti-na-tion, Sovereign grace we here re-ceive:

82 (226)

2 Every fallen soul, by sinning,
  Merits everlasting pain ;
But thy love, without beginning,
  Has restored thy sons again ;
    Countless millions
  Shall in life through Jesus reign.

3 Pause, my soul, adore and wonder!
  Ask, "O why such love to me?"
Grace hath put me in the number
  Of the Saviour's family:
    Hallelujah!
  Thanks, eternal thanks to thee!

4 Since that love had no beginning,
  And shall never, never cease;
Keep, O keep me, Lord, from sinning!
  Guide me in the way of peace!
    Make me walk in
  All the paths of holiness.

5 When I quit this feeble mansion,
  And my soul returns to thee;
Let the power of thy ascension
  Manifest itself in me:
    Through thy Spirit
  Give the final victory.
                JOHN ADAMS. 1751-1835.

SICILIAN HYMN. 8s. 7s. & 4s. Sicilian Melody.

1. { Sons we are through God's e-lec-tion, Who in Je-sus Christ believe;
   { By e-ter-nal des-ti-na-tion, Sovereign grace we here receive:
Lord, thy mer-cy, Lord, thy mer-cy Does both grace and glo-ry give.

ELECTION AND DECREES OF GOD.

WILMOT. 7s. — C. M. VON WEBER. 1786–1826

1. Sov-'reign Rul-er of the skies! Ev-er gra-cious, ev-er wise!
All my times are in thy hand,—All e-vents at thy com-mand.

83 (239) Psalm 31: 15; 34: 1.

1 SOVEREIGN Ruler of the skies!
Ever gracious, ever wise!
All my times are in thy hand,—
All events at thy command.

2 His decree, who formed the earth,
Fixed my first and second birth:
Parents, native place, and time,—
All appointed were by him.

3 He that formed me in the womb,
He shall guide me to the tomb;
All my times shall ever be
Ordered by his wise decree.

4 Times of sickness, times of health,
Times of penury and wealth;
Times of trial and of grief,
Times of triumph and relief:

5 Times the tempter's power to prove;
Times to taste a Saviour's love:
All must come, and last, and end,
As shall please my heavenly friend.

6 Plagues and deaths around me fly;
Till he bids, I cannot die:
Not a single shaft can hit
Till the God of love sees fit.

7 O thou Gracious, Wise, and Just,
In thy hands my life I trust:
Have I somewhat dearer still?—
I resign it to thy will.

8 Thee, at all times, will I bless:
Having thee, I all possess:
How can I bereaved be,
Since I cannot part with thee
Ryland.

84 (329) 7s. Matt. 1: 23.

1 *God with us!* O glorious name!
Let it shine in endless fame:
God and man in Christ unite:
Oh, mysterious depth and height!

2 *God with us!* Amazing love
Brought him from his courts above;
Now, ye saints, his grace admire,
Swell the song with holy fire.

3 *God with us!* but tainted not
With the first transgressor's blot;
Yet, did he our sins sustain,
Bear the guilt, the curse, the pain.

4 *God with us!* Oh, wondrous grace!
Let us see him face to face,
That we may Emmanuel sing,
As we ought, our God and King.
Miss Sarah Slinn.

COVENANT OF GRACE.

GRATITUDE. L. M.

1. From deep dis-tress and troubled thoughts, To thee, my God, I raised my cries; If thou se-vere-ly mark our faults, No flesh can stand be-fore thine eyes.

85 (250)

1 From deep distress and troubled tho'ts,
  To thee, my God, I raised my cries;
  If thou severely mark our faults,
  No flesh can stand before thine eyes.

2 But thou has built thy throne of grace,
  Free to dispense thy pardons there,
  That sinners may approach thy face,
  And hope and love, as well as fear.

3 As the benighted pilgrims wait,
  And long, and wish for breaking day,
  So waits my soul before thy gate;
  When will my God his face display?

4 My trust is fixed upon the Word,
  Nor shall I trust thy Word in vain;
  Let mourning souls address the Lord,
  And find relief from all their pain.

5 Great is his love, and large his grace,
  Through the redemption of his Son;
  He turns our feet from sinful ways,
  And pardons what our hands have done.
  Watts.

86 (258) L. M.

1 Great source of all eternal grace,
  That saints shall know, or seraphs trace;
  Thee we'll attempt in songs to praise,
  For acts of grace in ancient days.

2 Long ere the day that Adam fell,
  The covenant stood in all things well;
  Grace had secured in Jesus then,
  Millions untold of chosen men.

3 By grace their names were all enrolled,
  As chosen sheep within its fold;
  'Tis grace secures their standing there
  In lines of love divinely fair.
  Kent.

87 (259) L. M.

1 When in the cloud, with colors fair,
  I see the ancient bow appear,
  Its beauteous form and lovely rays,
  Awake my soul to love and praise.

2 It tells me now how firm the base,
  The oath, the promise, and the grace,
  Which God of old, ere time begun,
  To Zion swear, in Christ his Son.

3 Dejected saint, dismiss thy fears,
  Still round the throne the bow appears,
  Portending peace and mercy free,
  And full salvation now to thee.

4 It points thy soul to Jesus now;
  Vindictive wrath once smote his brow,
  That on thy guilty soul and mine,
  No storms should beat of wrath divine.

5 Sweet sign, that God remembers now
  To guilty man his ancient vow;
  But sweeter far by faith to see
  A covenant God, all love to thee.

6 Here when thy fears begin to rise,
  And hope in disappointment dies,
  This covenant bow thy fears shall quell,
  'Twas made for thee, in all things well.
  Newton.

REDEMPTION.

HUBERT. C. M.

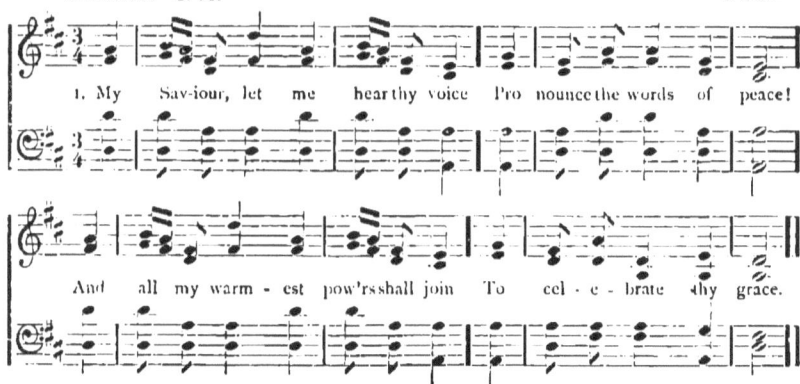

1. My Saviour, let me hear thy voice Pronounce the words of peace! And all my warmest pow'rs shall join To celebrate thy grace.

88 (264) Matt. 9: 2.

1 My Saviour, let me hear thy voice
  Pronounce the words of peace!
And all my warmest powers shall join
  To celebrate thy grace.

2 With gentle smiles call me thy child,
  And speak my sins forgiven;
The accents mild shall charm mine ear
  All like the harps of heaven.

3 Cheerful, where'er thy hand shall lead,
  The darkest path I'll tread;
Cheerful I'll quit these mortal shores,
  And mingle with the dead.

4 When dreadful guilt is done away,
  No other fears we know;
That hand which scatters pardons down,
  Shall crowns of life bestow. *Doddridge.*

89 (263) Matt. 9: 2.

1 How high a privilege 'tis to know
  Our sins are all forgiven;
To bear about this pledge below—
  This special grant of heaven!

2 To look on this when sunk in fears,
  While each repeated sight,
Like some reviving cordial, cheers,
  And makes temptations light;

3 Oh! what is honor, wealth, or mirth,
  To this well-grounded peace:
How poor are all the goods of earth,
  To such a gift as this!

4 This is a treasure rich indeed,
  Which none but Christ can give;
Of this the best of men have need;
  This I, the worst, receive. *Hart.*

MANOAH. C. M.

1. How high a priv'lege 'tis to know Our sins are all for-giv'n; To bear about this pledge below— This special grant of heav'n!

REDEMPTION.

FOUNTAIN. C. M. Arr. Dr. LOWELL MASON. 1830.

1. There is a fountain, fill'd with blood, Drawn from Immanuel's veins; And sinners, plunged be-neath that flood, Lose all their guilty stains, Lose all their guilty stains, Lose all their guilty stains.

90 (275) Zech. 13: 1; 1 John 1: 7.

2 The dying thief rejoiced to see
That fountain in his day;
O may I there, though vile as he,
Wash all my sins away.

3 Dear, dying Lamb! thy precious blood
Shall never lose its power,
Till all the ransomed church of God
Be saved, to sin no more.

4 E'er since, by faith, I saw the stream
Thy flowing wounds supply,
Redeeming love has been my theme,
And shall be till I die.

5 Then in a nobler, sweeter song,
I'll sing thy power to save,
When this poor, lisping, stamm'ring tongue
Lies silent in the grave.   Cowper.

DENFIELD. C. M. C. G. GLASER. 1784-1829.

1. On Zi-on's sa-cred mount I saw The Lamb for sin-ners slain;
His church redeem'd from end-less wo, Com-pos'd his glo-rious train.

91 (280)

2 This virgin throng, beloved of God,
All stood around him there,
With garments washed in his own blood,
Divinely bright and fair.

3 I strove this blood-bought host to count,
Thus to my sight revealed;
And found at last their full amount,
'Twas all that God had sealed.

4 They sung a song, for ever new,
And none could learn the same,
But ransomed slaves, and sinners, who
From tribulation came.

5 They hymned the great, the dread, I AM,
Whose sacred name they wore, [AM,
With endless honors to the Lamb,
'Till time shall be no more.   Kent.

REDEMPTION.

REFUGE. L. M.
FLORENCE VANE. Arr. by C. LEWIS.

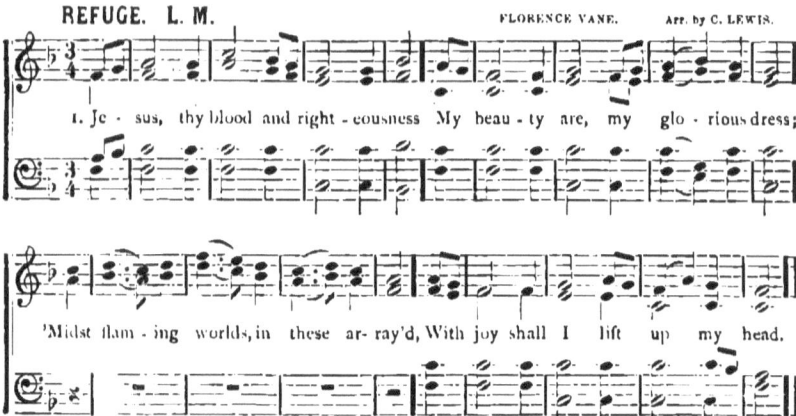

1. Je-sus, thy blood and right-eousness My beau-ty are, my glo-rious dress;
'Midst flam-ing worlds, in these ar-ray'd, With joy shall I lift up my head.

92 (299) Isa. 61: 10.

1 JESUS, thy blood and righteousness
My beauty are, my glorious dress;
'Midst flaming worlds, in these arrayed,
With joy shall I lift up my head.

2 When from the dust of death I rise,
To take my mansion in the skies,
E'en this shall then be all my plea,
"Jesus hath lived and died for me."

3 Bold shall I stand in that great day,
For who, aught to my charge shall lay,
While through thy blood absolved I am,
From sin's tremendous curse and shame?

4 Thus Abraham, the friend of God,
Thus all the armies bought with blood,
Saviour of sinners, thee proclaim—
Sinners of whom the chief I am.

5 This spotless robe the same appears,
When ruined nature sinks in years;
No age can change its glorious hue;
The robe of Christ is ever new.

6 O let the dead now hear thy voice;
Bid, Lord, thy banished ones rejoice;
Their beauty this, their glorious dress,
Jesus, the Lord, our righteousness.

Count Zinzendorf.

93 (394) L. M. Heb. 12: 2.

1 By various maxims, forms, and rules,
That pass for wisdom in the schools,
I strove my passion to restrain,
But all my efforts proved in vain.

2 But since the Saviour I have known,
My rules are all reduced to one,
To keep my Lord, by faith, in view;
This strength supplies, and motives, too.

3 I see him lead a suffering life,
Patient amidst reproach and strife;
And from his pattern courage take,
To bear and suffer for his sake.

4 Upon the cross I see him bleed,
And by the sight from guilt am freed;
This sight destroys the life of sin,
And quickens heavenly life within.

5 To look to Jesus as he rose,
Confirms my faith, disarms my foes;
Satan I shame and overcome,
By pointing to my Saviour's tomb.

6 Exalted on his glorious throne,
I see him make my cause his own;
Then all my anxious cares subside,
For Jesus lives, and will provide.

7 I see him look with pity down,
And hold in view the conqueror's crown;
If pressed with griefs and cares before,
My soul revives, nor asks for more.

8 By faith I see the hour at hand,
When in his presence I shall stand;
Then it will be my endless bliss,
To see him where, and as he is.

W——.

REDEMPTION.

GOSHEN. 11s. *German.*

1. O Zion! afflicted with wave upon wave, Whom no man can
D.S.—In toiling and

com-fort, whom no man can save; With dark-ness sur-round-ed, by terrors dismayed,
row-ing, thy strength is de-cayed.

94 (192)

1 O Zion! afflicted with wave upon wave,
Whom no man can comfort, whom no man
   can save;
With darkness surrounded, by terrors
   dismayed,
In toiling and rowing, thy strength is
   decayed.

2 Loud roaring, the billows now nigh overwhelm;
But skilful's the Pilot who stands at the
   helm;
His wisdom conducts thee, his power
   defends,
In safety and quiet thy warfare he ends.

3 "O fearful! O faithless!" in mercy he
   cries,
"My promise, my truth, are they light in
   thy eyes?
Still, still I am with thee, my promise
   shall stand,
Through tempest and tossing I'll bring
   thee to land.

4 "Forget thee, I will not, I cannot, thy
   name
Engraved on my heart, doth forever
   remain;

The palms of my hands, whilst I look on,
   I see
The wounds I received when suffering for
   thee.

5 "I feel at my heart all thy sighs and
   thy groans,
For thou art most near me, my flesh, and
   my bones;
In all thy distresses, thy Head feels the pain,
Yet all are most needful, not one is in vain.

6 "Then trust me and fear not, thy life
   is secure;
My wisdom is perfect, supreme is my
   power;
In love I correct thee, thy soul to refine,
To make thee at length in my likeness to
   shine.

7 "The foolish, the fearful, the weak are
   my care,
The helpless, the hopeless, I hear their
   sad prayer;
From all their afflictions, my glory shall
   spring,
And the deeper their sorrows, the louder
   they'll sing."

Grant.

REDEMPTION.

PROSPECT. L. M.
GRAHAM. Arr. F. L. A.

1. Poor, weak, and worth-less though I am, I have a rich al-might-y Friend; Je-sus, the Sav-iour, is his name;
D.S.—He freely loves, and with-out end.

95 (277) 2 Sam. 16: 17.

2 He ransomed me from hell with blood,
And by his power my foes controlled;
He found me, wandering far from God,
And brought me to his chosen fold.

3 He cheers my heart, my want supplies,
And says that I shall shortly be
Enthroned with him above the skies,
Oh! what a Friend is Christ to me.

4 But, ah! my inmost spirit mourns,
And well my eyes with tears may swim,
To think of my perverse returns;
I've been a faithless friend to him.

5 Often my gracious Friend I grieve,
Neglect, distrust, and disobey,
And often Satan's lies believe,
Sooner than all my Friend can say.

6 He bids me always freely come,
And promises whate'er I ask;
But I am straitened, cold and dumb,
And count my privilege a task.

7 Before the world, that hates his cause,
My treacherous heart has throbbed with shame;
Loth to forego the world's applause,
I hardly dare avow his name.

8 Sure, were not I most vile and base,
I could not thus my Friend requite!

And were not he the God of grace,
He'd frown and spurn me from his sight.
Newton.

96 (278) L. M.

1 How wondrous are the works of God,
Displayed through all the world abroad!
Immensely great! immensely small!
Yet one strange work exceeds them all.

2 He formed the sun, fair fount of light:
The moon and stars to rule the night:
But night, and stars, and moon, and sun,
Are little works compared with one.

3 He rolled the seas, and spread the skies,
Made valleys sink, and mountains rise;
The meadows clothed with native green,
And bade the rivers glide between.

4 But what are seas, or skies, or hills,
Or verdant vales, or gliding rills,
To wonders man was born to prove:
The wonders of redeeming love!

5 'Tis far beyond what words express,
What saints can feel or angels guess:
Angels, that hymn the great I AM,
Fall down, and veil before the Lamb.

6 The highest heavens are short of this;
'Tis deeper than the vast abyss;
'Tis more than thought can e'er conceive,
Or hope expect, or faith believe.
Hart.

REDEMPTION.

WOODBURY. L. M. S. K. WHITING.

1. Enslav'd by sin, and bound in chains Beneath its dreadful tyrant sway, And doom'd to everlasting pains, We wretched guilty captives lay.

97 (284) 1 Pet. 1: 18.

1 ENSLAVED by sin, and bound in chains
Beneath its dreadful tyrant sway,
And doomed to everlasting pains,
We wretched guilty captives lay.

2 Jesus the sacrifice became
To rescue guilty souls from hell:
The spotless, bleeding, dying Lamb,
Beneath avenging justice fell.

3 Amazing goodness! love divine!
O may our grateful hearts adore
The matchless grace; nor yield to sin,
Nor wear its cruel fetters more!

4 Dear Saviour, let thy love pursue
The glorious work it has begun;
Each secret lurking foe subdue,
And let our hearts be thine alone.
Mrs. Steele

98 (285) L. M. John 19: 30.

1 'TIS finished! so the Saviour cried,
And meekly bowed his head and died;
'Tis finished—yes, the race is run,
The battle fought, the victory won.

2 'Tis finished—all that Heaven decreed,
And all the ancient prophets said,
Is now fulfilled, as was designed,
In me, the Saviour of mankind.

3 'Tis finished—Aaron now no more
Must stain his robes with purple gore;
The sacred veil is rent in twain,
And Jewish rites no more remain.

4 'Tis finished—this my dying groan,
Shall sins of every kind atone:
Millions shall be redeemed from death
By this, my last expiring breath.

5 'Tis finished—Heaven is reconciled,
And all the powers of darkness spoiled;
Peace, love, and happiness again
Return, and dwell with sinful men.

6 'Tis finished—let the joyful sound
Be heard through all the nations round:
'Tis finished—let the echo fly
Thro' heaven and hell, thro' earth and sky.
Stennett.

99 (297) L. M. Micah 5: 5.

1 PEACE, by his cross, hath Jesus made,
The Church's everlasting Head;
O'er hell and sin hath victory won,
And with a shout to glory gone.

2 Then why, dejected saint, dost thou
Thy sorrows nurse, thy head thus bow?
Eternal truth declares to thee
This glorious Man thy peace shall be.

3 When o'er thy head the billows roll,
And shades of sin obscure thy soul;
When thou can'st no deliverance see,
Yet still this Man thy peace shall be.

4 In tribulation's thorny maze,
Or on the mount of sovereign grace,
Or in the fire, or through the sea,
This glorious Man thy peace shall be.
Kent.

REDEMPTION.

COWPER. C. M. Dr. LOWELL MASON. 1792-1872.

1. Plunged in a gulf of dark despair, We wretched sinners lay, Without one cheerful beam of hope, Or spark of glimm'ring day, Or spark of glimm'ring day.

100 (283)

1 PLUNGED in a gulf of dark despair,
  We wretched sinners lay,
Without one cheerful beam of hope,
  Or spark of glimmering day.

2 With pitying eyes, the Prince of Grace
  Beheld our helpless grief,
He saw, and (O amazing love!)
  He ran to our relief.

3 Down from the shining seats above
  With joyful haste he fled,
Entered the grave in mortal flesh,
  And dwelt among the dead.

4 He spoiled the powers of darkness thus,
  And brake our iron chains;
Jesus has freed our captive souls
  From everlasting pains.

5 O for such love, let rocks and hills
  Their lasting silence break,
And all harmonious human tongues
  The Saviour's praises speak.
                                Watts.

101 (288) C. M. Phil. 2: 8.

1 AND did the Holy and the Just,
  The Sovereign of the skies,
Stoop down to wretchedness and dust,
  That guilty worms might rise?

2 Yes, the Redeemer left his throne,
  His radiant throne on high,
(Surprising mercy! love unknown!)
  To suffer, bleed, and die!

3 He took the dying traitor's place,
  And suffered in his stead;
For man, (O, miracle of grace!)
  For man the Saviour bled.

4 Dear Lord, what heavenly wonders
  In thy atoning blood!   [dwell
By this are sinners snatched from hell,
  And rebels brought to God.

5 What glad return can I impart
  For favors so divine!
O! take my all, this worthless heart,
  And make it wholly thine.
                              Mrs. Steele.

102 (291) C. M. Ps. 110: 4; Rev. 5: 12.

1 THOU dear Redeemer, dying Lamb,
  We love to hear of thee;
No music's like thy charming name,
  Nor half so sweet can be.

2 O let us ever hear thy voice;
  In mercy to us speak;
And in our Priest we will rejoice,
  Thou great Melchisedec!

3 Our Jesus shall be still our theme,
  While in this world we stay;
We'll sing our Jesus' lovely name,
  When all things else decay.

4 When we appear in yonder cloud,
  With all thy favored throng,
Then will we sing more sweet, more loud,
  And Christ shall be our song.
                              Cennick.

REDEMPTION. 43

CAMBRIDGE. C. M.   JOHN RANDALL. 1715-1799.

1. Fa-ther, I sing thy wondrous grace, I bless my Saviour's name; He brought salvation for the poor, And bore the sinner's shame, And bore the sinner's shame, And bore the sinner's shame.

103 (293)

1 Father, I sing thy wondrous grace,
  I bless my Saviour's name ;
He brought salvation for the poor,
  And bore the sinner's shame.

2 His deep distress has raised us high,
  His duty and his zeal
Fulfilled the law which mortals broke
  And finished all thy will.

3 His dying groans, his living songs
  Shall better please my God,
Than harp or trumpet's solemn sound,
  Than goats' or bullocks' blood.

4 This shall his humble followers see,
  And set their hearts at rest ;
They by his death draw near to thee,
  And live for ever blest.

5 Let heaven and all that dwell on high
  To God their voices raise.
While lands and seas assist the sky,
  And join t' advance his praise.
                                Watts.

104 (302) C. M. Rom. 3: 19-22.

1 Vain are the hopes the sons of men
  On their own works have built ;
Their hearts by nature all unclean,
  And all their actions guilt.

2 Let Jew and Gentile stop their mouths,
  Without a murmuring word,
And the whole race of Adam stand
  Guilty before the Lord.

3 In vain we ask God's righteous law
  To justify us now,
Since to convince and to condemn,
  Is all the law can do.

4 Jesus, how glorious is thy grace !
  When in thy name we trust,
Our faith receives a righteousness
  That makes the sinner just.
                                Watts.

105 (305) C. M. Heb. 10. 19.

1 Great God ! from thee there's naught
    concealed,
  Thou seest my inward frame ;
To thee I always stand revealed,
  Exactly as I am !

2 Since I can hardly, therefore, bear
    What in myself I see ;
How vile and black must I appear,
  Most holy God, to thee !

3 But since my Saviour stands between,
  In garments dyed in blood ;
'Tis he, instead of me, is seen,
  When I approach to God.

4 Thus, though a sinner, I am safe,
  He pleads, before the throne,
His life and death in my behalf,
  And calls my sins his own.

5 What wondrous love, what mysteries,
  In this appointment shine ;
My breaches of the law are his,
  And his obedience mine.
                                Newton.

RIGHTEOUSNESS.

MIDDLETON. 8s. & 7s.
WM. SHIELDS, 1796.

1. Come, thou long-expected Jesus!
   Born to set thy people free;
   From our fears and sins release us,
   Let us find our rest in thee;
D.C.—Dear Desire of ev'ry nation,
   Joy of ev'ry longing heart.

Israel's strength and consolation,
Hope of all the saints thou art;

106 (324) Luke 2: 25.

Born, thy people to deliver;
Born a child, and yet a king;
Born to reign in us for ever,
  Now thy gracious kingdom bring:
By thine own eternal Spirit,
  Rule in all our hearts alone;
By thine all-sufficient merit,
  Raise us to thy glorious throne.
C. Wesley.

107 (335) 8s. & 7s. Isaiah 9: 2.

1 LIGHT of those whose dreary dwelling
  Borders on the shades of death,
Come! and, thy dear self revealing,
  Dissipate the clouds beneath;
The new heaven's and earth's Creator,
  In our deepest darkness rise!
Scattering all the night of nature,
  Pouring day upon our eyes.

2 Still we wait for thine appearing,
  Life and joy thy beams impart,
Chasing all our fears, and cheering
  Every poor benighted heart;
Come, and manifest the favor
  Thou hast for the ransomed race:
Come, thou dear exalted Saviour!
  Come, and bring thy gospel grace.

3 Save us in thy great compassion,
  O thou mild pacific Prince!
Give the knowledge of salvation,
  Give the pardon of our sins:

By thine all-sufficient merit,
  Every burdened soul release;
By the influence of thy Spirit,
  Guide us into perfect peace.
C. Wesley.

108 (380) 8s. & 7s.

1 JESUS heals the broken-hearted,
  Oh! how sweet that sound to me!
Once beneath my sin he smarted,
  Groaned, and bled, to set me free.
By his sufferings, death and merits,
  By his Godhead, blood and pain,
Broken hearts or wounded spirits,
  Are at once made whole again.

2 Broken by the law's loud thunder,
  To the cross for refuge flee;
O'er his pungent sorrows ponder,
  'Tis his stripes that healeth thee.
Oil and wine, to heal and cherish,
  Jesus still to Israel gives;
Nor shall e'er a sinner perish,
  Who in his dear name believes.

3 In his righteousness confiding,
  Sheltered safe beneath his wing,
Here they find a sure abiding,
  And of covenant mercy sing;
Seek, my soul, no other healing,
  But in Jesus' balmy blood;
He, beneath the Spirit's sealing,
  Stands the great High Priest with God.
Kent.

RIGHTEOUSNESS.

BRAY. C. M. HERMANN. 1544.

1. Awake, my heart, a-rise, my tongue, Pre-pare a tuneful voice; In God, the life of all my joys, A-loud will I re-joice....... A-loud will I re-joice.

109 (311) Isa. 61:10.

1 AWAKE, my heart, arise, my tongue,
  Prepare a tuneful voice;
  In God, the life of all my joys,
  Aloud will I rejoice.

2 'Tis he adorned my naked soul,
  And made salvation mine;
  Upon a poor, polluted worm
  He makes his graces shine.

3 And, lest the shadow of a spot
  Should on my soul be found,
  He took the robe the Saviour wrought,
  And cast it all around.

4 How far the heavenly robe exceeds
  What earthly princes wear;
  These ornaments, how bright they shine;
  How white the garments are.

5 The Spirit wrought my faith, and love,
  And hope, and every grace;
  But Jesus spent his life to work
  The robe of righteousness.

6 Strangely, my soul, art thou arrayed
  By the great sacred Three;
  In sweetest harmony of praise
  Let all thy powers agree. Watts.

110 (316) C. M. Psa. 87:7.

1 Now, dearest Lord, to praise thy name,
  Let all our powers agree;
  Worthy art thou of endless fame;
  Our springs are all in thee.

2 Here in thy love will we rejoice,
  All sovereign, rich, and free;
  Singing, we hope with heart and voice,
  Our springs are all in thee.

3 To whom, dear Jesus, O, to whom
  Shall needy sinners flee,
  But to thyself, who bidst us come?
  Our springs are all in thee.

4 Some tempted, weak, and trembling saint
  Before thee now may be;
  Let not his hopes or wishes faint;
  His springs are all in thee.

5 The poor supply, the wounded heal;
  Let sinners, such as we,
  Salvation's blessings taste and feel;
  Our springs are all in thee.

6 When we arrive at Zion's hill,
  And all thy glory see,
  Our joyful songs shall echo still,
  Our springs are all in thee. Medley.

P. G. LESTER.
FINE.

HASSELL. C. M.

D.C.

CHARACTER AND OFFICES OF CHRIST.

CORONATION. C. M.
OLIVER HOLDEN 1765-1844.

1. All hail the power of Jesus' name! Let angels prostrate fall; Bring forth the royal di-a-dem, And crown him Lord of all; Bring forth the royal di - a - dem, And crown him Lord of all.

111 (331) Cant. 3: 11.

1 ALL hail the power of Jesus' name!
  Let angels prostrate fall;
  Bring forth the royal diadem,
  And crown him Lord of all.

2 Crown him, ye martyrs of our God,
  Who from his altar call;
  Extol the stem of Jesse's rod,
  And crown him Lord of all.

3 Ye chosen seed of Israel's race,
  A remnant weak and small!
  Hail him who saves you by his grace,
  And crown him Lord of all.

4 Ye Gentile sinners, ne'er forget
  The wormwood and the gall;
  Go—spread your trophies at his feet,
  And crown him Lord of all.

5 Let every kindred, every tribe,
  On this terrestrial ball,
  To him all majesty ascribe,
  And crown him Lord of all.

6 Oh that, with yonder sacred throng,
  We at his feet may fall;
  We'll join the *everlasting* song,
  And crown him Lord of all.
  Perronet.

112 (328) C. M. 1 Pet. 2: 7.

1 JESUS, I love thy charming name,
  'Tis music to my ear;
  Fain would I sound it out so loud
  That earth and heaven might hear.

2 Yes, thou art precious to my soul!
  My transport and my trust:
  Jewels to thee are gaudy toys,
  And gold is sordid dust.

3 All my capacious powers can wish,
  In thee doth richly meet;
  Nor to my eyes is light so dear,
  Nor friendship half so sweet.

4 Thy grace shall dwell upon my heart,
  And shed its fragrance there;
  The noblest balm for all its wounds,
  The cordial for its care.

5 I'll speak the honors of thy name
  With my last laboring breath;
  And, dying, clasp thee in my arms—
  The antidote of death.
  Doddridge.

113 (326) C. M. Eph. 4: 15, 16.

1 JESUS, I sing thy wondrous grace
  That calls a worm thy own;
  Gives me among thy saints a place
  To make thy glories known.

2 Allied to thee, our vital Head,
  We act, and grow, and thrive;
  From thee divided, each is dead
  When most he seems alive.

3 Thy saints on earth, and those above,
  Here join in sweet accord:
  One body all in mutual love,
  And thou our common Lord.
  Doddridge.

CHARACTER AND OFFICES OF CHRIST. 47

NOTTING HILL. C. M.   C. H. PURDAY.

1. The Saviour! O what endless charms Dwell in the blissful sound! Its influence ev'ry fear disarms, And spreads sweet comfort round.

114 (348)

1 THE Saviour! O what endless charms
Dwell in the blissful sound!
Its influence every fear disarms,
And spreads sweet comfort round.

2 Here pardon, life, and joys divine,
In rich effusion flow,
For guilty rebels lost in sin,
Deserving endless wo.

3 O the rich depths of love divine,
Of bliss a boundless store!
Dear Saviour, let me call thee mine;
I cannot wish for more.

4 On thee alone my hope relies;
Beneath thy cross I fall;
My Lord, my life, my sacrifice,
My Saviour, and my all.
                 Mrs. Steele.

115 (365)   C. M.

1 MY SHEPHERD will supply my need,
Jehovah is his name;
In pastures fresh he makes me feed,
Beside the living stream.

2 He brings my wandering spirit back,
When I forsake his ways;
And leads me, for his mercy's sake,
In paths of truth and grace.

3 When I walk through the shades of
Thy presence is my stay;   [death,
A word of thy supporting breath
Drives all my fears away.

4 Thy hand, in sight of all my foes,
Doth still my table spread;
My cup with blessings overflows,
Thine oil anoints my head.

5 The sure provisions of my God
Attend me all my days;
O may thy house be mine abode,
And all my work be praise!

6 There would I find a settled rest,
(While others go and come,)
No more a stranger or a guest,
But like a child at home.
                 Watts.

116 (330)   C. M.

1 COME, ye that love the Saviour's name,
And joy to make it known;
The sovereign of your heart proclaim,
And bow before his throne.

2 When in his earthly courts we view
The glories of our King,
We long to love as angels do,
And wish like them to sing.

3 And shall we long and wish in vain?
Lord, teach our song to rise!
Thy love can animate the strain,
And bid it reach the skies.

4 Oh, happy period! glorious day!
When heaven and earth shall raise,
With all their powers, the raptured lay,
To celebrate thy praise.
                 Mrs. Steele.

CHARACTER AND OFFICES OF CHRIST.

BRIDGEWATER. L. M.
L. EDSON, 1782.

1. The Saviour calls his people sheep, And bids them on his love rely;
For he alone their souls can keep, And he alone their wants supply, And he alone their wants supply.

117 (319)

2 Jehovah is our Shepherd's name,
Then what have we, though weak, to
Our sin and folly we proclaim, [fear?
If we despond while he is near.

3 When Satan threatens to devour;
When troubles press on every side;
Think of our Shepherd's care and power,
He can defend, he will provide.

4 See the rich pastures of his grace,
Where, in full streams, salvation flows!
There he appoints our resting place,
And we may feed, secure from foes.

5 There, 'midst the flock, the Shepherd
The sheep around in safety lie; [dwells.
The wolf, in vain, with malice swells,
For he protects them with his eye.

6 Dear Lord, if I am one of thine,
From anxious thoughts I would be free
To trust, and love, and praise, is mine
The care of all belongs to thee.
Sonnets.

118 (327) L. M. John 3: 16; 2 Cor. 9: 15.

1 JESUS, my love, my chief delight,
For thee I long, for thee I pray,
Amid the shadows of the night,
Amid the business of the day.

2 When shall I see thy smiling face—
That face which I have often seen?
Arise, thou Sun of Righteousness!
Scatter the clouds that intervene.

3 Thou art the glorious Gift of God
To sinners weary and distrest ;
The first of all his gifts bestowed,
And certain pledge of all the rest.

4 Could I but say this Gift is mine,
I'd tread the world beneath my feet,
No more at poverty repine,
Nor envy the rich sinner's state.

5 The precious jewel I would keep,
And lodge it deep within my heart ;
At home, abroad, awake, asleep,
It never should from thence depart!
Beddome.

CHARACTER AND OFFICES OF CHRIST. 49

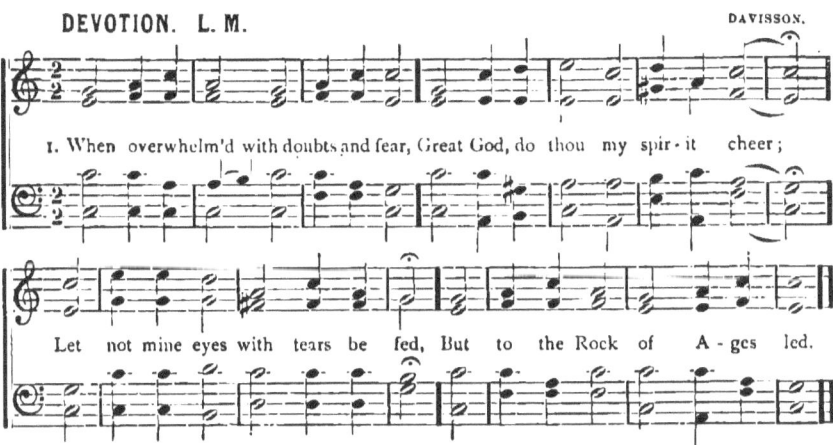

DEVOTION. L. M. — DAVISSON.

1. When overwhelm'd with doubts and fear, Great God, do thou my spir-it cheer; Let not mine eyes with tears be fed, But to the Rock of A-ges led.

119 (318)

1 WHEN overwhelmed with doubts and
Great God, do thou my spirit cheer; [fear,
Let not mine eyes with tears be fed,
But to the Rock of Ages led.

2 When storms of sin and sorrow beat,
Lead me to this divine retreat;
Thy perfect righteousness and blood,
My Rock, my Fortress, and my God.

3 When guilt lies heavy on my soul,
And waves of fierce temptation roll,
I'll to the Rock for shelter flee,
And take my refuge, Lord, in thee.

4 When called the vale of Death to tread,
Then to his Rock may I be led;
Nor fear to cross that gloomy sea,
Since thou hast tasted death for me.
Kent.

120 (334) L. M. John 11: 10.

1 WHEN sins and fears prevailing rise,
And fainting hope almost expires,
Jesus, to thee, I lift my eyes—
To thee I breathe my soul's desires.

2 Art thou not mine, my living Lord?
And can my hope—my comfort die?
Fixed on thy everlasting word; [sky?
That word which built the earth and

3 If my immortal Saviour lives,
Then my immortal life is sure;
His word a firm foundation gives;
Here let me build and rest secure.

4 Here let my faith unshaken dwell;
Immovable the promise stands;
Not all the powers of earth or hell,
Can e'er dissolve the sacred bands.

5 Here, O my soul, thy trust repose!
If Jesus is for ever mine,
Not death itself, that last of foes,
Shall break a union so divine.
Mrs. Steele.

121 (338) L. M. Acts 4: 12.

1 JESUS, the spring of joys divine,
Whence all our hopes and comforts
Jesus, no other name but thine [flow;
Can save us from eternal wo.

2 In vain would boasting reason find
The way to happiness and God;
Her weak directions leave the mind
Bewildered in a dubious road.

3 No other name will heaven approve;
Thou art the true, the living way,
Ordained by everlasting love,
To the bright realms of endless day.

4 Here let our constant feet abide,
Nor from the heavenly path depart:
O let thy Spirit, gracious Guide!
Direct our steps, and cheer our heart.

5 Safe lead us through this world of night,
And bring us to the blissful plains,
The regions of unclouded light,
Where perfect joy for ever reigns.
Mrs. Steele.

CHARACTER AND OFFICES OF CHRIST.

THATCHER. S. M. — HANDEL.

122 (353)
1 IN Sharon's lovely Rose
Immortal beauties shine;
Its sweet refreshing fragrance shows
Its origin divine.

2 How blooming and how fair!
O may my happy breast
This lovely rose for ever wear,
And be supremely blest. John Dobell.

LEBANON. S. M. D. — J. ZUNDEL. 1815-1882.

123 (367) S. M.
3 If e'er I go astray,
  He doth my soul reclaim,
And guides me in his own right way,
  For his most holy name.
4 While he affords his aid,
  I cannot yield to fear; [shade,
Though I should walk thro' death's dark
  My Shepherd's with me there.

5 In sight of all my foes,
  Thou dost my table spread;
My cup with blessings overflows,
  And joy exalts my head.
6 The bounties of thy love
  Shall crown my following days;
Nor from thy house will I remove,
  Nor cease to speak thy praise. Watts.

CHARACTER AND OFFICES OF CHRIST. 51

DUANE STREET. L. M.   Rev. G. COLES 1792–1858.

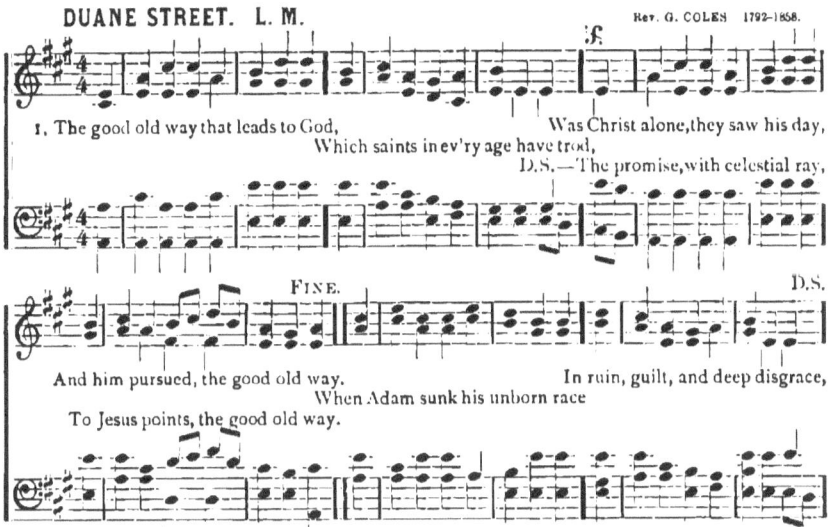

1. The good old way that leads to God,
Which saints in ev'ry age have trod,
Was Christ alone, they saw his day,
And him pursued, the good old way.

D.S.—The promise, with celestial ray,
In ruin, guilt, and deep disgrace,
When Adam sunk his unborn race
To Jesus points, the good old way.

124 (357)

1 THE good old way that leads to God,
Which saints in every age have trod,
Was Christ alone, they saw his day,
And him pursued, the good old way.

2 When Adam sunk his unborn race
In ruin, guilt, and deep disgrace,
The promise, with celestial ray,
To Jesus points, the good old way.

3 Th' apostles all proclaimed him thus,
Jesus the Lord, or God with us,
Who did by death our ransom pay,
The truth, the life, the good old way.

4 'Tis true, there's one exceeding broad,
Cast up by men, a dangerous road,
Where thousands to destruction stray,
Who never found this good old way.

5 Cheer up, believer, courage take;
Why should thy heart with sorrow break?
Eternal joys shall soon repay,
The sorrows of the good old way.

6 Should foes and fears on every hand,
Thick as the leaves in autumn stand,
Still forward press, the day is yours;
The good old way the crown secures.

Kent.

125 (358)   L. M.

1 JESUS, my All, to heaven is gone,
He whom I fix my hopes upon!
His track I see, and I'll pursue
The narrow way, till him I view.

2 The way the holy prophets went,
The road that leads from banishment,
The King's highway of holiness,
I'll go; for all his paths are peace.

3 This is the way I long have sought,
And mourned because I found it not;
My grief and burden long have been,
Because I could not cease from sin.

4 The more I strove against its power,
I sinned and stumbled but the more;
Till late I heard my Saviour say,
"Come hither, soul, *I am the way.*"

5 Lo! glad I come! and thou, blest Lamb,
Shalt take me to thee as I am!
My sinful self to thee I give:
Nothing but love shall I receive.

6 Then will I tell to sinners round
What a dear Saviour I have found:
I'll point to thy redeeming blood,
And say, *Behold the way to God.*

Cennick.

CHARACTER AND OFFICES OF CHRIST.

TOPLADY. 7s. 6l. Dr. THOS. HASTINGS. 1784-1872.

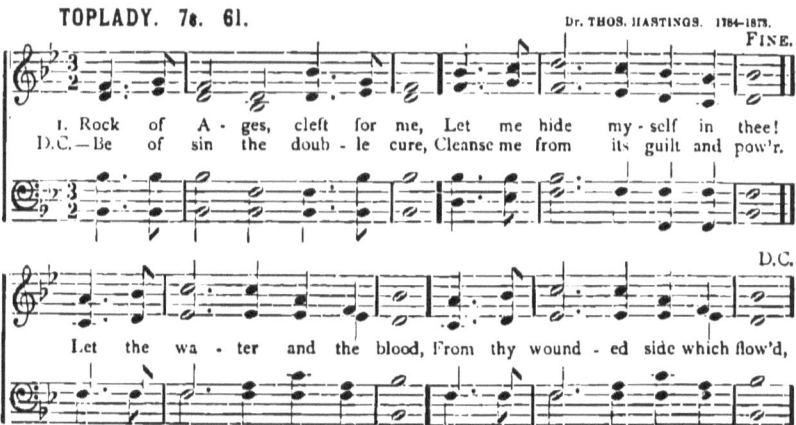

1. Rock of A-ges, cleft for me, Let me hide my-self in thee!
D.C.—Be of sin the doub-le cure, Cleanse me from its guilt and pow'r.

Let the wa-ter and the blood, From thy wound-ed side which flow'd,

126 (368) 1 Cor. 10: 4.

2 Not the labors of my hands
Can fulfil thy law's demands;
Could my zeal no respite know,
Could my tears for ever flow,
All for sin could not atone;
Thou must save, and thou alone.

3 Nothing in my hand I bring!
Simply to thy cross I cling;
Naked, come to thee for dress;
Helpless, look to thee for grace;
Black, I to the fountain fly;
Wash me, Saviour, or I die!

4 While I draw this fleeting breath,
When my eyelids close in death,
When I soar to worlds unknown,
See thee on thy judgment throne,—
Rock of Ages, cleft for me,
Let me hide myself in thee!
Toplady.

127 (552) 7s.

1 Quiet, Lord, my froward heart;
Make me teachable and mild,
Upright, simple, free from art;
Make me as a weaned child:
From distrust and envy free,
Pleased with all that pleases thee.

2 What thou shalt to-day provide,
Let me as a child receive;
What to-morrow may betide,
Calmly to thy wisdom leave:

'Tis enough that thou wilt care;
Why should I the burden bear?

3 As a little child relies
On a care beyond his own,
Knows he's neither strong nor wise,
Fears to stir a step alone,
Let me thus with thee abide,
As my Father, Guard, and Guide.

4 Thus preserved from Satan's wiles,
Safe from dangers, free from fears,
May I live upon thy smiles,
Till the promised hour appears,
When the sons of God shall prove
All their Father's boundless love.
Newton.

128 (929) 7s.

1 Christ, whose glory fills the skies,
Christ, the true, the only light,
Sun of Righteousness, arise,
Triumph o'er the shades of night;
Day-spring from on high, be near;
Day-Star, in our hearts appear.

2 Dark and cheerless is the morn,
If it bring no ray from thee;
Joyless is the day's return,
Till thy mercy's beams we see.
Lord, thine inward light impart,
Cheering each benighted heart.
Wesley.

PRIESTHOOD OF CHRIST.

WOODLAND. C. M. N. D. GOULD. 1181 1864.

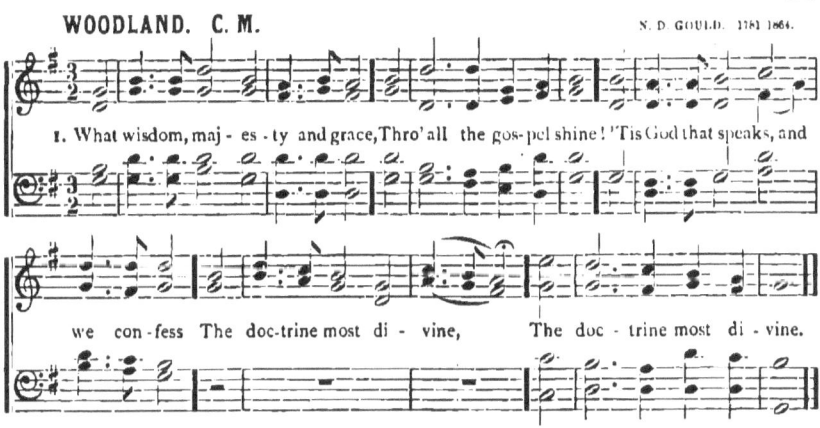

1. What wisdom, maj-es-ty and grace, Thro' all the gospel shine! 'Tis God that speaks, and we con-fess The doc-trine most di-vine, The doc-trine most di-vine.

129 (373) 1 Tim. 1: 11.

1 WHAT wisdom, majesty and grace,
Through all the gospel shine!
'Tis God that speaks, and we confess
The doctrine most divine.

2 Down from his shining throne on high,
The almighty Saviour comes;
Lays his bright robes of glory by,
And feeble flesh assumes.

3 The mighty debt his chosen owed,
Upon the cross he pays;
Then through the clouds ascends to God,
Midst shouts of loftiest praise.

4 There he, our great High Priest, appears
Before his Father's throne;
There on his breast our names he wears
And counts our cause his own.
Stennett.

130 (374) C. M. Matt. 12: 20.

1 WITH joy we meditate the grace
Of our High Priest above;
His heart is made of tenderness;
His bowels melt with love.

2 Touched with a sympathy within,
He knows our feeble frame;
He knows what sore temptations mean,
For he has felt the same.

3 But spotless, innocent, and pure,
The great Redeemer stood,
While Satan's fiery darts he bore,
And did resist to blood.

4 He, in the days of feeble flesh,
Poured out his cries and tears,
And, in his measure, feels afresh
What every member bears.

5 He'll never quench the smoking flax,
But raise it to a flame;
The bruised reed he never breaks,
Nor scorns the meanest name.

6 Then let our humble faith address
His mercy and his power;
We shall obtain delivering grace,
In the distressing hour.
Watts.

131 (379) C. M.

1 CHRIST bears the name of all his saints,
Deep on his heart engraved;
Attentive to the state and wants
Of all his love has saved.

2 In him a holiness complete,
Light and perfection shine;
And wisdom, grace, and glory meet;
A Saviour all divine.

3 The blood, which, as a priest, he bears
For sinners, is his own;
The incense of his prayers and tears
Perfumes the holy throne.

4 In him my weary soul has rest,
Though I am weak and vile;
I read my name upon his breast,
And see the Father smile.
Newton.

PRIESTHOOD OF CHRIST.

CHIMES. C. M.
Dr. LOWELL MASON. 1830.

1. To all e-ter-ni-ty our Priest And King shall be a-dor'd;
Sin-ners from Sa-tan's pow'r re-leas'd Shall ev-er praise the Lord.

132 (392) Zech. 6: 13.

2 The Lamb that died shall be our song
To cheer the night of time ;
Nor will the painful way be long
Through this unfriendly clime.

3 Our loving Lord and living Head
Our every sorrow feels ;
And when through trials sharp we're led,
He all our anguish heals.

4 A Priest so tender and so kind
Is suited to our need ;
While in this world we are confined,
For us he'll intercede.
Wm. L. Beebe

133 (458) C. M. Exodus 28: 29.

2 Though raised to a superior throne,
Where angels bow around,

And high o'er all the shining train,
With matchless honors crowned ;

3 The names of all his saints he bears
Deep graven on his heart ;
Nor shall the meanest Christian say
That he hath lost his part.

4 Those characters shall fair abide,
Our everlasting trust,
When gems, and monuments, and crowns
Are mouldered down to dust.

5 So, gracious Saviour! on my breast
May thy dear name be worn,—
A sacred ornament and guard,
To endless ages borne!
Doddridge.

PETERBOROUGH. C. M.
R. HARRISON. 1718-1810.

1. Now let our cheer-ful eyes sur-vey Our great High-Priest a-bove,
And cel-e-brate his con-stant care And sym-pa-thet-ic love.

REVELATION.

SHELDON. C. M.   Rev. G. WHEELER.

1. Nor eye hath seen, nor ear hath heard, Nor sense, nor reason known, What joys the Father hath pre-par'd For those that love the Son.

134 (393)   1 Cor. 2: 9, 10. Rev. 21: 27.

1 Nor eye hath seen, nor ear hath heard,
   Nor sense, nor reason known,
What joys the Father hath prepared
   For those that love the Son.

2 But the good Spirit of the Lord,
   Reveals a heaven to come;
The beams of glory in his word
   Allure and guide us home.

3 Pure are the joys above the sky,
   And all the region peace;
No wanton lips nor envious eye
   Can see or taste the bliss.

4 Those holy gates for ever bar
   Pollution, sin, and shame;
None shall obtain admittance there
   But followers of the Lamb.

5 He keeps the Father's Book of life,
   There all their names are found;
The hypocrite in vain shall strive
   To tread the heavenly ground.   Watts.

135 (395)   C. M.

1 The Spirit breathes upon the word,
   And brings the truth to sight;
Precepts and promises afford
   A sanctifying light.

2 A glory gilds the sacred page,
   Majestic like the sun;
It gives a light to every age;
   It gives, but borrows none.

3 Let everlasting thanks be thine,
   For such a bright display,
As makes a world of darkness shine
   With beams of heavenly day.

4 My soul rejoices to pursue
   The steps of him I love,
Till glory breaks upon my view
   In brighter worlds above.
                                  Cowper.

136 (397)   C. M.

1 The moon has but a borrowed light,
   A faint and feeble ray;
She owes her beauty to the night,
   And hides herself by day.

2 No cheering warmth her beam conveys,
   Though pleasing to behold;
We might upon her brightness gaze
   Till we were starved with cold.

3 Just such is all the light to man
   Which reason can impart;
It cannot show one object plain,
   Nor warm the frozen heart.

4 The gospel, like the sun at noon,
   Affords a glorious light;
Then fallen reason's boasted moon
   Appears no longer bright.

5 And grace not light alone bestows,
   But adds a quickening power;
The desert blossoms like the rose,
   And sin prevails no more.
                                  Newton.

56. GOVERNMENT OF CHRIST.

FREDERICKSBURG. H. M.

By per. R. M. McINTOSH.

137 (398) Phil. 4: 4.

1 REJOICE, the Lord is King;
  Your God and King adore;
Mortals, give thanks and sing,
  And triumph ever more!
Lift up the heart, lift up the voice,
Rejoice aloud, ye saints, rejoice.

2 Rejoice, the Saviour reigns,
  The God of truth and love;
When he had purged our stains,
  He took his seat above:
Lift up the heart, lift up the voice,
Rejoice aloud, ye saints, rejoice.

3 His kingdom cannot fail;
  He rules o'er earth and heaven;
The keys of death and hell
  Are to our Jesus given:
Lift up the heart, lift up the voice,
Rejoice aloud, ye saints, rejoice.

4 He all his foes shall quell;
  Shall all our sins destroy;
And every bosom swell
  With pure seraphic joy:
Lift up the heart, lift up the voice,
Rejoice aloud, ye saints, rejoice.

5 Rejoice in glorious hope,
  Jesus the Judge shall come,
And take his servants up
  To their eternal home:
We soon shall hear the Archangel's voice;
The trump of God shall sound; Rejoice.
                                     C. W.

GOVERNMENT OF CHRIST.

HARWICH. H. M.

1. Rejoice, the Saviour reigns Among the sons of men; He breaks the pris'ners' chains, And makes them free again: Let hell oppose God's only Son; In spite of foes his cause goes on.

138 (410)

2 The cause of righteousness,
   And truth and holy peace,
   Designed our world to bless,
   Shall spread and never cease:
Gentile or Jew, their souls shall bow,
Allegiance due with rapture vow.

3 The baffled prince of hell
   In vain new projects tries,
   Truth's empire to repel
   By cruelty and lies:
Th' infernal gates shall rage in vain;
Conquest awaits the Lamb once slain.

4 He died, but soon arose,
   Triumphant o'er the grave;
   And now himself he shows
   Omnipotent to save:
Let rebels kiss the victor's feet;
Eternal bliss his subjects meet.

5 All power is in his hand,
   His people to defend;
   To his most high command
   Shall millions more attend:
All heaven with smiles approves his cause,
And distant isles receive his laws.

6 This little seed from heaven
   Shall soon become a tree;
   This ever-blessed leaven
   Diffused abroad must be:

Till God the Son shall come again,
It must go on. Amen! Amen!
Ryland.

139 H. M. Psa. 81.

1 How amiable, how fair,
   O Lord of Hosts to me,
   Thy tabernacles are!
   My flesh cries out for thee;
My heart and soul, with heavenward fire,
To thee, the living God aspire.

2 Lord God of Hosts, give ear,
   A gracious answer yield;
   O God of Jacob, hear;
   Behold, O God, our shield;
Look on thine own Anointed One,
And save through thy beloved Son.

3 Lord, I would rather stand
   A keeper at thy gate,
   Than on the king's right hand
   In tents of worldly state;
One day within thy courts, one day,
Is worth a thousand cast away.

4 God is a sun of light,
   Glory and grace to shed;
   God is a shield of might,
   To guard the faithful head;
O Lord of Hosts, how happy he,
The man who puts his trust in thee.
Montgomery.

GOVERNMENT OF CHRIST.

DE FLEURY. 8s. D.

1. O come, let us sing to the Lord, In God our salvation rejoice; In psalms of thanksgiving record His praise, with one spirit, one voice! 2. For Jehovah is King, and he reigns, The God of all gods, on his throne;

D.C.—The strength of the hills he maintains, The ends of the earth are his own.

140 (413) Psa. 95.

1 O COME, let us sing to the Lord,
　In God our salvation rejoice ;
In psalms of thanksgiving record
　His praise, with one spirit, one voice !

2 For Jehovah is King, and he reigns,
　The God of all gods, on his throne ;
The strength of the hills he maintains,
　The ends of the earth are his own.

3 The sea is Jehovah's; he made
　The tide its dominion to know ;
The land is Jehovah's ;—he laid
　Its solid foundations below :

4 Oh come, let us worship, and kneel
　Before the Creator, our God !
The people who serve him with zeal,
　The flock whom he guides with his rod.

5 As Moses, the fathers of old
　Through the sea and the wilderness led,
His wonderful works we behold,
　With manna from heaven are fed :

6 To-day, let us hearken, to-day,
　To the voice that yet speaks from above,
And all his commandments obey,
　For all his commandments are love.

7 His wrath let us fear to provoke,
　To dwell in his favor unite ;
His service is freedom, his yoke
　Is easy, his burden is light :

8 But, oh ! of rebellion beware,
　Rebellion, that hardens the breast,
Lest God in his anger should swear
　That *we* shall not enter his rest.
　　　　　　　　　　　　Montgomery.

141 (349)　8s. D.

1 WHAT think ye of Christ ? is the test
　To try both your state and your scheme ;
You cannot be right in the rest,
　Unless you think rightly of him.

2 As Jesus appears in your view,
　As he is beloved or not,
So God is disposed toward you,
　And mercy or wrath is your lot.

3 Some take him a creature to be,
　A man, or an angel at most ;
Sure these have not feelings like me,
　Nor know themselves wretched and lost:

4 So guilty, so helpless am I,
　I durst not confide in his blood,
Nor on his protection rely,
　Unless I were sure he is God.

5 If asked, what of Jesus I think,
　Though still my best thoughts are but
I say, he's my meat and my drink, [poor,
　My life, and my strength, and my store,

6 My Shepherd, my husband, my friend,
　My Saviour from sin and from thrall,
My hope from beginning to end,
　My portion, my Lord, and my all.
　　　　　　　　　　　　Newton.

SUFFERINGS AND DEATH OF CHRIST. 59

SILOAM. C. M. — I. B. WOODBURY. 1819-1858.

1. Oh! what a sad and dole-ful night Pre-ced-ed that day's morn.,
When dark-ness seiz'd the Lord of light, And sin by Christ was borne.

142 (420)

2 When our intolerable load
 Upon his soul was laid,
And the vindictive wrath of God
 Flamed furious on his head.
3 We in our Jesus well may boast,
 For none but God alone,
Can know how dear the victory cost,
 How hardly it was won.
4 Forth from the garden, fully tried,
 Our bruised champion came,

To suffer what remained beside,
 Of pain, and grief, and shame.
5 Mocked, spit upon, and crowned with
 A spectacle he stood; [thorns,
His back with scourges lashed and torn,
 A victim bathed in blood.
6 Nailed to the cross through hands and
 He hung in open view; [feet,
To make his sorrows quite complete,
 By God deserted, too.   Hart.

MELODY. C. M. — A. CHAPIN. 1813.

1. Yon-der, a-maz-ing sight! I see Th'in-car-nate Son of God,
Ex-pir-ing on the ac-curs'd tree, And welt'ring in his blood.

143 (429) C. M. John 12: 32.

2 Behold a purple torrent run
 Down from his hands and head:
The crimson tide puts out the sun;
 His groans awake the dead.

3 The trembling earth, the darkened sky
 Proclaim the truth aloud;
And, with the amazed centurion, cry,
 "This is the Son of God!"   Stennett.

SUFFERINGS AND DEATH OF CHRIST.

LYNN. L. M. — LOWELL MASON.

1. Now be my heart inspir'd to sing The glories of my Saviour-King, Jesus the Lord; how heav'nly fair His form! how bright his beauties are!

144 (406)

1 Now be my heart inspired to sing
The glories of my Saviour-King,
Jesus the Lord; how heavenly fair
His form! how bright his beauties are!

2 O'er all the sons of human race
He shines with a superior grace;
Love from his lips divinely flows,
And blessings all his state compose.

3 Dress thee in arms, most mighty Lord,
Gird on the terror of thy sword;
In majesty and glory ride,
With truth and meekness at thy side.

4 Thine anger, like a pointed dart,
Shall pierce thy foes of stubborn heart;
Or words of mercy, kind and sweet,
Shall melt the rebels at thy feet.

5 Thy throne, O God, for ever stands;
Grace is the sceptre in thy hands:
Thy laws and works are just and right;
Justice and grace are thy delight.

6 God, thine own God, has richly shed
His oil of gladness on thy head,
And with his sacred Spirit blest
His first-born Son above the rest.
Watts.

145 (428) L. M.

1 LORD, when my thoughts with wonder
O'er the sharp sorrows of thy soul, [roll
And read my Maker's broken laws
Repaired and honored by thy cross;

2 My passions rise and soar above;
I'm winged with faith, and fired with love;
Fain would I reach eternal things,
And learn the notes that Gabriel sings.

3 But my heart fails, my tongue complains
For want of their immortal strains;
And in such humble notes as these
Falls far below thy victories.

4 Well, the kind minute must appear
When we shall leave these bodies here,
These clogs of clay, and mount on high
To join the songs above the sky.
Watts.

146 (431) L. M.

1 'Tis midnight; and on Olive's brow
The star is dimmed that lofty shone:
'Tis midnight; in the garden now
The suffering Saviour prays alone.

2 'Tis midnight; and from all removed,
Emmanuel wrestles lone with fears;
E'en the disciple that he loved
Heeds not his Master's grief and tears.

3 'Tis midnight; and for others' guilt
The Man of Sorrows weeps in blood;
Yet he that hath in anguish knelt,
Is not forsaken by his God.

4 'Tis midnight; from the heav'nly plains
Is borne the songs that angels know;
Unheard by mortals are the strains
That sweetly soothe the Saviour's wo.
W. B. Tappan.

RESURRECTION AND ASCENSION OF CHRIST.

LABAN. S. M. — LOWELL MASON.

1. In vain the sealed cave, In vain the Roman guard; My Lord will quit his silent grave Just at the time pre-par'd.

147 (441)

1 In vain the sealed cave,
  In vain the Roman guard;
  My Lord will quit his silent grave
  Just at the time prepared.

2 An earthquake tells the hour,
  Of Jesus' second birth;
  An angel opes the prison door,
  And lo! he springeth forth!

3 All hail, my risen Lord,
  Triumphant Saviour now!
  Sin, death, and hell, with one accord
  Before thy footstool bow.

4 The fight is bravely fought,
  The work is nobly done;
  A full salvation thou hast wrought
  And endless honors won.   *Sonnets.*

148 (449)   S. M.

1 Welcome, sweet day of rest,
  That saw the Lord arise;
  Welcome to this reviving breast,
  And these rejoicing eyes!

2 The King himself comes near,
  And feasts his saints to-day;
  Here may we sit, and see him here,
  And love, and praise, and pray.

3 One day amidst the place,
  Where my dear God hath been,
  Is sweeter than ten thousand days
  Of pleasurable sin.

4 My willing soul would stay
  In such a frame as this,
  And sit and sing herself away
  To everlasting bliss.   *Watts.*

DAYTON. S. M. — W. B. BRADBURY.

1. Welcome, sweet day of rest, That saw the Lord a-rise; Welcome to this re-viv-ing breast, And these re-joic-ing eyes! And these re-joic-ing eyes!

RESURRECTION AND ASCENSION OF CHRIST.

MAITLAND. C. M. — GEORGE N. ALLEN. 1812–1877.

149 (438) Luke 24: 51–53.

1 Now for a theme of thankful praise
To tune the stammerer's tongue:
Christians, your hearts and voices raise,
And join the joyful song.

2 The Lord's ascended up on high,
Decked with resplendent wounds:
While shouts of victory rend the sky,
And heaven with joy resounds.

3 See, from the regions of the dead,
Through all th' ethereal plains,
The powers of darkness captive led—
The dragon dragged in chains.

4 Ye eternal gates, your leaves unfold;
Receive the conquering King:
Ye angels, strike your harps of gold,
And, saints, triumphant sing.

5 Children, rejoice; he died for you;
For you prepares a place:
His Spirit sends to guide you through,
With every gift of grace.

6 His blood, which did your sins atone,
For your salvation pleads;
And, seated on his Father's throne,
He reigns and intercedes.
Hart.

150 (443) C. M.

1 HOSANNA to the Prince of light
That clothed himself in clay,
Entered the iron gates of death,
And tore the bars away.

2 Death is no more the king of dread
Since our Immanuel rose,
He took the tyrant's sting away,
And spoiled our hellish foes.

3 Bright angels, strike your loudest strings,
Your sweetest voices raise;
Let heaven and all created things
Sound our Immanuel's praise.
Watts.

151 (444) C. M. 1 Pet. 1: 3–5.

1 BLESSED be the everlasting God,
The Father of our Lord;
Be his abounding mercy praised,
His majesty adored.

2 When from the dead he raised his Son,
And called him to the sky,
He gave our souls a lively hope
That they should never die.

3 What though our inbred sins require
Our flesh to see the dust;
Yet as the Lord our Saviour rose,
So all his followers must.

4 There's an inheritance divine
Reserved against that day;
'Tis uncorrupted, undefiled,
And cannot waste away.

5 Saints by the power of God are kept
Till the salvation come;
We walk by faith as strangers here
Till Christ shall call us home.
Watts.

RESURRECTION AND ASCENSION OF CHRIST. 63

HARWELL. 8s. & 7s. LOWELL MASON.

1. Hark! ten thou-sand harps and voices Sound the note of praise a-bove;
D.C.—See, he sits on yon-der throne; Je-sus rules the world a-lone.
Jesus reigns, and heav'n re-joic-es; Je-sus reigns the God of love:

152 (454)

2 Jesus, hail! whose glory brightens
All above, and gives it worth ;
Lord of life, thy smile enlightens,
Cheers, and charms thy saints on earth :
When we think of love like thine,
Lord, we own it love divine.

3 King of glory, reign for ever ;
Thine's an everlasting crown :
Nothing from thy love shall sever
Those whom thou hast made thine own ;
Happy objects of thy grace,
Destined to behold thy face.

4 Saviour, hasten thine appearing ;
Bring, oh, bring the glorious day,
When, the awful summons hearing,
Heaven and earth shall pass away :
Then, with golden harps, we'll sing,—
"Glory, glory to our King,"
Kelly.

153 (940) 8s. & 7s. 1 Cor. 6: 11.

1 LET us love, and sing, and wonder ;
Let us praise the Saviour's name ;
He has hushed the law's loud thunder ;
He has quenched Mount Sinai's flame :
He has washed us in his blood ;
He has brought us home to God !

2 Let us love the Lord who bought us ;
Pitied us when enemies ;
Called us by his grace, and taught us ;
Gave us ears, and gave us eyes :
He has washed us in his blood ;
He has brought us home to God !

3 Let us sing, though fierce temptation
Threatens hard to bear us down ;
Jesus is our strong salvation :
He will surely give the crown :
He has washed us in his blood ;
He has brought us home to God !

4 Let us wonder ! grace and justice
Join and point to mercy's store ; [is,
When, through grace, in Christ our trust
Justice smiles, and asks no more :
He has washed us in his blood ;
He has brought us home to God !

5 Let us praise and join the chorus
Of the saints enthroned on high :
Here they trusted him before us,
Now their praises fill the sky :
He has washed us in his blood ;
He has brought us home to God !

6 Yes, we praise thee, gracious Saviour ;
Wonder, love, and bless thy name ;
Pardon, Lord, our poor endeavor ;
Pity, for thou know'st our frame :
Wash our souls and songs with blood,
For by thee we come to God !
Newton.

64 RESURRECTION AND ASCENSION OF CHRIST.

DUKE STREET. L. M.
J. HATTON. 1790.

1. Lord, when thou didst ascend on high, Ten thousand angels fill'd the sky; Those heav'nly guards around thee wait, Like chariots that attend thy state.

154 (445)

1 LORD, when thou didst ascend on high,
Ten thousand angels filled the sky;
Those heavenly guards around thee wait,
Like chariots that attend thy state.

2 Not Sinai's mountain could appear
More glorious when the Lord was there;
While he pronounced his dreadful law,
And struck the chosen tribes with awe.

3 How bright the triumph none can tell,
When the rebellious powers of hell,
That thousand souls had captive made,
Were all in chains, like captives, led.

4 Raised by his Father to the throne,
He sent the promised Spirit down,
With gifts and grace for rebel men,
That God might dwell on earth again.
Watts.

INDIAN'S LAMENT. L. M.

1. { He dies! the friend of sinners dies! Lo! Salem's daughters weep around;
   { A solemn darkness veils the skies, A sudden trembling shakes the ground.
D.S. —He shed a thousand drops for you, A thousand drops of richer blood.

2. Come, saints, and drop a tear or two For him who groan'd beneath your load;

155 (446)

3 Here's love and grief beyond degree:
    The Lord of Glory died for men;
But lo! what sudden joys we see;
Jesus, the dead, revives again!

4 The rising God forsakes the tomb;
    The tomb in vain forbids his rise;
Cherubic legions guard him home,
    And shout him welcome to the skies.

5 Break off your tears, ye saints, and tell
    How high our great Deliverer reigns;
Sing how he spoiled the hosts of hell,
    And led the monster, Death, in chains.

6 Say, Live for ever, wondrous King!
    Born to redeem, and strong to save;
Then, ask the monster, where's thy sting?
    And, where's thy victory, boasting
        grave?
Watts

RESURRECTION AND ASCENSION OF CHRIST. 65

MENDON. L. M. German. 1822.

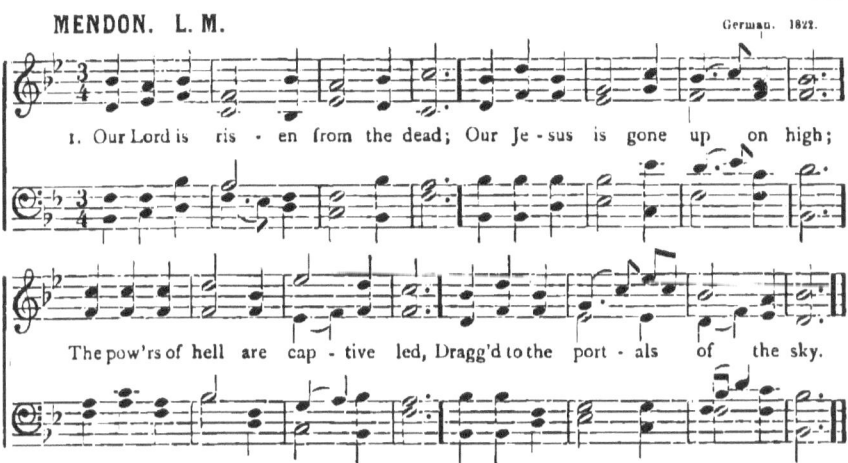

1. Our Lord is ris-en from the dead; Our Je-sus is gone up on high;
The pow'rs of hell are cap-tive led, Dragg'd to the port-als of the sky.

156 (452) Ps. 24: 7.

1 Our Lord is risen from the dead;
 Our Jesus is gone up on high;
The powers of hell are captive led,
 Dragged to the portals of the sky.

2 There his triumphal chariot waits,
 And angels chant the solemn lay:
"Lift up your heads, ye heavenly gates!
 Ye everlasting doors, give way!"

3 Loose all your bars of massy light,
 And wide unfold the radiant scene;
He claims those mansions as his right:
 Receive the King of Glory in.

4 Who is the King of Glory, who?
 The Lord that all his foes o'ercame,
The world sin, death, and hell o'erthrew;
 And Jesus is the Conqueror's name.

5 Lo! his triumphal chariot waits,
 And angels chant the solemn lay:
"Lift up your heads, ye heavenly gates!
 Ye everlasting doors, give way!"

6 Who is the King of Glory, who?
 The Lord, of boundless pow'r possessed,
The King of saints and angels, too,
 God over all, forever blessed.
   Wesley.

157 (453) L. M.

1 Now let us raise our cheerful strains,
 And join the blissful choir above;
There our exalted Saviour reigns,
 And there they sing his wondrous love.

2 While seraphs tune th' immortal song,
 Oh, may we feel the sacred flame;
And every heart, and every tongue,
 Adore the Saviour's glorious name!

3 Jesus, who once upon the tree
 In agonizing pains expired;
Who died for rebels—yes, 'tis he!
 How bright! how lovely! how admired!

4 Jesus, who died that we might live,
 Died in the wretched traitor's place;
Oh, what returns can mortals give
 For such immeasurable grace?

5 Were universal nature ours,
 And art, with all their boasted store,
Nature and art, with all their powers,
 Would still confess the offering poor.

6 Yet though for bounty so divine
 We ne'er can equal honors raise;
Dear Jesus, may our hearts be thine,
 And all our tongues proclaim thy praise.
  Mrs. A. Steele.

158 (408) L. M

1 From all that dwell below the skies
 Let the Creator's praise arise;
Let the Redeemer's name be sung
 Through every land, by every tongue.

2 Eternal are thy mercies, Lord;
 Eternal truth attends thy word:
Thy praise shall sound from shore to shore,
 Till suns shall rise and set no more.
   Watts.

SALVATION.

AVON. C. M. HUGH WILSON. 1768.

1. Be-gin, my tongue, some heav'nly theme, And speak some bound-less thing; The might-y works, or might-ier name Of our e-ter-nal King.

159 (461)

2 Tell of his wondrous faithfulness,
And sound his power abroad;
Sing the sweet promise of his grace,
And the performing God.

3 Proclaim salvation from the Lord,
For wretched, dying men;
His hand has writ the sacred word
With an immortal pen.

4 Engraved as in eternal brass
The mighty promise shines;
Nor can the powers of darkness 'rase
Those everlasting lines.

5 O, might I hear thine heavenly tongue
But whisper, "Thou art mine,"
Those gentle words should raise my song
To notes almost divine.

6 How would my leaping heart rejoice
And think my heaven secure;
I'd trust the all-creating voice,
And faith desires no more. *Watts.*

160 (471) C. M.

1 SALVATION! O the joyful sound!
'Tis pleasure to our ears;
A sovereign balm for every wound,
A cordial for our fears.

2 Buried in sorrow and in sin,
At hell's dark door we lay;
But we arise by grace divine,
To see a heavenly day.

3 Salvation! let the echo fly
The spacious earth around,
While all the armies of the sky
Conspire to raise the sound. *Watts*

161 (474) C. M. Luke 23: 42.

1 As on the cross the Saviour hung,
And wept, and bled, and died,
He poured salvation on a wretch
That languished at his side.

2 His crimes, with inward grief and
The penitent confessed; [shame,
Then turned his dying eyes to Christ,
And thus his prayer addressed:

3 "Jesus, thou Son and heir of heaven!
Thou spotless Lamb of God!
I see thee bathed in sweat and tears,
And weltering in thy blood.

4 "Yet quickly, from these scenes of wo,
In triumph thou shalt rise,
Burst through the gloomy shades of death,
And shine above the skies.

5 "Amid the glories of that world,
Dear Saviour, think on me,
And in the victories of thy death
Let me a sharer be."

6 His prayer the dying Jesus hears
And instantly replies:
"To-day thy parting soul shall be
With me in Paradise." *Stennett*

SALVATION. 67

HILLSIDE. L. M.
L. O. EMERSON.

1. Now to the pow'r of God supreme, Be everlasting honors giv'n;
He saves from hell, (we bless his name,) He calls our wandering feet to heav'n.

By per. O. DITSON & CO.

162 (473) 2 Tim. 1: 9.

1 Now to the power of God supreme,
Be everlasting honors given ;
He saves from hell, (we bless his name,)
He calls our wandering feet to heaven.

2 Not for our duties or deserts,
But of his own abounding grace,
He works salvation in our hearts,
And forms a people for his praise.

3 'Twas his own purpose that begun
To rescue rebels doomed to die ;
He gave us grace in Christ, his Son,
Before he spread the starry sky.

4 Jesus, the Lord, appears at last,
And makes his Father's counsels known;
Declares the great transactions past,
And brings immortal blessings down.

5 He dies; and in that dreadful night
Did all the powers of hell destroy ;
Rising he brought our heaven to light,
And took possession of the joy.
Watts.

163 (475) L. M. Micah 6: 6-8.

1 Wherewith, O Lord, shall I draw near,
Or bow myself before thy face?
How, in thy purer eyes appear?
What shall I bring to gain thy grace?

2 Will gifts delight the Lord Most High?
Will multiplied oblations please?
Thousands of rams his favor buy?
Or slaughtered millions e'er appease?

3 Can these assuage the wrath of God?
Can these wash out my guilty stain?
Rivers of oil, or seas of blood?
Alas! they all must flow in vain.

4 I plead the merits of thy Son,
Who died for sinners on the tree ;
I plead his righteousness alone,
O put the spotless robe on me.
C. W.

164 (478) L. M. Ps. 46: 4.

1 Indulgent God! to thee I raise
My spirit fraught with joy and praise :
Grateful I bow before thy throne,
My debt of mercy there to own.

2 Rivers descending, Lord, from thee,
Perpetual glide to solace me:
Their varied virtues to rehearse,
Demands an everlasting verse.

3 And yet there is, beyond the rest,
One stream, the widest and the best;
Salvation! Lo, the purple flood
Rolls rich with my Redeemer's blood.

4 I taste—delight succeeds to wo ;
I bathe—no waters cleanse me so:
Such joy and purity to share,
I would remain enraptured there,

5 Till death shall give this soul to know
The fullness sought in vain below ;
The fullness of that boundless sea
Whence flowed the river down to me.
Stennett.

SALVATION.

AMAZING GRACE. C. M.

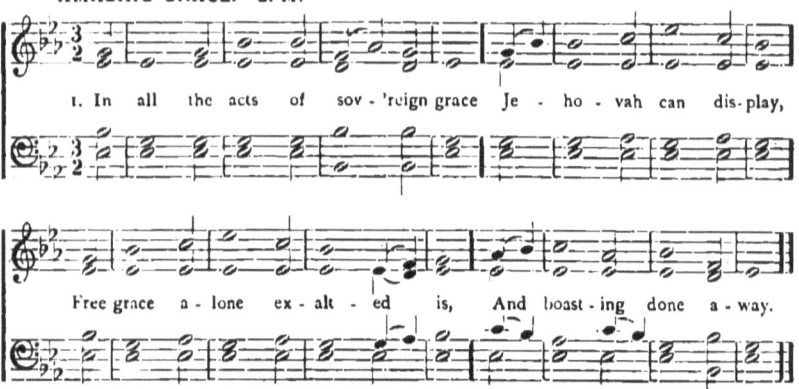

1. In all the acts of sov-'reign grace Je-ho-vah can dis-play, Free grace a-lone ex-alt-ed is, And boast-ing done a-way.

165 (469)

2 From sin to God could sinners turn,
  And make their natures clean,
Then incense to their shrine should burn,
  And Christ had died in vain.

3 But where the sovereign grace of God
    Shall set the guilty free,
  His only hope is Jesus' blood;
    The worst of sinners he.

4 Thus grace triumphant keeps the
    Without a rival there; [throne,
  While mercy shines in Christ alone
    In rays divinely clear.

166 (477) C. M. Psa. 35: 3.

1 SALVATION!—Oh, melodious sound
  To wretched dying men!
Salvation that from God proceeds,
  And leads to God again.

2 Rescued from hell's eternal gloom,
    From fiends, and fires, and chains;
  Raised to a paradise of bliss,
    Where love triumphant reigns!

3 But may a poor bewildered soul,
    Sinful and weak as mine,
  Presume to raise a trembling eye
    To blessings so divine?

4 The lustre of so bright a bliss
    My feeble heart o'erbears;
  But unbelief almost perverts
    The promise into tears.

5 My Saviour-God, no voice but thine
    These dying hopes can raise:
  Speak thy salvation to my soul,
    And turn my prayer to praise.
                                Doddridge.

167 (480) C. M.

1 SALVATION! what a glorious plan;
    How suited to our need!
  The grace that raises fallen man
    Is wonderful indeed.

2 'Twas wisdom formed the vast design,
    To ransom us when lost;
  And love's unfathomable mine
    Provided all the cost.

3 Strict Justice, with approving look,
    The holy covenant sealed;
  And Truth and Power undertook
    The whole should be fulfilled.

4 Truth, Wisdom, Justice, Power, am-
    In all their glory shone, [Love,
  When Jesus left the courts above,
    And died to save his own.

5 Truth, Wisdom, Justice, Power, and
    Are equally displayed: [Love,
  Now Jesus reigns enthroned above,
    Our Advocate and Head.

6 Now sin appears deserving death,
    Most hateful and abhorred;
  And yet the sinner lives by faith,
    And dares approach the Lord.
                                Newton.

GRACE.

HOME. C. M.

Used by per. R. M. McINTOSH.

168 (491)

1 Now, may the Lord reveal his face,
   And teach our stammering tongues
To make his sovereign, reigning grace,
   The subject of our songs.
No sweeter subject can invite
   A sinner's heart to sing,
Or more display the glorious right
   Of our exalted King.

2 This subject fills the starry plains
   With wonder, joy, and love;
And furnishes the noblest strains
   For all the harps above:
While the redeemed in praise combine
   To grace upon the throne,
Angels in solemn chorus join,
   And make the theme their own.

3 Grace reigns to pardon crimson sins,
   To melt the hardest hearts;
And from the work it once begins,
   It never more departs.
The world and Satan strive in vain
   Against the chosen few;
Secured by grace's conquering reign,
   They all shall conquer, too.

4 'Twas grace that called our souls at first;
   By grace thus far we're come;
And grace will help us through the worst,
   And lead us safely home.
Lord, when this changing life is past,
   If we may see thy face,

How should we praise and love at last,
   And sing the reign of grace!
                                    Newton.

169 (488)   C. M.   Eph. 2: 8.

1 AMAZING grace (how sweet the sound!)
   That saved a wretch like me;
I once was lost but now am found,
   Was blind, but now I see.

2 'Twas grace that taught my heart to fear,
   And grace my fears relieved:
How precious did that grace appear,
   The hour I first believed.

3 Through many dangers, toils, and snares,
   I have already come;
'Tis grace has brought me safe thus far,
   And grace will lead me home.

4 The Lord has promised good to me,
   His word my hope secures;
He will my shield and portion be
   As long as life endures.

5 Yes, when this flesh and heart shall fail,
   And mortal life shall cease,
I shall possess, within the vale,
   A life of joy and peace.

6 The earth shall soon dissolve like snow,
   The sun forbear to shine;
But God, who called me here below,
   Will be forever mine.
                                    Newton.

GRACE.

ROCHESTER. C. M.
JOHN PLAYFORD. 1676.

1. Hail, mighty Jesus! how divine Is thy victorious sword; The stoutest rebel must resign At thy commanding word.

170 (486) Psalm 45.

1 HAIL, mighty Jesus! how divine
Is thy victorious sword ;
The stoutest rebel must resign
At thy commanding word.

2 Deep are the wounds thy arrows give;
They pierce the hardest heart ;
Thy smiles of grace the slain revive.
And joy succeeds to smart.

3 Still gird thy sword upon thy thigh,
Ride with majestic sway :
Go forth, sweet Prince, triumphantly,
And make thy foes obey.

4 And when thy victories are complete,
When all the chosen race
Shall round the throne of glory meet,
To sing thy conquering grace :

5 O, may my blood-washed soul be found
Among that favored band ;
And I, with them, thy praise will sound
Throughout Immanuel's land.
Wallin and Toplady.

171 (492) C. M.

1 FREE grace to every heaven-born soul
Will be their constant theme :
Long as eternal ages roll
They'll still adore the Lamb.

2 Free grace alone can wipe the tears
From our lamenting eyes :
Can raise our souls from guilty fears
To joy that never dies.

3 Free grace can death itself outbrave,
And take its sting away ;
Can souls unto the utmost save,
And them to heaven convey.
Dracup.

172 (493) C. M.

1 BENEATH the sacred throne of God
I saw a river rise ;   [blood
The streams were peace and pardoning
Descending from the skies.

2 Angelic minds cannot explore
This deep, unfathomed sea ;
'Tis void of bottom, brim, or shore,
And lost in Deity.

3 I stood amazed, and wondered when,
Or why this ocean rose,
That wafts salvation down to men,
His traitors and his foes.

4 That sacred flood, from Jesus' veins,
Was free to take away
A Mary's or Manasseh's stains,
Or sins more vile than they.

5 Free to the sinner, dead to God,
Who sought the road to hell ;
That trampled on a Saviour's blood,
And on his buckler fell.

6 Triumphant grace, and man's free will,
Shall not divide the throne ;
For man's a fallen sinner still,
And Christ shall reign alone.
Kent.

GRACE.

ORTONVILLE. C. M.   T. HASTINGS.

1. If I must sing, I'll sing of grace Which rais'd me from the fall, And led me to a hiding-place, Jesus, my Lord, my all, Jesus, my Lord, my all.

173 (494)

1 IF I must sing, I'll sing of grace
Which raised me from the fall,
And led me to a hiding-place,
Jesus, my Lord, my all.

2 'Twas grace that brought my roving feet
From sin's destructive road,
And pointed out a sure retreat,
Jesus my blest abode.

3 Grace also first my soul inclined
At wisdom's door to wait,
And then assured me I should find
A Saviour good and great.

4 Grace likewise urged my soul to cry,
With fervency and zeal,
To God, who would not pass me by,
But would my pardon seal.

5 And when I've sank exceeding low,
Just ready to give up,
This grace hath raised my soul unto
A comfortable hope.

6 Of grace, I'll therefore loudly sing,
As long as I have breath;
Nor will I fear the dreadful sting,
That arms the monster, Death.

174 (498)   C. M.

1 HAPPY the birth where grace presides,
To form the future life;
In wisdom's paths the soul she guides,
Remote from noise and strife.

2 Since I have known the Saviour's name,
And what for me he bore,
No more I toil for empty fame,
I thirst for gold no more.

3 Placed by his hand in this retreat,
I make his love my theme;
And see that all the world calls great,
Is but a waking dream.

4 Since he has ranked my worthless name
Amongst the favored few,
Let the mad world, who scoff at them,
Revile and hate me, too.

5 O thou, whose voice the dead can raise,
And soften hearts of stone,
And teach the dumb to sing thy praise,
This work is all thine own.
                              Newton.

175 (525)   C. M.   Luke 12: 32.

1 YE little flock whom Jesus feeds,
Dismiss your anxious cares;
Look to the Shepherd of your souls,
And smile away your fears.

2 Though wolves and lions prowl around,
His staff is your defense: [voice
Midst sands and rocks, your Shepherd's
Calls streams and pastures thence.

3 Your Father will a kingdom give,
And give it with delight;
His feeblest child his love shall call
To triumph in his sight.
                              Doddridge.

GRACE.

HIDING-PLACE. L. M.
BENJ. SMITH. 1798.

1. Hail, sov'reign Grace, that first be-gan The scheme to res-cue fall-en man! Hail, matchless, free, e-ter-nal grace, That gave my soul a hid-ing-place!

176 (485) Isaiah 32: 2.

1 HAIL, sovereign Grace, that first began
The scheme to rescue fallen man!
Hail, matchless, free, eternal grace,
That gave my soul a hiding-place!

2 Against the God who rules the sky
I fought with hands uplifted high ;
Despised the mansions of his grace,
Too proud to seek a hiding-place !

3 But thus the Eternal Counsel ran,
"Almighty Love, arrest the man!"
I felt the arrows of distress,
And found I had no hiding-place !

4 Indignant Justice stood in view ;
To Sinai's fiery mount I flew ;
But Justice cried, with frowning face,
This mountain is no hiding-place !

5 Ere long a heavenly voice I heard,
And Mercy's angel-form appeared :
She led me on, with placid pace,
To Jesus, as my hiding-place !

6 Should storms of seven-fold thunder roll,
And shake the globe from pole to pole,
No thunder-bolt shall daunt my face
For Jesus is my hiding-place.

7 On him almighty vengeance fell,
That must have sunk a world to hell:
He bore it for his chosen race,
And thus became their hiding-place.

8 A few more rolling suns at most,
Will land me on the heavenly coast,
Where I shall sing the song of grace,
And see my glorious hiding-place.
Brewer.

177 (497) L. M.

1 ALMIGHTY King! whose wondrous hand
Supports the weight of sea and land,
Whose grace is such a boundless store,
No heart shall break that sighs for more.

2 Thy providence supplies my food,
And 'tis thy blessing makes it good ;
My soul is nourished by thy word,
Let soul and body praise the Lord.

3 My streams of outward comfort came
From him, who built this earthly frame ;
Whate'er I want his bounty gives,
By whom my soul for ever lives.

4 Either his hand preserves from pain,
Or, if I feel it, heals again ;
From Satan's malice shields my breast,
Or over-rules it for the best.

5 Forgive the song that falls so low
Beneath the gratitude I owe ;
It means thy praise, however poor ;
An angel's song can do no more.
Cowper.

GRACE. 73

FERGUSON. S. M. GEO. KINGSLEY. 1811.

1. Grace! 'tis a charm-ing sound! Har-mon-ious to the ear:
Heav'n with the ech-o shall re-sound, And all the saints shall hear.

178 (489) Eph. 2: 5-8.

2 Grace first ordained the way
   To save rebellious man,
And all the steps that grace display,
   Which drew the wondrous plan!
3 Grace first inscribed my name
   In God's eternal book;
'Twas grace that gave me to the Lamb,
   Who all my sorrows took.

4 Grace taught my soul to pray,
   And pardoning love to know;
'Twas grace that kept me to this day
   And will not let me go.
5 Grace all the work shall crown,
   Through everlasting days:
It lays in heaven the topmost stone,
   And well deserves the praise. Doddridge.

SMITHFIELD. S. M.

1. Be-hold the lep-'rous Jew, Op-press'd with pain and grief,
Pour-ing his tears at Je-sus' feet For pit-y and re-lief.

179 (476) Matt. 8: 2, 3

2 "O speak the word," he cries,
   "And heal me of my pain:
Lord, thou art able, if thou wilt,
   To make a leper clean."
3 Compassion moves his heart,
   He speaks the gracious word;
The leper feels his strength return,
   And all his sickness cured.

4 To thee, dear Lord, I look,
   Sick of a worse disease;
Sin is my painful malady,
   And none can give me ease.
5 But thy Almighty grace
   Can heal my lep'rous soul:
O bathe me in thy precious blood,
   And that will make me whole. Stennett.

GRACE.

SAMANTHRA. 11s. & 8s. D. HUMPHREYS. Arr. by F. L. ARMSTRONG.

180 (495) Jer. 31: 3.

1 IN songs of sublime adoration and praise,
Ye pilgrims for Zion who press,
Break forth, and extol the great Ancient of Days,
His rich and distinguishing grace.

2 His love, from eternity fixed upon you,
Broke forth and discovered its flame,
When each with the cords of his kindness he drew,
And brought you to love his great name.

3 O had he not pitied the state you were in,
Your bosoms his love had ne'er felt;
You all would have lived, would have died too in sin,
And sunk with the load of your guilt.

4 What was there in you that could merit esteem,
Or give the Creator delight?
'Twas "even so, Father!" you ever must sing,
"Because it seemed good in thy sight."

5 'Twas all of thy grace we were brought to obey,
While others were suffered to go
The road which by nature we chose as our way,
Which leads to the regions of wo.

6 Then give all the glory to his holy name;
To him all the glory belongs;
Be yours the high joy still to sound forth his fame,
And crown him in each of your songs.
K——.

181 (947) 11s. & 8s. D.

1 'TIS Jesus I sing, and salvation by grace,
How sweet and delightful the theme;
Come, Christians, no longer to sorrow give place,
But give honor and glory to him.

2 In him, as the Father's eternal delight,
Jehovah the Great and Supreme,
The saints without blemish appear in his sight
The perfection of beauty in him.

3 He saw them in Adam all sunk in disgrace,
Exposed unto vengeance extreme;
Yet wonder, O heavens, so great was his grace,
He sent them redemption in him.

4 When death he had vanquished, and spoiled all his foes,
Mysterious howe'er it may seem,
With him from the tomb all his members arose
And ascended to glory with him.
Kent.

THE HOLY SPIRIT.

NEW BRITAIN. C. M. CHAPIN.

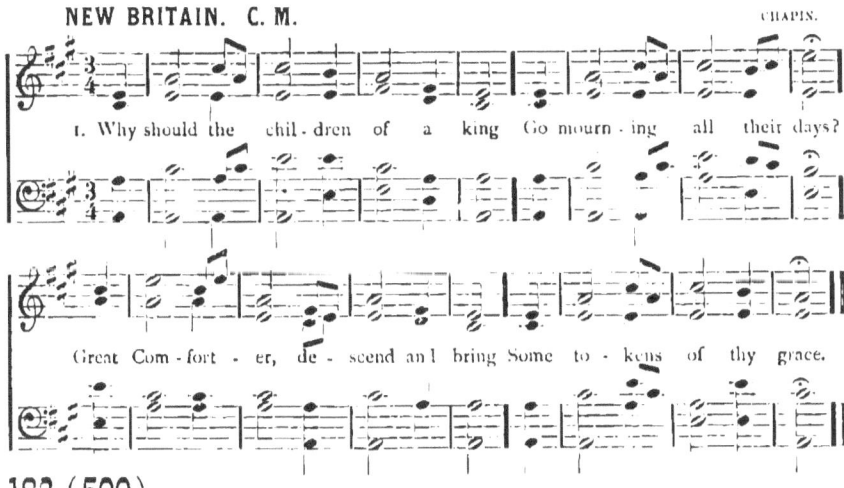

1. Why should the chil-dren of a king Go mourn-ing all their days? Great Com-fort-er, de-scend and bring Some to-kens of thy grace.

182 (500)

1 Why should the children of a king
Go mourning all their days?
Great Comforter, descend and bring
Some tokens of thy grace.

2 Dost thou not dwell in all the saints,
And seal the heirs of heaven?
When wilt thou banish my complaints,
And show my sins forgiven?

3 Assure my conscience of her part
In the Redeemer's blood;
And bear thy witness with my heart,
That I am born of God.

4 Thou art the earnest of his love,
The pledge of joys to come:
And thy soft wings, celestial Dove,
Will safe convey me home.
Watts.

183 (501) C. M.

1 Come, Holy Spirit, heavenly Dove!
With all thy quickening powers,
Kindle a flame of sacred love
In these cold hearts of ours.

2 Look! how we grovel here below,
Fond of these trifling toys;
Our souls can neither fly nor go
To reach eternal joys.

3 In vain we tune our formal songs;
In vain we strive to rise;
Hosannas languish on our tongues,
And our devotion dies.

4 Dear Lord, and shall we ever live
At this poor, dying rate?
Our love so faint, so cold to thee,
And thine to us so great?

5 Come, Holy Spirit, heavenly Dove,
With all thy quickening powers;
Come, shed abroad a Saviour's love,
And that shall kindle ours.
Watts.

184 (506) C. M.

1 My God, what silken cords are thine;
How soft, and yet how strong; [bine
While power, and truth, and love com-
To draw our souls along.

2 Thou sawest us crushed beneath the yoke
Of Satan and of sin:
Thy hand the iron bondage broke,
Our worthless hearts to win.

3 The guilt of twice ten thousand sins
One moment takes away;
And grace, when first the war begins,
Secures the crowning day.

4 Comfort through all this vale of tears,
In rich profusion flows,
And glory of unnumbered years
Eternity bestows.

5 Drawn by such cords, we onward move,
Till round thy throne we meet:
And captives in the chains of love,
Embrace our Conqueror's feet.
Doddridge.

THE HOLY SPIRIT.

EVENING HYMN. L. M. — THOS. TALLIS. 1529–1585.

1. Descend from heav'n, immortal Dove! Stoop down and take us on thy wings, And mount and bear us far above The reach of these inferior things:

185 (502)

1 Descend from heaven, immortal Dove!
Stoop down and take us on thy wings,
And mount and bear us far above
The reach of these inferior things:

2 Beyond, beyond this lower sky,
Up where eternal ages roll;
Where solid pleasures never die,
And fruits immortal feast the soul.

3 O for a sight, a pleasing sight
Of our Almighty Father's throne!
There sits our Saviour crowned with light,
Clothed in a body like our own.

4 Adoring saints around him stand,
And thrones and powers before him fall;
The God shines gracious through the man,
And sheds sweet glories on them all.

5 O what amazing joys they feel
While to their golden harps they sing,
And sit on every heavenly hill,
And spread the triumphs of their King.

6 When shall the day, dear Lord, appear,
That I shall mount to dwell above,
And stand and bow among them there,
And view thy face, and sing, and love!
Watts.

186 (503) L. M.

1 At anchor laid, remote from home,
Toiling, I cry, "*Sweet Spirit*, come!
Celestial breeze, no longer stay,
But swell my sails, and speed my way!

2 "Fain would I mount, fain would I glow,
And loose my cable from below;
But I can only spread my sail;
Thou, thou must breathe th' auspicious gale!"
Toplady.

187 (507) L. M.

1 Come, blessed Spirit! source of light!
Whose power and grace are unconfined,
Dispel the gloomy shades of night,
The thicker darkness of the mind.

2 To mine illumined eyes display
The glorious truth thy words reveal;
Cause me to run the heavenly way,
Make me delight to do thy will.

3 Thine inward teaching make me know,
Thy wonders of redeeming love,
The vanity of things below,
And excellence of things above.

4 While through these dubious paths I stray,
Spread like the sun thy beams abroad;
O show the dangers of the way,
And guide my feeble steps to God.

5 Let thy kind Spirit in my heart
Forever dwell, O God of love;
And light and heavenly peace impart,
Sweet earnest of the joys above.
Beddome.

THE HOLY SPIRIT.

ERNAN. L. M.   Dr. L. MASON.

1. Dear Lord! and shall thy Spirit rest In such a wretched heart as mine? Unworthy dwelling! glorious guest! Favor astonishing, divine!

188 (504) John 14: 16, 17.

1 Dear Lord! and shall thy Spirit rest
In such a wretched heart as mine?
Unworthy dwelling! glorious guest!
Favor astonishing, divine!

2 When sin prevails, and gloomy fear,
And hope almost expires in night,
Lord, can thy Spirit then be here,
Great Spring of comfort, life and light?

3 Sure the blest Comforter is nigh!
'Tis he sustains my fainting heart;
Else would my hopes for ever die,
And every cheering ray depart.

4 When some kind promise glads my soul,
Do I not find his healing voice
The tempest of my fears control,
And bid my drooping powers rejoice!

5 Whene'er to call the Saviour mine,
With ardent wish my heart aspires;
Can it be less than power divine
Which animates these strong desires?

6 And, when my cheerful hope can say,
"I love my God, and taste his grace,"
Lord, is it not thy blissful ray
Which brings this dawn of sacred peace?

7 Let thy kind Spirit in my heart
For ever dwell, O God of love!
And light and heavenly peace impart,—
Sweet earnest of the joys above.
                     Steele.

189 (505) L. M.

1 I'm in a world of hopes and fears,
A wilderness of toils and tears,
Where foes alarm, and dangers threat,
And pleasures kill, and glories cheat.

2 Shed down, O Lord, a heavenly ray,
To guide me in the doubtful way;
And o'er me hold thy shield of power,
To guard me in the dangerous hour.

3 Teach me the flattering path to shun,
In which the thoughtless many run,
Who for a shade the substance miss,
And grasp their ruin in their bliss.

4 Each sacred principle impart;
The faith that sanctifies the heart;
Hope, that to heaven's high vault aspires;
And love that warms with holy fires.

5 Whate'er is noble, pure, refined,
Just, generous, amiable, and kind,
That may my constant thought pursue;
That may I love and practice, too.

6 Let neither pleasure, wealth, nor pride,
Allure my wandering soul aside;
But, through this maze of mortal ill,
Safe lead me to thy heavenly hill.

7 There glories shine, and pleasures roll,
That charm, delight, transport the soul;
And every panting wish shall be
Possessed of boundless bliss in thee.
                  C. Wesley.

FAITH.

BALERMA. C. M. R. SIMPSON.

1. Faith is the brightest evidence Of things beyond our sight;
Breaks thro' the clouds of flesh and sense, And dwells in heav'nly light.

190 (509) Heb. 11.

1 FAITH is the brightest evidence
Of things beyond our sight;
Breaks thro' the clouds of flesh and sense,
And dwells in heavenly light.

2 It sets time past in present view,
Brings distant prospects home,
Of things a thousand years ago,
Or thousand years to come.

3 By faith we know the worlds were made
By God's almighty word:
Abra'm, to unknown countries led,
By faith obeyed the Lord.

4 He sought a city fair and high,
Built by th' eternal hands ;
And faith assures us, though we die,
That heavenly building stands.
Watts.

191 (530) C. M. Gen. 12: 14.

1 THE saints should never be dismayed,
Nor sink in hopeless fear :
For when they least expect his aid,
The Saviour will appear.

2 This Abra'm found ; he raised the knife,
God saw, and said, "Forbear:
Yon ram shall yield his meaner life ;
Behold the victim there !"

3 When Jonah sunk beneath the wave,
He thought to rise no more ;
But God prepared a fish to save,
And bear him to the shore.

4 Blessed proofs of power and grace divine,
That meet us in his word!
May every deep felt care of mine
Be trusted with the Lord.

5 Wait for his seasonable aid,
And though it tarry, wait;
The promise may be long delayed,
But cannot come too late.
Cowper.

192 (533) C. M.

1 OF all the gifts thine hand bestows,
Thou Giver of all good !
Not heaven itself a richer knows,
Than my Redeemer's blood.

2 Faith, too, the blood receiving grace,
From the same hand we gain ;
Else, sweetly as it suits our case,
That gift had been in vain.

3 Till thou thy teaching power apply,
Our hearts refuse to see;
And weak, as a distempered eye,
Shut out the view of thee.

4 Blind to the merits of thy Son,
What misery we endure ;
Yet fly that hand, from which alone
We could expect a cure.

5 We praise thee, and would praise thee more,
To thee our all we owe ;
The precious Saviour and the power
That makes him precious, too.
Cowper.

FAITH. 79

193 (512) 2 Cor. 5: 7.

1 'Tis by the faith of joys to come
We walk through deserts dark as night;
Till we arrive at heaven our home,
Faith is our guide, and faith our light.

2 The want of sight she well supplies;
She makes the pearly gates appear;
Far into distant worlds she pries,
And brings eternal glories near.

3 Cheerful we tread the desert through,
While faith inspires a heavenly ray,
Though lions roar, and tempests blow,
And rocks and dangers fill the way.

4 So Abraham, by divine command,
Left his own house to walk with God;
His faith beheld the promised land,
And fired his zeal along the road.
Watts.

194 (527) L. M. Mark 9: 24.

1 JESUS, our souls' delightful choice,
In thee, believing, we rejoice;
Yet still our joy is mixed with grief,
While faith contends with unbelief.

2 Thy promises our hearts revive,
And keep our fainting hopes alive:
But guilt, and fears, and sorrows rise,
And hide the promise from our eyes.

3 O let not sin and Satan boast,
While saints lie mourning in the dust;
Nor see that faith to ruin brought,
Which thy own gracious hand hath
 wrought.

4 Do thou the dying spark inflame;
Reveal the glories of thy name;
And put all anxious doubts to flight,
As shades dispersed by opening light.
Doddridge.

195 (529) L. M.

1 By faith in Christ I walk with God,
With heaven, my journey's end, in view,
Supported by his staff and rod,
My road is safe and pleasant, too.

2 I travel through a desert wide,
Where many round me blindly stray;
But he vouchsafes to be my guide,
And will not let me miss my way.

3 Though snares and dangers throng my
 path,
And earth and hell my course withstand,
I triumph over all by faith,
Guarded by his almighty hand.

4 The wilderness affords no food,
But God for my support prepares;
Provides me every needful good,
And frees my soul from want and cares.

5 With him sweet converse I maintain,
Great as he is, I dare be free;
Tell him of all my grief and pain,
And he reveals his love to me.

6 Some cordial from his word he brings,
Whene'er my feeble spirit faints;
At once my soul revives and sings,
And yields no more to sad complaints.
Newton.

FAITH.

LYONS. 10s. & 11s. F. J. HAYDN. 1732-1809.

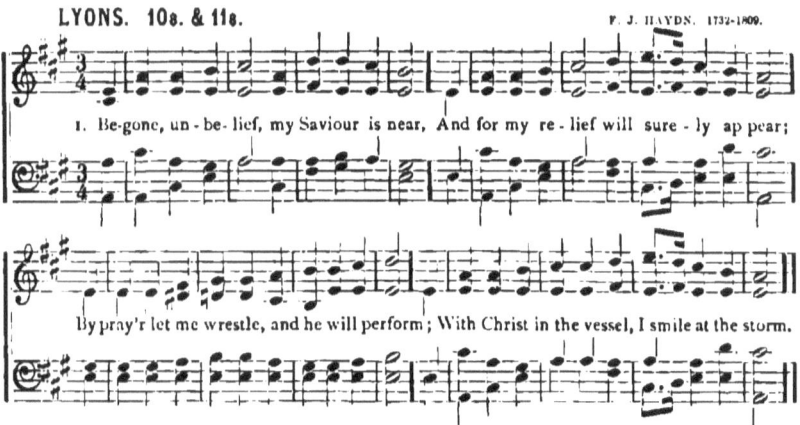

1. Be-gone, un-be-lief, my Saviour is near, And for my re-lief will sure-ly appear; By pray'r let me wrestle, and he will perform; With Christ in the vessel, I smile at the storm.

196 (515) Isaiah 12: 2.

1 BEGONE, unbelief, my Saviour is near,
And for my relief will surely appear;
By prayer let me wrestle, and he will perform; [storm.
With Christ in the vessel, I smile at the

2 Though dark be my way, since he is my Guide,
'Tis mine to obey, 'tis his to provide;
Though cisterns be broken, and creatures all fail, [vail.
The word he has spoken shall surely pre-

3 His love in time past forbids me to think
He'll leave me at last in trouble to sink:
Each sweet Ebenezer I have in review,
Confirms his good pleasure to help me quite through.

4 Determined to save, he watched over my path, [death.
When, Satan's blind slave, I sported with
And can he have taught me to trust in his name, [to shame?
And thus far have brought me to put me

5 Why should I complain of want or distress,
Temptation or pain? He told me no less;
The heirs of salvation, I know from his word, [their Lord.
Through much tribulation must follow

6 How bitter that cup, no heart can conceive, [might live.
Which he drank quite up that sinners

His way was much rougher and darker than mine; [repine?
Did Christ, my Lord, suffer, and shall I

7 Since all that I meet shall work for my good,
The bitter is sweet, the medicine is food:
Though painful at present, 'twill cease before long, [song.
And then, O how pleasant the conqueror's
Newton.

197 (712) 10s. & 11s. Lam. 3: 25.

1 THOU Fountain of bliss, thy smile I entreat; [thy feet:
O'erwhelmed with distress, I mourn at
The joy of salvation, when shall it be mine?
The high consolation of friendship divine!

2 Awakened to see the depth of my fall,
For mercy on thee I earnestly call:
'Tis thine the lost sinner to save and renew;
Faith's mighty beginner and finisher, too.

3 Thy Spirit alone repentance implants,
And gives me to groan at feeling my wants;
'Midst all my dejection, dear Lord, I can trace [grace.
Some marks of election, some tokens of

4 Thou wilt not despise a sinner distressed;
All-kind and all-wise, thy season is best.
To thy sovereign pleasure, resigned I would be,
And tarry thy leisure, and hope still in thee.
Toplady.

FAITH. 81

198 (516) Acts 16: 31; Pet. 2: 6.

1 THE sinner that truly believes,
  And trusts in his crucified Lord,
His justification receives,
  Redemption in full through his blood;
Though thousands and thousands of foes
  Against him in malice unite,
Their rage he through Christ can oppose,
  Led forth by the spirit to fight.

2 Not all the delusions of sin
  Shall ever seduce him to death;
He now has the witness within,
  Rejoicing in Jesus by faith.
This faith shall eternally fail
  When Jesus shall fall from his throne;
For hell against both must prevail,
  Since Jesus and he are but one.

3 The faith that lays hold on the Lamb
  And brings such salvation as this,
Is more than mere notion or name;
  The work of God's Spirit it is:
A principle, active and young,
  That lives under pressure and load;
That makes out of weakness more strong,
  And draws the soul upward to God.

4 It says to the mountains, "Depart,"
  That stand betwixt God and the soul;
It binds up the broken in heart, [whole:
  And makes their sore consciences
Bids sins of a crimson-like dye
  Be spotless as snow, and as white;

And proves such a sinner as I
  As pure as an angel of light.
                                    Hart.

199 (528) 8s. D.

1 A DEBTOR to mercy alone,
  Of covenant mercy I sing;
Nor fear, with thy righteousness on,
  My person and offering to bring:
The terrors of law and of God
  With me can have nothing to do;
My Saviour's obedience and blood
  Hide all my transgressions from view.

2 The work which his goodness began,
  The arm of his strength will complete;
His promise is Yea and Amen,
  And never was forfeited yet:
Things future, nor things that are now,
  Not all things below, nor above,
Can make him his purpose forego,
  Or sever my soul from his love.

3 My name from the palms of his hands
  Eternity will not erase;
Impressed on his heart it remains,
  In marks of indelible grace:
Yes! I to the end shall endure,
  As sure as the earnest is given;
More happy, but not more secure,
  The glorified spirits in heaven.
                                 Toplady.

FAITH.

ALEXANDER. 7s. & 6s.

1. If to Jesus for relief My soul has fled by pray'r,
Why should I give way to grief, Or heart-consuming care?
Are not all things in his hands? Has he not his promise pass'd?
Will he then regardless stand, And let me sink at last?

200 (534)

2 While I know his providence
  Disposes each event,
Shall I judge by feeble sense,
  And yield to discontent?
If he worms and sparrows feed,
Clothes the grass in rich array,
Can he see a child in need,
  And turn his eye away?

3 When his name was quite unknown,
  And sin my life employed,
Then he watched me as his own,
  Or I had been destroyed;
Now his mercy-seat I know,
Now by grace am reconciled
Would he spare me as a foe,
  To leave me as a child?

4 If he all my wants supplied,
  When I disdained to pray,
Now his spirit is my guide,
  How can he say me, Nay?
If he would not give me up,
When my soul against him fought,
Will he disappoint the hope
  Which he himself has wrought.

5 If he shed his precious blood
  To bring me to his fold,
Can I think that meaner good
  He ever will withhold!

Satan, vain is thy device!
Here my hope rests well assured,
In that great redemption-price,
  I see the whole secured.

Newton.

201 (550)   7s. & 6s.

1 Sin enslaved me many years,
  And led me bound and blind;
Till at length a thousand fears
  Came swarming o'er my mind.
Where, I said in deep distress,
Will these sinful pleasures end?
How shall I secure my peace,
  And make the Lord my friend?

2 Friends and ministers said much
  The gospel to enforce;
But my blindness still was such,
  I chose a legal course:
Much I fasted, watched, and strove,
Scarce would show my face abroad;
Feared, almost, to speak or move,—
  A stranger still to God.

3 Thus, afraid to trust his grace,
  Long time did I rebel;
Till, despairing of my case,
  Down at his feet I feel;
Then my stubborn heart he broke,
And subdued me to his sway,
By a simple word he spoke,
  "Thy sins are done away."

Cowper.

CONVERSION.   83

BROWN. C. M.   W. B. BRADBURY.

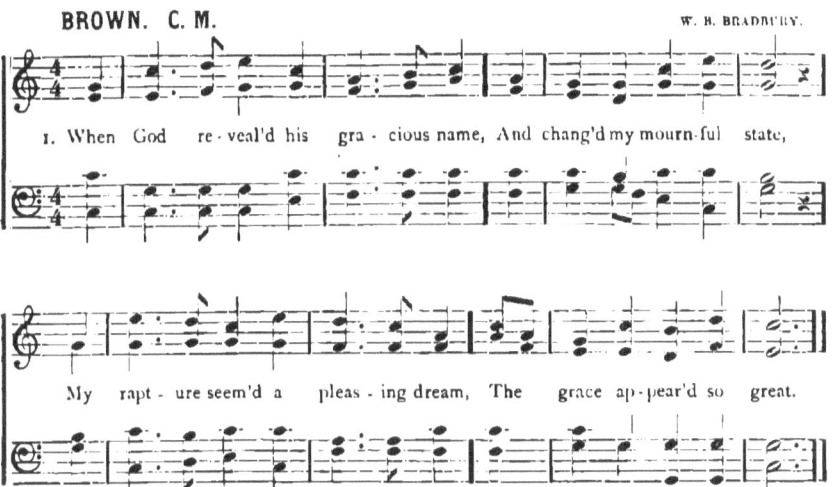

1. When God revealed his gracious name, And chang'd my mournful state,
My rapture seem'd a pleasing dream, The grace appear'd so great.

202 (541)

1 When God revealed his gracious name,
And changed my mournful state,
My rapture seemed a pleasing dream,
The grace appeared so great.

2 The world beheld the glorious change,
And did thy hand confess;
My tongue broke out in unknown strains,
And sung surprising grace.

3 "Great is the work," my neighbors cried,
And owned thy power divine;
"Great is the work," my heart replied,
"And be the glory thine."

4 The Lord can clear the darkest skies,
Can give us day for night,
Make drops of sacred sorrow rise
To rivers of delight.

5 Let those that sow in sadness wait
Till the fair harvest come;
They shall confess their sheaves are great,
And shout the blessings home.

6 Though seed lie buried long in dust,
It shan't deceive their hope;
The precious grain can ne'er be lost,
For grace ensures the crop.
Watts.

203 (543)   C. M.

1 Let worldly minds the world pursue,
It has no charms for me;
Once I admired its trifles, too,
But grace has set me free.

2 Its pleasures now no longer please,
No more content afford;
Far from my heart be joys like these,
Since I have known the Lord.

3 As by the light of opening day
The stars are all concealed,
So earthly objects fade away
When Jesus is revealed.

4 Creatures no more divide my choice,
I bid them all depart;
His name, and love, and gracious voice,
Have fixed my roving heart.

5 Now, Lord, I would be thine alone,
And wholly live to thee;
But may I hope that thou wilt own
A worthless worm like me?

6 Yes, though of sinners I'm the worst,
I cannot doubt thy will;
For if thou had'st not chose me first,
I had refused thee still.
Newton.

CONVERSION.

GARDEN. C. P. M.
J. INGALLS. 1764–1828.

1. Awaked by Sinai's awful sound, My soul in guilt and thrall I found, And knew not where to go, And knew not where to go: O'erwhelm'd in sin, with anguish slain, 'Twas said I must be born again, Or sink in endless wo, Or sink in endless wo.

204 (546) John 3: 7.

2 Amazed I stood, but could not tell
Which way to shun the gates of hell,
   For death and hell drew near;
I strove indeed, but strove in vain;
The sinner must be born again,
   Still sounded in my ear.

3 The saints I heard with rapture tell
How Jesus conquered death and hell,
   And broke the fowler's snare;
Yet when I found this truth remain,
The sinner must be born again,
   I sunk in deep despair.

4 But while I thus in anguish lay,
Jesus of Nazareth passed that way;
   It was the time of love:
He then relieved me from my pain,
And showed me I was born again,
   To dwell with him above.

5 To heaven my joyful praises flew,
Singing that song for ever new,
   To Christ my voice did raise:
All hail the Lamb that once was slain,
Unnumbered millions born again
   Shall shout thine endless praise.
S. Occom.

205 (521) C. P. M.

1 TELL me no more of earthly toys,
Of sinful mirth and carnal joys,
   The things I loved before;
Let me but view my Saviour's face,
And feel his animating grace,
   And I desire no more.

2 Tell me no more of praise and wealth,
Of great prosperity and health,
   For these have all their snares;
Let me but know my sins forgiven,
And see my name enrolled in heaven,
   I'm then quite free from cares.

3 Give me the bible in my hand,
A heart to read and understand,
   And faith to trust the Lord;
I'd sit alone from day to day,
Nor urge gay company to stay,
   Nor wish to rove abroad. Susanna Harrison.

REPENTANCE. 85

SOCIAL BAND. L. M.　　INGALLS.

1. { Show pity, Lord, O Lord, forgive, Let a repenting rebel live:
    { Are not thy mercies large and free? May not a sinner trust in thee? }
D.C.—Great God, thy nature hath no bound, So let thy pard'ning love be found.

2. My crimes are great, but can't surpass The pow'r and glory of thy grace;

206 (563)

1 SHOW pity, Lord, O Lord, forgive,
Let a repenting rebel live;
Are not thy mercies large and free?
May not a sinner trust in thee?

2 My crimes are great, but can't surpass
The power and glory of thy grace;
Great God, thy nature hath no bound,
So let thy pardoning love be found.

3 O wash my soul from every sin,
And make my guilty conscience clean;
Here on my heart the burden lies,
And past offenses pain my eyes.

4 My lips with shame my sins confess
Against thy law, against thy grace;
Lord, should thy judgment grow severe,
I am condemned, but thou art clear.

5 Should sudden vengeance seize my breath,
I must pronounce thee just in death;
And if my soul were sent to hell,
Thy righteous law approves it well.

6 Yet save a trembling sinner, Lord,
Whose hope still hovering round thy word,
Would light on some sweet promise there,
Some sure support against despair.
　　　　　　　　　　　Watts.

207 (554)　L. M.

1 WITH melting heart and weeping eyes,
My guilty soul for mercy cries;
What shall I do, or whither flee,
T' escape the vengeance due to me?

2 Till late I saw no danger nigh;
I lived at ease, nor feared to die!
Wrapped up in self-deceit and pride,
"I shall have peace at last," I cried.

3 But when, great God, thy light divine
Had shone in this dark soul of mine,
Then I beheld, with trembling awe,
The terrors of thy holy law.

4 How dreadful now my guilt appears,
In childhood, youth, and growing years;
Before thy pure discerning eye,
Lord, what a filthy wretch am I!

5 Should vengeance still my soul pursue,
Death and destruction are my due!
Yet mercy can my guilt forgive,
And bid a dying sinner live!

6 Does not thy sacred word proclaim
Salvation free in Jesus' name?
To him I look and humbly cry,
"O save a wretch condemned to die!
　　　　　　　　　　　Fawcett.

208 (565)　L. M.

1 LORD, with a grieved and aching heart
To thee I look, to thee I cry;
Supply my wants and ease my smart;
O help me soon, or else I die.

2 Here on my soul a burden lies!
No human power can it remove;
My numerous sins like mountains rise:
Do thou reveal thy pardoning love.
　　　　　　　　　　　Beddome.

REPENTANCE.

LEANDER. C. M. D.

209 (562)

1 Alas! and did my Saviour bleed,
And did my Sovereign die?
Would he devote that sacred head
For such a worm as I?

2 [Thy body slain, dear Jesus, thine,
And bathed in its own blood,
While all exposed to wrath divine
The glorious sufferer stood.]

3 Was it for crimes that I have done
He groaned upon the tree?
Amazing pity! Grace unknown!
And love beyond degree!

4 Well might the sun in darkness hide,
And shut his glories in,
When Christ, the mighty Saviour, died
For man, the creature's sin.

5 Thus might I hide my blushing face
While his dear cross appears,
Dissolve my heart in thankfulness,
And melt my eyes in tears.

6 But drops of grief can ne'er repay
The debt of love I owe;
Here, Lord, I give myself away,
'Tis all that I can do.
Watts.

210 (558) C. M. D.

1 How oft, alas! this wretched heart
Has wandered from the Lord!
How oft my roving thoughts depart,
Forgetful of his word;

2 Yet sovereign mercy calls "Return!"
Dear Lord, and may I come?
My vile ingratitude I mourn;
O, take the wanderer home.

3 Almighty grace, thy healing power
How glorious, how divine!
That can to life and bliss restore
So vile a heart as mine!

4 Thy pardoning love, so free, so sweet,
Dear Saviour, I adore;
O keep me at thy sacred feet,
And let me rove no more.
Mrs. Steele.

211 (561) C. M. D.

1 O God of mercy! hear my call,
My load of guilt remove;
Break down this separating wall
That bars me from thy love.

2 Give me the presence of thy grace,
Then my rejoicing tongue
Shall speak aloud thy righteousness,
And make thy praise my song.
Watts.

REPENTANCE.

AMAZING GRACE. C. M.

1. Dear Saviour! when my thoughts recall
The wonders of thy grace,
Low at thy feet a-sham'd, I fall,
And hide this wretched face.

212 (568)

2 Shall love like thine be thus repaid?
Ah, vile, ungrateful heart!
By earth's low cares detained, betrayed
From Jesus to depart.

3 From Jesus, who alone can give
True pleasure, peace, and rest:
When absent from my Lord, I live
Unsatisfied, unblessed.

4 But he, for his own mercy's sake,
My wandering soul restores;
He bids the mourning heart partake
The pardon it implores.

5 Oh, while I breath to thee, my Lord,
The penitential sigh
Confirm the kind, forgiving word,
With pity in thine eye!

6 Then shall the mourner at thy feet
Rejoice to seek thy face;
And grateful own how kind, how sweet,
Thy condescending grace.
Mrs. Steele.

213 (569) C. M. John 20: 13.

1 WHY, O my soul, why weepest thou?
Tell me from whence arise
Those briny tears that often flow,
Those groans that pierce the skies.

2 Is sin the cause of thy complaint,
Or the chastising rod?
Dost thou an evil heart lament,
And mourn an absent God?

3 Lord, let me weep for naught but sin!
And after none but thee!
And then I would—O, that I might!—
A constant weeper be!
Beddome.

214 (570) C. M. Isa. 57: 15.

1 THE Lord will happiness divine
On contrite hearts bestow;
Then tell me, gracious God! is mine
A contrite heart or no?

2 I hear, but seem to hear in vain,
Insensible as steel;
If aught is felt, 'tis only pain
To find I cannot feel.

3 I sometimes think myself inclined
To love thee, if I could;
But often feel another mind,
Averse to all that's good.

4 My best desires are faint and few,
I fain would strive for more;
But, when I cry, "My strength renew,"
Seem weaker than before.

5 Thy saints are comforted, I know,
And love thy house of prayer;
I sometimes go where others go,
But find no comfort there.

6 Oh, make this heart rejoice or ache;
Decide this doubt for me;
And, if it be not broken, break;
And heal it if it be.
Cowper.

HOPE.

BARBY. C. M. W. TANSUR.

1. Our Jesus is the Christian's hope, Wrought in us by God's pow'r; It holds the weak believer up In the distressing hour.

215 (574) Lam. 3: 24.

1 Our Jesus is the Christian's hope,
  Wrought in us by God's power;
It holds the weak believer up
  In the distressing hour.

2 The darkest cloud hope pierces through,
  And waits upon the Lord;
Expects to prove that all is true
  Throughout the sacred word.

3 True hope looks out for blessings great;
  And, though they're long delayed,
Yet hope's determined still to wait,
  Until they are conveyed.

4 Hope long will wait, and wait again,
  And ne'er can give it up,
Till the blessed Lamb, who once was slain,
  Appears the God of hope.
                             Burnham.

3 Were I in heaven without my God,
  'Twould be no joy to me;
And whilst this earth is my abode,
  I long for none but thee.

4 What if the springs of life were broke,
  And flesh and heart should faint!
God is my soul's eternal rock,
  The strength of every saint.

5 Behold, the sinners that remove
  Far from thy presence die;
Not all the idol gods they love
  Can save them when they cry.

6 But to draw near to thee, my God,
  Shall be my sweet employ;
My tongue shall sound thy works abroad,
  And tell the world my joy.
                             Watts.

216 (578) C. M. Psa. 73: 23-28.

1 God, my Supporter, and my Hope,
  My Help for ever near,
Thine arm of mercy held me up
  When sinking in despair.

2 Thy counsels, Lord, shall guide my feet
  Through this dark wilderness;
Thine hand conduct me near thy seat,
  To dwell before thy face.

217 (588) C. M.

1 We seek a rest beyond the skies,
  In everlasting day;
Thro' floods and flames the passage lies,
  But Jesus guards the way.

2 The swelling flood, and raging flame,
  Hear, and obey his word;
Then let us triumph in his name,
  Our Saviour is the Lord.

HOPE. 89

DEVIZES. C. M.   TUCKER.

1. How can I sink with such a prop As my e-ter-nal God, Who bears the earth's huge pil-lars up, And spreads the heav'ns a-broad, And spreads the heav'ns a-broad?

218 (579)

1 How can I sink with such a prop
  As my eternal God,
Who bears the earth's huge pillars up,
  And spreads the heavens abroad?

2 How can I die while Jesus lives,
  Who rose and left the dead?
Pardon and grace my soul receives
  From mine exalted Head.

3 All that I am, and all I have,
  Shall be for ever thine:
Whate'er my duty bids me give,
  My cheerful hands resign.

4 Yet if I might make some reserve,
  And duty did not call,
I love my God with zeal so great
  That I should give him all.
                        Watts.

219 (580)   C. M.

1 Give me the wings of faith to rise
  Within the veil, and see
The saints above, how great their joys,
  How bright their glories be.

2 Once they were mourning here below,
  And wet their couch with tears;
They wrestled hard, as we do now,
  With sins, and doubts, and fears.

3 I ask them whence their victory came?
  They, with united breath,
Ascribe their conquest to the Lamb,
  Their triumph to his death.

4 Our glorious Leader claims our praise
  For his own pattern given,
While the long cloud of witnesses
  Shows the same path to heaven.
                        Watts.

220 (584)   C. M.

1 Ye trembling souls! dismiss your fears;
  Be mercy all your theme:
Mercy, which, like a river, flows
  In one continued stream.

2 *Fear not* the powers of earth and hell;
  God will these powers restrain;
His mighty arm their rage repel,
  And make their efforts vain.

3 *Fear not* the want of outward good:
  He will for his provide;
Grant them supplies of daily food,
  And all they need beside.

4 *Fear not* that he will e'er forsake,
  Or leave his work undone;
He's faithful to his promises,
  And faithful to his Son.

5 *Fear not* the terrors of the grave,
  Or death's tremendous sting:
He will from endless wrath preserve,
  To endless glory bring.

6 You, in his wisdom, power, and grace
  May confidently trust;
His wisdom guides, his power protects,
  His grace rewards the just.
                        Beddome.

90 HOPE.

RETREAT. L. M. — Dr. THOS. HASTINGS. 1784–1872.

1. We travel through a barren land, With dangers thick on ev'ry hand; But Jesus guides us thro' the vale; The Christian's hope can never fail.

221 (575)   Heb. 6:19.

1 We travel through a barren land,
With dangers thick on every hand;
But Jesus guides us through the vale;
The Christian's hope can never fail.

2 Huge sorrows meet us as we go,
And devils aim our overthrow;
But vile infernals can't prevail:
The Christian's hope shall never fail.

3 Sometimes we're tempted to despair,
But Jesus makes us then his care:
Though numerous foes our souls assail,
The Christian's hope shall never fail.

4 We trust upon the sacred word,
The oath and promise of our Lord;
And safely through each tempest sail:
The Christian's hope shall never fail.
Gadsby's Col.

222 (582)   L. M.

1 O God, my Sun, thy blissful rays
Can warm, rejoice, and guide my heart:
How dark, how mournful are my days,
If thy enlivening beams depart.

2 Scarce through the shades a glimpse of
Appears to these desiring eyes;   [day
But shall my drooping spirit say,
The cheerful morn will *never* rise?

3 Oh, let me not despairing mourn!
Though gloomy darkness spreads the
My glorious Sun will yet return,   [sky,
And night with all its horrors fly.

4 Oh, for the bright, the joyful day,
When hope shall in fruition die:
So tapers lose their feeble ray
Beneath the Sun's refulgent eye.
Rippon's Col.

223 (583)   L. M.

1 Why sinks my weak desponding mind?
Why heaves my heart the anxious sigh?
Can sovereign goodness be unkind?
Am I not safe if God is nigh?

2 He holds all nature in his hand:
That gracious hand on which I live
Doth life, and time, and death command,
And has immortal joys to give.

3 'Tis he supports this fainting frame;
On him alone my hopes recline:
The wondrous glories of his name,
How wide they spread! how bright
they shine!

4 Infinite wisdom! boundless power!
Unchanging faithfulness and love!
Here let me trust, while I adore,
Nor from my refuge ere remove.

5 My God, if thou art mine indeed,
Then I have all my heart can crave;
A present help in times of need;
Still kind to hear, and strong to save.

6 Forgive my doubts, O gracious Lord!
And ease the sorrows of my breast;
Speak to my heart the healing word,
That thou art mine, and I am blest.
Mrs. Steele.

HOPE. 91

ZION. 8s. 7s. & 4s. Dr. THOS. HASTINGS, 1784-1873.

224 (589)

1 On the mountain's top appearing,
Lo! the sacred herald stands,
Welcome news to Zion bearing,
Zion long in hostile lands;
  Mourning captive,
God himself will loose thy bands.

2 Has thy night been long and mournful?
Have thy friends unfaithful proved?
Have thy foes been proud and scornful,
By thy sighs and tears unmoved?
  Cease thy mourning;
Zion still is well-beloved.

3 God, *thy* God, will now restore thee;
He himself appears thy friend;
All thy foes shall flee before thee;
Here their boasts and triumphs end;
  Great deliverance
Zion's King will surely send.

4 Peace and joy shall now attend thee;
All thy warfare now is past;
God thy Saviour will defend thee;
Victory is thine at last:
  All thy conflicts
End in everlasting rest.
Thos. Kelly.

225 (774) 8s. 7s. & 4s. Psa. 43: 3-5.

1 O my soul! what means this sadness?
Wherefore art thou thus cast down?
Let thy griefs be turned to gladness;
Bid thy restless fears be gone;
  Look to Jesus,
And rejoice in his dear name.

2 What though Satan's strong tempta-
Vex and tease thee, day by day, [tions
And thy sinful inclinations
Often fill thee with dismay;
  Thou shalt conquer,
Through the Lamb's redeeming blood.

3 Though ten thousand ills beset thee,
From without and from within,
Jesus saith, he'll ne'er forget thee,
But will save from hell and sin:
  He is faithful,
To perform his gracious word.

4 Though distresses shall attend thee,
And thou treadst the thorny road,
His right hand shall still defend thee;
Soon he'll bring thee home to God:
  Therefore praise him;
Praise the great Redeemer's name.

5 O that I could now adore him,
Like the heavenly host above,
Who for ever bow before him,
And unceasing sing his love!
  Happy songsters!
When shall I your chorus join?
Fawcett

LOVE.

DURAND. C. M.   EMERSON.

1. O Lord, I would delight in thee, And on thy care depend; To thee in all my troubles flee, My best, my only Friend.

226 (595) Psa. 27: 4.

1 O LORD, I would delight in thee,
   And on thy care depend;
To thee in all my troubles flee,
   My best, my only Friend.

2 When all created streams are dried,
   Thy fulness is the same;
May I with this be satisfied,
   And glory in thy name.

3 No good in creatures can be found,
   But may be found in thee;
I must have all things, and abound,
   While God is good to me.

4 He that has made my heaven secure
   Will here all good provide;
While Christ is rich, I can't be poor;
   What can I want beside?

5 O Lord, I cast my care on thee;
   I triumph and adore;
Henceforth my great concern shall be
   To love and praise thee more.   Ryland

227 (599) C. M. Gen. 17: 38.

1 WHEN Jesus, with his matchless love,
   Visits my troubled breast,
My doubts subside, my fears remove,
   And I'm completely blest.

2 I love the Lord with mind and heart,
   His people and his ways;
Envy, and pride, and lust depart,
   And all his works I praise.

3 But ah! when these short visits end,
   Though not quite left alone,
I miss the presence of my Friend,
   Like one whose comfort's gone.

4 I to my own sad place return,
   My wretched state to feel;
I tire, and faint, and droop, and mourn,
   And am but barren still.

5 More frequent let thy visits be,
   Or let them longer last;
I can do nothing without thee;
   Make haste, my God, make haste.
                                          Hart.

228 (604) C. M.

1 HAPPY the heart where graces reign,
   Where love inspires the breast:
Love is the brightest of the train,
   And strengthens all the rest.

2 'Tis love that makes our cheerful feet
   In sweet obedience move;
The devils know and tremble, too,
   But Satan cannot love.

3 This is the grace that lives and sings
   When faith and hope shall cease;
'Tis this shall strike our joyful strings
   In the sweet realms of bliss.

4 Before we quite forsake our clay,
   Or leave this dark abode,
The wings of love bear us away
   To see our smiling God.
                                     Watts.

LOVE. 93

DE FLEURY. 8s. D. German Melody.

1. How tedious and tasteless the hours When Jesus no longer I see; Sweet prospects, sweet birds, and sweet flow'rs
D.C.—But when I am hap-py in him, De-cem-ber's as pleasant as May.

Have lost all their sweetness to me: The mid-summer sun shines but dim; The fields strive in vain to look gay;

229 (603) Psa. 73: 25.

1 How tedious and tasteless the hours,
  When Jesus no longer I see;
Sweet prospects, sweet birds, and sweet
    flowers
  Have lost all their sweetness to me :
The mid-summer sun shines but dim;
  The fields strive in vain to look gay;
But when I am happy in him,
  December's as pleasant as May.

2 His name yields the richest perfume,
  And sweeter than music his voice;
His presence disperses my gloom,
  And makes all within me rejoice:
I should, were he always thus nigh,
  Have nothing to wish or to fear;
No mortal so happy as I,
  My summer would last all the year.

3 Content with beholding his face,
  My all to his pleasure resigned,
No changes of season or place,
  Would make any change in my mind;
While blessed with a sense of his love,
  A palace a toy would appear;
And prisons would palaces prove,
  If Jesus would dwell with me there.

4 Dear Lord, if indeed I am thine,
  If thou art my sun and my song,
Say, why do I languish and pine,
  And why are my winters so long?

O drive these dark clouds from my sky;
  Thy soul-cheering presence restore;
Or take me unto thee on high,
  Where winter and clouds are no more.
                                Newton.

230 (594) 8s. D. John 21: 17.

1 My gracious Redeemer I love;
  His praises aloud I'll proclaim,
And join with the armies above,
  To shout his adorable name:
To gaze on his glories divine
  Shall be my eternal employ;
And feel them incessantly shine,
  My boundless, ineffable joy.

2 He freely redeemed with his blood,
  My soul from the confines of hell,
To live on the smiles of my God,
  And in his sweet presence to dwell:
To shine with the angels of light,
  With saints and with seraphs to sing;
To view with eternal delight,
  My Jesus, my Saviour, my King.

3 In Meshech, as yet, I reside,—
  A darksome and restless abode;
Molested with foes on each side,
  And longing to dwell with my God.
O, when shall my spirit exchange
  This cell of corruptible clay
For mansions celestial, and range
  Through realms of ineffable day.
                                Francis.

LOVE.

FAIRFIELD. C. M.
HITCHCOCK.

1. Lo! what an entertaining sight Are brethren that agree; Brethren whose cheerful hearts unite In bands of u - ni - ty. Brethren whose cheerful hearts unite In bands of u - ni - ty.

231 (605)

2 When streams of love from Christ, the
Descend to every soul;   [spring,
And heavenly peace, with balmy wing,
Shades and bedews the whole.
3 'Tis like the oil divinely sweet,
On Aaron's reverend head;

The trickling drops perfumed his feet,
And o'er his garments spread.
4 'Tis pleasant as the morning dews
That fall on Zion's hill,
Where God his mildest glory shews,
And makes his grace distil.   Watts.

COMMUNION. C. M.
STEPHEN JENKS.

1. And have I, Christ, no love to thee,—No pas-sion for thy charms? No wish my Sav-iour's face to see, And dwell with-in his arms?

232 (608)

2 Is there no spark of gratitude
In this cold heart of mine,
To him whose generous bosom glowed
With friendship all divine?
3 Can I pronounce his charming name,
His acts of kindness tell,

And, while I dwell upon the theme,
No sweet emotion feel?
4 A very wretch, Lord, I should prove,
Had I no love to thee:
Rather than not my Saviour love,
O may I cease to be!   Stennett.

LOVE. 95

ELIZABETHTOWN. C. M.   GEORGE KINGSLEY.

1. Do not I love thee, O my Lord? Behold my heart and see; And turn each curs-ed i-dol out That dares to ri-val thee.

233 (613) John 21: 15.

1 Do not I love thee, O my Lord?
  Behold my heart and see;
And turn each cursed idol out
  That dares to rival thee.

2 Do not I love thee from my soul?
  Then let me nothing love;
Dead be my heart to every joy,
  When Jesus cannot move.

3 Is not thy name melodious still
  To mine attentive ear?
Doth not each pulse with pleasure bound
  My Saviour's voice to hear?

4 Hast thou a lamb in all thy flock
  I would disdain to feed?
Hast thou a foe, before whose face
  I fear thy cause to plead?

5 Thou know'st I love thee, dearest Lord;
  But, O! I long to soar
Far from the sphere of mortal joys,
  And learn to love thee more.
                        Doddridge.

234 (612) C. M.

1 PERMIT me, Lord, to seek thy face,
  Obedient to thy call;
To seek the presence of thy grace,
  My strength, my life, my all.

2 All I can wish is thine to give;
  My God, I ask thy love;
That greatest boon I can receive;
  That bliss of heaven above.

3 To heaven my restless heart aspires;
  Oh! for a quickening ray,
To animate my faint desires,
  And cheer the tiresome way.

4 While sin and Satan join their art
  To keep me from my Lord,
Dear Saviour, guard my trembling heart,
  And guide me by thy word.

5 My Guardian, my almighty Friend,
  On thee my soul would rest;
On thee alone my hopes depend;
  In thee I'm ever blest.
                        Mrs. Steele.

235 (617) C. M.

1 BLEST Jesus, when my soaring thoughts
  O'er all thy graces rove,
How is my soul in transport lost,
  In wonder, joy, and love!

2 Not softest strains can charm mine ears,
  Like thy beloved name;
Nor aught beneath the skies inspire
  My heart with equal flame.

3 No; thou art precious to my heart,
  My portion and my joy;
For ever let thy boundless grace
  My sweetest thoughts employ.

4 When nature faints, around my bed
  Let thy bright glories shine,
And death shall all its terrors lose
  In raptures so divine.
                        Heginbotham.

LOVE

GIVE. C. M.
J. GRIGG. 1815–1851.

1. How sweet, how heav'n-ly is the sight, When those who love the Lord
In one an-oth-er's peace de-light, And thus ful-fil his word:

236 (614)

1 How sweet, how heavenly is the sight,
When those who love the Lord
In one another's peace delight,
And thus fulfil his word:

2 When each can feel his brother's sigh,
And with him bear a part;
When sorrow flows from eye to eye,
And joy from heart to heart:

3 When free from envy, scorn, and pride,
Our wishes all above,
Each can his brother's failings hide,
And show a brother's love:

4 When love in one delightful stream
Through every bosom flows;
And union sweet, and dear esteem,
In every action glows!

5 Love is the golden chain that binds
The happy souls above;
And he's an heir of heaven that finds
His bosom glow with love.
Swain.

237 (615) C. M.

1 Thou lovely source of true delight,
Whom I unseen adore,
Unveil thy beauties to my sight,
That I may love thee more.

2 Thy glory o'er creation shines,
But in thy sacred word
I read, in fairer, brighter lines,
My bleeding, dying Lord.

3 Jesus, my Lord, my Life, my Light,
O come with blissful ray;
Break radiant through the shades of night,
And chase my fears away.

4 Then shall my soul with rapture trace
The wonders of thy love;
But the full glories of thy face
Are only known above.
Steele.

238 (624) C. M.

1 Jesus, my Lord, how rich thy grace!
Thy bounties how complete!
How shall I count the matchless sum?
How pay th' almighty debt?

2 High on a throne of radiant light
Dost thou exalted shine;
What can my poverty bestow,
When all the worlds are thine?

3 But thou hast brethren here below,
The partners of thy grace;
And wilt confess their humble names
Before thy Father's face.

4 In them thou mayest be clothed and fed,
And visited and cheered;
And in their accents of distress,
My Saviour's voice is heard.

5 Thy face, with reverence and love,
We in thy poor would see;
O, let us rather beg our bread
Than keep it back from thee!
Doddridge.

LOVE.

WOODLAND. C. M. P. N. D. GOULD.

1. With eyes of faith and wings of love My soul would upward rise, And converse hold with things above, And all that heav'nly influence prove, Which gave di-vine sup-plies.

239 (623)

2 But sin will oft my heart betray,
And cares from morn till e'en
Command my laboring thoughts away,
And my affections far astray
From happiness and heaven.

3 Heaven is the portion of my soul,
My treasure and my joy;
There's 'naught on earth, from pole to pole,
Where mountains rise or oceans roll,
That should my heart employ.

4 Upward, still upward, let me soar,
While in this vale of tears;
Till earthly cares and toils are o'er,
And sin shall wound my heart no more,
And heaven itself appears.

LOVE. C. M. D. WM. COLE. 1850.

1. { To thee, my Shepherd and my Lord, A grateful song I'll raise; } 2. Vain the attempt! what
   { O let the mean-est of thy flock Attempt to sing thy praise. }   Do jus-tice to so
tongue can speak A sub-ject so di-vine?
vast a theme, *Omit* .... And praise a love like thine?

240 (618)

1 To thee, my Shepherd and my Lord,
A grateful song I'll raise:
O let the meanest of thy flock
Attempt to sing thy praise.

2 Vain the attempt! what tongue can
A subject so divine?   [speak
Do justice to so vast a theme,
And praise a love like thine?

3 Love, that could bring thy willing feet
From that blessed world on high,
From thy great Father's dear embrace,
To suffer, bleed, and die!

4 My life, my joy, my hope, I owe
To this amazing love;
Ten thousand thousand comforts here,
And nobler bliss above.   Heginbotham.

LOVE

GUIDE. 7s. D.
M. M. WELLS.

1. Jesus, Lord, we look to thee; Let us in thy name agree:
   Show thyself the Prince of Peace; Bid all jars for ever cease.
   D.C.—Each to each unite, endear; Come and spread thy banner here.

2. By thy reconciling love, Ev'ry stumbling block remove:

241 (596)

3 Make us of one heart and mind,
Courteous, pitiful, and kind;
Lowly, meek, in thought and word;
Altogether like our Lord.
4 Let us each for other care;
Each another's burden bear;

To thy church the pattern give;
Show how true believers live.
5 Let us then with joy remove
To the family above;
On the wings of angels fly;
Show how true believers die.   c. w.

HEDDING. C. P. M.
D. READ.

1. O love divine, how sweet thou art! When shall I find my willing heart
   D.S.—The greatness of redeeming love,
   All taken up by thee? I thirst, and faint, and die to prove
   The love of Christ to me.

242 (597)

2 Stronger his love than death or hell;
Its riches are unsearchable;
The first-born sons of light
Desire in vain its depth to see;
They cannot reach the mystery,
The length, the breadth, and height.

3 God only knows the love of God;
O that it now were shed abroad
In this poor stony heart!
For this I sigh, for this I pine;
This only portion, Lord, be mine;
Be mine this better part.   c. w.

LOVE. 99

BAVARIA. 8s. & 7s. D. German Air.

1. Lamb of God, we fall before thee, Humbly trusting in thy cross;
That a-lone be all our glo-ry; All things else are dung and dross.
D.C.—Ev-'ry grace, and ev-'ry fa-vor Comes to us through Je-sus' blood.

Thee we own a per-fect Sav-iour, On-ly source of all that's good;

243 (559)

1 Lamb of God, we fall before thee,
  Humbly trusting in thy cross;
That alone be all our glory;
  All things else are dung and dross.
Thee we own a perfect Saviour,
  Only source of all that's good;
Every grace, and every favor
  Comes to us through Jesus' blood.

2 Jesus gives us true repentance:
  By his spirit sent from heaven
Jesus whispers this sweet sentence:
  "Son, thy sins are all forgiven:"
Faith he gives us to believe it;
  Grateful hearts his love to prize:
Want we wisdom? he must give it;
  Hearing ears, and seeing eyes.

3 Jesus gives us pure affections;
  Wills to do what he requires;
Makes us follow his directions,
  And what he commands, inspires:
All our prayers, and all our praises,
  Rightly offered in his name,
He that dictates them is Jesus;
  He that answers is the same.

4 When we live on Jesus' 'merit,
  Then we worship God aright;
Father, Son, and Holy Spirit,
  Then we savingly unite.
Hear the whole conclusion of it:
  Great or good, whate'er we call,

God, or King, or Priest, or Prophet,
  Jesus Christ is All in all!
  J. Hart.

244 (600) 8s. & 7s. D. Psa. 133: 1.

1 Jesus, Source of our salvation,
  May we now thy nature know:
Then, more bowels of compassion
  We to thy dear saints shall show.
May the grace thou hast imparted,
  In relieving our complaints,
Make us kind and tender-hearted
  To the feeblest of thy saints.

2 When they are severely tempted,
  We their sorrows would assuage,
Knowing we are not exempted
  From the tempter's furious rage.
If by sin they're overtaken,
  We'll their faults to them declare;
But in strains of much compassion,
  Lest we drive them to despair.

3 Keep us from a proud appearance,
  In whate'er we do or say;
Fill us with divine forbearance;
  Then how happy we shall be!
Hand in hand we would be walking,
  Eyeing Jesus' new command;
Of his love we'd e'er be talking,
  Till we reach the heavenly land.
  Burnham.

100 LOVE

EVENING. S. M.
INGALLS. 1804

1. Blest be the tie that binds Our hearts in Christian love!
The fellowship of kindred minds Is like to that above.

245 (609)

2 Before our Father's throne
  We pour our ardent prayers;
Our fears, our hopes, our aims are one,
  Our comforts and our cares.

3 We share our mutual woes;
  Our mutual burdens bear;
And often for each others flows
  The sympathizing tear.

4 When we asunder part,
  It gives us inward pain;
But we shall still be joined in heart,
  And hope to meet again.

5 This glorious hope revives
  Our courage by the way;
While each in expectation lives,
  And longs to see the day.

6 From sorrow, toil. and pain,
  And sin we shall be free:
And perfect love and friendship reign
  Through all eternity.
                              Fawcett.

246 (620)   S. M.

1 I LOVE the sons of grace,
  The heirs of bliss divine,
Who walk in paths of righteousness,
  And fly from every sin.

2 They will my faults reprove
  When heedlessly I err;
How do I prize their faithful love!
  Their kind and tender care.

3 They Jesus' image bear;
  How lovely is the sight:
They shall at length with him appear
  In everlasting light.

4 They love the Father's name,
  And gladly do his will;
They humbly follow Christ, the Lamb,
  In purity and zeal.

5 It is a sweet employ
  To join in worship here;
But how divine will be the joy
  To see each other there!
                           Baltimore Col.

247 (621)   S. M.

1 LOVE is the fountain, whence
  All true obedience flows;
The Christian serves the God he loves,
  And loves the God he knows.

2 He treads the heavenly road,
  And neither faints nor tires;
That generous love which warms his breast
  With fortitude inspires.

3 No burden seems so great,
  No task so hard appears,
But this he cheerfully performs,
  And that he meekly bears.

4 May love—that shining grace—
  O'er all my powers preside;
Direct my thoughts, suggest my words,
  And every action guide.

LOVE. 101

UNION. 8s.   BILLINGS.

1. From whence doth this union arise, That hatred is conquer'd by love?
It fastens our souls in such ties, As distance and time can't remove.

248 (619)

1 From whence doth this union arise,
  That hatred is conquered by love?
It fastens our souls in such ties,
  As distance and time can't remove.

2 It cannot in Eden be found,
  Nor yet in a Paradise lost;
It grows on Immanuel's ground,
  And Jesus' rich blood it did cost.

3 My friends now so dear unto me,
  Our hearts so united in love;
Where Jesus is gone we shall be,
  In yonder blest mansions above.

4 Why then so reluctant to part?
  Since there we shall all meet again?
Engraved on Immanuel's heart,
  At distance we cannot remain.

5 And soon we shall see that bright day,
  And join with the armies above;
Set free from these prisons of clay;
  United in mansions of love.

6 With Jesus we ever shall reign;
  His glory eternally see;
We'll sing hallelujah, Amen;
  Amen! even so let it be.
                            Baldwin

249 (591)   Tune—Wells, page 14.   L M   Sol. Song, 4:12.

1 We are a garden walled around,
  Chosen and made peculiar ground;
A little spot enclosed by grace
  Out of the worlds wide wilderness.

2 Like trees of myrrh and spice we stand,
  Planted by God the Father's hand;
And all his springs in Zion flow
  To make the young plantation grow.

3 Awake, O heavenly wind, and come,
  Blow on this garden of perfume;
Spirit divine, descend and breathe
  A gracious gale on plants beneath.

4 Our Lord into his garden comes,
  Well pleased to smell our poor perfumes,
And calls us to a feast divine,
  Sweeter than honey, milk, or wine.
                            Watts.

250 (622)   Tune—Wells, page 14.   L. M.

1 Jesus, thy boundless love to me
  No thought can reach, no tongue declare;
O knit my thankful heart to thee,
  And reign without a rival there.

2 Thy love, how cheering is its ray;
  All pain before its presence flies:
Care, anguish, sorrow, melt away,
  Where'er its healing beams arise.

3 O let thy love my soul inflame,
  And to thy service sweetly bind;
Transfuse it through my inmost frame,
  And mould me wholly to thy mind.

4 Thy love in sufferings be my peace;
  Thy love in weakness make me strong;
And when the storms of life shall cease,
  Thy love shall be my heaven and song.
            Paul Gerhardt   Tr. by J. Wesley.

102 HUMILITY.

HAMBURG. L. M. Arr. by Dr. LOWELL MASON, from Gregorian. Tone VIII.

1. Je-sus, be-fore thy face I fall, My Lord, my life, my hope, my all;

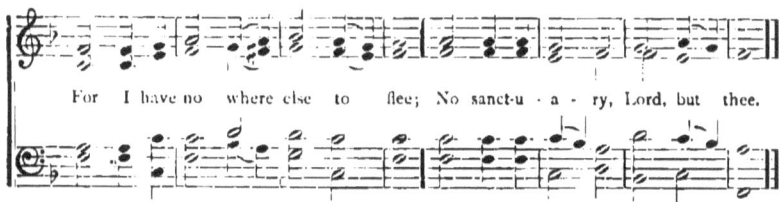

For I have no where else to flee; No sanct-u-a-ry, Lord, but thee.

251 (627) Isa. 8: 21.

1 JESUS, before thy face I fall,
My Lord, my life, my hope, my all;
For I have no where else to flee;
No sanctuary, Lord, but thee.

2 In thee I every glory view,
Of safety, strength, and beauty, too:
Beloved Saviour, ever be
A sanctuary unto me.

3 Whatever woes and fears betide,
In thy dear bosom let me hide;
And, while I pour my soul to thee,
Do thou my sanctuary be.

4 Through life and all its changing scenes,
And all the grief that intervenes,
'Tis this supports my fainting heart,
That thou my sanctuary art.

5 Apace the solemn hour draws nigh.
When I must bow my head and die;
But O, what joy this witness gives,—
Jesus, my sanctuary, lives.

6 He from the grave my dust will raise;
I in the heavens will sing his praise;
And when in glory I appear,
He'll be my sanctuary there.
                              Medley.

252 (628) L. M. 1 Pet. 2: 7.

1 JESUS is precious, saith the Word;
What comfort does this truth afford!
And those who in his name believe,
With joy this precious truth receive.

2 To them he is more precious far
Than life and all its comforts are;
More precious than their daily food;
More precious than their vital blood.

3 He's precious in his precious blood,
That pardoning and soul-cleansing flood;
He's precious in his righteousness,
That everlasting, heavenly dress.

4 In every office he sustains,
In every victory he gains,
In every counsel of his will,
He's precious to his people still.

5 As they draw near their journey's end,
How precious is their heavenly Friend!
And, when in death they bow their head,
He's precious on a dying bed.

6 In glory, Lord, may I be found,
And, with thy precious mercy crowned,
Join the glad song, and there adore
A precious Christ for evermore.
                              Medley

HUMILITY.
103

LUTON. L. M. *Spirited.*   BURDEN.

1. Ye humble souls, complain no more; Let faith sur-vey your fut-ure store: How hap-py, how di-vine-ly blest, The sa-cred words of truth at-test.

253 (630) Matt. 5: 3.

1 YE humble souls, complain no more;
Let faith survey your future store:
How happy, how divinely blest,
The sacred words of truth attest.

2 In vain the sons of wealth and pride
Despise your lot, your hope deride;
In vain they boast their little stores:
Trifles are theirs, a kingdom yours.

3 A kingdom of immense delight,
Where health, and peace, and joy unite:
Where undeclining pleasures rise,
And every wish hath full supplies.

4 A kingdom which can ne'er decay,
While time sweeps earthly thrones away;
The state which power and truth sustain,
Unmoved for ever must remain.

5 There shall your eyes with rapture view
The glorious Friend that died for you;
That died to ransom, died to raise
To crowns of joy and songs of praise.

6 Jesus, to thee I breathe my prayer;
Reveal, confirm my interest there:
Whate'er my humble lot below,
This, this my soul desires to know.
                          Mrs. Steele.

254 (639) L. M.

1 SEE a poor sinner, gracious Lord,
Whose soul, encouraged by thy word,
At mercy's footstool would remain,
And there would look, and look again.

2 Ah, bring a wretched wanderer home,
And to thy footstool let me come,
And tell thee all my grief and pain,
And wait, and look, and look again.

3 Take courage, then, my trembling soul;
One look from Christ will make thee whole;
Trust thou in him, 'tis not in vain, [
But wait, and look, and look again.

4 Look to the Lord, his word, his throne;
Look to his strength, and not thy own;
There wait, and look, and look again;
Thou shalt not wait, nor look in vain.
                         Medley.

255 (641) L. M.

1 OH, could I find some peaceful bower,
Where sin has neither place nor power;
This traitor vile I fain would shun,
But cannot from his presence run.

2 When to the throne of grace I flee,
He stands between my God and me:
Where'er I rove, where'er I rest,
I feel him working in my breast.

3 When I attempt to soar above,
To view the heights of Jesus' love,
This monster seems to mount the skies,
And veils his glory from my eyes.

4 Lord, free me from this deadly foe,
Which keeps my faith and hope so low;
I long to dwell in heaven my home,
Where not one sinful thought can come.
                         Harrison.

HUMILITY.

AYLESBURY. S. M. — JAMES GREEN 1715.

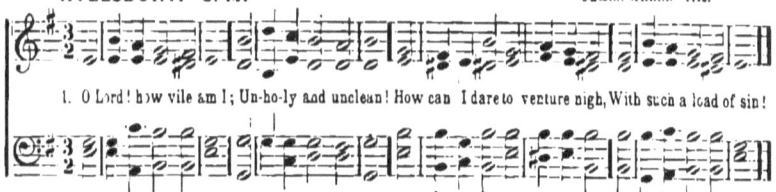

1. O Lord! how vile am I; Un-ho-ly and unclean! How can I dare to venture nigh, With such a load of sin!

256 (629) Job 10: 1; Rom. 7: 24.

1 O Lord! how vile am I;
Unholy and unclean!
How can I dare to venture nigh,
With such a load of sin!

2 Is this polluted heart
A dwelling fit for thee?
Swarming, alas! in every part,
What evils do I see!

3 If I attempt to pray,
And lisp thy holy name,
My thoughts are hurried soon away;
I know not where I am.

4 If in thy word I look,
Such darkness fills my mind,
I only read a sealed book,
And no relief can find.

5 Myself can hardly bear
This wretched heart of mine;
How hateful then, must it appear
To those pure eyes of thine;

6 And must I then indeed
Sink in despair and die?
Fain would I hope that thou didst bleed
For such a wretch as I.

7 That blood which thou hast spilt,
That grace which is thine own,
Can cleanse the vilest sinner's guilt
And soften hearts of stone.

8 Low at thy feet I bow;
O, pity and forgive!
Here will I lie, and wait till thou
Shalt bid me rise and live.
Newton.

257 (635) Psalm 140: 4.

1 Ye humble souls, rejoice,
And cheerful praises sing!
Wake all your harmony of voice,
For Jesus is your King!

2 That meek and lowly Lord,
Whom here your souls have known,
Pledges the honor of his word,
T' avow you for his own.

3 He brings salvation near;
For you his blood was paid!
How beauteous shall you all appear,
Thus sumptuously arrayed!

4 Salvation, Lord, is thine,
And all the saints confess
The royal robes, in which they shine,
Were wrought by sovereign grace.
Doddridge.

GEORGIA. S. M. — JOSEPH B. MOON. 1853.

1. Ye humble souls, rejoice, And cheerful praises sing! Wake all your harmony of voice, For Jesus is your King!

HUMILITY. 105

WOODSIDE. C. M.   L. O. EMERSON.

1. Je-sus the great, the might-y God, A man of grief be-came;
In paths of meek-ness here he trod, And bore the sin-ner's shame.

Used by per. O. Ditson & Co.

258 (631)

1 Jesus the great, the mighty God,
  A man of grief became;
In paths of meekness here he trod,
  And bore the sinner's shame.

2 Humility, how bright it shined
  In every act he wrought;
What lowliness of heart and mind,
  Appeared in all he taught.

3 His love to men of sinful race,
  Glowed in his tender breast;
For man he yielded to disgrace,
  Forsaken and distressed.

4 Led as a lamb to meet the sword,
  He bowed beneath the stroke;
Not one revengeful angry word,
  The dear Redeemer spoke.

5 O may his meekness be my guide,
  The pattern I pursue;
How can I bear revenge or pride,
  With Jesus in my view?

259 (633) C. M.

1 Is there ambition in my heart?
  Search, gracious God, and see;
Or do I act a haughty part?
  Lord, I appeal to thee.

2 I charge my thoughts, be humble still,
  And all my carriage mild;
Content, my Father, with thy will,
  And quiet as a child.

3 The patient soul, the lowly mind
  Shall have a large reward;
Let saints in sorrow lie resigned,
  And trust a faithful Lord.   *Watts.*

260 (646) C. M. Psalm 42.

1 With earnest longings of the mind,
  My God, to thee I look;
So pants the hunted hart to find
  And taste the cooling brook.

2 When shall I see the courts of grace,
  And meet my God again?
So long an absence from thy face
  My heart endures with pain.

3 Temptations vex my weary soul,
  And tears are my repast;
The foe insults without control:
  "And where's your God at last?"

4 'Tis with a mournful pleasure now
  I think on ancient days;
Then to thy house did numbers go,
  And all our work was praise.

5 But why, my soul, sunk down so far
  Beneath this heavy load?
Why do my thoughts indulge despair,
  And sin against my God?

6 Hope in the Lord, whose mighty hand
  Can all thy woes remove;
For I shall yet before him stand,
  And sing restoring love.   *Watts.*

RESIGNATION.

NAOMI. C. M. Dr. LOWELL MASON. 1792-1872.

261 (649)

1 O LORD! my best desires fulfil,
  And help me to resign
Life, health, and comfort to thy will,
  And make thy pleasure mine.

2 Why should I shrink at thy command,
  Whose love forbids my fears?
Or tremble at the gracious hand
  That wipes away my tears?

3 No! let me rather freely yield
  What most I prize to thee,
Who never hast a good withheld,
  Nor wilt withhold, from me.

4 Thy favor all my journey through
  Thou art engaged to grant;
What else I want, or think I do,
  'Tis better still to want.

5 But, ah! my inmost spirit cries,
  Still bind me to thy sway;
Else the next cloud, that veils my skies,
  Drives all these thoughts away.
           Cowper.

262 (650) C. M. Heb. 12: 7.

1 AND can my heart aspire so high,
  To say, "My Father, God!"
Lord, at thy feet I fain would lie
  And learn to kiss the rod.

2 I would submit to all thy will,
  For thou art good and wise,
Let every anxious thought be still,
  Nor one faint murmur rise.

3 Thy love can cheer the darksome gloom,
  And bid me wait serene,
Till hopes and joys immortal bloom,
  And brighten all the scene.

4 "My Father,"—O permit my heart
  To plead her humble claim;
And ask the bliss those words impart,
  In my Redeemer's name.
           Mrs. Steele.

263 (656) C. M.

1 My times of sorrow and of joy,
  Great God! are in thy hand;
My choicest comforts come from thee,
  And go at thy command.

2 If thou shouldst take them all away,
  Yet would I not repine;
Before they were possessed by me,
  They were entirely thine.

3 Nor would I drop a murmuring word,
  Though the whole world were gone;
But seek enduring happiness
  In thee, and thee alone.

4 What is the world, with all its store?
  'Tis but a bitter sweet;
When I attempt to pluck the rose,
  A prickly thorn I meet.

5 Here perfect bliss can ne'er be found,
  The honey's mixed with gall:
Midst changing scenes, and dying friends,
  Be thou my All in all.
           Beddome.

RESIGNATION.

DUNDEE. C. M. G. FRANC. 1520-1570.

1. Fa-ther, what-e'er of earth-ly bliss Thy sov-'reign will de-nies,
Ac-cept-ed at thy throne of Grace, Let this pe-ti-tion rise:

264 (657)

1 FATHER, whate'er of earthly bliss
Thy sovereign will denies,
Accepted at thy throne of Grace,
Let this petition rise:

2 Give me a calm and thankful heart,
From every murmur free;
The blessing of thy grace impart,
And make me live in thee:

3 Let the sweet hope that thou art mine,
My life and death attend;
Thy presence through my journey shine,
And crown my journey's end.
Mrs. Steele.

265 (663) C. M.

1 SUBMISSIVE to thy will, my God,
I all to thee resign,
And bow before thy chastening rod;
I mourn, but not repine.

2 Why should my foolish heart complain,
When wisdom, truth, and love,
Direct the stroke, inflict the pain,
And point to joys above?

3 How short are all my sufferings here!
How needful every cross!
Away, my unbelieving fear,
Nor call my gain my loss.

4 Then give, dear Lord, or take away,
I'll bless thy sacred name;
My Jesus yesterday, to-day,
Forever is the same.
Haweis.

266 (664) C. M.

1 THROUGH all the downward tracks of
God's watchful eye surveys;   [time,
Oh! who so wise to choose our lot,
Or regulate our ways?

2 I cannot doubt his bounteous love,
Immeasurably kind;
To his unerring, gracious will,
Be every wish resigned.

3 Good when he gives, supremely good,
Nor less when he denies;
E'en crosses from his sovereign hand
Are blessings in disguise.
Hervey.

267 (665) C. M.

1 My God, my Father—blissful name—
O may I call thee mine!
May I with sweet assurance claim
A portion so divine!

2 This only can my fears control,
And bid my sorrows fly;
What harm can ever reach my soul,
Beneath my Father's eye?

3 Whate'er thy holy will denies,
I calmly would resign;
For thou art good, and just, and wise;
O bend my will to thine.

4 Whate'er thy sacred will ordains,
O give me strength to bear;
And let me know my Father reigns,
And trust his tender care.
Mrs. Steele.

RESIGNATION.

VERNON. L. M. 6l.
INGALLS.

1. 'Tis hard, when we are sick and poor, And they who loved us, love no more,
When riches, health, and friends are gone, To say, "O Lord, thy will be done:"
Yet, Lord, I would to thee re-sign, And say, "My Father's will be mine."

268 (667)

2 'Tis hard, when in our souls distress,
All, all around is wilderness,
When herbs and quenching streams there's none,
To say, "My Father's will be done."
Yet, Lord, I would to thee resign,
And say, "My Father's will be mine."

3 And yet, how light our sorrows be,
To his, in dark Gethsemane,
Who drank the cup, with stifled groan,
And said, "My Father's will be done."
Dear Lord, may I to thee resign,
And say, "My Father's will be mine."

JUDAH. 8s. & 7s.
Judkin.

1. Jesus, while our hearts are bleeding, O'er the spoils that death has won, We would at this solemn meeting, Calmly say, "Thy will be done," Calmly say, "Thy will be done."

269 (668)

2 Though cast down, we're not forsaken,
Though afflicted, not alone;
Thou didst give, and thou has taken,
Blessed Lord, "Thy will be done."

3 Tho' to-day we're filled with mourning,
Mercy still is on the throne;
With thy smiles of Love returning,
We can sing, "Thy will be done."

4 By thy hands the boon was given,
Thou hast taken but thine own;
Lord of earth and God of heaven,
Evermore, "Thy will be done."

T. Hastings.

PEACE AND JOY. 109

DUNBAR. S. M.   E. W. DUNBAR.

270 (670)

1 BLEST are the sons of peace,
Whose hearts and hopes are one ;
Whose kind designs to serve and please
Through all their actions run.

2 Blest is the favored house
Where zeal and friendship meet ;
Their songs of praise, their mingled vows,
Make their communion sweet.

3 Thus when on Aaron's head
They poured the rich perfume,
The oil through all his raiment spread,
And pleasure filled the room.

4 Thus on the heavenly hills
The saints are blest above,
Where joy like morning dew distils,
And all the air is love.

5 There'll be no sorrow there,
There'll be no sorrow there,
In heaven above where all is love,
There'll be no sorrow there.
                         Watts.

271 (676)   S. M.

1 COME, we that love the Lord,
And let our joys be known ;
Join in a song with sweet accord,
And thus surround the throne.

2 The sorrows of the mind
Be banished from the place !
Religion never was designed
To make our pleasures less.
H

3 Let those refuse to sing
That never knew our God ;
But children of the heavenly King
Should speak their joys abroad.

4 The God that rules on high,
And thunders when he please,
That rides upon the stormy sky,
And manages the seas ;

5 This awful God is ours,
Our Father and our love ;
He will send down his heavenly powers
To carry us above.

6 There we shall see his face,
And never, never sin ;
There from the rivers of his grace
Drink endless pleasures in.

7 Yes, and before we rise
To that immortal state,
The thoughts of such amazing bliss
Should constant joys create.

8 The men of grace have found
Glory begun below ;
Celestial fruits in them abound,
For God ordained it so.

9 Then let our songs abound,
And every tear be dry ;
We're marching thro' Immanuel's ground
To fairer worlds on high.
                         Watts.

PEACE AND JOY.

BROWN. C. M.   W. B. BRADBURY, 1816-1868.

1. Far from the world, O Lord, I flee, From strife and tumult far; From scenes where Satan wages still His most successful war.

272 (672)

1 FAR from the world, O Lord, I flee,
From strife and tumult far;
From scenes where Satan wages still
His most successful war.

2 The calm retreat, the silent shade,
With prayer and praise agree,
And seem by thy sweet bounty made,
For those who follow thee.

3 There, if thy Spirit touch the soul,
And grace her mean abode,
Oh! with what peace, and joy, and love,
She communes with her God.

4 Author and guardian of my life,
Sweet source of light divine,
And (all harmonious names in one)
My Saviour, thou art mine.

5 What thanks I owe thee, and what love;
A boundless, endless store,
Shall echo through the realms above,
When time shall be no more.   Cowper.

273 (675)   C. M.

1 HENCE from my soul, sad thoughts, begone,
And leave me to my joys,
My tongue shall triumph in my God,
And make a joyful noise.

2 Darkness and doubts had veiled my mind,
And drowned my head in tears,
Till sovereign grace, with shining rays,
Dispelled my gloomy fears.

3 O what immortal joys I felt,
And raptures all divine,
When Jesus told me I was his,
And my Beloved mine.

4 In vain the tempter frights my soul,
And breaks my peace in vain,
One glimpse, dear Saviour, of thy face
Revives my joys again.   Watts.

274 (680)   C. M.   Neh. 8: 10.

1 JOY is a fruit that will not grow
In nature's barren soil;
All we can boast, till Christ we know,
Is vanity and toil.

2 But where the Lord has planted grace,
And made his glories known,
There fruits of heavenly joy and peace
Are found, and there alone.

3 A bleeding Saviour, seen by faith,
A sense of pardoning love,
A hope that triumphs over death,
Give joys like those above.

4 To take a glimpse within the veil,
To know that God is mine,
Are springs of joy that never fail,
Unspeakably divine!

5 These are the joys which satisfy,
And sanctify the mind;
Which make the spirit mount on high,
And leave the world behind.   Newton.

PEACE AND JOY. 111

275 (673)

1 SOMETIMES a light surprises
The Christian while he sings
It is the Lord who rises
   With healing in his wings;
When comforts are declining,
He grants the soul again
A season of clear shining,
   To cheer it after rain.

2 In holy contemplation,
   We sweetly then pursue
The theme of God's salvation,
   And find it ever new:
Set free from present sorrow,
   We cheerfully can say,
E'en let the unknown morrow
   Bring with it what it may.

3 It can bring with it nothing,
   But he will bear us through;
Who gives the lilies clothing,
   Will clothe his people, too;
Beneath the spreading heavens,
   No creature but is fed;
And he who feeds the ravens,
   Will give his children bread.

4 Though vine nor fig-tree neither
   Their wonted fruit shall bear,
Though all the field should wither,
   Nor flocks nor herds be there;
Yet God the same abiding,
   His praise shall tune my voice;

For while in him confiding
   I cannot but rejoice.   Cowper.

276 (671) Tune—MERDIN, page 154. 7s

1 'TIS religion that can give
Sweetest pleasures while we live
'Tis religion must supply
Solid comfort when we die:

2 After death, its joy will be
Lasting as eternity!
Be the living God my friend,
Then my bliss shall never end.
   Mary Masters. 1755.

277 (681) Tune—MERDIN, page 154. 7s

1 FIX my heart and eyes on thine!
   What are other objects worth?
But to see thy glory shine
   Is a heaven begun on earth:

2 Trifles can no longer move;
   Oh! I tread on all beside,
When I feel my Saviour's love,
   And remember how he died!

3 Take my heart, 'tis all thine own,
   To thy will my spirit frame;
Thou shalt reign, and thou alone,
   Over all I have or am:

4 Thus whatever may betide,
   I shall safe and happy be,
Still content and satisfied,
   Having all in having thee.   Newton

JOY.

NEW CONCORD. 6s. & 9s.
DAVISSON.

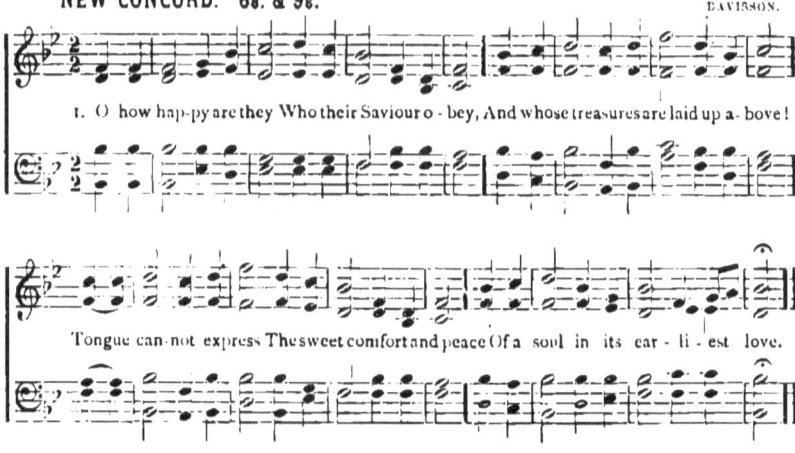

1. O how happy are they Who their Saviour obey, And whose treasures are laid up above! Tongue cannot express The sweet comfort and peace Of a soul in its earliest love.

278 (679)

1 O how happy are they
  Who their Saviour obey,
And whose treasures are laid up above!
  Tongue cannot express
  The sweet comfort and peace
Of a soul in its earliest love.

2 That sweet comfort was mine
  When the favor divine
I first found in the blood of the Lamb:
  When my heart first believed,
  O what joy I received!
What a heaven in Jesus' name!

3 'Twas a heaven below
  The Redeemer to know,
And the angels could do nothing more
  Than to fall at his feet,
  And the story repeat,
And the Saviour of sinners adore!

4 Jesus, all the day long,
  Was my joy and my song;
O that more his salvation might see;
  He hath loved me, I cried;
  He hath suffered and died
To redeem such a rebel as me.

5 On the wings of his love
  I was carried above,
All sin and temptation and pain;
  And I could not believe
  That I ever should grieve,
That I ever should suffer again.

6 I then rode on the sky,
  Freely justified I,
Nor envied Elijah his seat;
  My glad soul mounted higher
  In a chariot of fire,
And the world was put under my feet.

7 O! the rapturous height
  Of that holy delight
Which I felt in the life-giving blood!
  Of my Saviour possessed,
  I was perfectly blessed,
Overwhelmed with the fulness of God.

8 What a mercy is this,
  What a heaven of bliss!
How unspeakably favored am I!
  Gathered into the fold,
  With believers enrolled,
With believers to live and to die!

9 Now, my remnant of days
  Would I spend to his praise,
Who hath died my poor soul to redeem;
  Whether many or few,
  All my years are his due,
May they all be devoted to him.

C. Wesley

279 (682) 2 Tim. 1: 12.

1 I'M not ashamed to own my Lord,
  Or to defend his cause,
  Maintain the honor of his word,
  The glory of his cross.

2 Jesus, my God! I know his name,
  His name is all my trust;
  Nor will he put my soul to shame,
  Nor let my hope be lost.

3 Firm as his throne his promise stands,
  And he can well secure
  What I've committed to his hands,
  Till the decisive hour.

4 Then will he own my worthless name
  Before his Father's face,
  And, in the New Jerusalem,
  Appoint my soul a place.
  Watts.

280 (684) C. M. I Cor. 16: 13.

1 AM I a soldier of the cross,
  A follower of the Lamb?
  And shall I fear to own his cause,
  Or blush to speak his name?

2 Must I be carried to the skies
  On flowery beds of ease,
  While others fought to win the prize,
  And sailed through bloody seas?

3 Are there no foes for me to face?
  Must I not stem the flood?
  Is this vile world a friend to grace,
  To help me on to God?

4 Sure, I must fight, if I would reign;
  Increase my courage, Lord!
  I'll bear the toil, endure the pain,
  Supported by thy word.

5 Thy saints, in all this glorious war,
  Shall conquer though they die;
  They see the triumph from afar,
  And seize it with their eye.

6 When that illustrious day shall rise,
  And all thy armies shine
  In robes of victory through the skies,
  The glory shall be thine.
  Watts.

ZEAL.

WOODWORTH. L. M. — WM. B. BRADBURY. 1816-1868.

1. No more, my God, I boast no more Of all the duties I have done; I quit the hopes I held before, To trust the merits of thy Son.

281 (685) Phil. 3: 7-9.

1 No more, my God, I boast no more
Of all the duties I have done;
I quit the hopes I held before,
To trust the merits of thy Son.

2 Now for the love I bore his name,
What was my gain I count my loss;
My former pride I call my shame,
And nail my glory to his cross.

3 Yes, and I must and will esteem
All things but loss for Jesus' sake:
O may my soul be found in him,
And of his righteousness partake.

4 The best obedience of my hands
Dares not appear before thy throne;
But faith can answer thy demands,
By pleading what my Lord has done.
Watts.

282 (686) L M 2 Cor 12: 7-9, 10.

1 LET me but hear my Saviour say,
"Strength shall be equal to thy day,"
Then I'll rejoice in deep distress,
Leaning on all-sufficient Grace.

2 I glory in infirmity,
That Christ's own power may rest on me;
When I am weak, then am I strong;
Grace is my shield, and Christ my song.

3 I can do all things, or can bear
All sufferings, if my Lord be there;
Sweet pleasures mingle with the pains,
While his strong hand my head sustains.

4 But if the Lord be once withdrawn,
And we attempt the work alone,
When new temptations spring and rise
We find how great our weakness is.
Watts

283 (1129) L. M.

1 JESUS! and shall it ever be,
A mortal man ashamed of thee!
Ashamed of thee, whom angels praise;
Whose glories shine through endless days!

2 Ashamed of Jesus! sooner far
Let evening blush to own a star;
He sheds the beams of light divine
O'er this benighted soul of mine.

3 Ashamed of Jesus! just as soon
Let midnight be ashamed of noon:
'Tis midnight with my soul, till he,
Bright Morning Star! bids darkness flee.

4 Ashamed of Jesus! that dear friend
On whom my hopes of heaven depend!
No; when I blush—be this my shame,
That I no more revere his name.

5 Ashamed of Jesus! who can say,
Who that has sins to wash away,
Or tears to wipe, or good to crave,
Or fears to quell, or soul to save?

6 O then, nor is my boasting vain,
O then, I boast a Saviour slain;
And O, may this my glory be,
That Christ is not ashamed of me. *Gregg.*

TRUST.

WAVERLY. L. M. From "The Psalmist."

1. Lord, didst thou die, but not for me? Am I for-bid to trust thy blood? Hast thou not par-dons, rich and free? And grace, an o-ver-whelm-ing flood?

284 (696)

1 LORD, didst thou die, but not for me?
  Am I forbid to trust thy blood?
  Hast thou not pardons, rich and free
  And grace, an overwhelming flood?

2 Who, then shall drive my trembling soul
  From thee to regions of despair?
  Who has surveyed the sacred scroll,
  And found my name not written there?

3 Presumptuous thought! to fix the bound,
  To limit mercy's sovereign reign:
  What other happy souls have found,
  I'll seek, nor shall I seek in vain.

4 I own my guilt; my sins confess;
  Can men or devils make them more?
  Of crimes, already numberless,
  Vain the attempt to swell the score

5 Were the black list before my sight
  While I remember thou hast died,
  'Twould only urge my speedier fligh
  To seek salvation at thy side.

6 Low at thy feet I'll cast me down,
  To thee reveal my guilt and fear;
  And, if thou spurn me from thy throne,
  I'll be the *first* that perished there.
  Cruttenden.

285 (691)   L. M.

1 My spirit looks to God alone;
  My rock and refuge is his throne
  In all my fears, in all my straits,
  My soul on his salvation waits.

2 Trust him, ye saints, in all your ways,
  Pour out your hearts before his face:
  When helpers fail, and foes invade,
  God is our all-sufficient aid.
  Watts.

286 (704)   L. M.

1 As when the weary traveler gains
  The height of some o'erlooking hill,
  His eye revives, if 'cross the plains
  He sees his home, though distant still;

2 While he surveys the much-loved spot,
  He sights the space that lies between;
  His past fatigues are now forgot,
  Because his journey's end is seen;

3 Thus when the Christian pilgrim views,
  By faith, his mansion in the skies,
  The sight his fainting strength renews,
  And wings his speed to reach the prize.

4 The thought of home his spirit cheers;
  No more he grieves for troubles past;
  Nor any future trial fears,
  So he may safe arrive at last.

5 'Tis there, he says, I am to dwell
  With Jesus, in the realms of day;
  Then I shall bid my cares farewell,
  And he will wipe my tears away.

6 Jesus, on thee our hope depends
  To lead us on to thine abode;
  Assured our home will make amends
  For all our toil while on the road.
  Newton.

TRUST.

CONDESCENSION. C. M.
DAVISSON. Arr. by WM. HAUSER, M. D.

1. Kind are the words that Jesus speaks To cheer the drooping saint;
"My grace suf-fi-cient is for you, Though na-ture's pow'rs may faint.

287 (694)

1 KIND are the words that Jesus speaks
To cheer the drooping saint;
"My grace sufficient is for you,
Though nature's powers may faint.

2 "My grace its glories shall display,
And make your griefs remove:
Your weakness shall the triumphs tell
Of boundless power and love."

3 What though my griefs are not removed,
Yet why should I despair?
While my kind Saviour's arms support,
I can the burden bear.

4 Jesus, my Saviour, and my Lord,
'Tis good to trust thy name:
Thy power, thy faithfulness, and love,
Will ever be the same.

5 Weak as I am, yet through thy grace
I all things can perform;
And, smiling, triumph in thy name
Amid the raging storm.
Needham.

288 (697) C. M.

1 IF God is mine, then present things,
And things to come are mine;
Yea, Christ, his word, and spirit, too,
And glory all divine.

2 If he is mine, then from his love,
He every trouble sends;
All things are working for my good,
And bliss his rod attends.

3 If he is mine, let friends forsake,
Let wealth and honors flee;
Sure, he who giveth me *himself*,
Is more than these to me.

4 If he is mine, I'll boldly pass
Through death's tremendous vale:
He is a solid comfort, when
All other comforts fail.

5 Oh, tell me, Lord! that thou art mine;
What can I wish beside?
My soul shall at the *fountain* live,
When all the *streams* are dryed.
Beddome.

289 (698) C. M.

1 DEAR Lord, why should I doubt thy love,
Or disbelieve thy grace?
Sure thy compassions ne'er remove,
Although thou hide thy face.

2 Thy smiles have freed my heart from pain,
My drooping spirits cheered;
And wilt thou not appear again
Where thou hast once appeared?

3 Dost thou repent? wilt thou deny
The gifts thou hast bestowed?
Or, are those streams of mercy dry,
Which once so freely flowed?

4 Lord, let not groundless fears destroy
The mercies now possessed;
I'll *praise* for blessings I enjoy,
And *trust* for all the rest.
Rippon's Col.

TRUST.   117

SELGGUR. C. M.   Arr. by G. P. L.

1. Be-gone, ye gild-ed van-i-ties, I seek sub-stan-tial good:
To re-al bliss my wish-es rise—The fa-vor of my God.

290 (689) Psalm 4: 6.

1 BEGONE, ye gilded vanities,
  I seek substantial good:
To real bliss my wishes rise—
  The favor of my God.

2 Thy smiles immortal joys impart;
  Heaven dawns in every ray;
One glimpse of thee will cheer my heart,
  And turn my night to day.

3 Let the sweet hope that thou art mine,
  My life and death attend;
Thy presence through my journey shine,
  And crown my journey's end.

4 Grant, O my Father and my God,
  This sweet, this one request;
Be thou my guide to thine abode,
  And mine eternal rest.
                Mrs. Steele.

291 (728)   C. M.

1 With joy let each afflicted saint
  This cheering truth behold,
That when he's tried he shall not faint,
  But shall come forth as gold.

2 This privilege, dear Lord, I plead,
  Nor am I here too bold,
That from the fire as thou hast said,
  I may come forth as gold.

3 What though the furnace burns on high,
  Still to this truth I'll hold;
'Tis but designed my soul to try-
  I shall come forth as gold.

4 Herein his wisdom and his love
  Will God to me unfold;
And from the furnace I shall prove,
  He'll bring me forth as gold.

5 Thus will I sing his praises here,
  Whose mercies are of old;
And when in glory I appear,
  I shall appear as gold.
                Parkinson's Col.

292 (729) C. M.   Matt. 11: 27.

1 WHEN storm and tempest loudly howl,
  And clouds obscure the sky;
When lightnings flash and thunders roll,
  Be not afraid—'tis I.

2 If doubts about a future state
  Extort the serious cry,
"What shall I do? my sins how great!"
  Be not afraid—'tis I.

3 While Satan aims a fiery dart,
  Temptations make thee sigh;
Believe in me; I'll keep thy heart;
  Be not afraid—'tis I.

4 Should health and wealth, and friends
  And death itself draw nigh; [forsake,
Tho' heart should break, and nature shake,
  Be not afraid—'tis I.

5 'Tis I who lived—'tis I who died,
  That thou might'st reign on high;
Behold my hands, my feet, my side,
  And be convinced 'tis I.   Parkinson's Col.

TRUST.

WARD. L. M. — Dr. LOWELL MASON. 1830.

1. Je - sus, the glorious Head of grace, Knows ev - 'ry saint's pe - cul - iar case;
What sor rows by their souls are borne, And how for sin they dai - ly mourn.

293 (713) Matt. 5: 4.

1 JESUS, the glorious Head of grace,
Knows every saint's peculiar case;
What sorrows by their souls are borne,
And how for sin they daily mourn.

2 He knows how deep their groanings are
And what their secret sighs declare:
And, for their comfort, has expressed
That all such mourning souls are blessed.

3 They're blessed on earth; for 'tis by grace
They see and know their mournful case;
Blessed mourners! they shall shortly rise
To endless comfort in the skies.

4 There all their mourning day's will cease,
And they be filled with joy and peace:
Comforts eternal they shall prove,
And dwell for ever in his love.
Medley.

294 (716) L. M. Psa. 46: 10.

1 LET me, thou sovereign Lord of all,
Low at thy footstool humbly fall;
And while I feel affliction's rod,
Be still and know that thou art God.

2 Let me not murmur nor repine,
Under these trying strokes of thine!
But while I walk the mournful road,
Be still and know that thou art God.

3 When and wherever thou shalt smite,
Teach me to own thy sovereign right:
And underneath the heaviest load,
Be still and know that thou art God.

4 Still let this truth support my mind,
Thou canst not err nor be unkind;
And thus approve thy chastening rod,
And know thou art my Father-God!

5 When this afflicted soul shall rise
To ceaseless joys above the skies,
I shall, as ransomed by thy blood,
For ever sing, "Thou art my God!"
Medley.

295 (717) L. M. Lam. 1: 16.

1 O FOR a heart to seek my God,
Encouraged by his gracious word;
To view my Saviour all complete,
And lie submissive at his feet.

2 To thee, Almighty God, to thee,
My Rock and Refuge, would I flee;
Now tides of sorrow, rolling high,
Appear to mingle earth and sky.

3 To see thy saints in mourning clad,
And foes by their distress made glad,
O'erwhelms my soul with poignant grief:
Lord, send thy servant sweet relief.

4 Arise, O God, the cause defend;
Deliverance unto Zion send:
Arise, arise, O God of might,
And put thy threatening foes to flight.

5 Pity thy poor dejected few;
Our souls revive, our strength renew;
Collect thy scattered flock once more,
And open wide the gospel-door.
Horne.

TRUST. 119

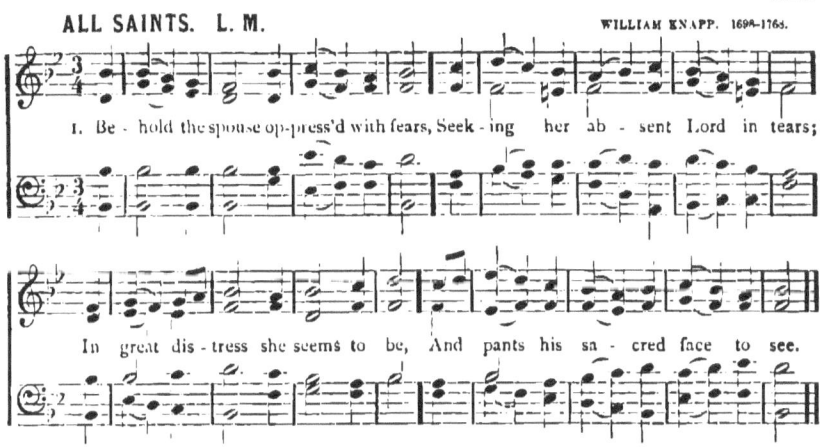

296 (719)

1 BEHOLD the spouse oppressed with fears,
Seeking her absent Lord in tears;
In great distress she seems to be,
And pants his sacred face to see.

2 Like her, my soul has often been,
When clouds and darkness intervene;
I've sought in vain that face to see,
Disfigured once with blood for me.

3 I sought him in his temple, where
His saints, to worship, oft repair;
Yet even here, so hard my lot,
I sought him, but I found him not.

4 I sought to find him, on my knees;
I sought him in his promises;
But his dear face I ne'er could see,
'Twas like the barren heath to me.

5 The sacred page no hope revealed;
This book divine to me was sealed;
Nor hope nor comfort could afford,
For I had lost my only Lord.

6 At length his lovely face he showed,
And joys divine my heart o'erflowed;
My sorrows fled when Jesus smiled,
And called me still his undefiled.
Sonnets

297 (653) L. M. Gen. 22: 6.

1 SAINTS, at your heavenly Father's word
Give up your comforts to the Lord;
He shall restore what you resign,
Or grant you blessing more divine.

2 So Abraham with obedient hand
Led forth his son at God's command;
The wood, the fire, the knife he took,
His arm prepared the dreadful stroke.

3 "Abraham, forbear," (the angel cried,)
"Thy faith is known, thy love is tried;
Thy son shall live, and in thy seed
Shall the whole earth be blessed indeed."

4 Just in the last distressing hour
The Lord displays delivering power;
The mount of danger is the place
Where we shall see surprising grace.
Watts.

298 (726) L. M. Mark 4: 39.

1 THE billows swell, the winds are high,
Clouds overcast my wintry sky;
Out of the depth to thee I call;
My fears are great, my strength is small.

2 O Lord, the pilot's part perform,
And guide and guard me thro' the storm;
Defend me from the threatening ill;
Control the waves, say, "Peace, be still."

3 Amidst the roaring of the sea
My soul still hangs its hopes on thee;
Thy constant love, thy faithful care,
Is all that saves me from despair.

4 Dangers of every shape and name
Attend the followers of the Lamb,
Who leave the world's deceitful shore
And leave it to return no more.
Cowper.

120 TRUST.

HENDON. 7s.
C. H. MALAN, 1787-1864.

1. Wait, my soul, up - on the Lord, To his gra - cious promise flee, Lay-ing hold up - on his word: "As thy days, thy strength shall be," "As thy days, thy strength shall be."

299 (708)

1 Wait, my soul, upon the Lord,
  To his gracious promise flee,
  Laying hold upon his word:
  "As thy days, thy strength shall be."

2 If the sorrows of thy case,
  Seem peculiar still to thee,
  God has promised needful grace:
  "As thy days, thy strength shall be."

3 Days of trial, days of grief,
  In succession thou mayst see;
  This is still thy sweet relief:
  "As thy days, thy strength shall be."

4 Rock of Ages, I'm secure,
  With my promise, full and free,
  Faithful, positive and sure:
  "As thy days, thy strength shall be."
  W. F. Lloyd.

300 (714) 7s. Isa. 56: 5-11.

1 Pensive, doubting, fearful heart,
  Hear what Christ the Saviour says;
  Every word should joy impart—
  Change thy mourning into praise.

2 Yes, he speaks, and speaks to thee;
  May he help thee to believe;
  Then thou presently wilt see,
  Thou hast little cause to grieve:

3 "Fear thou not, nor be ashamed;
  All thy sorrows soon shall end;
  I, who heaven and earth have framed,
  Am thy Husband and thy Friend:

4 I, the High and Holy One,
  Israel's God, by all adored,
  As thy Saviour will be known,
  Thy Redeemer and thy Lord.

5 "For a moment I withdrew,
  And thy heart was filled with pain,
  But my mercies I'll renew;
  Thou shalt soon rejoice again:

6 Though I seem to hide my face,
  Very soon my wrath shall cease;
  'Tis but for a moment's space,
  Ending in eternal peace!

7 "Though afflicted, tempest-tossed,
  Comfortless a while thou art,
  Do not think thou canst be lost;
  Thou art graven on my heart;

8 All thy wastes I will repair;
  Thou shalt be rebuilt anew;
  And in thee it shall appear
  What the God of love can do."
  Newton.

ENCOURAGEMENT. 121

THERON. L. M. — L. O. EMERSON.

1. When darkness long has veiled my mind, And smiling day once more appears, Then, my Redeemer, then I find The folly of my doubts and fears.

By per. O. DITSON & CO.

301 (749)

1 WHEN darkness long has veiled my mind,
And smiling day once more appears,
Then, my Redeemer, then I find
The folly of my doubts and fears.

2 I chide my unbelieving heart;
And blush that I should ever be
Thus prone to act so base a part,
Or harbor one hard thought of thee.

3 O let me then at length be taught
(What I am still so slow to learn,)
That God is love, and changes not,
Nor knows the shadow of a turn.

4 Sweet truth, and easy to repeat!
But when my faith is sharply tried,
I find myself a learner yet,
Unskillful, weak, and apt to slide.

5 But O, my Lord, one look from thee
Subdues the disobedient will;
Drives doubts and discontent away,
And thy rebellious worm is still.

6 Thou art as ready to forgive,
As I am ready to repine;
Thou, therefore, all the praise receive;
Be shame, and self-abhorrence mine.
Cowper.

302 (750) L. M. Deut. 33: 25.

1 AFFLICTED saint, to Christ draw near;
Thy Saviour's gracious promise hear;
His faithful word declares to thee
That, as thy days, thy strength shall be.

2 Let not thy heart despond, and say,
How shall I stand the trying day?
He has engaged, by firm decree,
That, as thy days, thy strength shall be.

3 Thy faith is weak, thy foes are strong;
And, if the conflict should be long,
Thy Lord will make the tempter flee;
For, as thy days, thy strength shall be.

4 Should persecution rage and flame,
Still trust in thy Redeemer's name;
In fiery trials thou shalt see
That, as thy days, thy strength shall be.

5 When called to bear the weighty cross,
Or sore affliction, pain, and loss,
Or deep distress, or poverty,
Still, as thy days, thy strength shall be.

6 When ghastly death appears in view,
Christ's presence shall thy fears subdue,
He comes to set thy spirit free;
And, as thy days, thy strength shall be.
Fawcett.

303 (744) L. M.

1 WHO is the trembling sinner, who
That owns eternal death his due?
Who mourns his sin, his guilt, his thrall,
And does on God for mercy call?

2 Peace, troubled soul, dismiss thy fear,
Hear, Jesus speaks, be of good cheer;
Upon his cleansing grace rely,
And thou shalt never, never die.
Rippon's Col.

ENCOURAGEMENT.

I DO BELIEVE. C. M.

1. 'Tis to his spouse that Je-sus speaks, He chides her long de-lay; How sweet his sa-cred ac-cent breaks, "My fair one, come a-way.

304 (761)

1 'Tis to his spouse that Jesus speaks,
   He chides her long delay;
   How sweet his sacred accent breaks,
   "My fair one, come away.

2 "No howling tempests rend the skies,
   Creation now looks gay;
   My love, my undefiled, arise,
   My fair one, come away.

3 "Should guilt still hover o'er thy mind,
   My love shall ne'er decay;
   I've thy release from bondage signed;
   My fair one, come away.

4 "Should earth, with her ten thousand
   Invite thy soul to stay, [charms,
   Yet, still, to thy Redeemer's arms,
   My fair one, come away.

5 "The sacred turtle's voice within,
   Proclaims the same to-day;
   It sweetly whispers pardoned sin;
   My fair one, come away."

305 (768) C. M.

1 His master taken from his head,
   Elisha saw him go,
   And in desponding accents said,
   "Ah! what must Israel do?"

2 But he forgot the Lord who lifts
   The beggar to the throne;
   Nor knew that all Elijah's gifts
   Would soon be made his own.

3 What! when a Paul has run his course,
   Or when Apollos dies,
   Is Israel left without resource?
   And have we no supplies?

4 Yes! while the dear Redeemer lives,
   We have a boundless store,
   And shall be fed with what he gives,
   Who lives for evermore.
   Cowper.

306 (769) C. M.

1 COURAGE, my soul, behold the prize
   The Saviour's love provides:
   Eternal life beyond the skies
   For all whom here he guides.

2 The wicked cease from troubling there,
   The weary are at rest;
   Sorrow, and sin, and pain, and care,
   No more approach the blest.

3 A wicked world, and wicked heart,
   With Satan now are joined;
   Each acts a too successful part
   In harassing my mind.

4 But fighting in my Saviour's strength,
   Though mighty are my foes,
   I shall a conqueror be at length
   O'er all that can oppose.

5 Then why, my soul, complain or fear?
   The crown of glory see!
   The more I toil and suffer here,
   The sweeter rest will be.
   Newton.

ENCOURAGEMENT.

CONSOLATION. C. M.
DEAN.

1. By the poor wid-ow's oil and meal E-li-jah was sus-tained; Though small the stock, it last-ed well, For God the store main-tained.

307 (763) 1 Kings 17: 16.

1 By the poor widow's oil and meal
  Elijah was sustained;
Though small the stock, it lasted well,
  For God the store maintained.

2 It seemed as if from day to day,
  They were to eat and die;
But still, though in a secret way,
  He sent a fresh supply.

3 Thus to his poor he still will give
  Just for the present hour:
But for to-morrow they must live
  Upon his word and power.

4 No barn or store-house they possess,
  On which they can depend;
Yet have no cause to fear distress,
  For Jesus is their Friend.

5 Then let no doubt your mind assail;
  Remember God has said,
"The cruise and barrel shall not fail;
  My people shall be fed."

6 And thus, though faint, it often seems,
  He keeps their grace alive;
Supplied by his refreshing streams,
  Their dying hopes revive.
  Newton.

308 (753) C. M.

1 A FRIEND there is—your voices join,
  Ye saints, to praise his name;
Whose truth and kindness are divine,
  Whose love's a constant flame.

2 When most we need his helping hand,
  This Friend is always near;
With heaven and earth at his command,
  He waits to answer prayer.

3 His love no end nor measure knows;
  No change can turn its course;
Immutably the same it flows
  From one eternal source.

4 When frowns appear to veil his face,
  And clouds surround his throne,
He hides the purpose of his grace,
  To make it better known.

5 And if our dearest comforts fall
  Before his sovereign will,
He never takes away our all;
  Himself he gives us still!
  - Swain.

309 (738) C. M.

1 OUR God, how firm his promise stands,
  E'en when he hides his face!
He trusts in our Redeemer's hands
  His glory and his grace.

2 Then why, my soul, these sad complaints,
  Since Christ and we are one?
Thy God is faithful to his saints,
  Is faithful to his Son.

3 Beneath his smiles my heart has lived,
  And part of heaven possessed;
I praise his name for grace received,
  And trust him for the rest.
  Watts.

FOUNDATION. 11s.

1. How firm a foun-da-tion, ye saints of the Lord, Is laid for your faith in his ex-cel-lent word! What more can he say than to you he hath said, You, who un-to Je-sus for ref-uge have fled?

310 (751) 2 Pet. 1: 4.

1 How firm a foundation, ye saints of the Lord,
Is laid for your faith in his excellent word!
What more can he say than to you he hath said,—
You, who unto Jesus for refuge have fled?

2 In every condition, in sickness, in health,
In poverty's vale, or abounding in wealth,
At home, and abroad, on the land, on the sea,
As thy days may demand, shall thy strength ever be.

3 "Fear not, I am with thee; O, be not dismayed!
I, I am thy God, and will still give thee aid,
I'll strengthen thee, help thee, and cause thee to stand,
Upheld by my righteous, omnipotent hand.

4 "When through the deep waters I call thee to go,
The rivers of wo shall not thee overflow;
For I will be with thee thy troubles to bless,
And sanctify to thee thy deepest distress.

5 "When through fiery trials thy pathway shall lie,
My grace, all-sufficient, shall be thy supply;
The flame shall not hurt thee; I only design
Thy dross to consume, and thy gold to refine.

6 "E'en down to old age, all my people shall prove
My sovereign, eternal, unchangeable love;
And when hoary hairs shall their temples adorn,
Like lambs they shall still in my bosom be borne.

7 "The soul that on Jesus hath leaned for repose,
I will not, I will not desert to his foes;
That soul, though all hell should endeavor to shake,
I'll never, no never, no never forsake."

G. Keith.

ENCOURAGEMENT. **125**

THE BOWER OF PRAYER. 11s.

RICHERSON and WALKER.
Arr. by WM. HAUSER, M. D.

1. The Lamb is ex-alt-ed re-pent-ance to give, That sin may be hat-ed, while sin-ners be-lieve; Con-tri-tion is grant-ed, and God jus-ti-fied, The sin-ner is hum-bled, and self is de-nied, and self is de-nied.

311 (557) Acts 5: 31.

1 THE Lamb is exalted repentance to give,
That sin may be hated, while sinners believe;
Contrition is granted, and God justified,
The sinner is humbled, and self is denied.

2 Repentance flows freely through Jesus' rich blood, [God,
Produced by the spirit and goodness of
The living possess it, through faith, hope and love, [above.
And own it a blessing sent down from

3 All born of the Spirit are brought to repent; [relent:
Free grace can make adamant hearts to
Repentance is granted, God's justice to prove;
Remission is given, and both from his love.

4 The vilest of sinners forgiveness have found, [abound;
For Jesus was humbled that grace might
Whoever this grace has received of God,
Shall surely be pardoned through Jesus' rich blood. Gadsby's Col.

312 (577) 11s.

1 THE hope set before us is Jesus the Lord;
The gospel reveals it; we bless the record:
With strong consolation, for those, we are told, [hold.
Who once on his merits have fled to lay

2 If Satan assails thee, and guilt should intrude, [good;
None but the Redeemer can e'er do thee
Lay hold on his blood, 'tis sufficient for thee, [set thee free.
Thy conscience to cleanse, and from guilt

3 To this we are pressing, with ardent desire, [and fire;
Through floods of affliction, temptation,
Tho' often dejected, and filled with dismay,
Because of the trials attending the way.

4 Then lift him, ye heralds that speak in his name;
Proclaim him to-day and for ever the same;
The life of his people, which none can destroy; [of joy.
Their hope and their portion, and fulness

ENCOURAGEMENT.

HALL. S. M.

313 (760)

1 CHEER up, ye trembling souls
   On Jesus' aid rely:
   He sees us when we see not him
   And always hears our cry.

2 Without cessation pray;
   Your prayers will not prove vain:
   Our Joseph turns aside to weep,
   But cannot long refrain.

3 Sudden he stands confessed;
   We look, and all is light;
   The foe, confounded, swift as thought,
   Is vanquished from our sight.

4 Christ's presence clears the soul
   And smooths the rugged way;
   He often makes the crooked straight,
   And turns the night to day.

5 We then move cheerful on;
   The ground feels firm and good;
   And, lest we should mistake the way,
   He lines it out with blood.

6 Again we cannot see
   His helping hand; but feel:
   And, though we neither feel nor see,
   His hand sustains us still.

7 He gently leads us on;
   Protects from fatal harms;
   And, when we faint, and cannot walk,
   He bears us in his arms.

8 He guides and moves our steps,
   For, though we seem to move,
   His Spirit all the motion gives,
   By springs of fear and love.
   Hart.

314 (752) S. M.

1 YOUR harps, ye trembling saints,
   Down from the willows take;
   Loud to the praise of Christ, our Lord,
   Bid every string awake.

2 Though in a foreign land,
   We are not far from home;
   And nearer to our house above
   We every moment come.

3 His grace shall to the end
   Stronger and brighter shine;
   Nor present things, nor things to come,
   Shall quench the spark divine.

4 The time of love will come,
   When we shall clearly see,
   Not only that he shed his blood,
   But each shall say, "For me."

5 Tarry his leisure, then;
   Wait the appointed hour;
   Wait till the Bridegroom of your souls
   Reveals his love with power.

6 Blest is the man, O God!
   That stays himself on thee!
   Who waits for thy salvation, Lord!
   Shall thy salvation see.
   Watts.

ENCOURAGEMENT.

KING OF PEACE. 7s.   CHAPIN. Arr. by F. PRICE.

315 (764) John 21: 16.

1 HARK, my soul! it is the Lord;
'Tis the Saviour, hear his word;
Jesus speaks, and speaks to thee,
"Say, poor sinner, lovest thou me?

2 "I delivered thee when bound,
And, when wounded, healed thy wound;
Sought thee wandering, set thee right,
Turned thy darkness into light.

3 "Can a woman's tender care
Cease toward the child she bare?
Yes, she may forgetful be,
Yet will I remember thee.

4 "Mine is an unchanging love,
Higher than the heights above;
Deeper than the depths beneath;
Free and faithful, strong as death.

5 "Thou shalt see my glory soon,
When the work of grace is done;
Partner of my throne shalt be!
Say, poor sinner, lovest thou me?"

6 Lord, it is my chief complaint,
That my love is weak and faint;
Yet I love thee and adore:
O, for grace to love thee more!
Cowper.

316 (777) 7s. Cant. 2: 16.

1 CHRIST is mine, and I am his;
Center, source, and sum of bliss:
Earth and hell in vain combine
Me and Jesus to disjoin.

2 Thou my fortress art and tower;
Having thee I want no more:
Strong in thy full strength I stand;
None can pluck me from thy hand.

3 Nothing in myself I am;
All I have is in the Lamb:
While his face on me doth shine,
All in heaven and earth is mine.

4 In my Jesus' arms secure,
To the end I shall endure;
Join with me, ye angels, join!
Praise his name in hymns divine.
Hammond.

317 (781) 7s. Psalm 3: 1-3.

1 LORD, how many are my foes!
Many they that me oppose!
Thou my strong Protector be;
All my safety is in thee.

2 Satan and my wicked heart,
Often use their treacherous art!
Fain would make my soul to flee;
But my safety is in thee.

3 Thou hast said, and thou art true,
"As I live, ye shall live, too:"
Thou my Rock wilt ever be;
All my safety is in thee.

4 I'm a pilgrim here below;
Guide me all the desert through:
Let me, as I journey, see
All my safety is in thee.
Adams.

128 PRESERVATION OF THE SAINTS TO GLORY.

DOWNS. C. M. — Dr. LOWELL MASON 1792-1872.

1. For us the dear Re-deem-er died; Why are we then a-shamed?
We stand for ev - er jus - ti - fied, And can - not be con-demn'd.

318 (779) Psa. 89: 28-34.

2 Though we believe not, he is true;
The work is in his hand;
His gracious purpose he will do,
And all his word shall stand.

3 If once the love of Christ we feel
Upon our hearts impressed,
The mark of that celestial seal
Can never be erased!

4 The Lord will scourge us if we stray,
And wound us with distress:
But he will never take away
His covenant of peace.

5 The peace which Jesus' blood secures,
And fixes in our hearts,
To all eternity endures,
Nor finally departs.

Gadsby's Col.

319 (799) C. M.

1 'Twas when the seas, with horrid roar,
A little barque assailed,
And pallid fear, with awful power,
O'er each on board prevailed,

2 Save one, the captain's darling child,
Who fearless viewed the storm,
And playful, with composure smiled
At danger's threatening form.

3 "Why sporting thus," a seaman cries,
"While sorrows overwhelm?"
"Why yield to grief?" the boy replies,
"My father's at the helm!"

4 Poor doubting soul, from hence be
How groundless is thy fear; [taught
Think what the power of Christ hath
And he is ever near. [wrought,

5 Safe in his hand, whom seas obey,
When swelling surges rise;
He turns the darkest night to day,
And brightens lowering skies.

6 Then, upward look, howe'er distrest,
Jesus will guide thee home,
To that eternal port of rest
Where storms shall never come.

Madan.

320 (801) C. M.

1 It shall be well, let Zion know,
With those who love the Lord;
His saints have always found it so
When resting on his word.

2 Peace, then, ye chastened sons of God,
Why let your sorrows swell?
Wisdom directs our Father's rod;
His word says, it is well.

3 Though you may trials sharp endure,
From sin, or death, or hell;
Your heavenly Father's love is sure,
And, therefore, it is well.

4 Soon will your sorrows all be o'er,
And you shall sweetly tell,
On heaven's calm and pleasant shore,
That all at last is well.

PRESERVATION OF THE SAINTS TO GLORY.

SOUTHAMPTON. 8s.

1. A Sov-'reign Pro-tect-or I have, Un-seen, yet for-ev-er at hand:

Un-change-a-bly faith-ful to save; Al-might-y to rule and com-mand!

321 (780) Psalm 3: 3–6.

1 A SOVEREIGN Protector I have,
   Unseen, yet for ever at hand:
Unchangeably faithful to save;
   Almighty to rule and command!

2 He smiles, and my comforts abound;
   His grace as the dew shall descend;
And walls of salvation surround
   The souls he delights to defend!

3 Kind author and ground of my hope,
   Thee, thee for my God I avow;
My glad Ebenezer set up,
   And own thou hast helped me till now.

4 I muse on the years that are past,
   Wherein my defense thou hast proved:
Nor wilt thou relinquish at last
   A sinner so signally loved!
                              Toplady.

322 (791) 8s. D.

1 LET those who inhabit the Rock,
   And out of his fulness receive,
Proclaim him the tower of the flock,—
   Still precious to them that believe:
Our prophet, our priest and our king,
   'Tis life everlasting to know;

His blood and his merits we sing,
   For Christ is the end of the law.

2 'Tis here, when with sorrows oppressed,
   Believers in Jesus should flee;
For those that are weary, here's rest,—
   For sin-burdened sinners like me:
If justice pursues thee for blood,
   His righteousness stands without flaw;
And he that redeemed thee to God,
   Is Jesus, the end of the law.

3 The types and the shadows are fled,
   With all that prediction foretold;
Since Jesus on Calvary bled,
   His sheep shall return to the fold:
Shall build upon him as a Rock,
   Nor fear, when the tempests shall blow;
And nothing the building shall shock,
   For Christ is the end of the law.

4 How sweet and delightful the strain,
   Salvation by grace to repeat;
Shall sinners redeemed e'er refrain,
   Who stand thus in Jesus complete?
From him as the Fountain of life,
   His saints their existence shall draw,
And live, though encompassed with strife;
   For Christ is the end of the law.
                              Kent.

PRESERVATION OF THE SAINTS TO GLORY.

RAPTURE. L. M. D.

1. Stand up, my soul, shake off thy fears, And gird the gospel armor on; March to the gates of endless joy, Where thy great Captain Saviour's gone.

D.S.—Thy Jesus nailed them to the cross, And sung the triumph when he rose.

2. Hell and thy sins resist thy course, But hell and sin are vanquish'd foes;

By per. O. Ditson & Co.

323 (795)

1 STAND up, my soul, shake off thy fears,
And gird the gospel armor on;
March to the gates of endless joy, [gone.
Where thy great Captain-Saviour's

2 Hell and thy sins resist thy course,
But hell and sin are vanquished foes;
Thy Jesus nailed them to the cross,
And sung the triumph when he rose.

3 What tho' the prince of darkness rage,
And waste the fury of his spite?
Eternal chains confine him down
To fiery deeps and endless night.

4 What though thine inward lusts rebel?
'Tis but a struggling gasp for life;
The weapons of victorious grace
Shall slay thy sins and end thy strife.

5 Then let my soul march boldly on,
Press forward to the heavenly gate;
There peace and joy eternal reign, [wait.
And glittering robes for conquerors

6 There shall I wear a starry crown,
And triumph in almighty grace;
While all the armies in the skies
Join in my glorious Leader's praise.

Watts.

324 (785) L. M. D.

1 WITH Christ in God your life is hid:
These words at once thy fears forbid;
For he must God himself dethrone,
Who takes that life, with Jesus one.

2 Though but a spark, 'tis heavenly fire,
May dwindle oft, but ne'er expire,
Till brighter than the solar rays,
It shines through everlasting days.

3 Earth, hell, and sin, that hateful name,
Together strive to quench the same;
Yet still it burns, his power to show,
In spite of all that hell can do.

4 God is its shield; he guards it well,
When tempests rise, and billows swell:
'Tis hid by God, where none but he
By his omniscient eye can see.

5 'Tis that blest hope that never dies;
Beyond the reach of hell it lies;
'Twill flourish and immortal be,
When death is lost in victory.

6 Shall this, O Christian, make thee say,
I'll serve my lust, and from thee stray?
Nay rather thus, my God, to thee
Let every power devoted be.

325 (804) Matt. 11: 28.

2 Burdened with a load of sin;
   Harassed with tormenting doubt;
  Hourly conflicts from within;
   Hourly crosses from without:
  All my little strength is gone;
   Sink I must without supply;
  Sure upon the earth there's none
   Can more weary be than I!

3 In the ark the weary dove
   Found a welcome resting-place;
  Thus my spirit longs to prove
   Rest in Christ the ark of grace.
  Tempest-tossed I long have been,
   And the flood increases fast;
  Open, Lord, and take me in,
   Till the storm be overpast.   *Newton.*

326 (638)

2 Quiet as a weaned child,
   Weaned from the mother's breast;
  By no subtilty beguiled,
   On thy faithful word I rest.

Saints! rejoicing evermore,
   In the Lord Jehovah trust;
  Him in all his ways adore,
   Wise, and wonderful, and just.
                           Montgomery.

REST.

ZEPHYR. L. M.
W. B. BRADBURY. 1816—1868.

327 (806) Col. 1: 5, 6; Matt. 6: 21.

1 IN heaven my choicest treasure lies,
My hopes are placed above the skies;
'Tis Christ, the bright and morning star,
Draws my affections from afar.

2 O that my anxious mind were free
From this vile tenement of clay,
That I might view th' immortal word,
And live and reign with Christ my Lord.

3 Then should I see, and feel, and know,
What 'tis to rest from sin and woe;
And all my soul be tuned to sing
The praises due to Christ my King.

4 Hail, blessed time! Lord, bid me come,
And enter my celestial home,
And drown the sorrows of my breast,
In seas of unmolested rest. Gadsby's Col.

WARE. L. M.
GEO. KINGSLEY.

328 (808)

2 There, they, from sin and sorrow free,
Shall spend a long eternity;
No more to strive with flesh and blood,
But cease from sin, and rest in God.

3 Eternal love this rest ordained,
To soothe the breast with sorrows pained,
And fold his lambs from harm secure,
Long as eternal years endure.

4 Oh! sacred rest, for thee we groan,
And bid the wheels of time roll on,
To bring that hour, when we shall rise
To join the chorus of the skies.

5 Immortal love shall then repay
The transient sorrows of the way;
And Jesus' name swell every song,
A whole eternity along.

REST. 133

WOODWORTH. L. M. W. B. BRADBURY, 1816-1868.

1. "Come hith-er, all ye wea-ry souls, Ye heav-y la-den sin-ners, come, I'll give you rest from all your toils, And raise you to my heav'nly home.

329 (814) Matt. 11: 28-30.

1 "Come hither, all ye weary souls,
Ye heavy laden sinners, come,
I'll give you rest from all your toils,
And raise you to my heavenly home.

2 "They shall find rest that learn of me;
I'm of a meek and lowly mind;
But passion rages like the sea,
And pride is restless as the wind.

3 " Blest is the man whose shoulders take
My yoke, and bear it with delight;
My yoke is easy to his neck,
My grace shall make the burden light."

4 Jesus, we come at thy command,
With faith and hope and humble zeal,
Resign our spirits to thy hand,
To mould and guide us at thy will.
Watts.

330 (813) L. M.

1 Great Rock, for weary travelers made,
When storms of sin infest the soul;
Here let me rest my weary head   [roll.
When lightnings blaze, and thunders

2 Within the clifts of his dear side,
There all his saints in safety dwell;
And what from Jesus shall divide?
Not all the rage of earth or hell.

3 O sacred covert, from the beams
That on the weary traveler beat,
How welcome are thy shade and streams,
How blest, how sacred, and how sweet!

4 And when that awful storm takes place,
That hurls destruction far and near,
My soul shall refuge in thy grace,
And take her glorious shelter there.

5 To shake this rock thy saints are in,
Tempest or storm shall ne'er prevail;
'Twill stand the blast of hell and sin,
An anchor sure within the veil.
Kent.

331 (815) L. M. Psa. 92.

1 Sweet is the work, my God, my King,
To praise thy name, give thanks and sing;
To show thy love by morning light,
And talk of all thy truth at night.

2 Sweet is the day of sacred rest;
No mortal cares shall seize my breast;
O may my heart in tune be found,
Like David's harp of solemn sound:

3 My heart shall triumph in my Lord,
And bless his works, and bless his word;
Thy works of grace, how bright they shine!
How deep thy counsels! how divine!

4 Sin (my worst enemy before)
Shall vex my eyes and ears no more;
My inward foes shall all be slain,
Nor Satan break my peace again.

5 Then shall I see, and hear, and know
All I desired or wished below;
And every power find sweet employ
In that eternal world of joy.
Watts.

REST.

EVAN. C. M.
Arr. by W. H. HAVERGAL.

1. Where must a weary sinner go, But to the sinner's friend? He only can relieve my wo, And bid my sorrows end.

332 (809) C. M. Ps. 62: 1.

1 WHERE must a weary sinner go,
  But to the sinner's friend?
He only can relieve my wo,
  And bid my sorrows end.

2 Thou art, O Lord, my resting-place;
  The promised land I see,
And long to live upon thy grace,
  And lose myself in thee.

3 A glimpse of thee, and thy sweet store,
  Thou dost to me impart;
But kindly shew me more and more,
  Till thou dost fill my heart.

4 The wilderness I cannot bear,
  So far from thee to stand;
Nor yet from Pisgah's top to stare,
  Upon the promised land.

5 I want to eat and drink my fill
  Of Canaan's milk and wine;
Let Moses die upon the hill,
  And I be wholly thine.

6 'Tis self, that legal thing and base,
  Which keeps me from my rest;
Me from myself let Christ release,
  And soon I shall be blest.

I'LL LAY MY ARMOR DOWN. C. M.
JOSEPH B. MOON, 1883
CHORUS.

1. Where must a weary sinner go, But to the sinner's friend? He only can relieve my wo, And bid my sorrows end. Oh, let me mount and soar away, I'll lay my armor down; To that bright world of endless day, I'll lay my armor down.

REST. 135

O LAND OF REST. C. M.   Caldwell.

1. O land of rest, for thee I sigh; When will the moment come, When I shall lay my armor by, And dwell with Christ at home? And dwell with Christ at home?...... And dwell with Christ at home? When I shall lay my armor by, And dwell with Christ at home?

This vale of sin and gloom,
I long to leave th' unhallowed ground,
And dwell with Christ at home.
MRS. E. MILLS.

333 (807)

1 O LAND of rest, for thee I sigh;
When will the moment come,
When I shall lay my armor by,
And dwell with Christ at home?
No tranquil joys on earth I know,
No peaceful sheltering dome;
This world's a wilderness of wo;
This world is not my home.

2 To Jesus Christ I sought for rest;
He bade me cease to roam,
And fly for succor to his breast,
And he'd conduct me home.
I should at once have quit the field,
Where foes and fury roam;
But, ah! my passport was not sealed;
I could not yet go home.

3 When by affliction sharply tried,
I view the gaping tomb,
Although I dread death's chilling tide,
Yet still I sigh for home.
Weary of wandering round and round,

NOTE.—To sing double omit slur in third strain.

334 (816)   C. M.

1 FROM east to west let others roam,
And search in vain for bliss;
My soul is satisfied at home;
The Lord my portion is.
Jesus, who on his glorious throne
Rules heaven, and earth, and sea,
Is pleased to claim me for his own,
And give himself to me.

2 His person fixes all my love,
His blood removes my fear;
And while he fills his throne above,
His arm preserves me here.
His word of promise is my food,
The Spirit is my guide;
Thus daily is my strength renewed,
And all my wants supplied.

3 For him I count as gain each loss,
Disgrace for him renown;
Well may I glory in his cross,
While he prepares my crown!
Let worldlings then indulge their boast,
How much they gain or spend;
Their joys must soon give up the ghost,
But mine shall know no end.   Newton.

FAREWELL.

PARTING HAND. L. M. D.

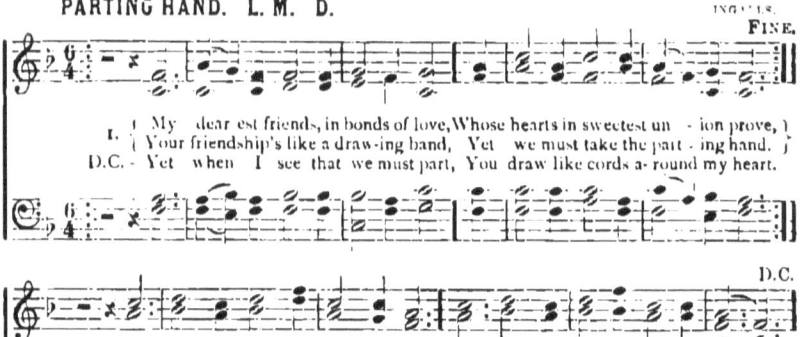

1. My dearest friends, in bonds of love, Whose hearts in sweetest union prove, Your friendship's like a drawing band, Yet we must take the parting hand.
D.C. Yet when I see that we must part, You draw like cords around my heart.

2. Your comp'ny's sweet, your union dear, Your words delightful to mine ear;

335 (820)

1 My dearest friends, in bonds of love,
Whose hearts in sweetest union prove,
Your friendship's like a drawing band,
Yet we must take the parting hand.

2 Your company's sweet, your union dear,
Your words delightful to mine ear;
Yet when I see that we must part,
You draw like cords around my heart.

3 How sweet the hours have passed away
Since we have met to sing and pray!
How loath we are to leave the place
Where Jesus shows his smiling face!

4 O could I stay with friends so kind,
How would it cheer my drooping mind!
But duty makes me understand
That we must take the parting hand.

5 And since it is God's holy will
We must be parted for awhile,
In sweet submission, all as one,
We'll say, our Father's will be done.

6 How oft I've seen your flowing tears,
And heard you tell your hopes and fears!
Your hearts with love were seen to flame,
Which makes me hope we'll meet again.

7 I hope you'll all remember me
If you on earth no more I see;
An interest in your prayers I crave,
That we may meet beyond the grave.

8 O glorious day! O blessed hope!
My soul leaps forward at the thought,
When in that happy, happy land,
We'll no more take the parting hand.
John Blair.

336 (825) L. M.

1 O HAPPY day, when saints shall meet,
To part no more! the thought is sweet!
No more to feel the rending smart,
Oft felt below when Christians part.

2 O happy place! I still must say,
Where all but love is done away;
All cause of parting there is past,
Their social feast will ever last.

3 On earth when friends together meet,
And find the passing moments sweet,
Time's rapid motions soon compel
With grief to say, dear friends, farewell.

4 The happy season soon will come,
When saints shall meet in heaven, their
Eternally with Christ to dwell, [home;
Nor ever hear the sound, farewell.
Barnard.

337 L. M.

1 COME, Christian brethren, ere we part,
Join every voice and every heart;
One solemn hymn to God we raise,
One final song of grateful praise.

2 Christians, we here may meet no more,
But there is yet a happier shore;
And there, released from toil and pain,
Dear brethren, we shall meet again.
Kirk White.

FAREWELL. 137

INDIAN'S FAREWELL. 7s. 6l. Arr. by WM. WALKER and WM. HAUSEL, M. D.

338 (824)

1 WHEN shall we all meet again?
When shall we all meet again?
Oft shall glowing hope expire,
Oft shall wearied love retire,
Oft shall death and sorrow reign,
Ere we all shall meet again.

2 Though in distant lands we sigh,
Parched beneath a burning sky,
Though the deep between us rolls,
Friendship shall unite our souls;
And in fancy's wide domain,
Oft shall we all meet again.

3 When the dreams of life are fled,
When its wasted lamps are dead,
When in cold oblivion's shade,
Beauty, fame, and wealth are laid,
Where immortal spirits reign,
There may we all meet again!

4 There shall we all be at rest,
Leaning on our Saviour's breast,
There shall we for ever be
Gazing on the Deity;
There shall we the Lamb adore,
Then shall we all part no more.

PRAYER. 7s. ASAHEL ABBOT.

339 (826)

2 When they move at duty's call,
He is with them by the way:
He is ever with them all,
Those who go, and those who stay.

3 For a season called to part,
Let us then ourselves commend
To the gracious eye and heart
Of our ever-present Friend.

4 Jesus, hear our humble prayer!
Tender Shepherd of thy sheep!

Let thy mercy and thy care
All our souls in safety keep.

5 In thy strength may we be strong,
Sweeten every cross and pain;
Give us, if we live, ere long
Here to meet in peace again.

6 Then, if thou thy help afford,
Ebenezers shall be reared,
And our souls shall praise the Lord,
Who our poor petitions heard. Newton

THE CHURCH.

AUTUMN. 8s. & 7s. D. — Spanish Melody from MARECHO.

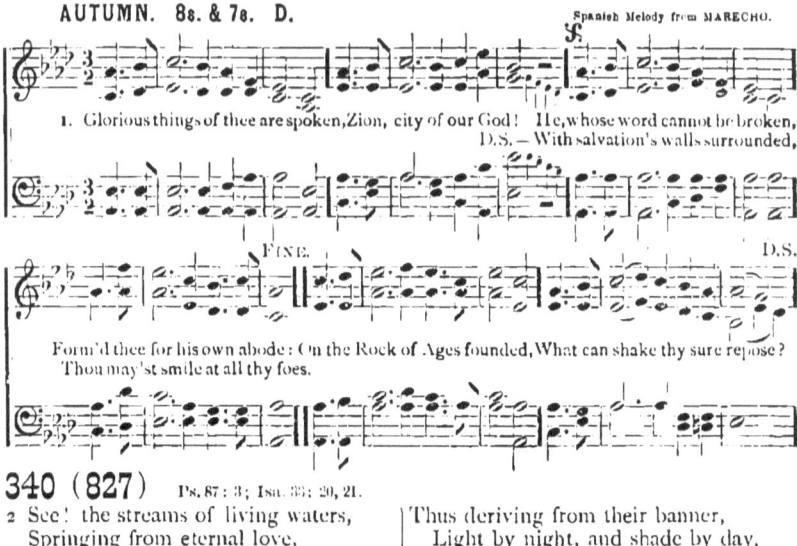

1. Glorious things of thee are spoken, Zion, city of our God! He, whose word cannot be broken,
D.S.—With salvation's walls surrounded,
Form'd thee for his own abode: On the Rock of Ages founded, What can shake thy sure repose?
Thou may'st smile at all thy foes.

340 (827) Ps. 87:3; Isa. 33:20, 21.

2 See! the streams of living waters,
   Springing from eternal love,
Well supply thy sons and daughters,
   And all fear of want remove.
Who can faint, while such a river
   Ever flows their thirst t' assuage?
Grace, which, like the Lord, the giver,
   Never fails from age to age.

3 Round each habitation hovering,
   See the cloud and fire appear,
For a glory and a covering,
   Showing that the Lord is near.

Thus deriving from their banner,
   Light by night, and shade by day,
Safe they feed upon the manna
   Which he gives them by the way.
4 Blessed inhabitants of Zion,
   Washed in the Redeemer's blood!
Jesus, whom their souls rely on,
   Makes them kings and priests to God:
'Tis his love his people raises
   Over self to reign as kings;
And as priests, his solemn praises
   Each for a thank-offering brings.
                                    Newton.

RIPLEY. 8s. & 7s. D. — From a Gregorian Chant.

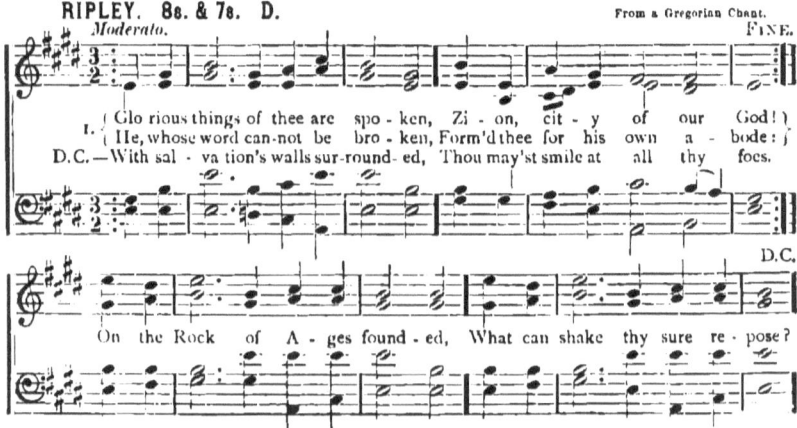

1. { Glorious things of thee are spoken, Zi-on, cit-y of our God! }
   { He, whose word can-not be bro-ken, Form'd thee for his own a-bode: }
D.C.—With sal-va-tion's walls sur-round-ed, Thou may'st smile at all thy foes.

On the Rock of A-ges found-ed, What can shake thy sure re-pose?

THE CHURCH. 139

DISCIPLE. 8s. & 7s. D.   MOZART.

1. Hear what God the Lord hath spoken,
O my people, faint and few;
Comfortless, afflicted, broken,
Fair abodes I build for you;
Scenes of heart-felt tribulation
Shall no more perplex your ways;
Walls Salvation, And your gates shall all be praise.

D.S.—You shall name your

Visit now thy needy Zion;
See thy people mourn and weep;
Day and night thy lambs are crying;
Come, good Shepherd, feed thy sheep.

2 Lord, in us there is no merit,
We've been sinners from our youth;
Guide us by thy Holy Spirit
Into all revealed truth;
On thy word of grace we'll venture,
Till in death's cold arms we sleep,
Love's our banner, Christ's our Leader;
Come, good Shepherd, feed thy sheep.

3 Saviour, still with courage arm us
That we may not yield to fear,
Nothing Lord, we know can harm us
While thy gracious aid is near.
Glory, glory be to Jesus,
At his name our hearts do leap;
He both comforts us and heals us:
Come, good Shepherd, feed thy sheep.

4 Christ alone our souls shall rest on;
Taught by him we own his name;
Sweetest of all names is Jesus;
How it doth our souls inflame!
Saints and angels chant the story,
Jesus all thy flock will keep;
He hath led the way to glory,
And will thither bring his sheep.
Granade.

341 (865) Isa. 60: 18-20.
2 There, like streams that feed the garden,
Pleasures without end shall flow;
For the Lord, your faith regarding,
All his bounty shall bestow:
Still in undisturbed possession,
Peace and righteousness shall reign;
Never shall you feel oppression,
Hear the voice of war again.

3 Ye no more your suns descending,
Waning moons no more shall see;
But, your griefs for ever ending,
Find eternal noon in me;
God shall rise, and shining o'er you,
Change to day the gloom of night;
He the Lord shall be your glory,
God your everlasting light.
Cowper.

342 (864) 8s. & 7s. D.
1 LET thy kingdom, blessed Saviour,
Come and bid our jarring cease;
Come, O come, and reign forever,
God of Love and Prince of Peace;

THE CHURCH.

MEAR. C. M. Welsh Air. A. WILLIAMS. 1762.

1. How did my heart rejoice to hear My friends devoutly say, In Zion let us all appear, And keep the solemn day!

343 (835)

1 How did my heart rejoice to hear
My friends devoutly say,
In Zion let us all appear,
And keep the solemn day!

2 I love her gates, I love the road;
The church, adorned with grace,
Stands like a palace built for God
To show his milder face

3 Up to her courts, with joys unknown,
The holy tribes repair:
The Son of David holds his throne,
And sits in judgment there.

4 He hears our praises and complaints,
And while his awful voice
Divides the sinners from the saints,
We tremble and rejoice.

5 Peace be within this sacred place,
And joy a constant guest!
With holy gifts and heavenly grace
Be her attendants blest!

6 My soul shall pray for Zion still,
While life or breath remains;
There my best friends, my kindred dwell,
There God my Saviour reigns.
Watts.

344 (839) C. M.

1 The Lord of glory is my light,
And my salvation, too;
God is my strength, nor will I fear
What all my foes can do.

2 One privilege my heart desires;
O grant me an abode
Among the churches of thy saints,
The temples of my God!

3 There shall I offer my requests,
And see thy beauty still,
Shall hear the messages of love,
And there inquire thy will.

4 When troubles rise, and storms appear,
There may his children hide;
God has a strong pavilion where
He makes my soul abide.
Watts.

345 (840) C. M.

1 What shall I render to my God
For all his kindness shown?
My feet shall visit thine abode,
My songs address thy throne.

2 Among the saints that fill thy house,
My offerings shall be paid;
There shall my zeal perform the vows
My soul in anguish made.

3 How much is mercy thy delight,
Thou ever-blessed God!
How dear thy servants in thy sight!
How precious is their blood!

4 How happy all thy servants are!
How great thy grace to me!
My life which thou hast made thy care,
Lord, I devote to thee.
Watts.

THE CHURCH. 141

LIVERPOOL. C. M. WM. BRADSHAW. 1824. Arr. by WM. HAUSER. M. D.

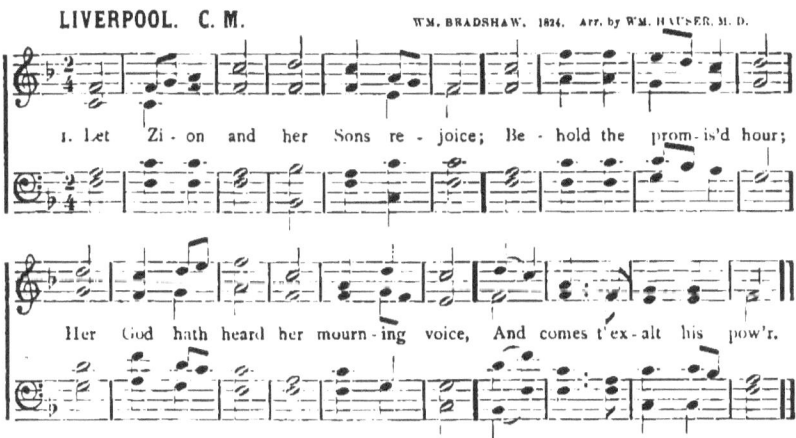

1. Let Zi-on and her Sons re-joice; Be-hold the prom-is'd hour;
Her God hath heard her mourn-ing voice, And comes t'ex-alt his pow'r.

346 (855)

1 Let Zion and her Sons rejoice;
   Behold the promised hour;
Her God hath heard her mourning voice,
   And comes t' exalt his power.

2 Her dust and ruins that remain
   Are precious in our eyes;
Those ruins shall be built again,
   And all that dust shall rise.

3 The Lord will raise Jerusalem,
   And stand in glory there;
Nations shall bow before his name,
   And kings attend with fear.

4 He sits a sovereign on his throne,
   With pity in his eyes;
He hears the dying prisoners groan,
   And sees their grief arise.

5 He frees the souls condemned to death,
   And when his saints complain,
It shan't be said that praying breath
   Was ever spent in vain.

6 This shall be known when we are dead,
   And left on long record;
That ages yet unborn may read,
   And trust, and praise the Lord.
                                    Watts.

347 (862) C. M.

1 A GARDEN fenced from common earth,
   By special sovereign grace,
Enriched by plants of heavenly birth,
   The Church of Jesus is.

2 His gospel is the open sky,
   His love the shining sun;
Rivers of peace, which never dry,
   Through all his garden run.

3 His spirit is the heavenly wind,
   That o'er his garden blows;
And opening each renewed mind,
   The Saviour's image shows.

4 Faith, like an ivy, to the rock
   (That stands forever,) cleaves;
And through the tempest's loudest shock,
   Eternal calm perceives.

5 Assurance, like a cedar, rears
   Its stately branches high,
Beyond the reach of doubts and fears,
   And blossoms in the sky.
                            Parkinson's Col.

348 (834) C. M.

1 My God, what endless pleasures dwell
   Above at thy right hand!
Thy courts below, how amiable,
   Where all thy graces stand!

2 The swallow near thy temple flies,
   And chirps a cheerful note;
The lark mounts upward to the skies,
   And tunes her warbling throat.

3 And we, when in thy presence, Lord,
   Do shout with joyful tongues,
Or sitting round our Father's board,
   We crown the feast with songs. Watts.

THE CHURCH.

FOREST. L. M. — CHAPIN.

1. When saint to saint, in days of old, Their sorrows, sins, and suff'rings told, Jesus, the Friend of sinners dear, His saints to bless, was present there.

349 (831)

1 When saint to saint, in days of old,
Their sorrows, sins, and sufferings told,
Jesus, the Friend of sinners dear,
His saints to bless, was present there.

2 As members of his mystic frame,
Together met, to bless his name,
While humbly at his throne we bow,
As God with us, he's present now.

3 Oh! blest devotion, thus to meet,
And spread our woes at his dear feet;
Call him our own in ties of blood,
And hold sweet fellowship with God.

350 (832) L. M. Ps. 48.

1 Zion's a city God hath blessed
With peace and everlasting rest;
A glorious city, strong and fair;
And Jesus dwells for ever there.

2 Her ancient walls appear to be
The workmanship of Deity;
Founded in grace, they still appear
Without a flaw or chasm there.

3 Oft has this city's strength been tried,
By mighty foes on every side;
But all in vain it yet has been,
She baffles Satan, hell, and sin.

4 Count ye her towers, how high they rise,
Her golden spires, they pierce the skies!
Her golden streets are fair to view;
Her palaces and bulwarks, too.

5 Then round her walk, her turrets tell;
Mark all her brazen bulwarks well;
Spread far and wide her deathless fame,
Her pearly gates and walls of flame.

6 Her founder's love has ever proved
Like Salem's mount, which ne'er was moved;
'Tis fixed on this eternal base,
The grace of God, and gift by grace.
<small>Kent.</small>

351 (836) L. M. Ps. 84.

1 How pleasant, how divinely fair,
O Lord of Hosts, thy dwellings are!
With long desire my spirit faints
To meet th' assemblies of thy saints.

2 My flesh would rest in thine abode,
My panting heart cries out for God;
My God! my King! why should I be
So far from all my joys and thee!

3 The sparrow chooses where to rest,
And for her young provides her nest;
But will my God to sparrows grant
That pleasure which his children want?

4 Blest are the souls that find a place
Within the temple of thy grace;
There they behold thy gentler rays,
And seek thy face, and learn thy praise.

5 Cheerful they walk with growing strength,
Till all shall meet in heaven at length;
Till all before thy face appear,
And join in nobler worship there. <small>Watts</small>

THE CHURCH.

DESIRE. L. M.

1 God is the ref-uge of his saints, When storms of sharp dis-tress in-vade; Ere we can of-fer our complaints, Be-hold him pres-ent with his aid.

352 (850) Ps. 46.

1 God is the refuge of his saints,
When storms of sharp distress invade;
Ere we can offer our complaints,
Behold him present with his aid.

2 Let mountains from their seats be hurled
Down to the deep, and buried there;
Convulsions shake the solid world,
Our faith shall never yield to fear.

3 Loud, may the troubled ocean roar,
In sacred peace our souls abide,
While every nation, every shore,
Trembles, and dreads the swelling tide.

4 There is a stream whose gentle flow
Supplies the city of our God;
Life, love and joy, still gliding through,
And watering our divine abode.

5 That sacred stream, thine holy word,
That all our raging fear controls;
Sweet peace thy promises afford,
And give new strength to fainting souls.

6 Sion enjoys her monarch's love,
Secure against a threatening hour;
Nor can her firm foundations move,
Built on his truth and armed with power.
Watts.

353 (857) L. M. Ps. 84.

1 How lovely, how divinely sweet,
O Lord, thy sacred courts appear!
Fain would my longing passions meet
The glories of thy presence there.

2 One day within thy sacred gate,
Affords more real joy to me,
Than thousands in the tents of state;
The meanest place is bliss with thee.
Mrs. Steele.

354 (861) L. M.

1 Kindred in Christ, for his dear sake,
A hearty welcome here receive;
May we together now partake
The joys which only he can give.

2 To you and us by grace 'tis given
To know the Saviour's precious name;
And shortly we shall meet in heaven,
Our hope, our way, our end the same.

3 May he, by whose kind care we meet,
Send his good Spirit from above;
Make our communications sweet,
And cause our hearts to burn with love.

4 Forgotten be each worldly theme,
When Christians see each other thus:
We only wish to speak of him,
Who lived, and died, and reigns for us.

5 We'll talk of all he did and said,
And suffered for us here below;
The path he marked for us to tread,
And what he's doing for us now.

6 Thus, as the moments pass away,
We'll love, and wonder, and adore;
And hasten on the glorious day,
When we shall meet to part no more.
Newton.

144 THE CHURCH.

EVENING SHADE. S. M.
STEPHEN JENKS. (1772-1856) 1804.

1. The church of God is fair; Her fame of old was known:
And Christ will dwell for ev-er there,
And Christ will dwell for ev-er there,
And Christ will dwell for ev-er there,
And Christ will dwell for ev-er there, And claim her for his own.

355 (833) Song 1: 15.

2 Here his affections rest,
   Nor shall from hence remove;
   'Tis his delight to make her blest,
   And live upon his love.

3 Her worthless name is found,
   Deep 'graven on his hand,
   In characters of grace profound,
   That shall for ever stand.

4 Though oft with tempest tost,
   Ne'er from her anchor drove;
   This chosen vessel can't be lost,
   Secured by covenant love.

5 Her bulwarks and her walls
   Are all the promises,
   Founded in potent *wills* and *shalls*
   In oaths and firm decrees.

356 (846) S. M. Ps. 48.

1 FAR as thy name is known
   The world declares thy praise;
   Thy saints, O Lord, before thy throne
   Their songs of honor raise.

2 With joy let Judah stand
   On Zion's chosen hill,
   Proclaim the wonders of thy hand,
   And counsels of thy will.

3 Let strangers walk around
   The city where we dwell,
   Compass and view thine holy ground,
   And mark the building well.

4 The orders of thy house,
   The worship of thy court,
   The cheerful songs, the solemn vows;
   And make a fair report.

5 How decent and how wise!
   How glorious to behold!
   Beyond the pomp that charms the eyes,
   And rites adorned with gold.

6 The God we worship now
   Will guide us till we die,
   Will be our God while here below,
   And ours above the sky.   Watts.

THE CHURCH.

STATE STREET. S. M. J. C. WOODMAN.

1. How charming is the place Where my Redeemer God Unveils the beauties of his face, And sheds his love abroad?

357 (856)
1 How charming is the place
  Where my Redeemer God
Unveils the beauties of his face,
  And sheds his love abroad?

2 Not the fair palaces,
  To which the great resort,
Are once to be compared with this,
  Where Jesus holds his court.

3 Here, on the mercy seat,
  With radiant glory crowned,
Our joyful eyes behold him sit,
  And smile on all around.

4 To him their prayers and cries
  Each humble saint presents;
He listens to their broken sighs,
  And grants them all their wants.

5 To them his sovereign will
  He graciously imparts;
And in return accepts, with smiles,
  The tribute of their hearts.

6 Give me, O Lord, a place
  Within thy blest abode,
Among the children of thy grace,
  The servants of my God.
  Stennett.

358 (866) S. M. Ps. 122.
1 GLAD was my heart to hear
  My old companions say,
Come, in the house of God appear,
  For 'tis an holy day.

2 Our willing feet shall stand
  Within the temple door;
While young and old, in many a band,
  Shall throng the sacred floor.

3 Thither the tribes repair,
  Where all are wont to meet,
And, joyful in the house of prayer,
  Bend at the mercy seat.

4 Pray for Jerusalem,
  The city of our God;
The Lord from heaven be kind to them
  That love the dear abode.

5 Within these walls may peace
  And harmony be found;
Zion! in all thy palaces,
  Prosperity abound!

6 For friends and brethren dear,
  Our prayer shall never cease;
Oft as they meet for worship here,
  God send his people peace!
  Montgomery.

359 (794) S. M. Jude 24: 25.
1 To God, the only wise,
  Our Saviour and our King,
Let all the saints below the skies
  Their humble praises bring.

2 'Tis his almighty love,
  His counsel, and his care,
Preserves us safe from sin and death,
  And every hurtful snare.
  Watts.

PRAYER

HURSLEY. L. M. PETER RITTER, 1760-1846.

1. My soul, take courage from the Lord; Believe and plead his holy word: To him, alone, do thou complain; Nor shalt thou seek his face in vain.

360 (872) Isa. 45: 19.

1 My soul, take courage from the Lord;
Believe and plead his holy word:
To him, alone, do thou complain;
Nor shalt thou seek his face in vain.

2 Upon him call in humble prayer;
Thou still art his peculiar care:
He'll surely turn and smile again;
Nor shalt thou seek his face in vain.

3 However sinful, weak and poor,
Still wait and pray at mercy's door;
Faithful Jehovah must remain;
Nor shalt thou seek his face in vain.

4 Though sharp afflictions still abound,
And clouds and darkness thee surround,
Still pray, for God will all explain;
Nor shalt thou seek his face in vain.

5 In him, and him alone, confide;
Still at the throne of grace abide;
Eternal victory thou shalt gain;
Nor shalt thou seek his face in vain.
Medley.

361 (879) L. M. Ps. 6: 4.

1 REGARD, great God! my mournful prayer;
Make my poor trembling soul thy care;
For me in pity undertake,
And save me, for thy mercy's sake.

2 My soul's cast down within me, Lord,
And only thou canst help afford;
Let not thy heart with sorrow break,
But save me, for thy mercy's sake.

3 I've foes and fears of every shape,
Nor from them can my soul escape;
Upon me, Lord, some pity take,
And save me, for thy mercy's sake.

4 I've scarce a glimmering ray of light;
With me 'tis little else but night;
O, for my help do thou awake,
And save me, for thy mercy's sake.

5 To me, dear Saviour, turn once more;
To my poor soul thy joys restore;
Let me again thy smiles partake;
Lord, save me, for thy mercy's sake.
Medley.

362 (906) L. M.

1 SPRINKLED with reconciling blood,
I dare approach thy throne, O God;
Thy face no frowning aspect wears;
Thy hand no vengeful thunder bears!

2 Th' encircling rainbow, peaceful sign,
Doth with refulgent brightness shine;
And while my faith beholds it near,
I bid farewell to every fear.

3 Let me my grateful homage pay,
With courage sing, with fervor pray;
And, though myself a wretch undone,
Hope for acceptance through thy Son.

4 Thy Son, who on th' accursed tree
Expired to set the vilest free,
On this I build my only claim,
And all I ask is in his name.
Beddome.

PRAYER. 147

PLEYEL'S HYMN. 7s.   IGNACE PLEYEL, 1757-1831.

1. Lord, I can-not let thee go, Till a bless-ing thou be-stow! Do not turn a-way thy face; Mine's an ur-gent, press-ing case.

363 (871) Gen. 32: 26.

1 LORD, I cannot let thee go,
Till a blessing thou bestow!
Do not turn away thy face;
Mine's an urgent, pressing case.

2 Dost thou ask me who I am?
Ah, my Lord, thou knowest my name!
Yet the question gives a plea,
To support my suit with thee.

3 Thou didst once a wretch behold,
In rebellion blindly bold,
Scorn thy grace, thy power defy;
That poor rebel, Lord, was I.

4 Once a sinner near despair
Sought thy mercy seat by prayer;
Mercy heard and set him free;
Lord, that mercy came to me.

5 Many days have passed since then;
Many changes I have seen;
Yet have been upheld till now:
Who could hold me up but thou?

6 Thou hast helped in every need;
This emboldens me to plead:
After so much mercy past,
Canst thou let me sink at last?

7 No; I must maintain my hold;
'Tis thy goodness makes me bold;
I can no denial take,
When I plead for Jesus' sake.
                        Newton.

364 (874) 7s. 1 Kings 3: 5.

1 COME, my soul, thy suit prepare;
To thy God address thy prayer;
He himself has bid thee pray,
Therefore will not say thee nay.

2 Thou art coming to a King;
Large petitions with thee bring;
For his grace and power are such,
None can ever ask too much.

3 With my burden I begin:
Lord, remove this load of sin!
Let thy blood, for sinners spilt,
Set my conscience free from guilt.

4 Lord, I come to thee for rest;
Take possession of my breast;
There thy blood-bought right maintain,
And without a rival reign.

5 As the image in the glass
Answers the beholder's face,
Thus unto my heart appear,
Print thine own resemblance there

6 While I am a pilgrim here,
Let thy love my spirit cheer;
As my Guide, my Guard, my Friend,
Lead me to my journey's end.

7 Show me what I have to do,
Every hour my strength renew;
Let me live a life of faith,
Let me die thy people's death.
                        Newton.

148 PRAYER.

DETROIT. C. M. BRADSHAW.

Dear Lord! to us assembled here Reveal thy smiling face,
While we, by faith, with love and fear, Approach the Throne of Grace.

365 (877) Heb. 4: 16.

1 DEAR Lord! to us assembled here
Reveal thy smiling face,
While we, by faith, with love and fear,
Approach the Throne of Grace.

2 Thy house is called the house of prayer:
A solemn, sacred place;
O let us now thy presence share,
While at the Throne of Grace.

3 With holy boldness may we come,
Though of a sinful race,
Thankful to find there yet is room
Before the Throne of Grace.

4 Our earnest, fervent cry attend,
And all our faith increase,
While we our heavenly Friend address
Upon the Throne of Grace.

5 His tender pity and his love
Our every fear will chase;
And all our help, we then shall prove,
Come from the Throne of Grace.

6 Dear Lord, our many wants supply;
Attend to every case;
While humble in the dust we lie,
Low at the Throne of Grace.

7 We bless thee for thy word and laws;
We bless thee for thy peace;

And we do bless thee, Lord, because
There is a Throne of Grace.
Medley.

366 (882) C. M. Ps. 22: 5-7.

1 APPROACH, my soul, the mercy seat,
Where Jesus answers prayer;
There humbly fall before his feet,
For none can perish there.

2 Thy promise is my only plea;
With this I venture nigh:
Thou callest burdened souls to thee,
And such, O Lord, am I.

3 Bowed down beneath a load of sin;
By Satan sorely pressed;
By wars without and fears within,
I come to thee for rest.

4 Be thou my shield and hiding place,
That, sheltered near thy side,
I may my fierce accuser face,
And tell him, Jesus died.

5 O wondrous love! to bleed and die,
To bear the cross and shame,
That guilty sinners, such as I,
Might plead thy gracious name.

6 "Poor, tempest-tossed soul, be still;
My promised grace receive;
'Tis Jesus speaks! I must, I will,
I can, I do believe. Newton

PRAYER. 149

ST. MARTINS. C. M.   WM. TANSUR. 1755.

1. A crumb of mer-cy, Lord, I crave, Un-wor-thy to be fed
With dain-ties such as an-gels have, Or with the children's bread

367 (884)   Matt 15: 27.

2 Have pity on my needy soul;
Thy peace and pardon give;
Thy love can make the wounded whole,
And bid the dying live.

3 Behold me prostrate at thy gate;
Do not my suit deny;
With longing eyes for thee I wait;
O, help me, or I die!

4 When thou dost give a heart to pray,
Thou wilt incline thine ear;
From me turn not thy face away,
But my petition hear.

5 So shall my joyful soul adore
The riches of thy grace;
No sinner needed mercy more,
That ever sought thy face.
                         Fawcett.

368 (892)   C. M.

1 My business lies at wisdom's gate
Where needy sinners come;
And here I sue, and here I wait
For mercy's falling crumb.

2 My rags and wounds my wants proclaim,
And help from him implore;
The wounds do witness I am lame,
The rags, that I am poor.

3 My Lord, I hear, the hungry feeds,
And cheereth souls distrest;
He loves to bind up broken reeds,
And heal a bleeding breast.

4 His name is Jesus, full of grace,
Which draws me to his door;
And will not Jesus shew his face,
And bring his gospel-store?

5 Supplies of every grace I want,
And each day want supply;
And if no grace the Lord will grant,
I must lie down and die.

6 But, oh! my Lord, such news shall ne'er
Be told in Zion's street,
That some poor soul fell in despair,
And died at Jesus' feet.
                    Erskine and Berridge.

369 (897)   C. M.

1 Dear Shepherd of thy people, here
Thy presence now display;
As thou hast given a place for prayer,
So give us hearts to pray.

2 Within these walls let holy peace,
And love and concord dwell;
Here give the troubled conscience ease,
The wounded spirit heal.

3 Show us some token of thy love,
Our fainting hope to raise;
And pour thy blessings from above,
That we may render praise.

4 And may the gospel's joyful sound,
Enforced by mighty grace,
Awaken many sinners round
To come and fill the place.   Newton.

150 PRAYER.

HUBERT. C. M.   S. MAIN.

1. Lord! let me see thy beauteous face! It yields a heav'n be-low; And an-gels round the throne will say, 'Tis all the heav'n they know.

370 (902)

1 LORD! let me see thy beauteous face!
It yields a heaven below;
And angels round the throne will say,
'Tis all the heaven they know.

2 A glimpse, a single glimpse of thee
Would more delight my soul
Than this vain world, with all its joys,
Could I possess the whole.
Stennett.

371 (904)   C. M.   Matt. 26: 41.

1 ALAS! what hourly dangers rise!
What snares beset my way!
To heaven, O let me lift my eyes,
And hourly watch and pray.

2 How oft my mournful tho'ts complain,
And melt in flowing tears:
My weak resistance, ah! how vain!
How strong my foes and fears?

3 O gracious God, in whom I live,
My feeble efforts aid;
Help me to watch, and pray, and strive,
Though trembling and afraid.

4 Increase my faith, increase my hope,
When foes and fears prevail;
And bear my fainting spirit up,
Or soon my strength will fail.

5 Whene'er temptations fright my heart,
Or lure my feet aside,
My God, thy powerful aid impart;
My guardian and my guide.

6 O keep me in thy heavenly way,
And bid the tempter flee;
And let me never, never stray
From happiness and thee.
Mrs. Steele.

372 (920)   C. M.

1 BREATHE from the gentle South, O Lord,
And cheer me from the North;
Blow on the treasures of thy word,
And call the spices forth!

2 I wish, thou knowest, to be resigned,
And wait with patient hope;
But hope delayed fatigues the mind,
And drinks the spirits up.

3 Help me to reach the distant goal;
Confirm my feeble knee,
Pity the sickness of a soul
That faints for love of thee.

4 Cold as I feel this heart of mine,
Yet since I feel it so,
It yields some hope of life divine,
Within, however low.

5 I seem forsaken and alone,
I hear the lion roar,
And every door is shut but one,
And that is mercy's door.

6 There, till the dear Deliverer come,
I'll wait with humble prayer;
And when he calls his exile home,
The Lord shall find me there.
Newton.

PRAYER. 151

BELIEVER. C. M. American Melody. Arr. by H. P. M. 1856.

1. One thing, with all my soul's de-sire, I sought and will pur-sue;
What thine own Spir-it doth in-spire, Lord! for thy serv-ant do.

By per. H. P. Main.

373 (921) Psalm 27.

1 ONE thing, with all my soul's desire,
  I sought and will pursue;
What thine own Spirit doth inspire,
  Lord! for thy servant do.

2 Grant me within thy courts a place,
  Among thy saints a seat,
For ever to behold thy face,
  And worship at thy feet.

3 In thy pavilion to abide,
  When storms of trouble blow;
And in thy tabernacle hide,
  Secure from every foe.

4 "Seek ye my face;"—without delay,
  When thus I hear thee speak,
My heart would leap for joy, and say,
  "Thy face, Lord, will I seek."

5 Then leave me not when griefs assail,
  And earthly comforts flee;
When father, mother, kindred fail,
  My God! remember me.

6 Oft had I fainted and resigned
  Of every hope my hold;
But mine afflictions brought to mind
  Thy benefits of old.
                              Montgomery.

374 (931) C. M.

1 WHILST thee I seek, protecting Power!
  Be my vain wishes stilled;
And may this consecrated hour
  With better hopes be filled.

2 Thy love the power of tho't bestowed;
  To thee my thoughts would soar:
Thy mercy o'er my life has flowed;
  That mercy I adore.

3 In each event of life, how clear
  Thy ruling hand I see!
Each blessing to my soul most dear,
  Because conferred by thee.

4 In every joy that crowns my days,
  In every pain I bear,
My heart shall find delight in praise,
  Or seek relief in prayer.

5 When gladness wings my favored hour,
  Thy love my thoughts shall fill;
Resigned, when storms of sorrow lower,
  My soul shall meet thy will.

6 My lifted eye, without a tear,
  The gathering storm shall see;
My steadfast heart shall know no fear;
  That heart will rest on thee.
                          Helen M. Williams.

375 (912) C. M.

1 Now, Lord, inspire the preacher's heart,
  And teach his tongue to speak;
Food to the hungry soul impart,
  And cordials to the weak.

2 Furnish us all with light and powers
  To walk in Wisdom's ways;
So shall the benefit be ours,
  And thou shalt have the praise. Newton.

PRAYER.

BLISSFUL HOME. S. M.
Moderato.
EMERSON.

1. Be-hold the Throne of Grace! The prom-ise calls me near;
There Je-sus shows his smil-ing face, And waits to an-swer pray'r.

By per. O. Ditson & Co.

376 (885) Heb. 4: 16.

2 That rich atoning blood,
 Which, sprinkled round, I see,
Provides, for those who come to God,
 An all-prevailing plea.

3 My soul, ask what thou wilt,
 Thou canst not be too bold:
Since his own blood for thee he spilt,
 What else can he withhold?

4 Beyond my utmost wants
 His love and power can bless!
To praying souls he always grants
 More than they can express.
                               Newton.

377 (707) S. M. Ps. 31.

1 IN thee, O Lord, I trust;
 My hope is in thy name;
In righteousness deliver me,
 Nor put my soul to shame.

2 From heaven bow down thine ear,
 My cause in mercy plead:
My Rock, my Fortress, my Defense,
 Vouchsafe my soul to lead.

3 From every snare preserve;
 From every foe defend;
For thy name's sake, O God, my Strength,
 Divine protection send.

4 I will be glad, and praise,
 And in thy name rejoice;
In sorrow thou hast known my soul,
 And heard my suppliant voice.

378 (983) S. M.

1 WHEN overwhelmed with grief,
 My heart within me dies,
Helpless and far from all relief,
 To heaven I lift my eyes.

2 O lead me to the rock
 That's high above my head,
And make the covert of thy wings
 My shelter and my shade.

3 Within thy presence, Lord,
 Forever I'll abide;
Thou art the tower of my defense,
 The refuge where I hide.

4 Thou givest me the lot
 Of those that fear thy name;
If endless life be their reward,
 I shall possess the same.
                               Watts.

379 (913) S. M.

1 HUNGRY, and faint, and poor,
 Behold us, Lord, again
Assembled at thy mercy's door,
 Thy bounty to obtain.

2 Thy word commands us nigh,
 Or we must starve indeed;
For we no money have to buy,
 No righteousness to plead.

3 The food our spirits want
 Thy hand alone can give;
Oh! hear the prayer of faith; and grant
 That we may eat and live.
                               Newton.

PRAYER 153

SIBERIA. 8s. & 7s. P. M. S. B. POND.

Saviour, visit thy plantation, Grant us, Lord, a gracious rain! All will come to desolation, Omit............ Unless thou return again: Lord, revive us, Lord, revive us; All our help must come from thee!

380 (909)

2 Keep no longer at a distance;
  Shine upon us from on high,
Lest, for want of thine assistance,
  Every plant should droop and die:
Lord, revive us, Lord, revive us;
All our help must come from thee!

3 Surely, once thy garden flourished,
  Every plant looked gay and green;
Then thy word our spirits nourished,
  Happy seasons we have seen!
Lord, revive us, Lord, revive us;
All our help must come from thee!

4 But a drought has since succeeded,
  And a sad decline we see;
Lord, thy help is greatly needed;
  Help can only come from thee:
Lord, revive us, Lord, revive us;
All our help must come from thee!

5 Let our mutual love be fervent:
  Make us prevalent in prayers;
Let each one, esteemed thy servant,
  Shun the world's bewitching snares:
Lord, revive us, Lord, revive us;
All our help must come from thee!

6 Break the tempter's fatal power;
  Turn the stony heart to flesh;
And begin from this good hour
  To revive thy work afresh:
Lord, revive us, Lord, revive us;
All our help must come from thee!
                              Newton.

SHAWMUT. S. M. Arranged by Dr. L. MASON.

154 PRAISE.

MERDIN. 7s. D.
MASON. Arr. by P. G. L.

1. Chil-dren of the heav'n-ly King, As you jour-ney, sweet-ly sing;
Sing your Sav-iour's wor-thy praise, Glo-rious in his works and ways.
D.C.—They are hap-py now, and ye Soon their hap-pi-ness shall see.

Ye are trav'-ling home to God, In the way the fa-thers trod;

---

381 (190) Isa. 35: 10; Luke 12: 32.

2 O, ye banished seed, be glad!
Christ our Advocate is made;
Us, to save, our flesh assumes,
Brother to our souls becomes.
Shout, ye little flock, and blest!
You on Jesus' throne shall rest;
There your seat is now prepared—
There your kingdom and reward.

3 Fear not, brethren, joyful stand
On the borders of your land;
Christ, your Father's elder Son,
Bids you undismayed go on.
Lord! submissive make us go,
Gladly leaving all below;
Only thou our Leader be,
And we still will follow thee.
Cennick.

382 (933) 7s. D. Heb. 7: 22.

1 CHRIST, exalted, is our song,
Hymned by all the blood-bought throng;
To his throne our shouts shall rise;
God with us by sacred ties.
Shout, believer, to thy God;
He hath once the wine-press trod;
Peace procured by blood divine;
Cancelled all thy sins and mine.

2 Here thy bleeding wounds are healed;
Sin condemned and pardon sealed:
Grace her empire still maintains;
Christ without a rival reigns.

In thy Surety thou art free;
His dear hands were pierced for thee;
With his spotless vesture on;
Holy as the Holy One.

3 Oh! the heights, the depths of grace,
Shining with meridian blaze;
Here the sacred records show,
Sinners black, but comely, too.
Saints, dejected, cease to mourn;
Faith shall soon to vision turn;
Ye the kingdom shall obtain,
And with Christ exalted reign.
Kent.

383 (955) 7s. D. Isaiah 12.

1 I WILL praise thee every day,
Now thine anger's turned away!
Comfortable thoughts arise
From the bleeding sacrifice.
Here, in the fair gospel field,
Wells of free salvation yield
Streams of life a plenteous store,
And my soul shall thirst no more.

2 Jesus is become at length
My salvation and my strength;
And his praises shall prolong,
While I live, my pleasant song.
Praise ye, then, his glorious name;
Publish his exalted fame!
Still his worth your praise exceeds;
Excellent are all his deeds.
Cowper.

PRAISE. 155

AMERICA. 6s. & 4s.   Dr. JOHN BULL, 1606.

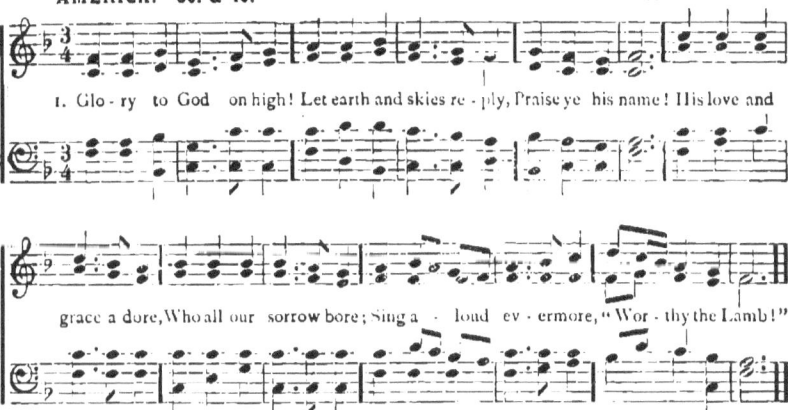

1. Glo-ry to God on high! Let earth and skies re-ply, Praise ye his name! His love and grace adore, Who all our sorrow bore; Sing a-loud ev-ermore, "Wor-thy the Lamb!"

384 (939)   Psa. 148: 13.

1 GLORY to God on high!
 Let earth and skies reply,
  Praise ye his name!
 His love and grace adore,
 Who all our sorrow bore;
 Sing aloud evermore,
  "Worthy the Lamb!"

2 Jesus, our Lord and God,
 Bore sin's tremendous load:
  Praise ye his name!
 Tell what his arms have done,
 What spoils from death he won;
 Sing his great name alone:
  "Worthy the Lamb!"

3 While they around the throne
 Cheerfully join in one,
  Praising his name,
 Ye who have felt his blood
 Sealing your peace with God,
 Sound his dear fame abroad;
  "Worthy the Lamb!"

4 Join, all ye ransomed race,
 Our Lord and God to bless;
  Praise ye his name!
 In him we will rejoice,
 And make a joyful noise,
 Shouting with heart and voice,
  "Worthy the Lamb!"
                    J. Allen.

385 (869)   6s. & 4s.

1 COME, thou Almighty King,
 Help us thy name to sing,
  Help us to praise:
 Father all-glorious,
 O'er all victorious,
 Come, and reign over us,
  Ancient of Days!

2 Jesus, our Lord, arise,
 Scatter our enemies,
  And make them fall!
 Let thy almighty aid
 Our sure defense be made,
 Our souls on thee be stayed:
  Lord, hear our call!

3 Come, thou incarnate Word,
 Gird on thy mighty sword;
  Our prayers attend:
 Come, and thy people bless,
 And give thy word success;
 Spirit of holiness,
  On us descend!

4 Come, holy Comforter!
 Thy sacred witness bear,
  In this glad hour:
 Thou, who almighty art,
 Now rule in every heart,
 And ne'er from us depart,
  Spirit of power!
                    C. Wesley.

156 PRAISE.

NETTLETON. 8s. & 7s. D.
J. WYETH'S Coll. 1812.

386 (934) 1 Sam. 7: 12.

1 COME, thou Fount of every blessing,
   Tune my heart to sing thy grace!
Streams of mercy, never ceasing,
   Call for songs of loudest praise.
Teach me some melodious sonnet,
   Sung by flaming tongues above:
Praise the mount! O, fix me on it!
   Mount of God's unchanging love.

2 Here I raise my Ebenezer;
   Hither by thy help I'm come;
And I hope, by thy good pleasure,
   Safely to arrive at home.

Jesus sought me, when a stranger,
   Wandering from the fold of God;
He, to save my soul from danger,
   Interposed his precious blood!

3 O to grace how great a debtor
   Daily I'm constrained to be:
Let thy grace, Lord, like a fetter,
   Bind my wandering heart to thee.
Prone to wander, Lord, I feel it!
   Prone to leave the God I love!
Here's my heart, Lord, take and seal it;
   Seal it for thy courts above!   Robinson.

WATCHMAN. 8s. & 7s. D.
H. D. PINNEY.

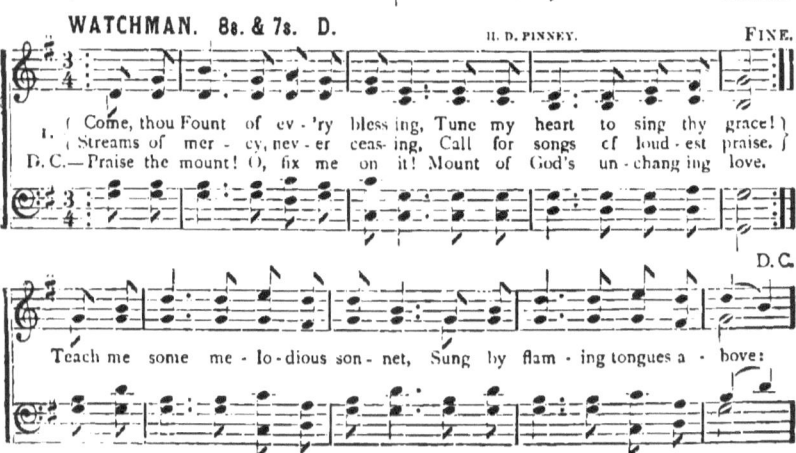

PRAISE.

SILVER STREET. S. M.
I. SMITH. 1770-1800.

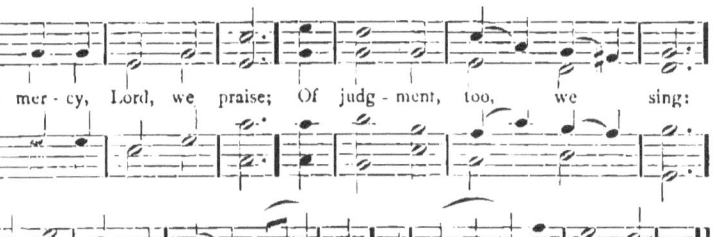

1. Thy mer-cy, Lord, we praise; Of judg-ment, too, we sing:

For all the rich-es of thy grace, Our grate - - ful trib-ute bring.

387 (945)

2 Mercy may justly claim
  A sinner's thankful voice;
And, judgment joining in the theme,
  We tremble and rejoice.

3 Thy mercies bid us trust;
  Thy judgments strike with awe:
We fear the last, we bless the first,
  And love thy righteous law.

4 Who can thy acts express,
  Or trace thy wondrous ways?
How glorious is thy holiness!
  How terrible thy praise!

5 Thy goodness how immense,
  To those that fear thy name!
Thy love surpasses thought or sense,
  And always is the same.

6 Thy judgments are too deep
  For reason's line to sound:
Thy tender mercy to thy sheep,
  No bottom knows, nor bound.

388 (956) S. M.

1 PREPARE a thankful song
  To the Redeemer's name!
His praises should employ each tongue,
  And every heart inflame!

2 He laid his glory by,
  And dreadful pains endured,
That rebels, such as you and I,
  From wrath might be secured.
L.

3 The world and Satan rage,
  But he their power controls;
His wisdom, love, and truth, engage
  Protection for our souls.

4 Though pressed, we will not yield,
  But shall prevail at length:
For Jesus is our sun and shield,
  Our righteousness and strength.

5 Assured that Christ, our King,
  Will put our foes to flight,
We on the field of battle sing,
  And triumph while we fight.
Newton.

389 (960) S. M.

1 AWAKE, and sing the song
  Of Moses and the Lamb;
Wake, every heart, and every tongue,
  To praise the Saviour's name.

2 Sing of his dying love,
  And sing his rising power;
Sing how he intercedes above,
  For those whose sins he bore.

3 Sing, on your heavenly way,
  Ye ransomed sinners, sing;
Sing on rejoicing, every day,
  In Christ, th' exalted King.

4 Soon shall your raptured tongue
  His endless praise proclaim;
And sweeter voices tune the song
  Of Moses and the Lamb. W Hammond.

PRAISE.

GREEN. C. M. — R. M. McINTOSH.

1. O, for a thou-sand tongues to sing My dear Re-deem-er's praise, The glo-ry of my God and King, The tri-umphs of his grace.

By per. R. M. McIntosh.

390 (962)

1 O, FOR a thousand tongues to sing
  My dear Redeemer's praise,
The glory of my God and King,
  The triumphs of his grace.

2 My gracious Master and my God,
  Let saints thy love proclaim,
And spread through all the earth abroad
  The honors of thy name.

3 Jesus, the name that calms our fears,
  That bids our sorrow cease;
'Tis music to our ravished ears;
  'Tis life, and health, and peace.

4 It breaks the power of reigning sin,
  And sets the prisoner free;
Thy blood can cleanse the foulest stain;
  And can avail for me.
      C. Wesley.

391 (954) C. M. Psa. 116: 12.

1 FOR mercies, countless as the sands,
  Which daily I receive
From Jesus my Redeemer's hands,
  My soul, what canst thou give?

2 Alas! from such a heart as mine,
  What can I bring him forth?
My best is stained and dyed with sin
  My all is nothing worth.

3 Yet this acknowledgment I'll make
  For all he has bestowed.
Salvation's sacred cup I'll take,
  And call upon my God.

4 The best returns for one like me,
  So wretched and so poor,
Is from his gifts to draw a plea,
  And ask him still for more.

5 I cannot serve him as I ought,
  No works have I to boast;
Yet would I glory in the thought,
  That I shall owe him most.
      Newton.

392 (402) C. M. Rev. 5: 11-13.

1 COME, let us join our cheerful songs
  With angels round the throne;
Ten thousand thousand are their tongues,
  But all their joys are one.

2 "Worthy the Lamb that died," they
  "To be exalted thus;"   [cry,
"Worthy the Lamb," our lips reply,
  "For he was slain for us."

3 Jesus is worthy to receive
  Honor and power divine;
And blessings more than we can give,
  Be, Lord, for ever thine.

4 Let all that dwell above the sky,
  And air, and earth, and seas,
Conspire to raise thy glories high,
  And speak thine endless praise.

5 The whole creation join in one
  To bless the sacred name
Of him that sits upon the throne,
  And to adore the Lamb.   Watts.

PRAISE. 159

BELOVED. 11s. & 8s. FREEMAN LEWIS. 1780-1859.

1. O thou in whose presence my soul takes delight, On whom in af-flictions I call, My comfort by day, and my song in the night, My hope, my sal-va-tion, my all.

393 (948)

2 Where dost thou at noontide resort with
thy sheep,
To feed on the pastures of love? [weep,
Say, why in the valley of death should I
Or alone in the wilderness rove?

3 O, why should I wander an alien from
thee,
And cry in the desert for bread? [see,
Thy foes will rejoice when my sorrows they
And smile at the tears I have shed.

4 Ye daughters of Zion, declare, have ye
The Star that on Israel shone? [seen
Say, if in your tents my Beloved has been,
And where, with his flocks, he is gone.

5 This is my Beloved; his form is divine;
His vestments shed odors around: [vine,
The locks on his head are as grapes on the
When autumn with plenty is crowned.

6 The roses of Sharon, the lilies that grow
In vales, on the banks of the streams:
On his cheeks, all the beauties of excel-
lence glow,
And his eyes are as quivers of beams.

7 His voice, as the sound of the dulcimer
sweet,
Is heard through the shadows of death;
The cedars of Lebanon bow at his feet,
The air is perfumed with his breath.

8 His lips as a fountain of righteousness
That waters the garden of grace, [flow,

From which their salvation, the Gentiles
shall know,
And bask in the smiles of his face.

9 Love sits in his eye-lids, and scatters
delight
Through all the bright mansions on high;
Their faces the cherubim veil in his sight,
And tremble with fulness of joy.

10 He looks, and ten thousands of angels
And myriads wait for his word; [rejoice,
He speaks, and eternity, filled with his
voice,
Re-echoes the praise of her Lord.
Swain.

394 (1037) 11s. & 8s. Gal. 5: 17.

1 How strange is the course that a Chris-
tian must steer;
How perplexed is the path he must tread!
The hope of his happiness rises from fear,
And his life he receives from the dead.

2 His fairest pretensions must wholly be
waived,
And his best resolutions be crossed;
Nor can he expect to be perfectly saved,
Till he finds himself utterly lost.

3 When all this is done, and his heart is
Of the total remission of sins, [assured
When his pardon is signed and his peace
is procured,
From that moment his conflict begins.
Hart.

PRAISE.

ARIEL. C. P. M.
Arr. by Dr. LOWELL MASON 1792-1872.

1. O, could I speak the matchless worth, O, could I sound the glories forth That in my Saviour shine;
{ I'd soar and touch the heav'nly strings, } { And vie with Gabriel while he sings } In notes that are divine, In notes that are divine.

395 (961)

2 I'd sing the characters he bears,
And all the forms of love he wears
Exalted on his throne;
In loftiest songs of sweetest praise,
I would, to everlasting days,
Make all his glories known.

3 Soon the delightful morn will come,
When my dear Lord will bring me home,
And I shall see his face;
There with my Saviour, Brother, Friend,
A blest eternity I'll spend,
Triumphant in his grace. Medley.

SESSIONS. L. M.
L. O. EMERSON.

1. What hath God wrought! might Israel say When Jordan roll'd its tide away,
And save a passage to their bands, Safely to march across its sands.

By per. O. Ditson & Co.

396 (953) Num. 23: 23.

2 What hath God wrought! might well be said,
When Jesus, rising from the dead,
Scattered the shades of Pagan night,
And blessed the nations with his light.

3 What hath God wrought! O blissful theme!
Are we redeemed and called by him?

Shall we be led the desert through,
And safe arrive at glory, too?

4 The news shall every heart employ;
Fill every tongue with rapturous joy;
When shall we join the heavenly throng,
To swell the triumph and the song!
Rippon's Col.

THE CHRISTIAN.

WARWICK. C. M. — S. STANLEY. 1767-1822.

1. I love the Lord; he heard my cries, And pit-ied ev-'ry groan; Long as I live, when troub-les rise, I'll has-ten to his throne.

397 (970)

1 I LOVE the Lord; he heard my cries,
 And pitied every groan:
Long as I live, when troubles rise,
 I'll hasten to his throne.

2 I love the Lord; he bowed his ear,
 And chased my griefs away;
O let my heart no more despair,
 While I have breath to pray!

3 My flesh declined, my spirits fell,
 And I drew near the dead,
While inward pangs, and fears of hell,
 Perplexed my wakeful head.

4 "My God," I cried, "thy servant save,
 Thou ever good and just;
Thy power can rescue from the grave,
 Thy power is all my trust."

5 The Lord beheld me sore distressed,
 He bade my pains remove;
Return, my soul, to God, thy rest,
 For thou hast known his love.

6 My God hath saved my soul from death,
 And dried my falling tears;
Now in his praise I'll spend my breath,
 And my remaining years. *Watts.*

398 (969) C. M.

1 INTO thine hand, O God of truth,
 My spirit I commit;
Thou hast redeemed my soul from death,
 And saved me from the pit.

2 'Twas in my haste, my spirit said,
 I must despair and die,
I am cut off before thine eyes,
 But thou hast heard my cry.

3 Thy goodness, how divinely free!
 How wondrous is thy grace
To those that fear thy majesty,
 And trust thy promises!

4 O love the Lord, all ye, his saints,
 And sing his praises loud;
He'll bend his ear to your complaints,
 And recompense the proud. *Watts.*

399 (979) C. M.

1 IN all my troubles and distress,
 The Lord my soul doth own;
Jehovah doth my griefs redress,
 And makes his mercy known.

2 He helps me on him to rely;
 He is my strength and tower;
'Tis he that hears me when I cry,
 And manifests his power.

3 In every storm, in every sea,
 My Jesus makes a way;
His light shall make the darkness flee,
 And turn the shade to day.

4 'Tis he in trouble bears me up,
 And leads me safely through;
My Jesus doth maintain my cup,
 And daily strength renew. *Franklin.*

THE CHRISTIAN.

ROCKINGHAM. L. M. — Dr. LOWELL MASON. 1792-1872.

1. Far from my tho'ts, vain world, be-gone; Let my re-lig-ious hours a-lone: Fain would my eyes my Sav-iour see; I wait a vis-it, Lord, from thee.

400 (974)

1 FAR from my thoughts, vain world,
  begone;
Let my religious hours alone:
Fain would my eyes my Saviour see;
I wait a visit, Lord, from thee.

2 My heart grows warm with holy fire,
And kindles with a pure desire:
Come, my dear Jesus, from above,
And feed my soul with heavenly love.

3 The trees of life immortal stand
In blooming rows at thy right hand;
And in sweet murmurs by thy side
Rivers of bliss perpetual glide.

4 Haste, then, but with a smiling face,
And spread the table of thy grace;
Bring down a taste of truth divine,
And cheer my heart with sacred wine.

5 Blessed Jesus, what delicious fare!
How sweet thy entertainments are!
Never did angels taste above
Redeeming grace and dying love.

6 Hail, great Immanuel, all divine,
In thee thy Father's glories shine;
Thou brightest, sweetest, fairest one,
That eyes have seen or angels known.
                                    Watts.

401 (977)   L. M.

1 I THIRST, but not as once I did,
  The vain delights of earth to share;
Thy wounds, Emmanuel, all forbid
  That I should seek my pleasures there.

2 It was the sight of thy dear cross,
  First weaned my soul from earthly
    things;
And taught me to esteem as dross
  The mirth of fools and pomp of kings.

3 I want that grace that springs from thee;
  That quickens all things where it flows;
And makes a wretched thorn like me,
  Bloom as the myrtle, or the rose.

4 Dear fountain of delight unknown!
  No longer sink below the brim;
But overflow, and pour me down
  A living and life-giving stream!

5 For sure, of all the plants that share
  The notice of thy Father's eye,
None proves less grateful to his care,
  Or yields him meaner fruit than I.
                                    Cowper.

402 (978)   L. M.   Col. 3: 11.

1 CHRIST is my All, my sure Defense;
Nor shall my soul depart from thence:
He is my Rock, my Refuge, too,
In spite of all my foes can do!

2 Christ is my All, and he will lead
My soul in pastures green to feed:
'Tis he supplies my every want,
And will all needful blessings grant.

3 Christ is my All: where should I go?
Without him I can nothing do!
Helpless and weak, a sinner great,
Yet in his righteousness complete. Adams.

SESSIONS. L. M. L. O. EMERSON.

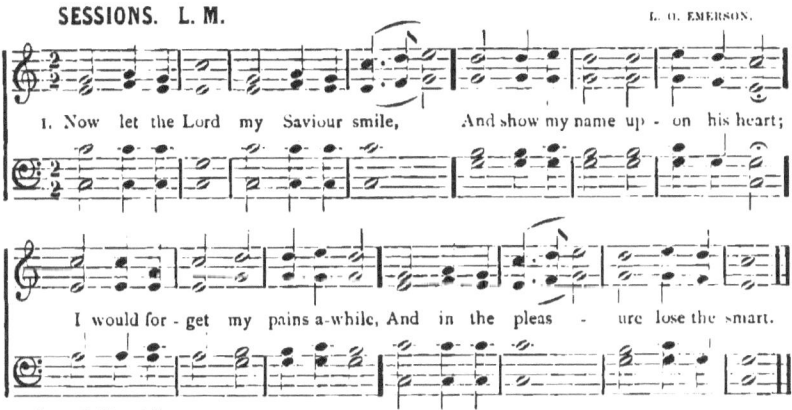

1. Now let the Lord my Saviour smile, And show my name up-on his heart; I would for-get my pains a-while, And in the pleas - ure lose the smart.

By per. O. Ditson & Co.

403 (987)

1 Now let the Lord my Saviour smile,
    And show my name upon his heart;
  I would forget my pains awhile,
    And in the pleasure lose the smart.

2 But, oh! it swells my sorrows high,
    To see my blessed Jesus frown;
  My spirits sink, my comforts die,
    And all the springs of life are down.

3 Yet why, my soul, why these complaints?
    Still while he frowns, his bowels move;
  Still on his heart he bears his saints,
    And feels their sorrows and his love.

4 My name is printed on his breast;
    His book of life contains my name;
  I'd rather have it there impressed
    Than in the bright records of fame.

5 Now shall my minutes smoothly run,
    Whilst here I wait my Father's will;
  My rising and my setting sun
    Roll gently up and down the hill.   Watts.

404 (994) L. M. Psa. 17.

1 LORD, I am thine; but thou wilt prove
  My faith, my patience, and my love:
  When men of spite against me join,
  They are the sword, the hand is thine.

2 Their hope and portion lie below;
  'Tis all the happiness they know;
  'Tis all they seek; they take their shares,
  And leave the rest among their heirs.

3 What sinners value, I resign;
  Lord, 'tis enough that thou art mine;
  I shall behold thy blissful face,
  And stand complete in righteousness.

4 This life's a dream, an empty show;
  But the bright world to which I go
  Hath joys substantial and sincere;
  When shall I wake, and find me there?

5 O glorious hour! O blest abode!
  I shall be near and like my God!
  And flesh and sin no more control
  The sacred pleasures of the soul.
                                Watts.

405 (997) L. M.

1 BLEST Jesus! source of grace divine,
  What soul-refreshing streams are thine!
  Oh, bring these healing waters nigh,
  Or we must droop, and fall, and die.

2 No traveler through desert lands,
  'Midst scorching suns, and burning sands,
  More needs the current to obtain,
  Or to enjoy refreshing rain.

3 Our longing souls aloud would sing,
  Spring up, celestial Fountain, spring;
  To a redundant river flow,
  And cheer this thirsty land below.

4 May this blest torrent near my side,
  Through all the desert, gently glide;
  Then, in Emmanuel's land above,
  Spread to a sea of joy and love! Doddridge.

DUNLAP. C. M.

SAMUEL McFARLAND.

1. My God, the spring of all my joys, The life of my delights, The glory of my brightest days, The comfort of my nights!

406 (990)

1 My God, the spring of all my joys,
  The life of my delights,
  The glory of my brightest days,
  The comfort of my nights!

2 In darkest shades if he appear,
  My dawning is begun;
  He is my soul's sweet morning star,
  And he my rising sun.

3 The opening heavens around me shine
  With beams of sacred bliss,
  While Jesus shows his heart is mine,
  And whispers *I am His!*

4 My soul would leave this heavy clay
  At that transporting word,
  Run up with joy the shining way
  To embrace my dearest Lord.

5 Fearless of hell and ghastly death
  I'd break through every foe;
  The wings of love, and arms of faith,
  Should bear me conqueror through.
  Watts.

407 (993) C. M.

1 ARISE, my soul, my joyful powers,
  And triumph in my God;
  Awake, my voice, and loud proclaim
  His glorious grace abroad.

2 He raised me from the deeps of sin,
  The gates of gaping hell,
  And fixed my standing more secure
  Than 'twas before I fell.

3 The arms of everlasting love
  Beneath my soul he placed;
  And on the rock of ages set
  My slippery footsteps fast.

4 The city of my blest abode
  Is walled around with grace,
  Salvation for a bulwark stands
  To shield the sacred place.

5 Satan may vent his sharpest spite,
  And all his legions roar;
  Almighty mercy guards my life,
  And bounds his raging power.

6 Arise, my soul, awake, my voice,
  And tunes of pleasure sing;
  Loud hallelujahs shall address
  My Saviour and my King.
  Watts.

408 (995) C. M.

1 I LOVE the windows of thy grace,
  Through which my Lord is seen,
  And long to meet my Saviour's face,
  Without a glass between.

2 O that the happy hour were come
  To change my faith to sight!
  I shall behold my Lord at home
  In a diviner light.

3 Haste, my Beloved, and remove
  These interposing days;
  Then shall my passions all be love,
  And all my powers be praise.
  Watts.

THE CHRISTIAN. 165

NINETY-FIFTH. C. M.

1. When I can read my title clear
To mansions in the skies,
I bid farewell, I bid farewell, I bid farewell to ev-'ry fear,
And wipe...... my weeping eyes.

409 (991)

2 Should earth against my soul engage,
And fiery darts be hurled,
Then I can smile at Satan's rage,
And face a frowning world.

3 Let cares like a wild deluge come,
And storms of sorrow fall,
May I but safely reach my home,
My God, my heaven, my all.

4 There shall I bathe my weary soul
In seas of heavenly rest,
And not a wave of trouble roll
Across my peaceful breast.
Watts

410 (999) C. M. 1 Cor. 13: 9.

1 Thy way, O God! is in the sea;
Thy paths I cannot trace;
Nor comprehend the mystery
Of thy unbounded grace.

2 Here the dark veils of flesh and sense
My captive soul surround;
Mysterious deeps of Providence
My wondering thoughts confound.

3 When I behold thy awful hand
My earthly hopes destroy,
In deep astonishment I stand,
And ask the reason, why?

4 As through a glass, I dimly see
The wonders of thy love;
How little do I know of thee,
Or of the joys above!

5 'Tis but in part I know thy will;
I bless thee for the sight;
When will thy love the rest reveal,
In glory's clearer light?

6 With rapture shall I then survey
Thy providence and grace;
And spend an everlasting day
In wonder, love and praise.
Fawcett

411 (980) C. M. Psa. 73: 25.

1 My God, my portion, and my love,
My everlasting all,
I've none but thee in heaven above,
Or on this earthly ball.

2 In vain the bright, the burning sun
Scatters his feeble light;
'Tis thy sweet beams create my noon;
If thou withdraw 'tis night.

3 And whilst upon my restless bed,
Among the shades I roll,
If my Redeemer shows his head,
'Tis morning with my soul.

4 Were I possessor of the earth,
And called the stars my own,
Without thy graces and thyself
I were a wretch undone.

5 Let others stretch their arms like seas,
And grasp in all the shore,
Grant me the visits of thy face,
And I desire no more.
Watts.

CONFLICTS AND DELIVERANCES.

FOREST. L. M. — CHAPIN.

1. My Captain sounds th' a-larm of war: A-wake! the pow'rs of hell are near! "To arms! to arms!" I hear him cry, "'Tis your's to con-quer or to die!"

412 (1001) Eph. 6: 13-17.

1 My Captain sounds the alarm of war:
Awake! the powers of hell are near!
"To arms! to arms!" I hear him cry,
"'Tis your's to conquer or to die!"

2 Rous'd by the animating sound,
I cast my eager eyes around;
Make haste to gird my armor on,
And bid each trembling fear begone.

3 Hope is my helmet; Christ my shield;
Thy word, my God, the sword I wield;
With sacred truth my loins are girt,
And holy zeal inspires my heart.

4 Thus armed, I venture on the fight;
Resolved to put my foes to flight:
While Jesus kindly deigns to spread
His conquering banner o'er my head.

5 In him I hope; in him I trust;
His bleeding Cross is all my boast;
Through troops of foes he'll lead me on
To victory and a victor's crown!
Stennett.

413 (1002) L. M. Heb. 11: 13.

1 PILGRIMS we are, and heav'nward bound;
Our journey lies along this road;
This wilderness we travel round,
To reach the city of our God.

2 And here as travelers we meet,
Before we reach the fields above,
To sit around our Master's feet,
And tell the wonders of his love.

3 Oft have we seen the tempests rise;
The world and Satan, hell and sin,
Like mountains seemed to reach the skies,
With scarce a gleam of hope between.

4 But still, as oft as troubles come,
Our Jesus sends some cheering ray;
And that strong arm shall guard us home,
Which thus protects us by the way.

5 A few more days, or months, or years,
In this dark desert to complain;
A few more sighs, a few more tears,
And we shall bid adieu to pain.
Swain.

414 (1016) L. M. Psa. 13.

1 How long, O Lord, shall I complain
Like one that seeks his God in vain?
Canst thou thy face for ever hide,
And I still pray, and be denied?

2 Shall I for ever be forgot
As one whom thou regardest not!
Still shall my soul thy absence mourn,
And still despair of thy return?

3 How long shall my poor troubled breast
Be with these anxious thoughts oppressed;
And Satan, my malicious foe,
Rejoice to see me sunk so low?

4 Hear, Lord, and grant me quick relief,
Before my death concludes my grief;
If thou withhold thy heavenly light,
I sleep in everlasting night.

CONFLICTS AND DELIVERANCES. 167

WARE. L. M. GEO. KINGSLEY.

1. O! for a glance of heav'nly day, To take this stubborn stone a-way! And thaw, with beams of love di-vine, This heart, this fro-zen heart of mine.

415 (1013) Isa. 61: 1; Ezek. 11: 19.

1 O! FOR a glance of heavenly day,
To take this stubborn stone away!
And thaw, with beams of love divine,
This heart, this frozen heart of mine.

2 The rocks can rend; the earth can quake;
The seas can roar; the mountains shake;
Of feeling, all things show some sign,
But this unfeeling heart of mine.

3 To hear the sorrows thou hast felt,
Dear Lord, an adamant would melt!
But I can read each moving line,
And nothing move this heart of mine.

4 Thy judgments, too, unmoved I hear,
(Amazing thought!) which devils fear;
Goodness and wrath in vain combine
To stir this stupid heart of mine.

5 But something yet can do the deed!
And that dear something much I need;
Thy Spirit can from dross refine,
And move and melt this heart of mine.
Hart.

416 (1007) L. M. Acts 11: 22.

1 I ASKED the Lord that I might grow
In faith, and love, and every grace;
Might more of his salvation know,
And seek more earnestly his face.

2 'Twas he who taught me thus to pray;
And he, I trust, has answered prayer;
But it has been in such a way
As almost drove me to despair.

3 I hoped that in some favored hour,
At once he'd answer my request;
And, by his love's constraining power,
Subdue my sins, and give me rest.

4 Instead of this, he made me feel
The hidden evils of my heart,
And let the angry powers of hell
Assault my soul in every part.

5 Yea, more, with his own hand he seemed
Intent to aggravate my wo;
Crossed all the fair designs I schemed,
Blasted my gourds, and laid me low.

6 "Lord, why is this?" I trembling cried;
"Wilt thou pursue thy worm to death?"
"'Tis in this way," the Lord replied,
"I answer prayer for grace and faith.

7 "These inward trials I employ,
From self and pride to set thee free;
And break thy schemes of earthly joy,
That thou mayest seek thy all in me."
Newton.

5 How will the powers of darkness boast,
If but one praying soul be lost!
But I have trusted in thy grace,
And shall again behold thy face.

6 Whate'er my fears or foes suggest,
Thou art my hope, my joy, my rest;
My heart shall feel thy love, and raise
My cheerful voice to songs of praise.
Watts.

RISSAH. C. M.

1. Why is my heart so far from thee, My God, my chief delight? Why are my tho'ts no more by day With thee, no more by night?

By per. Biglow & Main.

417 (1015)

1 Why is my heart so far from thee,
My God, my chief delight?
Why are my thoughts no more by day
With thee, no more by night?

2 Why should my foolish passions rove?
Where can such sweetness be
As I have tasted in thy love,
As I have found in thee?

3 When my forgetful soul renews
The savor of thy grace,
My heart presumes I cannot lose
The relish all my days.

4 But ere one fleeting hour is past,
The flattering world employs
Some sensual bait to seize my taste,
And to pollute my joys.

5 Trifles of nature or of art,
With fair deceitful charms,
Intrude upon my thoughtless heart,
And thrust me from thy arms.

6 Then I repent and vex my soul,
That I should leave thee so;
Where will those wild affections roll
That let a Saviour go!

7 Sin's promised joys are turned to pain,
And I am drowned in grief;
But my dear Lord returns again,
He flies to my relief.

8 Seizing my soul with sweet surprise,
He draws with loving bands;
Divine compassion in his eyes,
And pardon in his hands.

9 Wretch that I am to wander thus
In chase of false delight!
Let me be fastened to thy cross
Rather than lose thy sight.

10 Make haste, my days, to reach the goal,
And bring my heart to rest
On the dear center of my soul,
My God, my Saviour's breast. *Watts.*

418 (1021) C. M.

1 Now to thy praise, eternal King,
Be all my thoughts employed,
While of his precious truth I sing—
Cast down, but not destroyed.

2 Oft the united powers of hell
My soul have sore annoyed;
And yet I live, this truth to tell—
Cast down, but not destroyed.

3 In all the paths thro' which I've passed,
What mercies I've enjoyed!
And this shall be my song at last—
Cast down, but not destroyed.

4 When I in heaven with God appear,
There shall I him adore;
Destroyed shall be my sin and fear,
And I cast down no more. *Primitive.*

CONFLICTS AND DELIVERANCES.

BEVERLEY. C. M.
HALE.

1. My soul lies cleaving to the dust; Lord, give me life di-vine; From vain desires and ev-'ry lust Turn off these eyes of mine, Turn off these eyes of mine.

419 (1017)

1 My soul lies cleaving to the dust;
Lord, give me life divine;
From vain desires and every lust
Turn off these eyes of mine.

2 I need the influence of thy grace
To speed me in thy way,
Lest I should loiter in my race,
Or turn my feet astray.

3 Does not my heart thy precepts love,
And long to see thy face?
And yet how slow my spirits move
Without enlivening grace!

4 Then shall I love thy gospel more,
And ne'er forget thy word,
When I have felt its quickening power
To draw me near the Lord.
Watts.

420 (1019) C. M.

1 Dear Refuge of my weary soul,
On thee, when sorrows rise,
On thee, when waves of trouble roll,
My fainting hope relies.

2 To thee I tell each rising grief,
For thou alone canst heal;
Thy word can bring a sweet relief
For every pain I feel.

3 But O! when gloomy doubts prevail,
I fear to call thee mine;
The springs of comfort seem to fail,
And all my hopes decline.

4 Yet, gracious God, where shall I flee?
Thou art my only trust;
And still my soul would cleave to thee,
Though prostrate in the dust.

5 Thy mercy seat is open still,
Here let my soul retreat;
With humble hope attend thy will,
And wait beneath thy feet.
Mrs. Steele.

421 (1029) C. M.

1 Affliction is a stormy deep,
Where wave resounds to wave;
Though o'er my head the billows roll,
I know the Lord can save.

2 The hand that now witholds my joys,
Can re-instate my peace;
And he who bade the tempest roar,
Can bid the tempest cease.

3 In the dark watches of the night,
I'll count his mercies o'er;
I'll praise him for ten thousand past,
And humbly sue for more.

4 When darkness and when sorrow rose,
And pressed on every side;
The Lord has still sustained my steps,
And still has been my Guide.

5 Here will I rest, and build my hopes,
Nor murmur at his rod;
He's more than all the world to me,
My Health, my Life, my God!
Cotton.

170 CONFLICTS AND DELIVERANCES.

GOLDEN HILL. S. M.
Slow. — DAVISSON.

1. How sore a plague is sin, To those by whom 'tis felt: The Christian cries, "Unclean, un-clean!" E'en though 're - leased from guilt.

422 (1012) Rom. 7: 21.

1 How sore a plague is sin,
  To those by whom 'tis felt:
The Christian cries, "*Unclean, unclean!*"
  E'en though released from guilt.

2 O wretched, wretched man!
  What horrid scenes I view!
I find, alas! do all I can,
  That I can nothing do.

3 Of peace if I'm in quest,
  Or love my thoughts engage,
Envy and anger in my breast
  That moment rise and rage.

4 When for an humble mind
  To God I pour my prayer,
I look into my heart, and find
  That pride will still be there.

5 How long, dear Lord, how long
  Deliverance must I seek?
And fight with foes so very strong,
  Myself so very weak?

6 I'll bear th' unequal strife,
  And wage the war within;
Since death that puts an end to life,
  Shall put an end to sin.
                              Hart.

423 (733) S. M. Rom. 7: 19.

1 I WOULD, but cannot sing;
  Guilt has untuned my voice;
The serpent's sin-envenomed sting
  Has poisoned all my joys.

2 I know the Lord is nigh,
  And would but cannot pray;
For Satan meets me when I try,
  And frights my soul away.

3 I would, but can't repent,
  Though I endeavor oft;
This stony heart can ne'er relent,
  Till Jesus makes it soft.

4 I would, but cannot rest,
  In God's most holy will;
I know what he appoints is
  Yet murmur at it still.

5 O could I but believe!
  Then all would easy be;
I would, but cannot—Lord relieve;
  My help must come from thee.

6 But if indeed I would,
  Though I can nothing do,
Yet the desire is something good,
  For which my praise is due.

7 By nature prone to ill,
  Till thine appointed hour,
I was as destitute of will,
  As now I am of power.

8 Wilt thou not crown at length
  The work thou hast begun?
And with a will afford me strength,
  In all thy ways to run?
                           Newton.

CONFLICTS AND DELIVERANCES.

CONFLICT. L. M.   LEWIS.

1. I am a stranger here below, And what I am 'tis hard to know; I am so vile, so prone to sin, I fear that I'm not born again.

424 (1022)

1 I AM a stranger here below,
And what I am 'tis hard to know;
I am so vile, so prone to sin,
I fear that I'm not born again.

2 When I experience call to mind,
My understanding is so blind,
All feeling sense seems to be gone,
Which makes me fear that I am wrong.

3 I find myself out of the way,
My thoughts are often gone astray;
Like one alone I seem to be;
Oh! is there any one like me?

4 'Tis seldom I can ever see
Myself as I would wish to be;
What I desire, I can't attain;
From what I hate I can't refrain.

5 So far from God I seem to lie
Which makes me often weep and cry,
I fear at last that I shall fall;
For if a saint, the least of all.

6 I seldom find a heart to pray,
So many things come in my way;
Thus filled with doubts, I ask to know—
Come, tell me, is it thus with you?

7 So by experience do I know
There's nothing good that I can do;
I cannot satisfy the law,
Nor hope nor comfort from it draw.

8 My nature is so prone to sin,
Which makes my duty so unclean.

That when I count up all the cost,
Without free grace, I know I'm lost.

Primitive.

425 (1030) L. M.

1 AMIDST these various scenes of ills,
Each stroke some kind design fulfils;
And shall I murmur at my God,
When sovereign love directs the rod?

2 Peace, rebel thoughts! I'll not complain;
My Father's smiles suspend my pain;
Smiles, that a thousand joys impart,
And pour the balm that heals the smart.

3 Though Heaven afflicts. I'll not repine,
Each heartfelt comfort still is mine;
Comforts that shall o'er death prevail,
And journey with me through the vale.

4 Lord Jesus, smooth the rugged way,
And lead me to the realms of day,
To milder skies and brighter plains,
Where everlasting sunshine reigns.

426 (1053) L. M.

1 WHY should a son redeemed with blood
Born not of man, but born of God,
Feel an eternal war within,
'Twixt reigning grace and striving sin?

2 'Tis but to make him every day,
From self to Jesus turn away:
His very falls shall make him wise,
And teach him where his victory lies.

Ebenezer.

CONFLICTS.

CLARINGTON. 8s. D.

1. Constrain'd by their Lord to em-bark, And venture without him to sea,
   The sea son tem-pestu-ous and dark, How griev'd the dis-ci-ples must be!
   D.C.—They still were as safe as be-fore, And e-qual-ly un-der his care.

But though he re-main'd on the shore, He spent the night for them in pray'r;

427 (1026) John 6: 16-21.

2 We, like the disciples, are tossed
  By storms on a perilous deep;
  But cannot be possibly lost,
  For Jesus has charge of the ship.
  Though billows and winds are enraged,
  And threaten to make us their sport,
  This pilot his word has engaged
  To bring us in safety to port.

3 If sometimes we struggle alone,
  And he is withdrawn from our view,
  It makes us more willing to own
  We nothing without him can do:
  Then Satan our hopes would assail,
  But Jesus is still within call;
  And when our poor efforts quite fail,
  He comes in good time, and does all.

4 Yet, Lord, we are ready to shrink,
  Unless we thy presence perceive,
  O save us, we cry, or we sink:
  We would, but we cannot believe.
  The night has been long and severe;
  The winds and the seas are still high;
  Dear Saviour, this moment appear,
  And say to our souls, "It is I!"
  Newton.

428 (1035) 8s. D. Psa. 61: 2.

1 Encompassed with clouds of distress,
  And tempted all hope to resign,
  I pant for the light of thy face,
  That I in thy beauty may shine;
  Disheartened with waiting so long,
  I sink at thy feet with my load:
  All plaintive I pour out my song,
  And stretch forth my hands unto God.

2 Shine, Lord, and my terror shall cease;
  The blood of atonement apply:
  And lead me to Jesus for peace,
  The Rock that is higher than I:
  Speak, Saviour, for sweet is thy voice;
  Thy presence is fair to behold;
  I thirst for thy Spirit, with cries
  And groanings that cannot be told.

3 If sometimes I strive as I mourn,
  My hold of thy promise to keep,
  The billows more fiercely return,
  And plunge me again in the deep:
  While harassed and cast from thy sight,
  The tempter suggests with a roar,
  "The Lord hath forsaken thee quite;
  Thy God will be gracious no more."

4 Yet, Lord, if thy love hath designed
  No covenant blessing for me,
  Ah, tell me, how is it I find
  Some sweetness in waiting for thee?
  Almighty to rescue thou art,
  Thy grace is immortal and free;
  Lord, succor and comfort my heart,
  And make me live wholly to thee.
  Toplady.

COOK. 7s.

1. 'Tis my hap-pi-ness be-low, Not to live with-out the Cross;
But the Sav-iour's power to know, Sanc-ti-fy-ing ev-'ry loss.

429 (1032) 1 Pet. 1: 6, 7.

1 'Tis my happiness below,
   Not to live without the Cross;
   But the Saviour's power to know,
   Sanctifying every loss.

2 Trials must and will befall;
   But with humble faith to see
   Love inscribed upon them all,
   This is happiness to me.

3 Trials make the promise sweet;
   Trials give new life to prayer;
   Trials bring me to his feet,
   Lay me low, and keep me there.

4 Did I meet no trials here,
   No chastisement by the way,
   Might I not with reason fear,
   I should be a cast away?

5 Bastards may escape the rod,
   Sunk in earthly, vain delight;
   But the true-born child of God
   Must not, would not if he might.
   Cowper.

430 (1033) 7s. John 21: 16.

1 'Tis a point I long to know;
   Oft it causes anxious thought;
   Do I love the Lord or no?
   Am I his, or am I not?

2 If I love, why am I thus?
   Why this dull and lifeless frame?
   Hardly, sure, can they be worse
   Who have never heard his name.

3 Could my heart so hard remain,
   Prayer a task and burden prove,
   Every trifle give me pain,
   If I knew a Saviour's love?

4 When I turn my eyes within,
   All is dark, and vain, and wild;
   Filled with unbelief and sin,
   Can I deem myself a child?

5 If I pray, or hear, or read,
   Sin is mixed with all I do:
   You that love the Lord indeed,
   Tell me, is it thus with you?

6 Yet I mourn my stubborn will;
   Find my sin a grief and thrall:
   Should I grieve for what I feel,
   If I did not love at all?

7 Could I joy his saints to meet,
   Choose the ways I once abhorred,
   Find, at times, the promise sweet,
   If I did not love the Lord?

8 Lord, decide the doubtful case;
   Thou who art thy people's Sun,
   Shine upon thy work of grace,
   If it be indeed begun.

9 Let me love thee more and more,
   If I love at all, I pray:
   If I have not loved before,
   Help me to begin to-day.
   Newton

174. CONFLICTS AND DELIVERANCES.

HADDAM. H. M. — Dr. LOWELL MASON. 1792-1872

1. And must it, Lord, be so? And must thy children bear Such various kinds of wo, Such soul-perplexing fear? Are these the blessings we expect? Is this the lot of God's elect?

431 (1036) James 1: 12.

1 AND must it, Lord, be so?
  And must thy children bear
Such various kinds of wo,
  Such soul-perplexing fear?
Are these the blessings we expect?
Is this the lot of God's elect?

2 Boast not, ye sons of earth,
  Nor look with scornful eyes;
Above your highest mirth,
  Our saddest hours we prize;
For though our cup seems filled with gall,
There's something secret sweetens all.

3 How harsh soe'er the way,
  Dear Saviour, still lead on;
Nor leave us till we say,
  "Father, thy will be done:"
At most we do but taste the cup,
For thou alone hast drank it up.

4 Shall guilty man complain?
  Shall sinful dust repine?
And what is all our pain?
  How light compared with thine!
Finish, dear Lord, what is begun;
Choose thou the way, but still lead on.
Hart.

432 (1051) P. M.

1 JESUS! at thy command
  I launch into the deep,
And leave my native land,
  Where sin lulls all asleep:
For thee I would the world resign,
And sail to heaven with thee and thine.

2 Thou art my pilot wise:
  My compass is thy word:
My soul each storm defies,
  While I have such a Lord!
I trust thy faithfulness and power
To save me in the trying hour.

3 Though rocks and quicksands deep
  Through all my passage lie;
Yet Christ will safely keep
  And guide me with his eye:
My anchor hope shall firm abide,
And I each boisterous storm outride.

4 By faith I see the land—
  The port of endless rest
My soul, thy sails expand,
  And fly to Jesus' breast!
Oh, may I reach the heavenly shore,
Where winds and waves distress no more.

5 Whene'er becalmed I lie,
  And storms forbear to toss,
Be thou, dear Lord, still nigh,
  Lest I should suffer loss:
For more the treacherous calm I dread,
Than tempests bursting o'er my head.

6 Come, Holy Ghost! and blow
  A prosperous gale of grace;
Waft me from all below
  To heaven, my destined place!
Then, in full sail, my port I'll find,
And leave the world and sin behind.
Toplady.

CONFLICTS AND DELIVERANCES.

DUKE STREET. L. M. J. HATTON.

1. On Zi-on's glo-rious sum-mit stood A num'rous host, re-deem'd by blood;
They prais'd their King in strains di-vine; I heard the song, and strove to join.

433 (1040)

2 Here all who suffered sword or flame,
For truth, or Jesus' lovely name,
Shout victory now, and hail the Lamb,
And bow before the great I AM.

3 While everlasting ages roll,
Eternal love shall feast their souls;
And scenes of bliss for ever new,
Rise in succession to their view.

4 O sweet employ to sing and trace
Th' amazing heights and depths of grace;
And spend, from sin and sorrow free,
A blissful vast eternity!

5 O what a sweet exalted song,
When every tribe, and every tongue,
Redeemed by blood, with Christ appear,
And join in one full chorus there.

6 My soul anticipates the day,
Would stretch her wings and soar away,
To aid the song, a palm to bear,
And bow the chief of sinners there.
Kent.

434 (1050) L. M.

1 THOU only Sovereign of my heart,
My Refuge, my almighty Friend,
And can my soul from thee depart,
On whom alone my hopes depend?

2 Whither, ah! whither shall I go,
A wretched wanderer from my Lord?
Can this dark world of sin and wo
One glimpse of happiness afford?

3 Eternal life thy words impart,
On these my fainting spirit lives;
Here sweeter comforts cheer my heart
Than all the round of nature gives.

4 Let earth's alluring joys combine,
While thou art near, in vain they call;
One smile, one blissful smile of thine,
My dearest Lord, outweighs them all.
Mrs. Steele.

435 (1059) L. M.

1 WHEN God from sin's captivity
Set his afflicted people free,
Lost in amaze, their mercies seem
The transient raptures of a dream.

2 But soon their ransomed souls rejoice,
And mirth and music swell their voice,
Till foes confess, nor dare condemn,
"The Lord hath done great things for them."

3 They catch the strain and answer thus,
"The Lord hath done great things for us;
Whence gladness fills our hearts, and songs,
Sweet and spontaneous, wake our tongues."

4 Turn our captivity, O Lord!
As southern rivers, at thy word,
Bound from their channels, and restore
Plenty, where all was waste before.

5 Who sow in tears shall reap in joy;
Naught shall the precious seed destroy,
Nor long the weeping exiles roam,
But bring their sheaves rejoicing home.
Montgomery.

CONFLICTS AND DELIVERANCES.

WATCHMAN. 7s. D. Dr. LOWELL MASON. 1792-1872.

1. Jesus! lover of my soul, Let me to thy bosom fly,
While the raging billows roll, While the tempest still is nigh!
D.S.—the haven guide; Oh, receive my soul at last!

Hide me, O my Saviour! hide Till the storm of life is past; Safe into

436 (1052)

2 Other refuge have I none;
Hangs my helpless soul on thee;
Leave, ah! leave me not alone;
Still support and comfort me.
All my trust on thee is stayed;
All my help from thee I bring:
Cover my defenceless head
With the shadow of thy wing.

3 Thou, O Christ, art all I want;
More than all in thee I find;
Raise the fallen, cheer the faint,
Heal the sick, and lead the blind:

Just and holy is thy name,
I am all unrighteousness;
Vile and full of sin I am;
Thou art full of truth and grace.

4 Plenteous grace with thee is found—
Grace to pardon all my sin:
Let the healing streams abound;
Make and keep me pure within:
Thou of Life the fountain art!
Freely let me take of thee;
Spring thou up within my heart;
Rise to all eternity! C. Wesley.

MARTYN. 7s. D. S. B. MARSH. 1798-1854.

1. Jesus! lover of my soul, Let me to thy bosom fly,
While the raging billows roll, While the tempest still is nigh!
Hide me, O my Saviour! hide Till the storm of life is past;
D.C.—Safe into the haven guide; Oh, receive my soul at last.

CHRISTIAN EXPERIENCE.

IDUMEA. S. M.   DAVISSON.

1. Out of the depths of wo To thee, O Lord! I cry; Dark-ness sur-rounds me, but I know That thou art ev-er nigh.

437 (1060)

1 OUT of the depths of wo
  To thee, O Lord! I cry;
Darkness surrounds me, but I know
  That thou art ever nigh.

2 Then hearken to my voice,
  Give ear to my complaint;
Thou bidst the mourning soul rejoice,
  Thou comfortest the faint.

3 I cast my hope on thee,
  Thou canst, thou wilt forgive;
Wert thou to mark iniquity,
  Who in thy sight could live?

4 Glory to God above!
  The waters soon will cease:
For, lo! the swift returning dove
  Brings home the sign of peace.

5 Though storms his face obscure,
  And dangers threaten loud,
Jehovah's covenant is sure,
  His bow is in the cloud.   Montgomery

438 (1086) S. M. Psa. 66:16.

1 COME, ye that fear the Lord,
  And listen while I tell
How narrowly my feet escaped
  The snares of death and hell.

2 The flattering joys of sense
  Assailed my foolish heart,
While Satan, with malicious skill,
  Guided the poisonous dart.

3 I fell beneath the stroke,
  But fell to rise again;
My Lord for me laid down his life,
  And purged away my sin.

4 Darkness, and shame, and grief
  Oppressed my gloomy mind;
I looked around me for relief,
  But no relief could find.

5 At length to God I cried,
  He heard my plaintive sigh;
He heard, and instantly he sent
  Salvation from on high.

6 My drooping head he raised;
  My bleeding wounds he healed;
Pardoned my sins, and with a smile
  The gracious pardoned sealed.

7 Oh! may I ne'er forget
  The mercy of my God;
Nor ever want a tongue to spread
  His loudest praise abroad.   Stennett.

439 (1058) S. M.

1 THE Lord is on our side,
  His people now may say;
The Lord is on our side,—or we
  Had fallen a sudden prey.

2 Sin, Satan, Death, and Hell,
  Like fire, against us rose;
Then had the flames consumed us quick,
  But God repelled our foes. Montgomery.

CHRISTIAN EXPERIENCE.

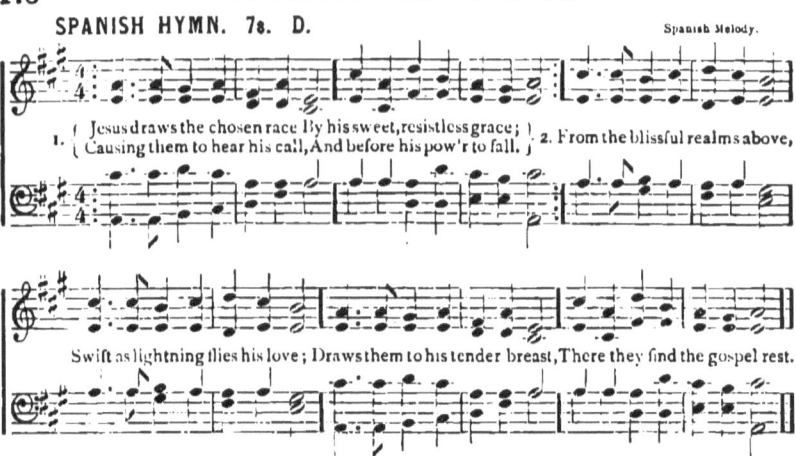

SPANISH HYMN. 7s. D. — Spanish Melody.

1. Jesus draws the chosen race By his sweet, resistless grace; Causing them to hear his call, And before his pow'r to fall. 2. From the blissful realms above, Swift as lightning flies his love; Draws them to his tender breast, There they find the gospel rest.

440 (1061) Jer. 21: 3.

1 JESUS draws the chosen race
By his sweet, resistless grace;
Causing them to hear his call,
And before his power to fall.

2 From the blissful realms above,
Swift as lightning flies his love;
Draws them to his tender breast,
There they find the gospel rest.

3 Then how eagerly they move
In the happy paths of love!
How they glory in the Lord,
Pleased with Jesus' sacred word!

4 When the Lord appears in view,
Old things cease, and all is new:
Love divine o'erflows the soul,
Love doth every sin control.
Burnham.

441 (1092) 7s. D.

1 PEOPLE of the living God,
I have sought the world around,
Paths of sin and sorrow trod,
Peace and comfort nowhere found.

2 Now to you my spirit turns,
Turns, a fugitive unblest;
Brethren, where your altar burns,
O receive me into rest!

3 Lonely I no longer roam,
Like the cloud, the wind, the wave;
Where you dwell shall be my home,
Where you die shall be my grave.

4 Mine the God whom you adore,
Your Redeemer shall be mine;
Earth can fill my soul no more,
Every idol I resign.
Montgomery.

442 (1034) 7s. D. Rev. 22: 20.

1 WHEN shall all my sorrows end?
When my days of mourning cease?
When shall I to Christ ascend?
Only place of happiness.

2 Thirsting, panting after home,
Longing for that happy day;
Still I cry, "My Saviour, come!
Come, Lord Jesus, come away."

3 See! what tribulations rise;
Earth and sin beset me round;
Sorrows, trickling from my eyes,
Moisten all the weary ground.

4 Lord, thy pardoning love reveal;
Let my cry ascend thy ears;
Sin, alas! I deeply feel!
Sin! but ah! thy blood appears!

5 Blood, that answers every claim,
Tells me, Jesus died for me:
Then, in his delightful name,
Sin's subdued, and I am free!
Langley.

CHRISTIAN EXPERIENCE.

NEW BRITAIN. C. M.   AARON CHAPIN.

1. O that the Lord would guide my ways To keep his stat-utes still!
O that my God would grant me grace To know and do his will!

443 (1046)

1 O THAT the Lord would guide my ways
To keep his statutes still!
O that my God would grant me grace
To know and do his will!

2 O send thy Spirit down to write
Thy law upon my heart!
Nor let my tongue indulge deceit,
Nor act the liar's part.

3 From vanity turn off my eyes;
Let no corrupt design,
Nor covetous desires arise
Within this soul of mine.

4 Order my footsteps by thy word,
And make my heart sincere;
Let sin have no dominion, Lord,
But keep my conscience clear.

5 My soul hath gone too far astray,
My feet too often slip;
Yet since I've not forgot thy way,
Restore thy wandering sheep.

6 Make me to walk in thy commands,
'Tis a delightful road;
Nor let my head, or heart, or hands,
Offend against my God.
Watts.

444 (1064) C. M. 2. Cor. 12: 9.

1 GRACE, like a fountain, ever flows,
Fresh succors to renew;
The Lord my wants and weakness knows,
My sins and sorrows, too.

2 He sees me often overcome,
And pities my distress;
And bids affliction drive me home,
To anchor on his grace.

3 'Tis he directs my doubtful ways,
When dangers line the road:
Here I my Ebenezer raise,
And trust the gracious God.
Montgomery.

445 (1066) C. M. 1 Peter 2:7.

1 EXCEEDING precious is my Lord,
His love divinely free!
And sure his name doth health afford
To sickly souls like me.

2 It cheers a debtor's gloomy face,
Unbolts his prison door;
It brings amazing stores of grace
To feed the gospel poor.

3 And if with lively faith we view
His dying toil and smart,
And hear him say, it was for you,
This breaks the stony heart.

4 An heavenly joy his words convey,
The bowels strangely move:
We blush, and melt, and faint away,
Quite overwhelmed with love.

5 In such sweet posture let me lie,
And wet thy feet with tears,
Till joined with saints above the sky,
I tune my harp with theirs.
Berridge.

CHRISTIAN EXPERIENCE.

PALESTRINA. C. M. G. P. A. PALESTRINA. 1524-1594

1. 'Twas in the night, when troub-les came, I sought, my God, for thee;
But found no ref-uge in that name, That once sup-port-ed me.

446 (1083)

1 'Twas in the night, when troubles came,
  I sought, my God, for thee;
But found no refuge in that name,
  That once supported me.

2 I sought thee, but I found thee not,
  For all was dark within;
Thy tender mercy I forgot,
  To me, when dead in sin.

3 I saw no day-star in the skies,
  Wrapped in perpetual gloom,
I said, "When will that sun arise
  That shall my soul illume?"

4 With cords of his eternal love,
  'Twas thus my soul he drew,
And taught my faithless heart to prove
  His oath and promise true.

5 The path was rugged to my feet,
  Yet still I followed thee;
Went often to my mercy seat,
  With—"God, remember me."

6 At length my Sun's refulgent beam
  Through the dark cloud appeared;
My night of wo was like a dream,
  My soul was blessed and cheered.

447 (1085) C. M. Job 29: 2.

1 Sweet was the time when first I felt
  The Saviour's pardoning blood
Applied to cleanse my soul from guilt,
  And bring me home to God.

2 Soon as the morn the light revealed,
  His praises tuned my tongue;
And, when the evening shades prevailed,
  His love was all my song.

3 In vain the tempter spread his wiles,
  The world no more could charm:
I lived upon my Saviour's smiles,
  And leaned upon his arm.

4 In prayer my soul drew near the Lord,
  And saw his glory shine;
And when I read his holy word,
  I called each promise mine.

5 Then to his saints I often spoke
  Of what his love had done;
But now my heart is almost broke,
  For all my joys are gone.

6 Now when the evening shade prevails,
  My soul in darkness mourns;
And when the morn the light reveals,
  No light to me returns.

7 My prayers are now a chattering noise,
  For Jesus hides his face!
I read, the promise meets my eyes,
  But will not reach my case.

8 Now Satan threatens to prevail,
  And make my soul his prey;
Yet, Lord, thy mercies cannot fail,
  O, come without delay! Newton.

CHRISTIAN EXPERIENCE.

MARLOW. C. M. — Rev. John Chetham

1. O Lord, how lovely is thy name, How faithful is thy heart! To-day and yesterday the same, And always kind thou art!

448 (1068).

1 O Lord, how lovely is thy name,
  How faithful is thy heart!
  To-day and yesterday the same,
  And always kind thou art!

2 No change of mind the Saviour knows,
  A true and constant friend!
  Where once the Lord his love bestows,
  He loves unto the end!

3 He well remembers we are flesh,
  At best a bruised reed;
  And fainting souls he will refresh,
  And well supply their need.

4 No danger can thy soul await,
  While resting on this rock;
  The winds may blow, the waves may beat,
  But he sustains the shock.

5 Dear Jesus, let me always rest
  Within thy arms divine;
  Thy daily care, to make me blest;
  To love and call thee mine.

449 (1084) C. M.

1 I waited patient for the Lord,
  Who bowed to hear my cry;
  He made me rest upon his word;
  He brought salvation nigh.

2 He raised me from a horrid pit,
  Where mourning long I lay,
  And from my bonds released my feet,
  Deep bonds of miry clay.

3 Firm on a rock he made me stand,
  And taught my cheerful tongue
  To praise the wonders of his hand,
  In a new thankful song.

4 I'll spread his works of grace abroad;
  The saints with joy shall hear,
  How I was brought to trust in God,
  My only hope and fear.

5 How many are thy thoughts of love!
  Thy mercies, Lord, how great!
  We have not words nor hours enough
  Their numbers to repeat.

6 When I'm afflicted, poor, and low,
  And light and peace depart,
  My God beholds my heavy wo,
  And bears me on his heart.
  Watts.

450 (1089) C. M.

1 When from the precepts to the cross
  The humble sinner turns,
  His brightest deeds he counts but dross,
  And o'er his vileness mourns.

2 God on the table of his heart
  Inscribes his love and fear;
  He loves the law in every part,
  But takes no refuge there.

3 Thus gospel, law, and justice, too,
  Unite to set him free;
  Reflect, my soul, admire and view
  What God hath done for thee.
  Kent.

CHRISTIAN EXPERIENCE.

GANGES. C. P. M. — S. CHANDLER.

1. Let Zion, in her songs, record The honors of her dying Lord,
Triumphant over sin: How sweet the song there's none can say,
But he whose sins are wash'd away, Who feels the same with-in.

451 (1065) 8.8.6

1 LET Zion, in her songs, record
The honors of her dying Lord,
  Triumphant over sin:
How sweet the song there's none can say,
But he whose sins are washed away,
  Who feels the same within.

2 We claim no merit of our own,
But, self-condemned before thy throne,
  Our hopes on Jesus place;
In heart, in lip, in life depraved,
Our theme shall be a sinner saved,
  And praise redeeming grace.

3 We'll sing the same while life shall last
And when, at the Archangel's blast,
  Our sleeping dust shall rise,
Then, in a song for ever new,
The glorious theme we'll still pursue,
  Throughout the azure skies.

4 Prepared of old, at God's right hand,
Bright everlasting mansions stand,
  For all the blood-bought race:
And till we reach those seats of bliss,
We'll sing no other song but this—
  A sinner saved by grace!
  Kent.

452 (1265) 8.8.6.

1 WHEN thou, my righteous Judge, shalt
  To take thy ransomed people home,[come
    Shall I among them stand?
Shall such a worthless worm as I,
Who sometimes am afraid to die,
    Be found at thy right hand?

2 I love to meet among them now,
Before thy gracious feet to bow,
    Though vilest of them all:
But can I bear the piercing thought?
What if my name should be left out,
    When thou for them shalt call!

3 Prevent, prevent it by thy grace;
Be thou, dear Lord, my hiding-place,
    In that most solemn day;
Thy pardoning voice, O let me hear,
And still my unbelieving fear;
    Nor let me fall, I pray.

4 Let me among thy saints be found
Whene'er th'Archangel's trump shall
    To see thy smiling face; [sound,
Then loudest of the crowd I'll sing,
While heaven's resounding mansions ring
    With shouts of sovereign grace.
  Lady Huntington

THIS WORLD IS POOR. C. M. 51.

GRAMBLING. Arr. by H. P. MAIN.

1. This world is poor from shore to shore, And like a baseless vision: Its loft-y domes and brilliant ore, Its gems and crowns are vain and poor; There's nothing rich but heaven.

453 (1093)

2 Empires decay, and nations die,
　Bright hopes to winds are given;
The vernal flowers in ruin lie,
Death conquers all below the sky;
　There's nothing lives but heaven.

3 A pilgrim stranger here I roam;
　From place to place I'm driven;

My friends are gone, and I'm in gloom,—
The earth is all a lonely tomb,—
I have no home but heaven.

4 The clouds disperse, the light appears,
　My sins are all forgiven!
Triumphant grace has quelled my fears;
Roll on, thou Sun,—fly swift, my years,—
I'm on my way to heaven. Charles Giles.

TAPPAN. P. M.

GEO. KINGSLEY.

1. There is an hour of peaceful rest, To mourning wan-d'rers giv'n; There is a joy for souls distress'd, A balm for ev-'ry wounded breast —'Tis found above— in heav'n.

454

2 There is a home for weary souls,
　By sin and sorrow driven;
When tossed on life's tempestuous shoals,
Where storms arise and ocean rolls,
And all is dark—but heaven.

3 Where faith lifts up her cheerful eye
To brighter prospects given;

And views the tempest passing by,
And evening shadows quickly fly,
And all serene—in heaven.

4 There fragrant flowers immortal bloom,
　And joys supreme are given;
There joys divine, disperse the gloom;
Beyond the confines of the tomb
Appears the dawn of heaven. Tappan.

CHRISTIAN EXPERIENCE.

UXBRIDGE. L. M. Dr. LOWELL MASON. 1792-1872.

1. What jarring natures dwell within— Immortal life, remaining sin! Nor can this reign, nor that prevail, Though each by turns my heart assail.

455 (1077)

1 WHAT jarring natures dwell within—
Immortal life, remaining sin!
Nor can this reign, nor that prevail,
Though each by turns my heart assail.

2 Now I complain, and groan, and die;
Now raise my songs of triumph high;
Sing a rebellious passion slain,
Or mourn to feel it live again.

3 One happy hour beholds me rise,
Borne upward to my native skies,
While faith assists my soaring flight
To realms of joy and worlds of light.

4 Scarce a few hours or minutes roll,
Ere earth reclaims my captive soul;
I feel its sympathetic force,
And headlong urge my downward course.

5 How short the joys thy visits give!
How long thine absence, Lord, I grieve;
What clouds obscure my rising sun,
Or intercept its rays at noon!

6 Again the Spirit lifts his sword,
And power divine attends the word;
I feel the aid its comforts yield,
And vanquished passions quit the field.

7 Great God, assist me through the fight,
Make me triumphant in thy might;
Thou the desponding heart can raise;
The victory mine, be thine the praise.
Cruttenden.

456 (1080) L. M.

1 OH! that my soul, as heretofore,
Could with delight and love explore
Those sacred sweets, in Jesus' name,
That once my raptured soul o'ercame.

2 Once I beheld his lovely face,
As full of truth, and full of grace;
Ten thousand thousand suns were dim
In lustre, then, compared with him.

3 With his delights my soul was cheered,
With rapture then his voice I heard;
The words he spake were sweet to me,
'Twas—"Sinner, I have loved thee."

4 But now those golden hours are fled,
My spirit mourns, with sorrow fed;
His promise in his word I see,
But fear, alas! 'tis not for me.

5 Why should a child whom thou hast blest,
In darkness walk, and find no rest; [
Feel unbelief, that cruel foe,
From whence all other evils flow?

6 Oh, that my Sun, with cheering ray,
Would chase those shades of night away;
Then shall my soul arise and sing
The healing virtue of his wing.
Sonnets.

CHRISTIAN EXPERIENCE. 185

STAR OF BETHLEHEM. L. M. D.
JAMES MILLAR. 1754.

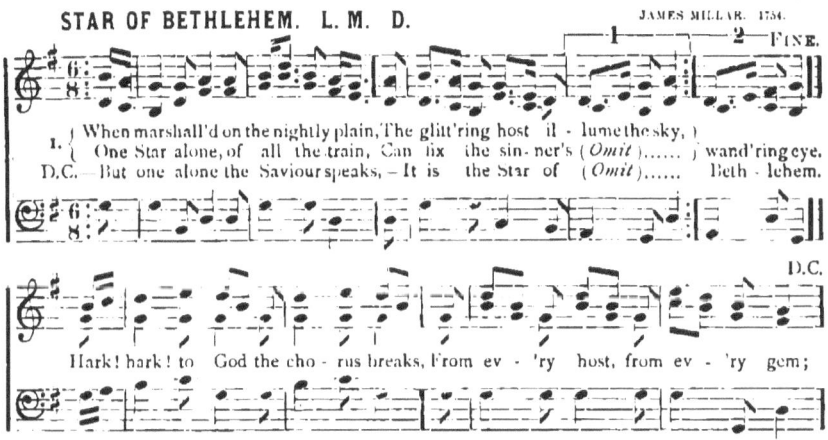

1. When marshall'd on the nightly plain, The glitt'ring host illume the sky,
   One Star alone, of all the train, Can fix the sinner's (*Omit*)...... wand'ring eye.
   D.C. But one alone the Saviour speaks,— It is the Star of (*Omit*)...... Beth-lehem.

Hark! hark! to God the cho-rus breaks, From ev-'ry host, from ev-'ry gem;

457 (1087)

1 WHEN marshalled on the nightly plain,
   The glittering host illume the sky,
   One Star alone, of all the train,
   Can fix the sinner's wandering eye.
   Hark! hark! to God the chorus breaks,
   From every host, from every gem;
   But one alone the Saviour speaks,—
   It is the Star of Bethlehem.

2 Once on the raging seas I rode,
   The storm was loud, the night was dark,
   The ocean yawned, and rudely blowed
   The wind that tossed my foundering bark
   Deep horror then my vitals froze,
   Death-struck, I ceased the tide to stem,
   When suddenly a star arose,
   It was the Star of Bethlehem.

3 It was my Guide, my Light, my All,
   It bade my dark forebodings cease;
   And through the storm and danger's thrall,
   It led me to the port of peace.
   Now safely moored, my perils o'er,
   I'll sing, first in night's diadem,
   For ever and for ever more,
   The Star, the Star of Bethlehem!
   Henry Kirke White.

458 (1088) L. M.

1 WHY, mourning soul, why flow these tears?
   Why thus indulge thy doubts and fears?
   Look to thy Saviour on the tree,
   Who bore the load of guilt for thee.

2 Then cease thy sorrows, banish grief,
   Though thou of sinners art the chief;
   The wounds that make poor sinners grieve,
   Are healed when they in Christ believe.

3 Whom Jesus wounds, he wounds to heal—
   Oh! 'tis a mercy thus to feel:
   There's none can mourn while dead in sin;
   Thine are the marks of life within.

4 Be of good cheer, on him rely,
   He'll pass the great transgressions by,
   And guide thee safely by his hand,
   Till thou shalt reach the heavenly land.
   Dobell.

459 (1097) L. M. Tit 2: 10-13.

1 So let our lips and lives express
   The holy gospel we profess,
   So let our works and virtues shine,
   To prove the doctrine all divine.

2 Thus shall we best proclaim abroad
   The honors of our Saviour-God;
   When the salvation reigns within,
   And grace subdues the power of sin.

3 Our flesh and sense must be denied,
   Passion and envy, lust and pride;
   While justice, temperance, truth and love,
   Our inward piety approve.

4 Religion bears our spirits up,
   While we expect that blessed hope,
   The bright appearance of the Lord,
   And faith stands leaning on his word.
   Watts.

186 BAPTISM.

RESTORATION. 8s. & 7s.
CARHOT. 1821. Arr. by WM. HAUSER, M. D.

1. Humble souls, who seek salvation Thro' the Lamb's redeeming blood, Hear the voice of revelation, Tread the path that Jesus trod;

460 (1108) Acts 2: 38; 22: 16.

1 HUMBLE souls, who seek salvation
Through the Lamb's redeeming blood,
Hear the voice of revelation,
Tread the path that Jesus trod;

2 Follow him, your only Saviour,
In his mighty name confide;
In the whole of your behavior,
Own him for your sovereign guide.

3 Hear the blessed Redeemer call you;
Listen to his gracious voice;
Dread no ills that can befall you,
While you make his ways your choice.

4 Jesus says, "Let each believer
Be baptized in my name;"
He himself, in Jordan's river,
Was immersed beneath the stream.

5 Plainly here his footsteps tracing,
Follow him without delay;
Gladly his command embracing;
Lo! your Captain leads the way.

6 View the rite with understanding,
Jesus' grave before you lies;
Be interred at his commanding:
After his example rise.
Fawcett.

461 (1150) Tune.—MARTYN, page 176. 7s.

1 CHRISTIANS, if your hearts be warm,
Ice and snow can do no harm;
If by Jesus you are prized,
Rise, believe, and be baptized.

2 Jesus drank the gall for you;
Bore the curse for sinners due;
Children, prove your love to him,
Never fear the frozen stream.

3 Never shun the Saviour's cross,
All on earth is worthless dross;
If the Saviour's love you feel,
Let the world behold your zeal.
Leland.

462 (1145) L. M.

1 COME, all ye sons of grace, and view
Your bleeding Saviour's love to you,
Behold him sink with heavy woes,
And give his life to save his foes.

2 When you behold the sacred wave,
You see the emblem of his grave;
Come, all who would his laws obey,
And view the place where Jesus lay.

3 When you ascend above the flood,
Then call to mind the rising God;
Ye saints, lift up your joyful eyes,
Exulting see your Saviour rise.

4 Ye too are buried with your Lord,
Who in the water own his word,
And joyfully behold therein
An emblem of your death to sin.

5 Fresh from the stream and filled with love, [
Far from the tents of sin remove;
Nobly from strength to strength proceed,
And rise to every righteous deed. Godwin.

BAPTISM. 187

WINDHAM. L. M.   DANIEL READ. 1757-1836.

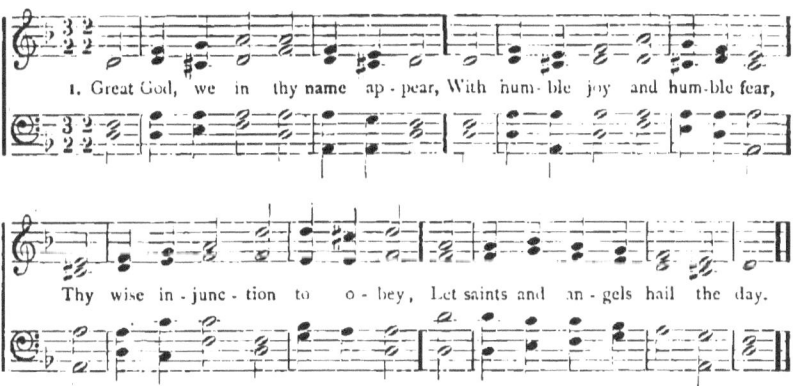

463 (1115) Matt. 11: 29.

1 GREAT God, we in thy name appear,
With humble joy and humble fear,
Thy wise injunction to obey;
Let saints and angels hail the day.

2 Great things, O everlasting Son,
Great things for us thy grace hath done;
Constrained by thy almighty love,
Our willing feet to meet thee move.

3 Here at the water side we stand,
Obedient to thy great command:
The liquid stream is full in view,
And thy sweet voice commands us through.

4 The Word, the Spirit, and the Bride,
Must not command and be denied;
Was not the Lord, who came to save,
Baptized in such a liquid grave?

5 Thus we, dear Saviour, own thy name;
Are buried with thee in the stream;
Then to thy table let us come,
And dwell in Zion as our home.
Fellows.

464 (1119) L. M.

1 COME, Holy Spirit, dove divine,
On these baptismal waters shine,
O teach our hearts, in highest strain,
To praise the Lamb for sinners slain.

2 We love thy name, we love thy laws,
We joyfully embrace thy cause;
We love thy cross, the shame, the pain,
O Lamb of God, for sinners slain!

3 We're plunged beneath the mystic flood;
Oh, plunge us in thy cleansing blood;
We die to sin, and seek a grave
With thee beneath the yielding wave.

4 And as we rise with thee to live,
O let the Holy Spirit give
The sealing unction from above,
The breath of life, the fire of love!
Judson.

465 (1151) L. M.

1 JESUS, behold thy children here
Met in thy name, do thou draw near
Remember Jordan, dearest Lord,
And gracious influence now afford.

2 Thy footsteps, O incarnate God,
Direct us in this pleasant road;
Nor would we e'er forsake this way,
Whatever friends or foes may say.

3 Though we this watery grave descend,
We on thy death alone depend,
And while ascending up again,
Thy resurrection would proclaim.

4 Thus in a figure here we see
The gospel's glorious mystery;
Christ dead and buried, raised again,
And all to save rebellious men.

5 In memory of this blessed theme,
We thus react this solemn scene,
And so proclaim to dying man,
Our only hope in Christ the Lamb.

BAPTISM.

BAPTISM. C. M.
WM. DOUGLAS 1871.

1. Thus was the great Redeemer plung'd In Jordan's swelling flood, To show he must be soon bap-tiz'd, In tears, and sweat, and blood.

466 (1118)

1 Thus was the great Redeemer plunged
In Jordan's swelling flood,
To show he must be soon baptized,
In tears, and sweat, and blood.

2 Thus was his sacred body laid
Beneath the yielding wave;
Thus was his sacred body raised
Out of the liquid grave.

3 Lord, we thy precepts would obey;
In thy own footsteps tread,
Would die, be buried, rise with thee,
Our ever-living Head.
Stennett.

467 (1120) C. M.

1 Meekly in Jordan's flowing stream
The great Redeemer bowed;
Bright was the glory's sacred beam,
That hushed the wondering crowd.

2 Thus God descended to approve
The deed that Christ had done;
Thus came the emblematic Dove,
And hovered o'er the Son.

3 So, blessed Spirit, come to-day
To our baptismal scene;
Ye thoughts of earth, be far away,
Ye bosoms, be serene.

4 This day we give to holy joy—
This day to heaven belongs;
Raised to new life, we will employ
In melody our tongues.
S. F. Smith.

468 (1123) C. M.

1 Buried beneath the yielding wave
The great Redeemer lies;
Faith views him in the watery grave,
And thence beholds him rise.

2 With joy we in his footsteps tread,
And would his cause maintain;
Like him be numbered with the dead,
And with him rise and reign.

3 Now, blest Redeemer, we to thee
Our grateful voices raise;
Washed in the fountain of thy blood,
Our lives shall be thy praise.
Beddome.

469 (1127) C. M. Gen. 21: 56.

1 In all my Lord's appointed ways,
My journey I'll pursue;
Hinder me not, ye much-loved saints,
For I must go with you.

2 Through floods and flames, if Jesus lead,
I'll follow where he goes;
Hinder me not, shall be my cry,
Though earth and hell oppose.

3 Through duty and through trials, too,
I'll go at his command;
Hinder me not, for I am bound
To my Immanuel's land.

4 And when my Saviour calls me home,
Still this my cry shall be,
Hinder me not—come, welcome death,
I'll gladly go with thee.
Ryland.

BAPTISM. 189

SALVATION. C. M. D. R. A. BOYD. 1817.

1. How great, how solemn is the work Which we attend to-day!
   Now for a holy, solemn frame, O God, to thee we pray.
2. O may we feel as once we felt, When pain'd and griev'd at heart,
   Thy kind, forgiving, melting look, Reliev'd our ev'ry smart.

470 (1130) Psa. 119: 32.

1 How great, how solemn is the work
 Which we attend to-day!
Now for a holy, solemn frame,
 O God, to thee we pray.

2 O may we feel as once we felt,
 When pained and grieved at heart,
Thy kind, forgiving, melting look,
 Relieved our every smart.

3 Let graces then in exercise
 Be exercised again;
And, nurtured by celestial power,
 In exercise remain.

4 Awake, our love, our fear, our hope,
 Wake, fortitude and joy;
Vain world, begone; let things above
 Our happy thoughts employ.

5 Whilst thee, our Saviour and our God,
 To all around we own;
Drive each rebellious rival lust,
 Each traitor, from the throne.

6 Instruct our minds, our wills subdue,
 To heaven our passions raise,
That hence our lives, our all, may be
 Devoted to thy praise.   Beddome.

471 (1152) C. M.

1 WHAT poor despised company
 Of travelers are these,
That's walking yonder narrow way,
 Along that rugged maze?

2 They all are of a royal line,
 They're children of a King,
Heirs of immortal crowns divine,
 And loud for joy they sing.

3 Why do they then appear so mean,
 And why so much despised?
Because of their rich robes unseen
 The world are not apprised.

4 Why some of them seem poor, distressed,
 And lacking daily bread?
Heirs of immortal wealth possessed,
 With hidden manna fed.

5 Why do they shun that pleasant path
 Which worldlings love so well?
Because it is the road to death—
 The certain way to hell.

6 Why do they walk the narrow road
 To Salem's happy ground?
Christ is the only way to God;
 No other can be found.   Maxwell.

BAPTISM.

BOYLSTON. S. M. — L. MASON.

1. Down to the sa-cred wave The Lord of life was led; And he who came, our souls to save, In Jordan bow'd his head.

472 (1122)

1 Down to the sacred wave
  The Lord of life was led;
And he who came, our souls to save,
  In Jordan bowed his head.

2 He taught the solemn way;
  He fix'd his holy rite;
He bade his ransomed ones obey,
  And keep the path in sight.

3 The Holy Ghost came down
  The baptism to approve;
The ordinance of Christ to crown,
  And stamp it with his love.

4 Dear Saviour, we will tread
  In thine appointed way;
Let glory o'er these scenes be shed,
  And smile on us to-day.
                        S. F. Smith.

473 (1124) S. M.

1 Come, and behold the place,
  Where once your Saviour lay;
Confess that he is Lord of all,
  And humble homage pay.

2 Laid in the watery grave,
  He quickly rose again;
Buried with him, we too shall rise,
  And endless life obtain.

3 Now may the Spirit crown,
  With tokens of his grace,

The solemn service of this day,
  And bid us go in peace.

474 (1147) S. M.

1 Thou great incarnate God!
  Behold thy children stand;
Warmed with the fire of love divine,
  They bow to thy command.

2 When buried with the Lord,
  May they his presence find,
Proving that pleasures from thy throne
  Are with obedience joined.

3 When rising from the wave,
  Lord, show thy lovely face;
May sacred joy from heaven descend,
  And glory fill the place.

4 Then may these happy saints
  In thy commandments run,
Till they shall reach the realms of bliss,
  And mount Emmanuel's throne.

5 There may they sit and sing
  The once baptized Lamb,
And make the courts of heaven resound
  With his beloved name.

6 With what ecstatic joy
  They'll tune the Saviour's praise!
While millions join the sacred theme,
  And swell the heavenly lays.

THE LORD'S SUPPER.

SHIRLAND. S. M.
S. STANLEY.

1. Let all our tongues be one To praise our God on high,
Who from his bo-som sent his Son To fetch us strangers nigh.

475 (1164) 1 John. 5: 6.

1 LET all our tongues be one
To praise our God on high,
Who from his bosom sent his Son
To fetch us strangers nigh.

2 Nor let our voices cease
To sing the Saviour's name;
Jesus, th' ambassador of peace,
How cheerfully he came!

3 It cost him cries and tears
To bring us near to God;
Great was our debt, and he appears
To make the payment good.

4 My Saviour's pierced side
Poured out a double flood;
By water we are purified,
And pardoned through the blood.

5 Infinite was our guilt,
But he our Priest atones:
On the cold ground his life was spilt,
And offered with his groans.

6 Look up, my soul, to him
Whose death was thy desert,
And humbly view the living stream
Flow from his breaking heart.
Watts.

476 (195) S. M. 1 Cor. 10: 16, 17.

1 JESUS commands his saints
To meet around his board;
Here pardoned rebels sit, and hold
Communion with their Lord.

2 For food he gives his flesh,
He bids us drink his blood;
Amazing favor! matchless grace
Of our descending God!

3 This holy bread and wine
Maintain our fainting breath,
By union with our living Lord,
And interest in his death.

4 Our heavenly Father calls
Christ and his members one;
We the young children of his love,
And he the first-born Son.

5 We are but several parts
Of the same broken bread;
One body with its several limbs,
But Jesus is the Head.

6 Let all our powers be joined
His glorious name to raise;
Pleasure and love fill every mind,
And every voice be praise.
Watts.

477 (1154) S. M. John 14: 21.

1 THE table now is spread;
We meet around the board;
Dear Jesus, bless the wine and bread,
And heavenly life afford.

2 O may the Lord appear,
With looks divinely mild,
And whisper in each humble ear,
"I love thee well, my child." *Berridge.*

THE LORD'S SUPPER.

WINDHAM. L. M. READ.

1. 'Twas on that dark, that doleful night, When pow'rs of earth and hell arose Against the Son of God's delight, And friends betray'd him to his foes;

478 (1159) 1 Cor. 11: 23.

1 'Twas on that dark, that doleful night,
When powers of earth and hell arose
Against the Son of God's delight,
And friends betrayed him to his foes;

2 Before the mournful scene began,
He took the bread, and blest, and brake.
What love through all his actions ran!
What wondrous words of grace he spake!

3 "This is my body, broke for sin;
Receive and eat the living food:"
Then took the cup, and blessed the wine;
"' Tis the new covenant in my blood."

4 "Do this (he cried) till time shall end,
In memory of your dying friend:
Meet at my table, and record
The love of your exalted Lord."
Watts.

479 (1162) L. M. John 16: 16.

1 Jesus is gone above the skies,
Where our weak senses reach him not;
And carnal objects court our eyes
To thrust our Saviour from our thought.

2 He knows what wandering hearts we have,
Apt to forget his lovely face;
And to refresh our minds he gave
These kind memorials of his grace.

3 The Lord of life this table spread
With his own flesh and dying blood;
We on the rich provision feed,
And taste the wine, and bless our God.

4 Let sinful sweets be all forgot,
And earth grow less in our esteem;
Christ and his love fill every thought,
And faith and hope be fixed on him.

5 Our eyes look upward to the hills
Whence our returning Lord shall come;
We wait thy chariot's awful wheels,
To fetch our longing spirits home.
Watts.

480 (1163) L. M. Gal. 6: 14.

1 When I survey the wondrous cross
On which the Prince of glory died,
My richest gain I count but loss,
And pour contempt on all my pride.

2 Forbid it. Lord, that I should boast,
Save in the death of Christ my Lord,
All the vain things that charm me most,
I sacrifice them to his blood.

3 See from his head, his hands, his feet,
Sorrow and love flow mingled down;
Did e'er such love and sorrow meet?
Or thorns compose so rich a crown?

4 His dying crimson like a robe
Spreads o'er his body on the tree,
Then I am dead to all the globe,
And all the globe is dead to me.

5 Were the whole realm of nature mine,
That were an offering far too small;
Love so amazing, so divine,
Demands my soul, my life, my all.
Watts.

THE LORD'S SUPPER.

HURSLEY. L. M.
W. H. MONK

1. The King of saints his table spreads for children in his courts below;
And while with them he sits and feeds Not one distressing thought they know.

481 (1157)

1 THE King of saints his table spreads
  For children in his courts below;
And while with them he sits and feeds
  Not one distressing thought they know.

2 His look enlivens every guest,
  Makes budding grace in blossom rise,
Rekindles love in every breast,
  And lifts the heart above the skies.

3 As morning suns refresh the earth,
  And make the blossoms open fair,
And draw the balmy fragrance forth,
  And scatter odors through the air;

4 So when the Sun of Righteousness
  Ariseth on the plants of grace,
They spring up into beauteous dress,
  And with their songs perfume the place.

O dearest, sweetest, heavenly friend,
  The spring of life and heavenly joys,
Some look afford, or message send,
  Or all devotion quickly dies.

482 (1166) L. M.

1 AT thy command, our dearest Lord,
  Here we attend thy dying feast;
Thy blood like wine adorns thy board,
  And thine own flesh feeds every guest.

2 Our faith adores thy bleeding love,
  And trusts for life in one that died:
We hope for heavenly crowns above
  Through a Redeemer crucified.

3 Let the vain world pronounce it shame,
  And fling their scandals on thy cause;
We come to boast our Saviour's name,
  And make our triumphs in his cross.

4 With joy we tell the scoffing age
  He that was dead has left his tomb,
He lives above their utmost rage,
  And we are waiting till he come.
                                  Watts.

483 (1168) L. M.

1 OUR spirits join t'adore the Lamb,
  O that our feeble lips could move
In strains immortal as his name,
  And melting as his dying love.

2 Was ever equal pity found?
  The Prince of Heaven resigns his breath,
And pours his life out on the ground
  To ransom guilty worms from death.

3 Rebels, we broke our Maker's laws;
  He from the threatening set us free;
Bore the full vengeance on his cross,
  And nailed the curses to the tree.

4 The law proclaims no terror now,
  And Sinai's thunder roars no more;
From all his wounds new blessings flow
  A sea of joy without a shore.
                                  Watts.

THE LORD'S SUPPER.

MEAR. C. M. Welsh Air. A. WILLIAMS. 1762.

1. Father of heav'n, almighty King, How wondrous is thy love, That worms of dust thy praise should sing, And thou their songs approve!

484 (1158)

1 Father of heaven, almighty King,
How wondrous is thy love,
That worms of dust thy praise should sing,
And thou their songs approve!

2 Since by a new and living way,
Access to thee is given,
Poor sinners may with boldness pray,
And earth converse with heaven.

3 Give each some token, Lord, for good;
And send the Spirit down
To feed us with celestial food,
The body of thy Son.

485 (1165) C. M. John 14: 17-22, 23.

1 How sweet and awful is the place
With Christ within the doors,
While everlasting love displays
The choicest of her stores!

2 Here every bowel of our God
With soft compassion rolls;
Here peace and pardon, through his blood,
Are food for dying souls.

3 While all our hearts and all our songs
Join to admire the feast,
Each of us cry with thankful tongues,
"Lord, why was I a guest?"

4 "Why was I made to hear thy voice,
And seek my heavenly home,
While thousands, left to their own choice,
Would rather starve than come?"

5 'Twas the same love that spread the feast,
That sweetly forced us in,
Or we, without a saving taste,
Had perished in our sin.
Watts.

486 (1170) C. M.

1 Jesus, O name divinely sweet!
How charming is the sound!
What joyful news! what heavenly sense
In that dear name is found!

2 Our souls all guilty, and condemned,
In hopeless fetters lay;
Our souls, with numerous sins depraved
To death and hell a prey.

3 Jesus, to purge away this guilt,
A willing victim fell,
And on his cross triumphant broke
The bands of death and hell.

4 Our foes were mighty to destroy,
He mighty was to save;
He died, but could not long be held
A prisoner in the grave.

5 Jesus! who mighty art to save,
Still push thy conquests on;
Extend the triumphs of thy cross,
Where'er the sun has shone.

6 O Captain of salvation! make
Thy power and mercy known;
Till crowds of willing converts come
And worship at thy throne. Stennett.

THE LORD'S SUPPER.

AVON. C. M. HUGH WILSON.

1. The cross of Christ in-spires my heart, To sing re-deem-ing grace; A-wake, my soul, and bear a part In my Re-deem-er's praise!

487 (1174)

1 THE cross of Christ inspires my heart,
   To sing redeeming grace;
   Awake, my soul, and bear a part
   In my Redeemer's praise!

2 Oh! who can be compared to him,
   Who died upon the tree?
   This is my dear delightful theme,
   That Jesus died for me.

3 When at the table of the Lord
   We humbly take our place,
   The death of Jesus we record,
   With love and thankfulness.

4 These emblems bring my Lord to view
   Upon the bloody tree;
   My soul believes and feels it true,
   That Jesus died for me.

5 His body broken, nailed and torn,
   And stained with streams of blood;
   His spotless soul was left forlorn,
   Forsaken of his God.

6 'Twas then his Father gave the stroke
   That justice did decree;
   All nature felt the dreadful shock,
   When Jesus died for me.

7 My guilt was on my surety laid,
   And therefore he must die;
   His soul a sacrifice was made
   For such a worm as I.

8 Was ever love so great as this?
   Was ever grace so free?
   This is my glory, joy and bliss,
   That Jesus died for me.
                                Primitive.

488 (1171) C. M.

1 LORD, at thy table I behold
   The wonders of thy grace;
   But most of all admire that I
   Should find a welcome place.

2 I that am all defiled with sin;
   A rebel to my God;
   I that have crucified his Son,
   And trampled on his blood.

3 What strange surprising grace is this,
   That such a soul has room!
   My Saviour takes me by the hand,
   My Jesus bids me come.

4 "Eat, O my friends," the Saviour cries,
   "The feast was made for you:
   For you I groaned, and bled, and died,
   And rose and triumphed, too."

5 With trembling faith, and bleeding
   Lord, we accept thy love: [hearts,
   'Tis a rich banquet we have had,
   What will it be above?

6 Ye saints below, and hosts of heaven,
   Join all your praising powers;
   No theme is like redeeming love,
   No Saviour is like ours.   Stennett.

BEFORE PREACHING.

ORTONVILLE. C. M.   Dr. T. HASTINGS. 1784-1872.

1. Once more we come before our God; Once more his blessing ask; O, may not du-ty seem a load, Nor wor-ship prove a task, Nor wor-ship prove a task.

489 (1182)   Cant. 4: 16.

1 ONCE more we come before our God;
Once more his blessing ask;
O, may not duty seem a load,
Nor worship prove a task.

2 Father, thy quickening Spirit send
From heaven, in Jesus' name,
To make our waiting minds attend,
And put our souls in frame.

3 May we receive the word we hear,
Each in an honest heart;
Hoard up the precious treasure there,
And never with it part.

4 To seek thee all our hearts dispose;
To each thy blessings suit;
And let the seed thy servant sows
Produce a copious fruit.

5 Bid the refreshing north wind wake;
Say to the south wind, Blow;
Let every plant the power partake,
And all the garden grow.

6 Revive the parched with heavenly show-
The cold with warmth divine; [ers;
And as the benefit is ours,
Be all the glory thine.
                         Hart.

490 (1184)   C. M.   Eph. 6: 14, 15.

1 LORD, fill thy servant's heart to-day
With pure seraphic fire,
And set his tongue at liberty,
And grant his soul's desire.

2 O may he preach the word of God
With energy and power;
May gospel blessings spread around,
Like a refreshing shower.

3 May God's eternal love and grace
Be sweetly felt within;
While he is preaching Christ the Lord,
Who took our curse and sin.

4 May burdened sinners lose their load,
And downcast souls rejoice;
May doubting souls believe to-day
They are Jehovah's choice.

5 May Christ be first, and Christ be last,
And Christ be all in all,
Who died to make salvation known,
And raise us from the fall.

6 O may thy servant now, to-day,
Proclaim salvation free;
As finished by the Son of God,
For such poor souls as we.
                         Herbert.

491 (1191)   L. M.

1 THE saints Emmanuel's portion are,
Redeemed by price, reclaimed by power;
His special choice, and tender care,
Owns them and guards them every hour.

2 He finds them in a barren land,
Beset with sins, and fears, and woes;
He leads and guides them by his hand,
And bears them safe from all their foes.
                         Newton.

BEFORE PREACHING.

PORTUGAL. L. M.

1. Come, dearest Lord, descend and dwell By faith and love in ev - 'ry breast;
Then shall we know, and taste, and feel The joys that can - not be express'd.

492 (1179) Eph. 3: 16, &c.

1 COME, dearest Lord, descend and dwell
By faith and love in every breast;
Then shall we know, and taste, and feel
The joys that cannot be expressed.

2 Come, fill our hearts with inward
   strength,
Make our enlarged souls possess,
And learn the height, and breadth, and
Of thine unmeasurable grace. [length

3 Now to the God, whose power can do
More than our thoughts or wishes know,
Be everlasting honors done
By all the church, thro' Christ his Son.
   Watts.

493 (1185) L. M.

1 Now, Lord, thy saving power display,
And magnify thy grace to-day;
All power is thine, in earth and seas,
Now from the grave dead sinners raise.

2 Make bare thy arm, thy power make
   known,
Let grace sit regent on the throne;
To it be endless honors paid,
For man's not half, but wholly dead.

3 He's far from God, conceived in sin,
Dark as chaotic night within;
A captive bound, his fetters show,
Say, Loose him, Lord, and let him go.

4 No voice but that which formed the
And gave the vast creation birth, [earth,
That bade the tempest cease to roar,
Can sinners dead to life restore.

5 Come, heavenly wind, celestial breath,
Awake the souls that sleep in death;
Their fetters break, of guilt and sin,
And gather, Lord, thy chosen in.

494 (1188) L. M.

1 WHEN Zion's sons, great God, appear,
In Zion's courts, for praise and prayer,
Then, in thy Spirit, deign to be
As one with those who worship thee.

2 Till thou shalt o'er the waters move,
'Twill but a barren season prove;
Lifeless and cold will be the song,
The preacher dull, the service long.

3 Without thy sovereign power, O Lord,
No sweets the gospel can afford;
No drops of heavenly love will fall
To cheer the weary, thirsty soul.

4 Winds, from the north and south, awake,
Take of the things of Jesus, take;
Diffuse thy kind celestial dew,
Bring pardon, peace, and healing, too.

5 Confirm the weak and feeble knees,
Unfold the gospel promises;
Thy truth impress on every mind;
May every heart a blessing find!

6 Then shall we count the season dear,
To those who speak, or those who hear;
And all conspire with sweet accord,
In hymns of joy, to praise the Lord.
   Kent.

AFTER PREACHING.

OLD HUNDRED. L. M.
L. BOURGEOIS.

1. Praise God, from whom all blessings flow; Praise him, all creatures here below; Praise him above, ye heav'nly host; Praise Fa-ther, Son, and Ho-ly Ghost.

495 (1306)

1 PRAISE God, from whom all blessings
Praise him, all creatures here below; [flow;
Praise him above, ye heavenly host;
Praise Father, Son, and Holy Ghost.
Thos Ken.

496 (1198) L. M.

1 DISMISS us with thy blessing, Lord!

Help us to feed upon thy word;
All that has been amiss forgive,
And let thy truth within us live.

2 Though we are guilty, thou art good;
Wash all our works in Jesus' blood;
Give every fettered soul release,
And bid us all depart in peace. *Hart*

ARLINGTON. C. M.
Dr. T. A. ARNE, 1710-1778.

1. Not un-to us, but thee a-lone, Blest Lamb, be glo-ry giv'n;
Here shall thy prais-es be be-gun, And car-ried on in heav'n.

497 (1195) Psa 115: 1.

2 The hosts of spirits now with thee
Eternal anthems sing:
To imitate them here, lo! we
Our hallelujahs bring.

3 Had we our tongues like them inspired,
Like theirs our songs should rise;
Like them we never should be tired,
But love the sacrifice.

4 Till we the veil of flesh lay down,
Accept our weaker lays;
And when we reach thy Father's throne

We'll give thee nobler praise.
Cennick.

498 (1200) C. M. Jer. 31: 14.

1 LORD, help us on thy word to feed;
In peace dismiss us hence;
Be thou, in every time of need,
Our Refuge and defense.

2 We now desire to bless thy name,
And in our hearts record,
And with our thankful tongues proclaim
The goodness of the Lord. *Hart.*

AFTER PREACHING.

499 (1196)

1 This God is the God we adore,
  Our faithful unchangeable Friend;
  Whose love is as large as his power,
  And neither knows measure nor end.

2 'Tis Jesus, the First and the Last,
  Whose Spirit shall guide us safe home;
  We'll praise him for all that is past,
  And trust him for all that's to come.
                                    Kent.

500 (1201) Heb 13: 20, 21.

2 Thanks we give and adoration,
  For thy gospel's joyful sound;
  May the fruits of thy salvation
  In our hearts and lives be found;
    May thy presence
    With us evermore abound.

3 So, whene'er the signal's given,
  Us from earth to call away,
  Borne on angel's wings to heaven,
  Glad to leave our cumbrous clay,
    May we ready,

  Rise and reign in endless day!
                                    Toplady.

501 (1302) 8s. & 7s. 2 Cor. 13: 14.

1 May the grace of Christ, our Saviour,
  And the Father's boundless love,
  With the Holy Spirit's favor,
  Rest upon us from above.
  Thus may we abide in union
  With each other and the Lord:
  And possess, in sweet communion,
  Joys which earth cannot afford. Newton.

200. WASHING THE SAINTS' FEET.
HEBRON. L. M. — Dr. Lowell Mason, 1792–1872.

1. If thou, dear Jesus, art my Lord, My Master, and my sovereign God, If well we say, when this we claim, Then teach us to revere thy name.

502 (1177) John 13: 13–16.

1 IF thou, dear Jesus, art my Lord,
My Master, and my sovereign God,
If well we say, when this we claim,
Then teach us to revere thy name.

2 If thou our Lord and Master meet,
Didst wash thy dear disciples' feet,
May we thy bright example see,
And meekly learn to follow thee.

3 If Christ, our Master and our Lord,
Has given the pattern and the word,
Shall we refuse his charge to keep,
By washing the disciples' feet?

503 (1178) L. M.

1 COME, brethren, ye who love the Lord,
And walk according to his word;
Let true humility abound,
And in his footsteps too be found.

2 When your dear Lord was here below,
He bowed to let his people know
How they should bow his saints to greet,
By washing one another's feet.

3 As in our Lord and Master, we
A meek, but clear example see;
We ought to follow, as 'tis meet,
And also wash each other's feet.

4 No servants should aspire to be
Above what in their Lord they see;
Enough, if we like him may greet,
And stoop and wash each other's feet.

5 If stronger brethren can't accord
In this, a precept of our Lord,
We'll not contend, but kindly greet;
Give us our herbs, give them their meat.

6 While to the letter we conform,
Regardless of contempt and scorn,
May we in spirit also meet,
And watch and cleanse each other's feet.

7 As through this wilderness we roam,
And onward march towards heaven our home,
Let not the filth of sin or earth
Defile our feet, or shame our birth.

8 Our feet with gospel grace well shod,
Dressed in the armor of our God,
In all our walk let us be seen
With hearts, and hands, and feet, all clean.

504 L. M.

1 GIVE me thy Spirit, O my God,
Then I can well all trials meet,
Deny myself, and all my pride,
And wash thy weakest servant's feet.

2 Give me thy Spirit, O my God,
Then shall I in thy footsteps trace,
And show to all who read thy word,
That I'm indeed renewed by grace.

3 Give me thy Spirit, O my God,
Then through my few remaining days
I'll yield obedience to thy word,
And as I go, I'll sing thy praise.

WASHING THE SAINTS' FEET.

BALERMA. C. M. — HUGH WILSON.

1. Jesus, by heav'nly hosts adored, The church's glorious Head,
With humble joy I call thee Lord, And in thy footsteps tread.

505

1 Jesus, by heavenly hosts adored,
The church's glorious Head,
With humble joy I call thee Lord,
And in thy footsteps tread.

2 Emptied of all thy greatness here,
While in the body seen,
Thou wouldst the least of all appear,
And minister to men.

3 A servant to thy servants thou,
In thy debased estate;
How meekly did thy goodness bow
To wash thy followers' feet.

4 I come, O God, to do thy will,
With Jesus in my view;
A servant to thy servants still,
My pattern I pursue.

5 The loving labor I repeat,
Obedient to his word,
And wash his dear disciples' feet,
And wait upon the Lord.

6 Shall I, a worm, refuse to stoop?
My fellow worm disdain?
I give my vain distinctions up,
Since Christ did wait on man.

506 C. M.

1 Did Christ the great example lead
For all his humble train,
In washing the disciples' feet
And wiping them again?

2 And did my Lord and Master say,
If I have washed your feet
Ye also ought to watch and pray,
And wash each other's feet?

3 In imitation of my Lord,
Who blood for me did sweat,
I yield unto his sacred word,
And wash the pilgrim's feet.

4 Yea, blessed Jesus, I like them,
Would Christians often meet;
The least of all the flock would be,
And wash his children's feet?

507 L. M.

1 Jesus, thou great exalted King,
Thy love, thy matchless love, I sing;
Descending from thy lofty seat,
I see thee wash thy servant's feet.

2 Here I behold at once displayed
The God in mortal flesh arrayed,
And an example set for me—
Set, Christian, by thy Lord, for thee.

3 Let us attend our Sovereign Lord,
And all his works and acts record;
"I have you an example set,
That you should wash each other's feet."

TIME AND ETERNITY.

KENTUCKY. S. M. INGALLS.

1. Great God! before thy throne We joyfully appear,
In songs to make thy glories known, And thus begin the year.

508 (1203) Psa. 52: 1.

1 GREAT God! before thy throne
We joyfully appear,
In songs to make thy glories known,
And thus begin the year.

2 What favors all divine!
What mercies shall we share!
What blessings all around us shine
To open this new year!

3 Indulgent goodness spares
And still preserves us here,
And bounty all divine prepares
Supplies for this new year.

4 Our follies past forgive;
Our souls divinely cheer;
And help us more on thee to live,
Dear Lord, in this new year.

5 Prepare us for thy will,
Whatever may appear;
And let thy loving-kindness still
Preserve us through the year.

6 Confirm our souls in thee,
In faith and holy fear;
And let a precious Jesus be
Our song through all the year.
Medley.

509 (1216) S. M.

1 THE day is past and gone,
The evening shades appear;
O may we all remember well
The night of death is near.

2 We lay our garments by,
Upon our beds to rest;
So death will soon disrobe us all
Of what we here possess.

3 Lord, keep us safe this night,
Secure from all our fears;
Thy angel guard us while we sleep,
Till morning light appears.

4 And when we early rise,
And view th' unwearied sun,
May we press on to reach the prize,
And after glory run.

5 And when our days are past,
And we from time remove,
O may we in thy bosom rest,
The bosom of thy love.
Leland.

510 (1213) C M.

1 LORD, what is man, poor feeble man,
Born of the earth at first!
His life a shadow, light and vain,
Still hasting to the dust.

2 O what is feeble, dying man,
Or any of his race,
That God should make it his concern
To visit him with grace!

3 That God who darts his lightnings
Who shakes the worlds above, [down,
And mountains tremble at his frown,
How wondrous is his love! Watts.

TIME AND ETERNITY. 203

KINGWOOD. C. P. M. HUMPHREYS.

511 (1218)

1 A FEW more days on earth to spend,
And all my toils and cares shall end,
And I shall see my God and friend,
  ' And praise his name on high :
No more to sigh or shed a tear,
No more to suffer pain or fear,
But God, and Christ, and heaven appear
  Unto the raptured eye.

2 Then, O my soul, despond no more,
The storm of life will soon be o'er,
And I shall find the peaceful shore
  Of everlasting rest.
O happy day! O joyful hour!
When freed from earth my soul shall tower,
Beyond the reach of Satan's power,
  To be for ever blessed.

3 My soul anticipates the day;
I'll joyfully the call obey
Which comes to summon me away
  To seats prepared above:
There I shall see my Saviour's face,
And dwell in his beloved embrace,
And taste the fulness of his grace,
  And sing redeeming love.

4 Adieu, ye scenes of noise and show,
And all this region here below,
Where naught but disappointments grow;
  A better world's in view.
My Saviour calls. I haste away;
I would not here for ever stay;
Hail! ye bright realms of endless day;
  Vain world, once more, adieu.

TIME AND ETERNITY.

JERUSALEM. C. M.
P. BURGMULLER. 1804—.

1. Time! what an empty va-por 'tis! And days how swift they are! Swift as an In - dian ar - row flies, Or like a shoot ing star, Or like a shoot ing star.

512 (1212)

1 TIME! what an empty vapor 'tis!
And days how swift they are!
Swift as an Indian arrow flies,
Or like a shooting star.

2 The present moments just appear,
Then glide away in haste,
That we can never say, "They're here,"
But only say, "They're past."

3 Our life is ever on the wing,
And death is ever nigh:
The moment when our lives begin,
We all begin to die.

4 Yet, mighty God, our fleeting days
Thy lasting favors share;
Yet with the bounties of thy grace
Thou load'st the rolling year.

5 'Tis sovereign mercy finds us food,
And we are clothed with love;
While grace sustains us in the road
That leads our souls above.

6 His goodness runs an endless round;
All glory to the Lord:
His mercy never knows a bound,
And be his name adored!
Watts.

513 (1211) C. M.

1 OUR days, alas! our mortal days,
Are short and wretched, too;
"Evil and few," the patriarch says,
And well the patriarch knew.

2 'Tis but at best a narrow bound
That heaven allows to men;
And pains and sins run through the round
Of three score years and ten.

3 Well, if ye must be sad and few,
Run on, my days, in haste;
Moments of sin, and months of wo,
Ye cannot fly too fast.

4 Let heavenly love prepare my soul,
And call me to the skies,
Where years of long salvation roll,
And glory never dies.
Watts

514 (1210) C. M.

1 GOD of my childhood and my youth,
The Guide of all my days,
I have declared thy heavenly truth,
And told thy wondrous ways.

2 Wilt thou forsake my hoary hairs,
And leave my fainting heart?
Who shall sustain my sinking years
If God, my strength, depart?

3 Let me thy power and truth proclaim
To the surviving age,
And leave a savor of thy name
When I shall quit the stage.

4 The land of silence and of death
Attends my next remove;
O may these poor remains of breath,
Teach the wide world thy love! *Watts*

TIME AND ETERNITY. 205

MANOAH. C. M.   From G. ROSSINI.

Teach me the measure of my days, Thou Maker of my frame!
I would survey life's narrow space, And learn how frail I am.

515 (1214)

1 TEACH me the measure of my days,
   Thou Maker of my frame!
I would survey life's narrow space,
   And learn how frail I am.

2 A span is all that we can boast,
   An inch or two of time;
Man is but vanity and dust
   In all his flower and prime.

3 See the vain race of mortals move
   Like shadows o'er the plain,
They rage and strive, desire and love,
   But all their noise is vain.

4 Some walk in honor's gaudy show,
   Some dig for golden ore,
They toil for heirs, they know not who,
   And straight are seen no more.

5 What should I wish or wait for then,
   From creatures, earth and dust?
They make our expectations vain,
   And disappoint our trust.

6 Now I forbid my carnal hope,
   My fond desires recall:
I give my mortal interest up,
   And make my God my all.   Watts.

516 (1215) C. M.

1 ETERNAL God, enthroned on high,
   Whom angel hosts adore,

Who yet to suppliant dust art nigh;
   Thy presence I implore.

2 O guide me down the steep of age,
   And keep my passions cool;
Teach me to scan the sacred page,
   And practise every rule.

3 My flying years time urges on
   What's human must decay;
My friends, my young companions gone,
   Can I expect to stay?

4 Can I exemption plead when death
   Projects his awful dart?
Can medicines then prolong my breath,
   Or virtue shield my heart?

5 Ah! no—then smooth the mortal hour,
   On thee my hope depends;
Support me with almighty power,
   While dust to dust descends.

6 Then shall my soul, O Gracious God,
   (While angels join the lay,)
Admitted to the blest abode,
   Its endless anthems pay,—

7 Through heaven, howe'er remote the bound,
   Thy matchless love proclaim,
And join the choir of saints that sound
   Their great Redeemer's name.

                         Rippon's Col.

206 DEATH.

RUSSIA. L. M. READ.

1. Why should we start and fear to die? What tim-'rous worms we mor-tals are!

Death is the gate of end-less joy, And yet we dread

- less joy, And yet we dread to en - ter there.
- ter there,

517 (1225)

2 The pains, the groans, and dying strife,
Fright our approaching souls away:
Still we shrink back again to life,
Fond of our prison and our clay.

3 O, if my Lord would come and meet,
My soul should stretch her wings in haste,
Fly fearless through death's iron gate,
Nor feel the terrors as she past.

4 Jesus can make a dying bed
Feel soft as downy pillows are,
While on his breast I lean my head,
And breathe my life out sweetly there.
Watts.

518 (1234) L. M.

1 Now let our souls, on wings sublime,
Rise from the vanities of time,
Draw back the parting veil, and see
The glories of eternity.

2 Born by a new celestial birth,
Why should we grovel here on earth?
Why grasp at transitory toys,
So near to heaven's eternal joys?

3 Shall aught beguile us on the road,
While we are walking back to God?
For strangers into life we come,
And dying is but going home.

4 Welcome, sweet hour of full discharge,
That sets our longing souls at large,
Unbinds our chains, breaks up our cell,
And gives us with our God to dwell.

5 To dwell with God, to feel his love,
Is the full heaven enjoyed above;
And the sweet expectation now
Is the young dawn of heaven below.
Gibbons.

DEATH. 207

REST. L. M. W. B. BRADBURY.

1. Asleep in Jesus! blessed sleep, From which none ever wake to weep! A calm and undisturb'd repose, Unbroken by the last of foes.

520 (1257)

2 Asleep in Jesus! O, how sweet,
To be for such a slumber meet!
With holy confidence to sing,
That death has lost his cruel sting.

3 Asleep in Jesus! peaceful rest,
Whose waking is supremely blest;
No fear, no wo shall dim that hour
That manifests the Saviour's power.

4 Asleep in Jesus! O, for me
May such a blissful refuge be;
Securely shall my ashes lie,
Waiting the summons from on high.

5 Asleep in Jesus! far from thee
Thy kindred and their graves may be;
But there is still a blessed sleep
From which none ever wake to weep.
Margaret Mackay.

521 (1233) L. M.

1 No, I'll repine at death no more,
But with a cheerful gasp resign
To the cold dungeon of the grave
These dying, withering limbs of mine.

2 Break, sacred morning, through the skies,
Bring that delightful, dreadful day;
Cut short the hours, dear Lord, and come,
Thy lingering wheels, how long they stay!

3 Our weary spirits faint to see
The light of thy returning face,
And hear the language of those lips
Where God has shed his richest grace.

4 Haste, then, upon the wings of love,
Rouse the redeemed, sleeping clay,
That we may join in heavenly joys,
And sing the triumph of the day. Watts.

519 (1252) L. M.

1 In hope of life eternal given,
Behold, a pardoned sinner dies;
A chosen blood-bought heir of heaven,
Called to his mansion in the skies.

2 He trod the shades of gloomy death,
Could set his zeal that God was true;
Finished his course, and kept the faith,
And died with glory full in view.

3 Methinks I see him now at rest,
In the bright mansion love ordained;
His head reclines on Jesus' breast,
No more by sin or sorrow pained.

4 Why should our eyes with sorrow flow,
Our bosoms heave the painful sigh!
When Jesus calls, the saint must go,
'Tis his eternal gain to die.

5 'Twas through the strength of Israel's King
He proved a conqueror when he fell;
'Tis to the praise of grace we sing,
Though of the dying saint we tell.

6 Fearless he entered death's cold flood,
In peace of conscience closed his eyes:
His only trust was Jesus' blood,
In sure and certain hope to rise.

208 DEATH

VARINA. C. M. D.
JOHANN C. H RINK. 1770-1843.

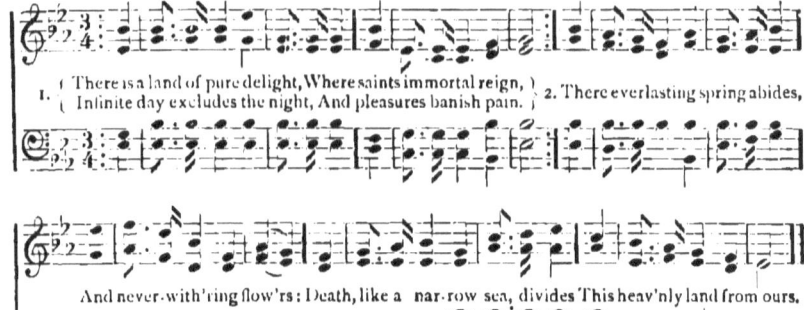

There is a land of pure delight, Where saints immortal reign, Infinite day excludes the night, And pleasures banish pain. 2. There everlasting spring abides, And never-with'ring flow'rs: Death, like a narrow sea, divides This heav'nly land from ours.

522 (1224)

1 THERE is a land of pure delight,
Where saints immortal reign,
Infinite day excludes the night,
And pleasures banish pain.

2 There everlasting spring abides,
And never-withering flowers:
Death, like a narrow sea, divides
This heavenly land from ours.

3 Sweet fields, beyond the swelling flood,
Stand dressed in living green;
So to the Jews old Canaan stood,
While Jordan rolled between.

4 But timorous mortals start and shrink
To cross this narrow sea,
And linger, shivering, on the brink,
And fear to launch away.

5 O! could we make our doubts remove,
Those gloomy doubts that rise,
And see the Canaan that we love,
With unbeclouded eyes:

6 Could we but climb where Moses stood,
And view the landscape o'er;
Not Jordan's stream nor death's cold flood
Should fright us from the shore. Watts.

523 (1223) C. M.

1 DEATH cannot make our souls afraid
If God be with us there;
We may walk through its darkest shade
And never yield to fear.

2 I could renounce my all below
If my Creator bid,
And run if I were called to go,
And die as Moses did.

3 Might I but climb to Pisgah's top,
And view the promised land,
My flesh itself would long to drop,
And pray for the command.

4 Clasped in my heavenly Father's arms,
I would forget my breath,
And lose my life among the charms
Of so divine a death. Watts.

524 (1222) C. M. Job 19: 25-27.

1 GREAT God, I own thy sentence just,
And nature must decay;
I yield my body to the dust,
To dwell with fellow-clay.

2 Yet faith may triumph o'er the grave,
And trample on the tomb;
My Jesus, my Redeemer lives,
My God, my Saviour comes.

3 The mighty Conqueror shall appear
High on a royal seat,
And Death, the last of all his foes,
Lie vanquished at his feet.

4 There shall I see thy lovely face
With strong immortal eyes,
And feast upon thy sovereign grace
With pleasure and surprise. Watts

DEATH.

CHINA. C. M.   TIMOTHY SWAN. 1754-1842.

1. Why do we mourn de-part-ing friends, Or shake at death's a-larms? 'Tis but the voice that Je-sus sends To call them to his arms.

525 (1228)

2 Are we not tending upward, too,
  As fast as time can move?
Nor would we wish the hours more slow,
  To keep us from our love.

3 Why should we tremble to convey
  Their bodies to the tomb?
There the dear flesh of Jesus lay,
  And left a long perfume.

4 The graves of all his saints he blessed,
  And softened every bed;
Where should the dying members rest,
  But with their living Head?

5 Thence he arose, ascended high,
  And showed our feet the way;
Up to the Lord our souls shall fly
  At the great rising-day.

6 Then let the last loud trumpet sound,
  And bid our kindred rise;
Awake, ye nations under ground,
  Ye saints, ascend the skies.   *Watts.*

526 (1227)   C. M.   2 Cor 5: 1, 5-8.

1 THERE is a house not made with hands,
  Eternal and on high;
And here my spirit waiting stands,
  Till God shall bid it fly.

2 Shortly this prison of my clay
  Must be dissolved and fall,
Then, O my soul, with joy obey
  Thy heavenly Father's call.

3 'Tis he, by his almighty grace,
  That forms thee fit for heaven,
And as an earnest of the place,
  Has his own Spirit given.

4 We walk by faith of joys to come,
  Faith lives upon his word;
But while the body is our home
  We're absent from the Lord.

5 'Tis pleasant to believe thy grace,
  But we had rather see;
We would be absent from the flesh,
  And present, Lord, with thee.   *Watts.*

527 (1245)   C. M.   Tit. 2: 13.

1 WHY should we shrink at death's cold
  Or dread the unknown way? [flood,
See, yonder rolls a stream of blood
  That bears the curse away!

2 Death lost his sting when Jesus bled:
  When Jesus left the ground,
Disarmed, the King of terrors fled,
  And felt a mortal wound.

3 And now his office is to wait
  Between the saints and sin:
A *porter* at the heavenly gate,
  To let the pilgrims in!

4 And though his pale and ghastly face
  May seem to frown the while;
We soon shall see the King of grace,
  And he'll for ever smile!

210 DEATH.

COLESHILL. C. M. — KIRBY 1590.

1. Death is no more a fright-ful foe; Since I with Christ shall reign, With joy I leave this world of wo: For me to die is gain.

528 (1246) Phil. 1: 21.

1 DEATH is no more a frightful foe;
Since I with Christ shall reign,
With joy I leave this world of wo:
For me to die is gain.

2 To darkness, doubts and fears adieu,
Adieu, thou world so vain!
Then shall I know no more of you:
For me to die is gain.

3 No more shall Satan tempt my soul;
Corruption shall be slain;
And tides of pleasure o'er me roll:
For me to die is gain.

4 Nor shall I know a Father's frown,
But ever with him reign,
And wear an everlasting crown:
For me to die is gain.

5 Sorrow for joy I shall exchange,
For ever freed from pain;
And in the heavenly regions range:
For me to die is gain.

6 Fain would my raptured soul depart,
Nor longer here remain,
But dwell, dear Jesus, where thou art:
For me to die is gain. *Horne.*

529 (1226) C. M.

1 DEATH may dissolve my body now,
And bear my spirit home:
Why do my minutes move so slow,
Nor my salvation come?

2 With heavenly weapons I have fought
The battles of the Lord,
Finished my course, and kept the faith,
And wait the sure reward.

3 God has laid up in heaven for me
A crown which cannot fade;
The righteous Judge, at that great day,
Shall place it on my head.

4 Nor hath the King of grace decreed
This prize for me alone;
But all that love, and long to see
Th' appearing of his Son. *Watts.*

530 (1229) C. M.

1 MY soul, come meditate the day,
And think how near it stands,
When thou must quit this house of clay,
And fly to unknown lands.

2 O could we die with those that die,
And place us in their stead,
Then would our spirits learn to fly,
And converse with the dead.

3 How we should scorn these clothes of flesh,
These fetters and this load!
And long for evening to undress,
That we may rest with God.

4 We should almost forsake our clay
Before the summons come,
And pray, and wish ourselves away
To our eternal home. *Watts.*

DEATH.

ATHENS. C. M. D. F. GIARDINI.

531 (1247) Psa. 101: 34.

1 WHEN languor and disease invade
This trembling house of clay,
'Tis sweet to look beyond our cage,
And long to fly away.

2 Sweet to look inward and attend
The whispers of his love;
Sweet to look upward to the place,
Where Jesus pleads above.

3 Sweet to look back, and see my name
In life's fair book set down;
Sweet to look forward, and behold
Eternal joys my own.

4 Sweet to reflect how grace divine
My sins on Jesus laid:
Sweet to remember that his blood
My debt of suffering paid.

5 Sweet in his righteousness to stand,
Which saves from second death;
Sweet to experience, day by day,
His Spirit's quickening breath.

6 Sweet in his faithfulness to rest,
Whose love can never end;
Sweet on his covenant of grace
For all things to depend.

7 Sweet in the confidence of faith
To trust his firm decrees;
Sweet to lie passive in his hands,
And know no will but his.

8 If such the sweetness of the streams,
What must the fountain be?
Where saints and angels draw their bliss
Immediately from thee!

Toplady.

532 (1249) C. M.

1 O HAPPY soul, who safely past,
Thy weary warfare here;
Arrived at Jesus' feet at last,
And ended all thy care!

2 No more shall sickness break thy rest,
Or pain create thee smart;
No more shall doubts disturb thy breast,
Or sin afflict thine heart.

3 No more the world on thee shall frown,
No longer Satan roar—
Thy man of sin is broken down,
And shall torment no more.

4 "Adieu, vain world," the spirit cries,
"All tears are wiped away;
My Jesus fills my cup with joys,
And fills it every day."

5 "A taste of love we have below,
To cheer a pilgrim's face;
But every saint must die to know
The feast of heav'nly grace."

6 "Delightful concord always reigns
In the fair realms above!
There hymns are sung in rapt'rous strains,
With ceaseless joy and love!"

Sonnets.

DEATH.

LITTLE MARLBOROUGH. S. M.
WILLIAMS.

1. And must this body die? This mortal frame decay?
And must these active limbs of mine Lie mould'ring in the clay?

533 (1232)

1 AND must this body die?
This mortal frame decay?
And must these active limbs of mine
Lie mouldering in the clay?

2 God, my Redeemer, lives,
And always, from the skies,
Looks down and watches all my dust,
Till he shall bid it rise.

3 Arrayed in glorious grace
Shall these vile bodies shine;
And every shape, and every face,
Look heavenly and divine.

4 These lively hopes we owe,
To Jesus' dying love;
We would adore his grace below,
And sing his power above.

5 Dear Lord, accept the praise
Of these our humble songs,
Till tunes of nobler sound we raise
With our immortal tongues.
Watts.

534 (1238) S. M. Matt. 21; 45.

1 PREPARE me, gracious God!
To stand before thy face!
Thy Spirit must the work perform,
For it is all of grace.

2 In Christ's obedience clothe,
And wash me in his blood;
So shall I lift my head with joy,
Among the sons of God.

3 Do thou my sins subdue;
Thy sovereign love make known;
The spirit of my mind renew,
And save me in thy Son.

4 Let me attest thy power,
Let me thy goodness prove,
Till my full soul can hold no more
Of everlasting love.
Elliott and Toplady

535 (1256) S. M.

1 IT is not death to die—
To leave this weary road,
And, 'midst the brotherhood on high,
To be at home with God.

2 It is not death to close
The eye long dimmed by tears,
And wake in glorious repose,
To spend eternal years.

3 It is not death to bear
The wrench that sets us free
From dungeon chain, to breathe the air
Of boundless liberty.

4 It is not death to fling
Aside this sinful dust,
And rise, on strong, exulting wing,
To live among the just.

5 Jesus, thou Prince of Life!
Thy chosen cannot die;
Like thee, they conquer in the strife
To reign with thee on high.
G. W. Bethune.

DEATH.   213

KENTUCKY. 8s. & 11s.   INGALLS.   Arr. by P. G. L.

1. While sorrows encompass me round, And endless distresses I see, Astonished, I cry, can a mortal be found Surrounded with troubles like me?

536 (1251)

2 Few minutes in praise I enjoy,
And they are succeeded by pain;
If a moment in praising of God I employ,
I have hours again to complain.

3 Oh! when shall my sorrows subside?
Oh! when shall my sufferings cease?
Oh! when to the bosom of Christ be conveyed
To the regions of glory and peace? [veyed

4 O may I, prepared for that day,
When Christ shall descend from above,

Be filled with his presence, go shouting away
To the arms of my heavenly love! [way
5 The spirit to glory conveyed,
My body laid low in the ground,
I wish not a tear on my grave to be shed,
But all join in praising around.

6 No sorrow be vented that day,
When Jesus has called me home, [say,
But, singing and shouting, let each brother
"He's gone from the evil to come."

Payton.

KEENE. 8s. & 11s.   H. BAKER.

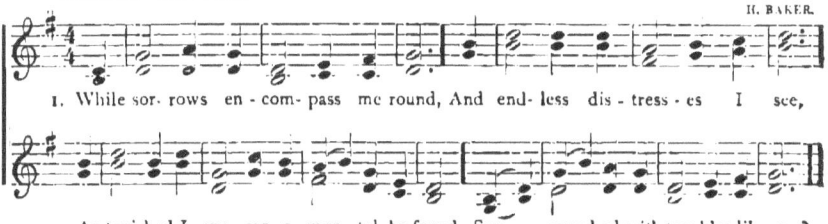

1. While sorrows encompass me round, And endless distresses I see, Astonished, I cry, can a mortal be found Surrounded with troubles like me?

537 (1250) S. M.

1 THE spirits of the just,
Confined in bodies, groan,
Till death consigns the corpse to dust,
And then the conflict's done

2 Jesus, who came to save,
The Lamb for sinners slain,
Perfumed the chambers of the grave,
And made e'en death our gain.

3 Why fear we then to trust
The place where Jesus lay?

In quiet rests our brother's dust,
And thus it seems to say:

4 "Forbear, my friends, to weep,
Since death has lost his sting;
Those Christians that in Jesus sleep,
Our God will with him bring."

5 This message then receive,
And grief indulge no more:
Return to work awhile; believe;
And wait the welcome hour.

Hart.

DEATH.

OLIPHANT. 8s. 7s. & 4s. BAILLOT. Arr. by Dr. LOWELL MASON, 1792-1872.

1. Guide me, O thou great Jehovah! Pilgrim thro' this barren land; I am weak, but thou art mighty, Hold me with thy pow'rful hand: Bread of heaven, Bread of heaven, Feed me till I want no more, Feed me till I want no more.

538 (1243)

1 GUIDE me, O thou great Jehovah!
  Pilgrim through this barren land;
I am weak, but thou art mighty,
  Hold me with thy powerful hand:
    Bread of heaven,
  Feed me till I want no more.

2 Open thou the crystal fountain,
  Whence the healing streams do flow,
Let the fiery, cloudy pillar,
  Lead me all my journey through:
    Strong Deliverer,
  Be thou still my strength and shield.

3 When I tread the verge of Jordan,
  Bid my anxious fears subside;
Death of death, and hell's destruction,
  Land me safe on Canaan's side:
    Songs of praises
  I will ever give to thee.
                    Wm. Williams. 1717-1791.

539 (1244)

Tune—BARTIMEUS, page 18.
8s. & 7s. 1 Cor 15: 42.

1 SONS of God, by blest adoption,
  View the dead with fearless eyes;
What is sown thus in corruption,
  Shall in incorruption rise;
What is sown in death's dishonor,
  Shall revive to glory's light;
What is sown in this weak manner,
  Shall be raised in matchless might.

2 Jesus, thy rich consolations
  To thy mourning people send!
May we all, with faith and patience,
  Wait for our approaching end:
Keep from courage, vain or vaunted,
  For our change our hearts prepare;
Give us confidence undaunted,
  Cheerful hope and godly fear.
                                    Hart.

RESURRECTION. **215**

CYPRESS. C. M. L. O. EMERSON.

1. Why should our mourn-ing thoughts de-light To grov-el in the dust?
Or why should streams of tears u-nite A-round th' ex-pir-ing just?

By per. O. Ditson & Co.

540 (1259) Rom. 8: 11.

2 Did not the Lord, our Saviour, die,
And triumph o'er the grave?
Did not our Lord ascend on high,
And prove his power to save?

3 Doth not the sacred Spirit come,
And dwell in all the saints?
And should the temples of his grace
Resound with loud complaints?

4 Awake, my soul, and like the sun
Burst through each sable cloud;
And thou, my voice, tho' broke with sighs,
Tune forth thy songs aloud.

5 The Spirit raised my Saviour up,
When he had bled for you;
And, spite of death and hell, shall raise
The friends of Jesus, too.

6 Awake, ye saints that dwell in dust,
Your hymns of victory sing;
And let his dying servants trust
Their ever-living King.
Rippon's Col.

541 (1255) C. M.

1 My soul, this curious house of clay,
Thy present frail abode,
Must quickly fall to worms a prey,
And thou return to God.

2 Canst thou, by faith, survey with joy
The change before it come?
And say, Let death this house destroy,
I have a heavenly home!

3 The Saviour whom I then shall see
With new-admiring eyes,
Already has prepared for me
A mansion in the skies.

4 I feel this earth-walled cottage shake,
And long to see it fall;
That I my willing flight may take
To him who is my all.

5 Burdened and groaning then no more,
My rescued soul shall sing,
As up the shining path I soar,
"Death, thou hast lost thy sting."
Newton.

542 (1279) C. M.

1 ALTHOUGH my Lord is now enthroned
Before his Father's face,
Yet here below he may be found
In gardens of his grace.

2 He sweetly waters every tree,
And makes them upward spring:
His grace affords that we may see
What rich increase they bring.

3 And he among the spicy beds,
Makes grace and mercy flow
And very cheerfully he feeds,
Where fruits both thrive and grow.

4 He likewise gathers there a crop
Of lilies without toil;
And when full ripe, he picks them up
To deck a heavenly soil.

HEAVEN.

COMPLAINER. 7s. & 6s.   WM. WALKER.

543 (1276) Luke 12: 32.

1 YES, I shall soon be landed
On yonder shores of bliss;
There, with my powers expanded,
Shall dwell where Jesus is.

2 Yes, I shall soon be seated
With Jesus on his throne;
My foes be all defeated,
And sacred peace made known.

3 With Father, Son, and Spirit,
I shall forever reign,
Sweet joy and peace inherit,
And every good obtain.

4 I soon shall reach the harbor,
To which I speed the way;
Shall cease from all my labor,
And there for ever stay.

5 Sweet Spirit, guide me over
This life's tempestuous sea;
Keep me, O holy Lover,
For I confide in thee.

6 O that in death's dark swelling
I may be helped to sing,
And pass the river, telling
The triumphs of my King.
Gadsby's Col.

544 (1235) 7s. & 6s.

1 AH! I soon shall be dying,
Time swiftly glides away;
But on my Lord relying,
I hail the happy day:

2 The day when I must enter
Upon a world unknown;
My helpless soul I venture
On Jesus Christ alone.

3 He once, a spotless victim,
Upon Mount Calvary bled!
Jehovah did afflict him,
And bruise him in my stead.

4 Hence all my hope arises
Unworthy as I am:
My soul most surely prizes
The sin-atoning Lamb.

5 To him, by grace united,
I joy in him alone;
And now, by faith delighted,
Behold him on his throne.

6 There he is interceding
For all who on him rest:
The grace from him proceeding,
Shall waft me to his breast.

7 Then with the saints in glory
The grateful song I'll raise,
And chant my blissful story,
In high seraphic lays.

8 Free grace, redeeming merit,
And sanctifying love,
Of Father, Son, and Spirit,
Shall charm the courts above.
Ryland.

HEAVEN.

FEDERAL STREET. L. M. H. K. OLIVER. 1800.

1. There is a land mine eye hath seen In visions of en-rapt-ur'd thought; So bright that all which spreads be-tween Is with its ra-diant glo-ry fraught.

545 (1290)

1 There is a land mine eye hath seen
In visions of enraptured thought;
So bright that all which spreads between
Is with its radiant glory fraught.

2 A land upon whose blissful shore
There rests no shadow, falls no stain;
There those who meet shall part no more,
And those long parted meet again.

3 Its skies are not like earthly skies,
With varying hues of shade and light;
It hath no need of suns to rise,
To dissipate the gloom of night.

4 There sweeps no desolating wind
Across that calm, serene abode:
The wanderer there a home shall find,
Within the paradise of God.
Gurdon Robins.

546 (1299) L. M.

1 With transport,Lord,our souls proclaim
Th' immortal honors of thy name;
Although ascended to thy throne,
Thou still art present with thine own.

2 High on his Father's royal seat,
Our Jesus shone divinely great;
Ere Adam's clay with life was warmed,
Or Gabriel's nobler spirit formed.

3 Through all succeeding ages, he
The same hath been—the same shall be;
Immortal radiance gilds his head,
While stars and suns wax old, and fade.

4 The same his power his flock to guard;
The same his bounty to reward:
The same his faithfulness and love,
To saints on earth and saints above.

5 Let nature change, and sink, and die;
Jesus shall raise his chosen high;
And fix them near his heavenly throne,
In glory changeless as his own.
Doddridge.

547 (1300) L. M.

1 With what delight faith lifts her eyes,
To view the courts where Jesus dwells;
Jesus, who reigns above the skies,
And here below his grace reveals.

2 Of God's own house the sacred key
Is borne by his majestic hand;
Mansions and treasures there I see
Subjected all to his command.

3 He shuts, and worlds might strive in vain
The mighty obstacle to move;
He looses all their bars again,
And who shall shut the gates of love!

4 Fixed in omnipotence, he bears
The glories of his Father's name;
Sustains his people's weighty cares,
Through every changing age the same.

5 My little all I here suspend,
Where the whole weight of heaven is
Secure I rest on such a friend, [hung;
And into raptures wake my tongue.

HEAVEN.

EXHORTATION. C. M. HIBBARD.

1. On Jordan's stormy banks I stand, And cast a wishful eye, To Canaan's fair and happy land, Where my possessions lie.

548 (1288)

2 Oh, the transporting, rapturous scene,
  That rises to my sight!
Sweet fields arrayed in living green,
  And rivers of delight!
3 All o'er those wide-extended plains
  Shines one eternal day;
There God the Sun for ever reigns,
  And scatters night away.
4 No chilling winds, or poisonous breath,
  Can reach that healthful shore;
Sickness and sorrows, pain and death,
  Are felt and feared no more.
5 When shall I reach that happy place,
  And be forever blest?
When shall I see my Father's face
  And in his bosom rest?
6 Filled with delight, my raptured soul
  Can here no longer stay;
Though Jordan's waves around me roll,
  Fearless I'd launch away.

Stennett.

549 (1286) C. M.

1 COME, Lord, and warm each languid
  Inspire each lifeless tongue;   [heart,
And let the joys of heaven impart
  Their influence to our song.
2 Sorrow and pain, and every care,
  And discord there shall cease;
And perfect joy, and love sincere,
  Adorn the realms of peace.
3 The soul, from sin for ever free,
  Shall mourn its power no more;
But, clothed in spotless purity,
  Redeeming love adore.
4 Lord, tune our hearts to praise and
  Our feeble notes inspire;   [love,
Till in thy blissful courts above,
  We join th' angelic choir. Mrs. Steele.

HEAVEN.

PLEASANT HILL. C. M. D. WM. NICHOLSON. Arr. by T. B. AUSMUS.

1. There is a place of hallow'd peace For those with cares oppress'd;
When sighs and sorrowing tears shall cease And all be hush'd to rest.
2. 'Tis then the soul is freed from fears, And doubts which here annoy; There they that oft had sown in tears

Shall reap again in joy.

550 (1289)

3 There is a home of sweet repose,
    Where storms assail no more ;
The stream of endless pleasure flows
    On that celestial shore.

4 There purity with love appears,
    And bliss without alloy;
There they that oft had sown in tears
    Shall reap again in joy.
                                    Tappan.

551 (1284) c. m.

1 From thee, my God, my joys shall rise,
    And run eternal rounds,
Beyond the limits of the skies,
    And all created bounds.

2 The holy triumphs of my soul
    Shall death itself outbrave
Leave dull mortality behind,
    And fly beyond the grave.

3 There, where my blessed Jesus reigns
    In heaven's unmeasured space,
I'll spend a long eternity
    In pleasure and in praise.

4 Millions of years my wondering eyes
    Shall o'er thy beauties rove,
And endless ages I'll adore
    The glories of thy love.

5 Sweet Jesus, every smile of thine
    Shall fresh endearments bring,
A thousand tastes of new delight
    From all thy graces spring.

6 Haste, my Beloved, fetch my soul
    Up to thy blest abode,
Fly, for my spirit longs to see
    My Saviour and my God.
                                    Watts.

552 (1285) c. m. Rom. 13: 11.

1 Awake, ye saints, and raise your eyes,
    And raise your voices high;
Awake, and praise that sovereign love
    That shows salvation nigh.

2 On all the wings of time it flies,
    Each moment brings it near ;
Then welcome each declining day,
    And each revolving year !

3 Not many years their round shall run,
    Nor many mornings rise,
Ere all its glories stand revealed
    To our admiring eyes.

4 Ye wheels of nature, speed your course!
    Ye mortal powers decay !
Fast as ye bring the night of death,
    Ye bring eternal day.
                                    Doddridge.

HEAVEN.

DRAVO. C. M.

1. Ah! when with saints, where Jesus reigns, My soul hath found a place, I'll sing in loud exalted strains, A song of boundless grace.

553 (1278)

1 AH! when with saints, where Jesus reigns,
My soul hath found a place,
I'll sing in loud exalted strains,
A song of boundless grace.

2 Nor will my pleasure, peace, and joy,
In that eternal noon,
Become extinct, decay, or cloy,
But e'er maintain their bloom.

3 I there will, also, raise a note
Of praise to Christ my King,
Which I shall with my warbling throat
Through endless ages sing.

4 There darksome clouds are never seen
To veil the happy mind;
But all is light, and all serene,
And God profusely kind.

5 Not plagued, and vexed with sin and care,
As is the case below;
But undisturbed, when seated there,
And naught but pleasure know.

6 With joyful lips I there shall own
God just in all his ways,
And bow to him who fills the throne,
And give him lasting praise.

554 (1291) C. M.

1 THERE is a world of perfect bliss
Above the starry skies;
Oppressed with sorrows and with sins,
I thither lift my eyes.

2 'Tis there the weary are at rest,
And all is peace within;
The mind, with guilt no more oppressed,
Is tranquil and serene.

3 Discord and strife are banished thence,
Distrust and slavish fear;
No more we hear the pensive sigh,
Or see the falling tear.

4 I long to see my Father's face,
And sing his praises, too;
Adieu, companions, dearest friends;
Vain world, once more, adieu.
                                                Beddome.

555 (1293) C. M.

1 FAR from these narrow scenes of night
Unbounded glories rise,
And realms of joy and pure delight,
Unknown to mortal eyes.

2 No cloud those blissful regions know,
Realms ever bright and fair;
For sin, the source of mortal wo,
Can never enter there.

3 O may the heavenly prospect fire
Our hearts with ardent love,
Till wings of faith and strong desire
Bear every thought above.

4 Prepare us, Lord, by grace divine,
For thy bright courts on high;
Then bid our spirits rise, and join
The chorus of the sky.   Steele.

HEAVEN. 221

VIGILS. C. M. S. WEBBE. 1740-1816.

1 How happy are the souls above! From sin and sorrow free,
With Jesus they are now at rest, And all his glory see.

556 (1292)

1 How happy are the souls above!
  From sin and sorrow free,
 With Jesus they are now at rest,
  And all his glory see.

2 "Worthy the Lamb," aloud they cry,
  "That brought us near to God!"
 In ceaseless hymns of praise they shout
  The virtue of his blood.

3 Sweet gratitude inspires their songs,
  Ambitious to proclaim,
 Before the Father's awful throne,
  The honors of the Lamb.

4 With wondering joy their lips recount
  Their fears and dangers past;
 And bless the wisdom, power, and love,
  Which brought them home at last.

5 Lord, let the merits of thy death
  To me, like them, be given;
 And I, like them, will shout thy praise
  Through all the courts of heaven.
  Elliott.

557 (1295) C. M.

1 O the delights, the heavenly joys,
  The glories of the place
 Where Jesus sheds the brightest beams
  Of his o'erflowing grace!

2 Sweet majesty and awful love
  Sit smiling on his brow,
 And all the glorious ranks above
  At humble distance bow.

3 Princes to his imperial name
  Bend their bright sceptres down;
 Dominions, thrones, and powers rejoice
  To see him wear the crown.

4 Those soft, those blessed feet of his,
  That once rude iron tore,
 High on a throne of light they stand,
  And all the saints adore.

5 His head, the dear majestic head,
  That cruel thorns did wound,
 See what immortal glories shine,
  And circle it around.

6 This is the man, th' exalted man,
  Whom we unseen adore:
 But when our eyes behold his face,
  Our hearts shall love him more.
  Watts.

558 (1297) C. M.

1 The sinner who, by precious faith,
  Has felt his sins forgiven,
 Is, from that moment, passed from death,
  And sealed an heir of heaven.

2 Though thousand snares enclose his feet,
  Not one shall hold him fast;
 Whatever dangers he may meet,
  He shall be safe at last.

3 Not as the world the Saviour gives;
  He is no fickle friend;
 Whom once he loves he never leaves,
  But loves him to the end.
  Hart.

HEAVEN.

REDEMPTION. 11s.

559 (1296)

2 He loved me of old, and he loveth me still;
Before the creation he gave me by will,
A portion worth more than the Indies of gold,
Which cannot be wasted, nor mortgaged, nor sold.

3 He gave me a Surety, a covenant Head,
To live in my name, and to die in my stead;
He gave me a righteousness wholly divine,
And viewed all the merits of Jesus as mine.

4 He gave a Preceptor infallibly wise,
And treasures of grace to be sent in supplies;
Yea, all that I ask for, my Father hath given
To help me on earth, and to crown me in heaven.

5 He gave me a will to accept what he gave,
Though I was averse to his purpose to save;
He wrote in his will my repentance and faith,
And all my enjoyments for life and for death.

6 My trials and sorrows, my conflicts and cares, [prayers,
The spirit of prayer and the answer of
The steps that I tread, and the station I fill,
My Father determined and wrote in his will.

7 My cross and my crown are both willed
by my God, [blood;
He swore to his will, and then sealed it with
'Tis proved by the Spirit, the witness within;
'Tis mine to inherit; I'll glory begin.

IMANDRA. 11s.

MISCELLANEOUS. 223

WOODSIDE. C. M. L. O. Emerson.

1. O for a clos-er walk with God, A calm and heav'nly frame; A light to shine up-on the road That leads me to the Lamb!

By per. O. Ditson & Co.

560 Gen. 5: 24.

2 Where is the blessedness I knew
When first I saw the Lord?
Where is the soul-refreshing view
Of Jesus, and his word?

3 What peaceful hours I then enjoyed!
How sweet their memory still!
But now I find an aching void
The world can never fill.

4 Return, O holy Dove! return,
Sweet messenger of rest!
I hate the sins that made thee mourn,
And drove thee from my breast.

5 The dearest idol I have known,
Whate'er that idol be,
Help me to tear it from thy throne,
And worship only thee.

6 So shall my walk be close with God,
Calm and serene my frame;
So purer light shall mark the road
That leads me to the Lamb.
Cowper.

561 C. M.

1 O, FOR a heart to praise my God,
A heart from sin set free!
A heart that's sprinkled with the blood
So freely shed for me.

2 O, for a heart submissive, meek,
My Great Redeemer's throne,
Where only Christ is heard to speak,
Where Jesus reigns alone!

3 O, for an humble, contrite heart;
Believing, true and clean,
Which neither life nor death can part
From him that dwells within.

4 Thy temper, gracious Lord, impart;
Come quickly from above;
O write thy name upon my heart;
Thy name, O God, is love.
Wesley.

562 C. M. Job 23: 3, 4.

1 O THAT I knew the secret place
Where I might find my God!
I'd spread my wants before his face,
And pour my woes abroad.

2 I'd tell him how my sins arise,
What sorrows I sustain;
How grace decays, and comfort dies,
And leaves my heart in pain.

3 He knows what arguments I'd take
To wrestle with my God;
I'd plead for his own mercy's sake,
And for my Saviour's blood.

4 My God will pity my complaints,
And heal my broken bones:
He takes the meaning of his saints,
The language of their groans.

5 Arise, my soul, from deep distress,
And banish every fear;
He calls thee to his throne of grace,
To spread thy sorrows there.
Watts.

MISCELLANEOUS.

WOODSTOCK. C. M. — D. DUTTON.

1. I love to steal a-while a-way From ev-'ry cum-b'ring care,
And spend the hours of set-ting day In hum-ble, grate-ful pray'r.

563

1 I LOVE to steal awhile away
  From every cumbering care,
And spend the hours of setting day
  In humble, grateful prayer.

2 I love in solitude to shed
  The penitential tear,
And all his promises to plead
  Where none but God can hear.

3 I love to think on mercies past,
  And future good implore,
And all my cares and sorrows cast
  On him whom I adore.

4 I love by faith to take a view
  Of brighter scenes in heaven;
The prospect doth my strength renew,
  While here by tempest driven.

5 Thus, when life's toilsome day is o'er,
  May its departing ray
Be calm as this impressive hour,
  And lead to endless day.
                                    Mrs. Brown.

564   C. M.

1 I THINK of thee, my God, by night,
  And talk of thee by day;
Thy love my treasure and delight,
  Thy truth my strength and stay.

2 The day is dark, the night is long,
  Unblest with thoughts of thee,
And dull to me the sweetest song,
  Unless its theme thou be.

3 So all day long, and all the night,
  Lord, let thy presence be,
Mine air, my breath, my shade, my light,
  Myself absorbed in thee.
                        John S. B Monsell. 1863.

565 (1280)   C. M.

1 OUR sins, alas, how strong they be!
  And like a raging sea
They break our duty, Lord, to thee,
  And hurry us away.

2 The waves of trouble how they rise!
  How loud the tempests roar!
But death shall land our weary souls
  Safe on the heavenly shore.

3 There to fulfil his sweet commands
  Our speedy feet shall move,
Nor sin shall clog our winged zeal
  Or cool our burning love.

4 There shall we sit, and sing, and tell
  The wonders of his grace,
And heavenly raptures fire our hearts,
  And smile in every face.

5 For ever his dear sacred name
  Shall dwell upon our tongue
And Jesus and salvation be
  The theme of every song.   Watts

MISCELLANEOUS. 225

By per. Biglow & Main.

566 (910)

1 PRAYER is the saint's sincere desire,
Unuttered or expressed;
The motion of a hidden fire,
That trembles in the breast.

2 Prayer is the burden of a sigh,
The falling of a tear;
The upward glancing of an eye,
When none but God is near.

3 Prayer is the simplest form of speech
That infant lips can try;
Prayer the sublimest strains that reach
The Majesty on high.

4 Prayer is the Christian's vital breath,
The Christian's native air;
The watchword at the gate of death;
He enters heaven with prayer.
Montgomery.

567   C. M.

1 O HOW melodious was that voice,
Which bade my sins depart!
That filled my soul with heavenly joys,
And healed my broken heart!

2 'Twas Jesus spake: and at his word,
My load of guilt was gone!
I leaped for joy, and praised the Lord,
For what his grace had done!

3 My soul was bordering on despair,
And sinking down with grief;

When Jesus, Saviour, saw me there,
And ran to my relief.

4 O! wondrous love! that snatched my feet,
From the abyss of wo!
Here, all my warmest passions meet,
And hence my comforts flow.
Vanmeter.

568 (981)   C. M.

1 How vain are all things here below!
How false, and yet how fair!
Each pleasure hath its poison, too,
And every sweet a snare.

2 The brightest things below the sky
Give but a flattering light;
We should suspect some danger nigh
Where we possess delight.

3 Our dearest joys, and nearest friends,
The partners of our blood,
How they divide our wavering minds,
And leave but half for God!

4 The fondness of a creature's love,
How strong it strikes the sense!
Thither the warm affections move,
Nor can we call them thence.

5 Dear Saviour, let thy beauties be
My soul's eternal food;
And grace command my heart away
From all created good.
Watts

MISCELLANEOUS.

THE HOUSE OF THE LORD. 12s.

1. In my sorrow I cried unto God with my voice,
And he heard me, and made my poor heart to rejoice;
And now of his love and his mercy I'll sing,
And speak of the glory of Jesus my King.

569 Psalm 77.

2 Mine eyes were held waking; my soul full of grief,
All comfort refused, and all hope of relief;
I considered the days that are passed, and the years [my fears.
When the Lord by his presence subdued all

3 I called to remembrance my song in the night, [delight;
When the favor of God filled my soul with I communed with my heart of his wonders of grace, [face.
And my spirit made diligent search for his

4 Has the Lord in his anger forgotten poor me?
His tender compassions no more shall I see?
Are his mercies clean gone? will his favor no more
To me the sweet joys of salvation restore?

5 Then a glorious light sweetly dawned on my heart,
Which bade all my fears in a moment depart;
'Twas the light of the knowledge of Jesus, that Friend [end.
Who, having once loved his own, loves to the

6 And I said, My infirmity causes this fear;
But now from all doubtings my soul shall be clear:
For I will remember thy wonders of old,
And the years of thy right hand again shall behold.

7 How sweet to recall thy past mercies to mind, [shined;
The light of thy face that upon me hath
And unspeakably sweet, while I think on thy name,
To remember that thou art forever the same.

Silas H. Durand.

570 12s. Luke 11: 31; 1 Kings 10: 1-13.

1 WHEN the Queen of the south heard of Solomon's fame, [came,
From the uttermost parts of the earth she
To prove him with questions deep-searching and hard,
And to see the wonderful house of the Lord.

2 And when she with him had communed, and his word, [she had heard,
Which searched all the depths of her heart,
And when all his wonderful work she had viewed,
Its perfection of beauty her spirit subdued.

3 So when the poor soul from the ends of the earth [sorrow, comes forth
Whose sins have o'erwhelmed him with
To Jesus in strong supplication and prayer,
What wonders untold are revealed to him there!

4 What wonders of wisdom, what riches of grace, [face!
What fulness of love in the dear Saviour's
Hard questions, that filled all his soul with dismay, [away.
In a moment are answered and scattered

5 The half was not told, and it never can be,
The glory and grace that in Jesus I see;
The sweetness and comfort I find in his word,
And the beauty I see in the house of the Lord.

Silas H. Durand.

MISCELLANEOUS.

FREDERICK. 11s. GEORGE KINGSLEY.

I would not live alway: I ask not to stay / Where storm after storm rises (*Omit*........) dark o'er the way; The few lurid mornings, that dawn on us here, Are followed by gloom, or beclouded with fear.

571 (1217) Job 7: 16.

2 I would not live alway thus fetter'd by sin,
Temptation without and corruption within:
E'en the rapture of pardon is mingled with tears,
And the cup of thanksgiving with penitent tears.

3 I would not live alway; no, welcome the tomb;
Since Jesus hath lain there I dread not its gloom:
There sweet be my rest till he bid me arise,
To hail him in triumph descending the skies.

4 Who, who would live alway, away from his God,
Away from that heaven, that blissful abode,
Where the rivers of pleasure flow o'er the bright plains,
And the noontide of glory eternally reigns.

5 There saints of all ages in harmony meet,
Their Saviour and brethren transported to greet;
While the anthems of rapture unceasingly roll,
And the smile of the Lord is the feast of the soul. *Muhlenberg.*

SUMMER. 11s. SWAN. Arr. by F. L. ARMSTRONG.

I would not live alway: I ask not to stay / Where storm after storm rises dark o'er the way; The few lurid mornings, that dawn on us here, Are follow'd by gloom, or be-clouded with fear.

MISCELLANEOUS.

GRATITUDE. L. M.

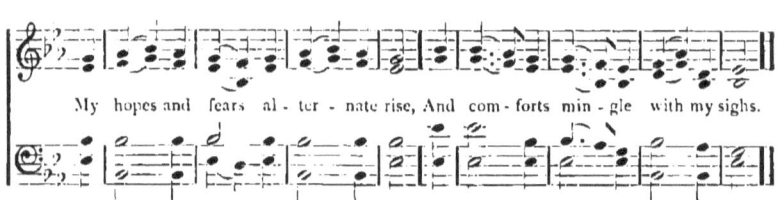

1. Thus far my God hath led me on, And made his truth and mercy known;
My hopes and fears alternate rise, And comforts mingle with my sighs.

572 (1298) Deut. 8: 2.

1 Thus far my God hath led me on,
And made his truth and mercy known;
My hopes and fears alternate rise,
And comforts mingle with my sighs.

2 Through this wide wilderness I roam,
Far distant from my blissful home;
Lord, let thy presence be my stay,
And guard me in this dangerous way.

3 Temptations everywhere annoy,
And sins and snares my peace destroy:
My earthly joys are from me torn,
And oft an absent God I mourn.

4 My soul, with various tempests tossed,
Her hopes o'erturned, her projects crossed,
Sees every day new straits attend,
And wonders where the scene will end.

5 Is this, dear Lord, that thorny road
Which leads us to the mount of God?
Are these the toils thy people know,
While in the wilderness below?

6 'Tis even so; thy faithful love
Doth all thy children's graces prove;
'Tis thus our pride and self must fall,
That Jesus may be All in all.
Fawcett.

573 L. M. Matt. 6: 28-30.

1 BEHOLD the lilies, how they grow!
They toil not, neither do they spin;

Yet Solomon could never show
Such raiment as God clothes them in.

2 And you, poor souls, who weep and mourn
Because your works cannot supply
That spotless robe that must be worn
By all who dwell with God on high;

3 Blessed are you if you strive in vain,
And all your works no comfort yield;
For when you cease to toil and spin,
You are as lilies of the field.

4 And he who richly clothes the flower,
Which passes almost as a breath,
Will show his richer grace and power,
In you, O ye of little faith.

5 Infinite wisdom, power and love
Prepared the robe that you shall wear;
And in the realms of bliss above
'Twill shine forever bright and fair.

6 As sun and dew afflictions come,
Making the heavenly lilies grow;
And bringing forth a lovelier bloom
Than all the fields of earth can show.

7 Through trials thus prepared to wear
The robe of righteousness, they prove
Their heavenly Father's tender care,
And reach the fullness of his love.
Silas H. Durand.

MISCELLANEOUS.

HEBRON. L. M. Dr. LOWELL MASON. 1792-1872.

1. Thus far the Lord has led me on, Thus far his pow'r pro-longs my days; And ev-'ry eve-ning shall make known Some fresh me-mo-rial of his grace.

574

1 Thus far the Lord has led me on,
Thus far his power prolongs my days;
And every evening shall make known
Some fresh memorial of his grace.

2 Much of my time has run to waste,
And I, perhaps, am near my home;
But he forgives my follies past,
He gives me strength for days to come.

3 I lay my body down to sleep,
Peace is the pillow for my head,
While well-appointed angels keep
Their watchful stations round my bed.

4 In vain the sons of earth or hell
Tell me a thousand frightful things,
My God in safety makes me dwell
Beneath the shadow of his wings.
                                     Watts.

575 L. M.

1 Glory to thee, my God, this night,
For all the blessings of the light;
Keep me, O keep me, King of kings,
Beneath thy own Almighty wings.

2 Forgive me, Lord, for thy dear Son,
The ill that I this day have done;
That with the world, myself, and thee,
I, ere I sleep, at peace may be.

3 Teach me to live, that I may dread
The grave as little as my bed;
Teach me to die, that so I may
Rise glorious at the awful day.

4 O let my soul on thee repose,
And may sweet sleep my eye-lids close;
Sleep that shall me more vigorous make
To serve my God when I awake.

5 If in the night I sleepless lie,
My soul with heavenly thoughts supply;
Let no ill dreams disturb my rest,
No power of darkness me molest.
                                     Bp. Ken.

576 L. M.

1 Lord, unto whom should sinners go?
Thou hast the words of endless life;
When sinking down with grief and wo,
Thy voice affords us quick relief.

2 Thou hast all power in heaven above,
And all below the shining sun;
The earth, and all the worlds that move,
Are subject to thy lofty throne.

3 Amidst temptations, sharp and long,
And tribulations here below;
Thy name is like a fortress strong
To which thy tempted children go.

4 When clouds and darkness veil the way,
And doubts and fears our souls annoy,
Thy presence turns our night to day,
And all our doubts and fears to joy.
                                     Vanmeter.

MISCELLANEOUS.

HE LIVES. L. M. D.

1. Blest are the humble souls that see Their emptiness and poverty; Treasures of grace to them are given, And crowns of joy laid up in heav'n.
D.C. The blood of Christ divinely flows, A healing balm for all their woes.

2. Blest are the men of broken heart, Who mourn for sin with inward smart;

577 (986) Matt. 5: 2-12.

1 BLEST are the humble souls that see
Their emptiness and poverty;
Treasures of grace to them are given,
And crowns of joy laid up in heaven.

2 Blest are the men of broken heart,
Who mourn for sin with inward smart;
The blood of Christ divinely flows,
A healing balm for all their woes.

3 Blest are the meek, who stand afar
From rage and passion, noise and war;
God will secure their happy state,
And plead their cause against the great.

4 Blest are the souls that thirst for grace,
Hunger and long for righteousness,
They shall be well supplied and fed
With living streams and living bread.

5 Blest are the men whose bowels move
And melt with sympathy and love:
From Christ the Lord shall they obtain
Like sympathy and love again.

6 Blest are the pure, whose hearts are clean
From the defiling power of sin,
With endless pleasure they shall see
A God of spotless purity.

7 Blest are the men of peaceful life,
Who quench the coals of growing strife,
They shall be called the heirs of bliss,
The sons of God, the God of peace.

8 Blest are the sufferers who partake
Of pain and shame for Jesus' sake;
Their souls shall triumph in the Lord,
Glory and joy are their reward.

Watts.

578 L. M.

1 I KNOW that my Redeemer lives;
What comfort this sweet sentence gives!
He lives, he lives, who once was dead,
He lives, my ever-living head.

2 He lives to bless me with his love,
He lives to plead for me above;
He lives my hungry soul to feed,
He lives to help in time of need.

3 He lives to grant me fresh supply,
He lives to guide me with his eye;
He lives to comfort me when faint,
He lives to hear my soul's complaint.

4 He lives to silence all my fears,
He lives to stoop and wipe my tears;
He lives to calm my troubled heart,
He lives all blessings to impart.

5 He lives, my kind, wise, heavenly Friend,
He lives and loves me to the end;
He lives, and while he lives I'll sing,
He lives, my Prophet, Priest and King.

6 He lives, all glory to his name!
He lives eternally the same;
O! the sweet joy this sentence gives,
I know that my Redeemer lives.

MISCELLANEOUS. 231

RETREAT. L. M. T. HASTINGS.

1. From ev-'ry storm-y wind that blows, From ev-'ry swell-ing tide of woes, There is a calm, a sure re-treat; 'Tis found be-neath the mer-cy-seat.

579

1 FROM every stormy wind that blows,
From every swelling tide of woes,
There is a calm, a sure retreat;
'Tis found beneath the mercy-seat.

2 There is a place where Jesus sheds
The oil of gladness on our heads,—
A place of all on earth most sweet;
It is the gracious mercy-seat.

3 There is a place where spirits blend,
Where friend holds fellowship with friend;
Though sundered far, by faith they meet
Around one common mercy-seat.

4 Ah! whither could I flee for aid
When tempted, desolate, dismayed?
Or how the hosts of hell defeat,
Had suffering saints no mercy-seat?

5 There, there, on eagle's wings to soar,
And sin and sense molest no more;
And heaven comes down our souls to greet,
And glory crowns the mercy-seat. [Stowell.

580   L. M. John 13: 15.

1 AND is the gospel peace and love?
Such let our conversation be;
The serpent blended with the dove,
Wisdom and meek simplicity.

2 Whene'er the angry passions rise,
And tempt our thoughts or tongues to strife,
To Jesus let us lift our eyes, [strife,
Bright pattern of the Christian life!

3 Oh, how benevolent and kind!
How mild! how ready to forgive!
Be this the temper of our mind,
And these the rules by which we live.

4 To do his heavenly Father's will
Was his employment and delight;
Humility and holy zeal
Shone through his life divinely bright!

5 Dispensing good where'er he came,
The labors of his life were love:
Oh, if we love the Saviour's name,
Let his divine example move!
                                  Steele.

581   L. M. Luke 15: 32.

1 THE mighty God will not despise
The contrite heart for sacrifice;
The deep-fetched sigh, the secret groan,
Rises accepted to the throne.

2 He meets, with tokens of his grace,
The trembling lip, the blushing face;
His bowels yearn when sinners pray;
And mercy bears their sins away.

3 When filled with grief, o'erwhelmed
           with shame,
He, pitying, heals their broken frame;
He hears their sad complaints, and spies
His image in their weeping eyes.

4 Thus what a rapturous joy possessed
The tender parent's throbbing breast,
To see his spendthrift son return,
And hear him his past follies mourn!
                                  Beddome.

MISCELLANEOUS.
WATCHMAN! TELL US OF THE NIGHT.
L. MASON.

582

1 WATCHMAN! tell us of the night,
What its signs of promise are:
Traveller! o'er yon mountain's height,
See that glory-beaming star!
Watchman! does its beauteous ray
Aught of hope or joy foretell?
Traveller! yes; it brings the day,—
Promised day of Israel!

2 Watchman! tell us of the night,
Higher yet that star ascends:
Traveller! blessedness and light,
Peace and truth its course portends!
Watchman! will its beams alone
Gild the spot that gave them birth?
Traveller! ages are its own,
See! it bursts o'er all the earth.

3 Watchman! tell us of the night,
For the morning seems to dawn:
Traveller! darkness takes its flight,
Doubt and terror are withdrawn.
Watchman! let thy wanderings cease;
Hie thee to thy quiet home;
Traveller! lo! the Prince of Peace,
Lo! the Son of God is come. Bowring.

MISCELLANEOUS.

PILGRIM. 8s. & 7s. CHAPIN.

1. "Whith-er goest thou, pil-grim stran-ger, Wan-d'ring thro' this lone-ly vale?
   Know'st thou not 'tis full of dan-ger, And will not thy cour-age fail?"
   D.C.—But no ill shall e'er be-fall me, While I'm blest with such a Guide."

2. "Pil-grim thou dost just-ly call me, Wand'ring thro' this lone-ly void,—

583

3 "Such a Guide? No guide attends thee—
Hence for thee my fears arise;
If some guardian power defend thee,
'Tis unseen by mortal eyes."

4 "Yes, unseen; but still, believe me,
Such a Guide my steps attend;
He'll in every strait befriend me,
He will guide me to the end."

GREENVILLE. 8s. & 7s. J. J. ROUSSEAU. 1754.

1. Je-sus is our great sal-va-tion; Wor-thy of our best es-teem;
   D.C.—He has sav'd us: He has sav'd us: Christ a-lone could us re-deem.

He has sav'd his favorite na-tion; Join to sing a-loud of him;

584 (499) 2 Tim. 1: 9.

2 When involved in sin and ruin,
And no helper there was found,
Jesus our distress was viewing;
Grace did more than sin abound.
He has called us,
With salvation in the sound.

3 Let us never, Lord, forget thee;
Make us walk as children here:
We will give thee all the glory,

Of that love that brought us near
Bid us praise thee,
And rejoice with holy fear.

4 Free election, known by calling,
Is a privilege divine;
Saints are kept from final falling;
All the glory, Lord, be thine:
All the glory!
All the glory, Lord, is thine! Adams

585

1 "For ever with the Lord!"
  Amen, so let it be;
Life for the dead is in that word,
  'Tis immortality.
Here in the body pent,
  Absent from him I roam;
Yet nightly pitch my moving tent
A day's march nearer home.
Nearer home, nearer home,
A day's march nearer home.

2 My Father's house on high,
  Home of my soul, how near,
At times, to faith's aspiring eye,
  The golden gates appear!
Ah, then my spirit faints
  To reach the land I love;
The bright inheritance of saints,
  Jerusalem above.
Home above, home above,
  Jerusalem above.

3 Yet doubts still intervene,
  And all my comfort flies;
Like Noah's dove I flit between
  Rough seas and stormy skies.
Anon the clouds depart,
  The winds and waters cease;
While sweetly o'er my gladdened heart
  Expands the bow of peace.
Bow of peace, bow of peace,
  Expands the bow of peace.

Montgomery.

MISCELLANEOUS.

BEALOTH. S. M. D.

586

1 I LOVE thy kingdom, Lord,
　The house of thine abode;
The church our blest Redeemer saved
　With his own precious blood.
I love thy church, O God,
　Her walls before thee stand,
Dear as the apple of thine eye,
　And graven on thy hand.

2 For her my tears shall fall,
　For her my prayers ascend,
To her my cares and toils be given
　Till cares and toils shall end.
Beyond my highest joy
　I prize her heavenly ways;
Her sweet communion, solemn vows,
　Her hymns of love and praise.

3 Jesus, thou friend divine,
　Our Saviour and our King,
Thy hand, from every snare and foe,
　Shall great deliverance bring.
Sure as thy truth shall last,
　To Zion shall be given
The brightest glories earth can yield,
　And brighter bliss of heaven.
　　　　　　　　　　　Dwight.

587　　　S. M.

1 O WHERE shall rest be found,
　Rest for the weary soul?
'Twere vain the ocean's depths to sound,
　Or pierce to either pole.

2 The world can never give,
　The bliss for which we sigh;
'Tis not the whole of life to live,
　Nor all of death to die.

3 Beyond this vale of tears,
　There is a life above,
Unmeasured by the flight of years,
　And all that life is love.　Montgomery.

MISCELLANEOUS.

FAITHFUL SOLDIER. 7s. & 6s.

1. O when shall I see Jesus, And reign with him above,
And from the flowing fountain Drink everlasting love?
D.C.—And with my blessed Jesus, Drink endless pleasure in?

When shall I be deliver'd From this vain world of sin,

588

1 O WHEN shall I see Jesus,
  And reign with him above,
  And from the flowing fountain
  Drink everlasting love?
  When shall I be delivered
  From this vain world of sin,
  And with my blessed Jesus,
  Drink endless pleasure in?

2 But now I am a soldier,
  My Captain's gone before,
  He's given me my orders,
  And bid me not give o'er;
  His promises are faithful,
  A crown of life he'll give,
  And all his valiant soldiers
  Eternally shall live.

3 Through grace he will support me,
  To conquer though I die,
  And then away to Jesus
  On wings of love I'll fly:
  Farewell to sin and sorrow,
  I bid you both adieu;
  And, O my friends, still trust him,
  And on your way pursue.

4 Whene'er you meet with troubles
  And trials on the way,
  Cast all your care on Jesus,
  And don't forget to pray:
  Gird on the gospel armor

Of faith, and hope, and love;
And when the combat's ended
He'll carry you above.

Tibbout.

589 7s. & 6s. Psa. 85: 9.

1 O CHRIST, he is the Fountain,
  The deep, sweet well of love!
  The streams on earth I've tasted,
  More deep I'll drink above:
  There to an ocean fulness
  His mercy doth expand,
  And glory, glory dwelleth
  In my Immanuel's land.

2 O I am my Beloved's,
  And my Beloved's mine!
  He brings a poor, vile sinner
  Into his "house of wine!"
  I stand upon his merit,
  I know no other stand,
  Not e'en where glory dwelleth
  In my Immanuel's land.

3 The bride eyes not her garment,
  But her dear Bridegroom's face;
  I will not gaze at glory,
  But on my King of grace;
  Not at the crown he giveth,
  But on his pierced hand;
  The Lamb is all the glory
  In my Immanuel's land. A. R. Cousin.

MISCELLANEOUS. 237

SELBORNE. 7s. & 6s. D.   Arr. from an Old Melody.

1. How lost was my con-dition Till Jesus made me whole!
   There is but one phy-si-cian Can cure a sin-sick soul.
   Next door to death he found me, And snatch'd me from the grave, To tell to all around me His wondrous pow'r to save.

590   Luke 29: 10.
2 The worst of all diseases
   Is light compared with sin;
   On every part it seizes,
   But rages most within:
   'Tis palsy, plague, and fever,
   And madness, all combined;
   And none, but a believer,
   The least relief can find.

3 From men, great skill professing,
   I sought a cure to gain;
   But this proved more distressing,
   And added to my pain:
   Some said that nothing ailed me,
   Some gave me up for lost;
   Thus every refuge failed me,
   And all my hopes were crossed.

4 At length this great Physician,
   How matchless is his grace,
   Accepted my petition,
   And undertook my case:
   First, gave me sight to view him—
   For sin my eyes had sealed—
   Then bade me look unto him:
   I looked and I was healed

5 A dying, risen Jesus,
   Seen by the eye of faith,
   At once from danger frees us,
   And saves the soul from death:
   Come then to this Physician,
   His help he'll freely give;
   He makes no hard condition,
   To Jesus—look and live!   Newton.

WEBB. 7s. & 6s. D.   G. J. WEBB. 1830.

1. How lost was my con-di-tion Till Je-sus made me whole! There is but one phy-si-cian
   D.S.—To tell to all a-round me
   Can cure a sin-sick soul. Next door to death he found me, And snatch'd me from the grave,
   His wondrous pow'r to save.

LONE PILGRIM. 11s. & 8s.

COMMACK.

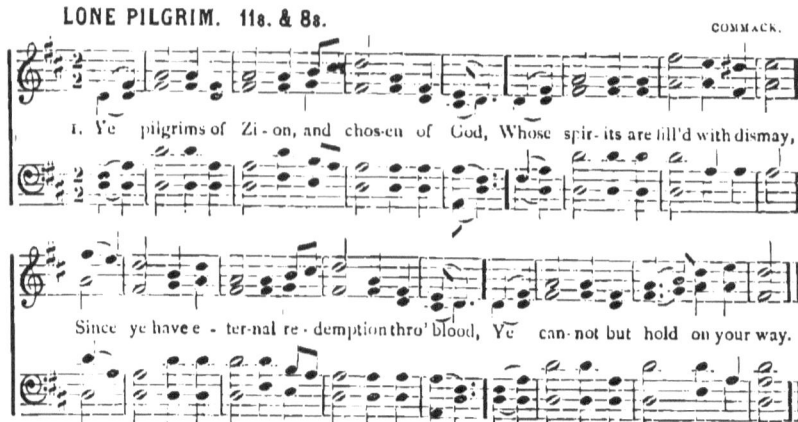

1. Ye pilgrims of Zi-on, and chosen of God, Whose spirits are fill'd with dismay, Since ye have e-ter-nal re-demption thro' blood, Ye can-not but hold on your way.

591 (784) Job 17:9.

2 As Jesus, in covenant love, did engage
  A fulness of grace to display,
  The powers of darkness in malice may rage,
  The righteous shall hold on his way.

3 This truth, like its Author, eternal shall
  Tho' all things in nature decay; [stand,
  Upheld by Jehovah's omnipotent hand,
  The righteous shall hold on his way.

4 They may on the main of temptation be
  tossed;
  Their sorrows may swell as the sea;
  But none of the ransomed shall ever be lost;
  The righteous shall hold on his way.

5 Surrounded with sorrows, temptations,
  and cares,
  This truth with delight we survey,
  And sing, as we pass through this valley
  of tears,
  The righteous shall hold on his way.

Fowler.

OLMUTZ. S. M.

LOWELL MASON. Arr.

1. Christians, dismiss your fear; Let hope and joy succeed; The great good news with gladness hear, The Lord is ris'n indeed.

592 (437) Luke 24:34.

2 The shades of death withdrawn,
  His eyes their beams display;
  So wakes the sun, when rosy dawn
  Unbars the gates of day.

3 The promise is fulfilled:
  Salvation's work is done;
  Justice with mercy's reconciled,
  And God has raised his Son.

4 He quits the dark abode,
  From all corruptions free;

5 The holy, harmless Son of God
  Could no corruption see.

5 My soul, thy Saviour laud,
  Who all thy sorrows bore:
  Who died for sin, but lives to God,
  And lives to die no more.

6 His death procured thy peace;
  His resurrection's thine:
  Rest and receive the full release;
  'Tis signed with blood divine.

Hart.

MISCELLANEOUS.

GENEVA. 7s. 6s. D. LOWELL MASON.

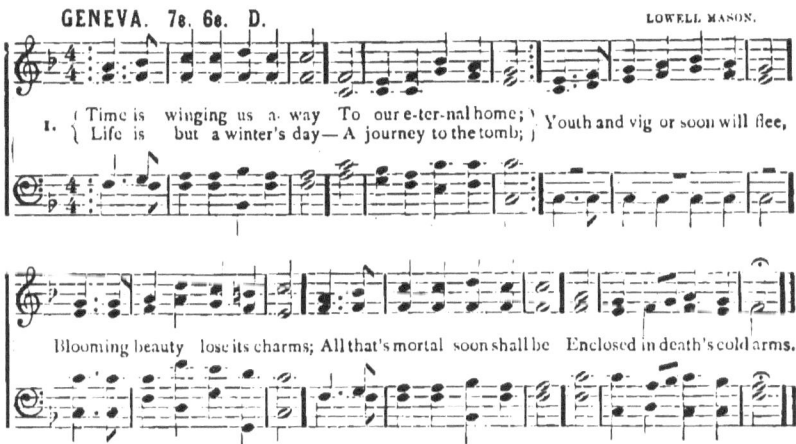

Time is winging us away To our eternal home; Life is but a winter's day—A journey to the tomb; Youth and vigor soon will flee, Blooming beauty lose its charms; All that's mortal soon shall be Enclosed in death's cold arms.

593

1 TIME is winging us away
  To our eternal home;
Life is but a winter's day—
  A journey to the tomb;
Youth and vigor soon will flee,
  Blooming beauty lose its charms;
All that's mortal soon shall be
  Enclosed in death's cold arms.

2 Time is winging us away
  To our eternal home;
Life is but a winter's day—
  A journey to the tomb;
But the Christian shall enjoy
  Health and beauty, soon, above,
Far beyond the world's annoy,
  Secure in Jesus' love.
                            J. Burton.

594 7s. 6s. D.

1 RISE, my soul, and stretch thy wings,
  Thy better portion trace;
Rise from transitory things
  Toward heaven, thy native place:
Sun and moon and stars decay;
  Time shall soon this earth remove;
Rise, my soul, and haste away
  To seats prepared above.

2 Rivers to the ocean run,
  Nor stay in all their course;

Fire ascending seeks the sun;
  Both speed them to their source:
So a soul that's born of God,
  Pants to view his glorious face;
Upward tends to his abode,
  To rest in his embrace.

3 Cease, ye pilgrims, cease to mourn,
  Press onward to the prize;
Soon our Saviour will return
  Triumphant in the skies:
Yet a season,—and you know
  Happy entrance will be given,
All our sorrows left below,
  And earth exchanged for heaven.
                          R. Seagrave.

595 7s.

1 "SERVANT of God, well done;
  Rest from thy loved employ;
The battle fought, the victory won,
  Enter thy Master's joy."

2 The pains of death are past;
  Labor and sorrow cease;
And life's long warfare closed at last,
  His soul is found in peace.

3 Soldier of Christ, well done;
  Praise be thy new employ;
And, while eternal ages run,
  Rest in thy Saviour's joy.
                  James Montgomery. 1825.

MISCELLANEOUS.

SWEET HOME. 11s.

1. 'Mid scenes of con-fus-ion and creat-ure complaints,
How sweet to my soul is com-mun-ion with ...... saints! To find at the banquet of mercy there's room, And feel in the presence of Jesus at home! Home, home, sweet, sweet home,
D.S.—Pre-pare me, dear Saviour, for glo-ry, my home.

596

2 Sweet bonds that unite all the children
   of peace,
And thrice blessed Jesus, whose love
   cannot cease;
Though oft from thy presence in sadness I
   roam,
I long to behold thee in glory at home.
   Home, home, &c.

3 I sigh from this body of sin to be free,
Which hinders my joy and communion
   with thee;
Though now my temptations like billows
   may foam,
All, all will be peace when I'm with thee at
   home.
   Home, home, &c.

4 While here in the valley of conflict I stay,
O give me submission and strength as my
   day;
In all my afflictions to thee I would come,
Rejoicing in hope of my glorious home.
   Home, home, &c.

5 Whate'er thou deniest, O give me thy
   grace,   [face;
The Spirit's sure witness, and smiles of thy
Indulge me with patience to wait at thy
   throne
And find even now a foretaste of my home.
   Home, home, &c.

6 I long, dearest Lord, in thy beauties to
   shine,
No more as an exile in sorrow to pine;
And in thy dear image arise from the tomb,
With glorified millions to praise thee at
   home.
   Home, home, sweet, sweet home,
Recieve me, dear Saviour, in glory, my
   home.
           Dennam.

597   7s.

1 JESUS, merciful and mild,
  Lead me as a helpless child;
  On no other arm but thine
  Would my weary soul recline;

2 Thou art ready to forgive,
  Thou canst bid the sinner live—
  Guide the wanderer day by day,
  In the straight and narrow way.

3 Thou canst fit me by thy grace
  For the heavenly dwelling-place;
  All thy promises are sure,
  Ever shall thy love endure;

4 Then what more could I desire,
  How to greater bliss aspire?
  All I need, in thee I see,
  Thou art all in all to me.   T. Hastings

MISCELLANEOUS.   241

MONTGOMERY. 7s.   THIBAUT.

1. Christ, the Lord, is ris'n to-day, Sons of men and an-gels say;
Raise your joys and tri-umphs high; Sing, ye heav'ns, and earth, re-ply.

598 (435)

2 Love's redeeming work is done;
Fought the fight, the battle won:
Lo! the sun's eclipse is o'er;
Lo! he sets in blood no more!

3 Vain the stone, the watch, the seal;
Christ hath burst the gates of hell;
Death in vain forbids his rise;
Christ hath opened Paradise.

4 Lives again our glorious King;
Where, O Death, is now thy sting?
Once he died our souls to save;
Where's thy victory, boasting Grave?
J. & C. W.

SEABURY. 7s.   F. L. ARMSTRONG.

1. Let the lit-tle chil-dren come; Suf-fer, and for-bid them not;
In my king-dom they have room; None of them shall be left out.

599   Mark 10: 14, 15; Isaiah 66: 13.

2 For these little ones I died;
They are precious in my sight;
And with me they shall abide
Evermore in realms of light.

3 All my people come to me,
Weak as little children are:
Only such my kingdom see;
Only such its glories share.

4 In their weakness is their strength;
All their wants a cry makes known;

And in all its breadth and length,
In each one my love is shown.

5 In each sorrowing, painful breath,
I am with them; and as one
Whom his mother comforteth,
So I comfort them alone.

6 Blessed are they now in me,
Resting in my arms of love;
Blessed shall they ever be
In the world of bliss above.   S. H. Durand.

MISCELLANEOUS.

MISSIONARY HYMN. 7s, 6s. D.
Dr. LOWELL MASON. 1792–1872.

1. Brief life is here our portion, brief sorrow, short-lived care; The life that knows no ending, The tearless life, is there. O happy retribution! Short toil, eternal rest; For mortals and for sinners A mansion with the blest.

600

1 BRIEF life is here our portion,
  Brief sorrow, short-lived care;
 The life that knows no ending,
  The tearless life, is there.
 O happy retribution!
  Short toil, eternal rest;
 For mortals and for sinners
  A mansion with the blest.

2 The morning shall awaken,
  The shadows shall decay,
 And each true-hearted servant
  Shall shine as doth the day.
 There God, our King and Portion,
  In fulness of his grace,
 Shall we behold forever,
  And worship face to face.

3 O sweet and blessed country,
  The home of God's elect,
 O sweet and blessed country,
  That eager hearts expect!
 Jesus, in mercy bring us
  To that dear land of rest;
 Who art with God the Father,
  And Spirit ever blest. St. Bernard.
                         J. M. Neale, Tr.

601 Tune—MANOAH, page 205.
C. M.

1 JERUSALEM, my happy home,
  Oh, how I long for thee!
 When will my sorrows have an end?
  Thy joys, when shall I see?

2 Thy walls are all of precious stone,
  Most glorious to behold;
 Thy gates are richly set with pearl,
  Thy streets are paved with gold.

3 Why should I shrink at pain and wo,
  Or feel at death dismay,
 With Canaan's goodly land in view,
  And realms of endless day?

4 Reach down, O Lord, thine arm of
  And cause me to ascend [grace,
 Where congregations ne'er break up,
  And Sabbaths never end.

5 When we've been there ten thousand
  Bright shining as the Sun, [years,
 We've no less days to sing God's praise
  Than when we first begun.

MISCELLANEOUS. 243

EVENTIDE. 10s.
W. H. MONK, 1861.

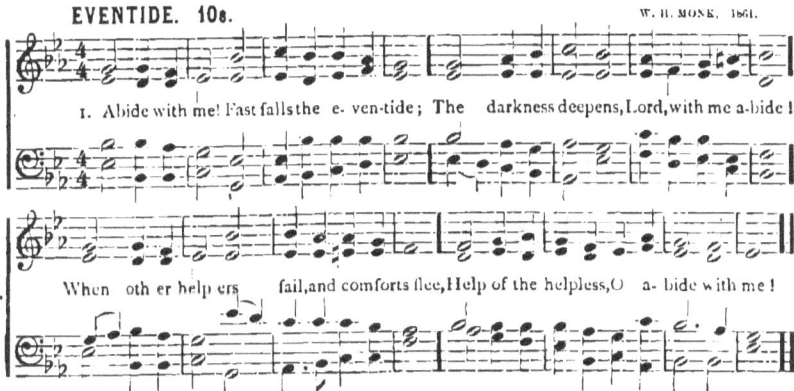

1. Abide with me! Fast falls the e-ventide; The darkness deepens, Lord, with me abide!
When other helpers fail, and comforts flee, Help of the helpless, O abide with me!

602
2 Swift to its close ebbs out life's little day;
Earth's joys grow dim, its glories pass away;
Change and decay in all around I see;
O thou, who changest not, abide with me!

3 I need thy presence every passing hour,
What but thy grace can foil the tempter's power?
Who, like thyself, my guide and stay can be?
Thro' cloud and sunshine, O abide with me!

4 Hold thou thy cross before my closing eyes;
Shine through the gloom, and point me to the skies;
Heaven's morning breaks, and earth's vain shadows flee!
In life, in death, O Lord, abide with me!
H. F. Lyte.

ST. PETERSBURG. L. M. 6l.
D. BORTNIANSKY. 1751-1825.

1. { When gath-'ring clouds a-round I view, And days are dark, and friends are few, }
   { On him I lean, who, not in vain, Ex-peri-enc'd ev-'ry hu-man pain; }
He feels my griefs, he sees my fears, And counts and treas-ures up my tears.

603 (803)
2 If aught should tempt my soul to stray,
From heavenly wisdom's narrow way,
To fly the good I would pursue,
Or do the ill I would not do;
Still he, who felt temptation's power,
Shall guard me in that dangerous hour.

3 When vexing thoughts within me rise,
And, sore dismayed, my spirit dies;
Then he who once vouchsafed to bear
The sickening anguish of despair,
Shall sweetly soothe, shall gently dry,
The throbbing heart, the streaming eye.
Grant.

MISCELLANEOUS.

WONDROUS LOVE. P. M. No. 1.

1. What wondrous love is this, O my soul, O my soul, What wondrous love is this, O my soul! What wondrous love is this, that caus'd the Lord of bliss
D.C.—To bear the dreadful curse for my soul, for my soul, To bear the dreadful curse for my soul!

604

2 When I was sinking down, sinking down,
    sinking down,
When I was sinking down, sinking down;
When I was sinking down beneath God's
    righteous frown,   [my soul,
Christ laid aside his crown for my soul, for
Christ laid aside his crown for my soul.

3 To God and to the Lamb I will sing, I
    will sing,
To God and to the Lamb I will sing;
To God and to the Lamb, and to the Great
    I AM,   [I will sing,
While millions join the theme, I will sing,
While millions join the theme, I will sing.

4 Ye sons of Zion's King, join the praise,
    join the praise,
Ye sons of Zion's King, join the praise;
Ye sons of Zion's King, with hearts and
    voices sing,   [in his praise,
And strike each tuneful string in his praise,
And strike each tuneful string in his praise.

5 And when to that bright world we ar-
    rive, we arrive,
And when to that bright world we arrive;
When to that world we go, free from all
    pain and wo,   [and sing on,
We'll join the happy throng, and sing on,
We'll join the happy throng, and sing on.

WONDROUS LOVE. P. M. No. 2.

1. What wondrous love is this, O my soul, O my soul, What wondrous love is this, O my soul!
D.S.—for my soul, To bear the dreadful curse for my soul!

What wondrous love is this, that caus'd the Lord of bliss To bear the dreadful curse for my soul,

MISCELLANEOUS.

THE ROCK. 11s. WAKEFIELD.

1. In seasons of grief to my God I'll repair, When my heart is o'erwhelmed with sorrow and care: From the ends of the earth unto thee will I cry: Lead me to the Rock that is higher than I. Higher than I, Higher than I! Lead me to the Rock that is higher than I.

605

2 When Satan, my foe, comes in like a flood,
To drive my poor soul from the fountain of
good,
I'll pray to the Saviour who kindly did die;
"Lead me to the Rock that is higher than I!"

3 And when I have ended my pilgrimage
here,
In Jesus' pure righteousness let me appear:
From the swellings of Jordan to thee will I cry;
"Lead me to the Rock that is higher than I!"
John Price.

606 11s. Psa. 61: 2
1 CONVINCED as a sinner, to Jesus I come,
Informed by the gospel for such there is room;
Overwhelmed with sorrow for sin, will I cry,
"Lead me to the Rock that is higher than I!"

2 When tempted by Satan my Saviour to
leave,
Who sets forth religion as meant to deceive,
I'll claim my relation to Jesus on high,
The Rock of Salvation that's higher than I!

3 When God from my soul shall his presence remove,
To try by his absence the strength of my love,
I'll rest on the promise of Jesus, and try
The force of that Rock which is higher than I!

4 When sorely afflicted and ready to faint,
Before my Redeemer I'll spread my complaint;   [rely
Midst storms and distresses, my soul shall
On Jesus, the Rock that is higher than I!
Bennett.

MISCELLANEOUS.

IT IS I. 12s. & 8s.　　　A. S. KIEFFER

1. When the storm in its fury on Gal-i-lee fell, And lift ed its waters on high,
And the faithless disciples were bound in the spell, Jesus whis, er'd, "Fear *Omit* not, it is I."
D.S.— "Fear not, trembling *Omit* ...... one, it is I."

"It is I, it is I, Fear not, trembling one, it is I," { In the midst of the storm,
in the midst of the gloom. }

By permission.

607

2 The storm could not bury that word in the wave,
'Twas taught through the tempest to fly,
It shall reach his disciples in every age,
Saying, "Be not afraid, it is I."

3 When the spirit is broken with sorrow and care,
And comfort is ready to die,

Then darkness shall pass, and the sunshine appear,
By the life-giving word, "It is I."

4 When death is at hand, and this cottage
Is left with a tremulous sigh, [of clay
The gracious Redeemer will light all the way,
Saying, "Be not afraid, it is I."

Rev. I. Baltzell.

I DO BELIEVE. C. M.

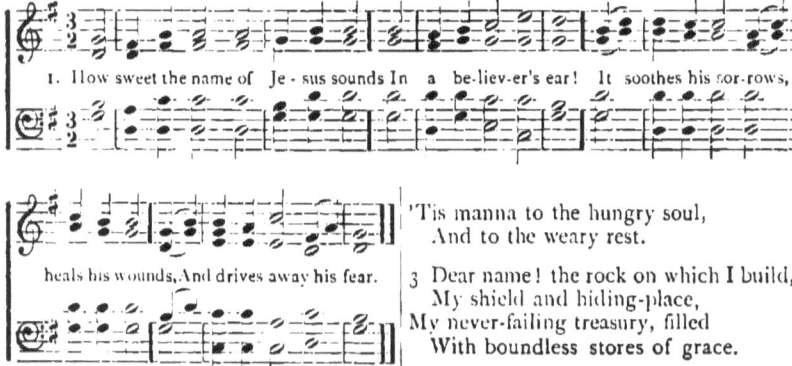

1. How sweet the name of Je - sus sounds In a be-liev-er's ear! It soothes his sor-rows,
heals his wounds, And drives away his fear.

'Tis manna to the hungry soul,
And to the weary rest.

3 Dear name! the rock on which I build,
My shield and hiding-place,
My never-failing treasury, filled
With boundless stores of grace.

608 (746)　Cant 1:3.

2 It makes the wounded spirit whole,
And calms the troubled breast;

4 Jesus, my Shepherd, Husband, Friend,
My Prophet, Priest, and King,
My Lord, my Life, my Way, my End,
Accept the praise I bring.　Newton.

MISCELLANEOUS. 247

BETHANY. 6s. & 4s. L. MASON.

1. Near-er, my God, to thee, Near-er to thee; E'en though it be a cross
D.S.—Near-er, my God, to thee,

That rais-eth me; Still all my song shall be, Near-er, my God, to thee,
Near-er to thee.

By permission.

609

2 Though like a wanderer,
  The sun gone down,
  Darkness be over me,
  My rest a stone;
  Yet in my dreams I'd be
  Nearer, my God, to thee,
  Nearer to thee.

3 There let the way appear
  Steps unto heaven;
  All that thou sendest me
  In mercy given;
  Angels to beckon me
  Nearer, my God, to thee,
  Nearer to thee.

4 Then, with my waking thoughts,
  Bright with thy praise,
  Out of my stony griefs,
  Bethels I'll raise;
  So by my woes to be
  Nearer, my God, to thee,
  Nearer to thee.

5 Or if on joyful wing,
  Cleaving the sky,
  Sun, moon, and stars forgot,
  Upward I fly;
  Still all my song shall be,
  Nearer, my God, to thee,
  Nearer to thee. S. F. Adams.

610 (321) C. M. Cant. 5: 10-16.

1 To Christ, the Lord, let every tongue
  Its noblest tribute bring:
  When he's the subject of the song,
  Who can refuse to sing?

2 Survey the beauties of his face,
  And on his glories dwell;
  Think of the wonders of his grace,
  And all his triumphs tell

3 Majestic sweetness sits enthroned
  Upon his awful brow;
  His head with radient glories crowned,
  His lips with grace o'erflow.

4 No mortal can with him compare
  Among the sons of men:
  Fairer he is than all the fair
  That fill the heavenly train.

5 To him I owe my life, and breath,
  And all the joys I have:
  He makes me triumph over death,
  And saves me from the grave.

6 To heaven, the place of his abode,
  He brings my weary feet;
  Shows me the glories of my God,
  And makes my joys complete. Stennett.

MISCELLANEOUS.

BELIEF. C. M. D. BRADBURY.

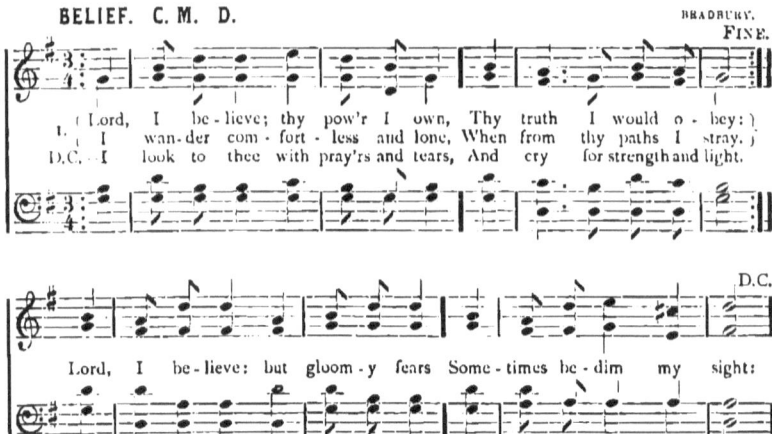

611

1 Lord, I believe; thy power I own,
   Thy truth I would obey:
I wander comfortless and lone,
   When from thy paths I stray.
Lord, I believe: but gloomy fears
   Sometimes bedim my sight:
I look to thee with prayers and tears,
   And cry for strength and light.

2 Lord, I believe a rest remains
   To all thy people known;
A rest where pure enjoyment reigns,
   And thou art loved alone.
A rest where all our soul's desire
   Is fixed on things above;
Where fear, and sin, and grief expire,
   Cast out by perfect love.

3 O that I now the rest might know,
   Believe, and enter in:
Now Saviour, now the power bestow,
   And let me cease from sin;
Remove this hardness from my heart;
   This unbelief remove;
To me the rest of faith impart,—
   The Sabbath of thy love.
                              Wreford.

612   C. M.

1 'Tis winter in my soul; my sins
   Like clouds o'erspread the sky;
While wailing winds and dreary rains
   To me all joys deny.

2 My heart lies hopeless of relief,
   And filled with deep alarm,
Like the cold earth, benumbed with grief,
   Under the pelting storm.

3 I try to look to God, but sin
   Forbids to lift my eyes;
My cries and prayers are all in vain,
   Guilt will not let them rise.

4 O weary winter of the soul,
   How sad and full of gloom!
The heavy hours, how slow they roll,
   While griefs my heart consume.

5 And must I thus fore'er remain?
   Will the sun shine no more?
May I not hope that yet again
   His beams will warmth restore?

6 Turn my captivity, O Lord!
   Once more to thee I call;
And let thy sweet forgiving word
   Make summer in my soul.

7 Then shall the streams of joyful praise,
   Loosed by thy gracious hand,
To thy blessed name flow all my days,
   In my heart's southern land.
                           Silas H. Durand.

MISCELLANEOUS.

SPRING. C. M.
L. C. EVERETT.

1. While winter's gloom was still o'er-spread, And on my spirit lay, The voice of my Be-lov-ed said, Rise up and come a-way.

By permission.

613

1 WHILE winter's gloom was still o'er-
 And on my spirit lay, [spread,
 The voice of my Beloved said,
 Rise up and come away.

2 For lo, the winter's past, the rain
 Is over now and gone;
 The flowers appear, and songs again
 Of praises are begun.

3 The power and sweetness of that voice
 Wrought wondrous change in me;
 Made my poor, drooping heart rejoice,
 And fears and sorrows flee.

4 In sweet amazement I came forth;
 What wonders met my eyes!
 Spring's glorious beauty on the earth,
 Her radiance in the skies.

5 Grace fills the garden of the Lord
 With blooming joys from heaven;
 The warm south wind is in that word
 Which shows my sins forgiven.

6 'Tis this makes winter clouds depart,
 And gives me brighter days;
 The sweet spring time is in my heart,
 And I am filled with praise.

7 What heavenly rest from cold and pain
 In these soft airs that come

 With blessed thoughts of Jesus' name,
 And breathing rich perfume.

8 Thanks that the weary days are o'er;
 Thanks for spring's gentle sway;
 Thanks for the love that says with power,
 Rise up and come away.
Silas H. Durand.

614 C. M.

1 JESUS, the very thought of thee,
 With sweetness fills my breast:
 But sweeter far thy face to see,
 And in thy presence rest.

2 No voice can sing, no heart can frame,
 Nor can the memory find
 A sweeter sound than Jesus' name,
 To those of heavenly mind.

3 O Hope of every contrite heart!
 O Joy of all the meek!
 To those who ask, how kind thou art!
 How good, to those who seek!

4 But what to those who find? Ah! this,
 No tongue nor pen can show;
 The love of Jesus, what it is,
 None but his loved ones know.
Bernard of Clairvaux. 1153.
Tr. by E. Caswall. 1849.

HOW CALM AND BEAUTIFUL. 8s, 6s & 8s.

THOS. HASTINGS.

1. How calm and beautiful the morn That gilds the sacred tomb, Where once the Crucifi'd was borne, And veil'd in midnight gloom! O weep no more the Saviour slain; The Lord is ris'n, He lives again.

615

1 How calm and beautiful the morn,
  That gilds the sacred tomb,
Where once the Crucified was borne,
  And veiled in midnight gloom!
O weep no more the Saviour slain;
The Lord is risen—He lives again.

2 Ye mourning saints, dry every tear
  For your departed Lord;
"Behold the place—He is not here,"
  The tomb is all unbarred;
The gates of death were closed in vain;
The Lord is risen—He lives again.

3 Now cheerful to the house of prayer,
  Your early footsteps bend,
The Saviour will himself be there,
  Your Advocate and Friend;
Once by the law your hopes were slain,
But now in Christ ye live again.

4 How tranquil now the rising day!
  'Tis Jesus still appears,
A risen Lord, to chase away
  Your unbelieving fears;
O weep no more your comforts slain;
The Lord is risen—He lives again.

5 And when the shades of evening fall,
  When life's last hour draws nigh,
If Jesus shines upon the soul,
  How blissful then to die!
Since he has risen who once was slain,
Ye die in Christ to live again.
                              T. Hastings.

616 (266) 8s, 6s & 8s.

1 LET others boast their ancient line
  In long succession great;
In the proud list, let heroes shine,
  And monarchs swell the state;
Descended from the King of kings,
Each saint a nobler title sings.

2 Pronounce me, gracious God! thy son,
  Own me an heir divine;
I'll pity princes on the throne,
  When I can call thee mine:
Sceptres and crowns unenvied rise,
And lose their lustre in mine eyes.

3 Content, obscure, I pass my days,
  To all I meet unknown;
And wait till thou thy child shalt raise,
  And seat me near thy throne:
No name, no honors here I crave,
Well pleased with those beyond the grave.

4 Jesus, my elder brother, lives;
  With him I too shall reign;
Nor sin, nor death, while he survives,
  Shall make the promise vain:
In him my title stands secure,
And shall while endless years endure.

5 When he, in robes divinely bright,
  Shall once again appear,
Thou too, my soul, shalt shine in light,
  And his full image bear;
Enough!—I wait th' appointed day;
Blessed Saviour, haste, and come away.
                              Cruttenden.

MISCELLANEOUS.

VOX ANGELICA. 11s. 10s. HENRY SMART. 1867—.

1. O God of love, how in-fi-nite and ho-ly, How great in wisdom and in pow'r thou art! And yet dost make thy dwelling with the lowly, And him who is of meek and con-trite heart, And him who is of meek and contrite heart.

617

2 Under the shadow of thy wing reposing,
I feel that all is best which comes to me;
I see thy circling arms my way enclosing,
And feel that e'en my life is hid with thee.

3 Thy grace divine, thy holy consolations,
Thy gift of faith, with its mysterious power,
Thy love, that heavenward wings my aspir-
  ations,
Hallow the silence of the midnight hour.

4 In songs of gratitude my heart would
  render
Unto thy holy name the praises due,
For pardon, peace, and countless mercies
  [new.
For old things passed away, and all things

5 Each secret breathing of sincere devotion
Reaches thy pitying, ever-listening ear,
And thy great love, exhaustless as the ocean,
Fills and encircles all thy children here.

6 Throughout the darkness and the silence
  lonely,   [and song;
Thou art my light and hope, my strength
I find no rest but in thy favor only,
To whom the issues of my life belong.
James B. Durand.

618
11s. 10s.

1 My God, my Keeper, thou doest never
  slumber,
But looking on me from thy throne above,
Dost hear my sighings, all my heart-throbs
  number,
And watch me ever with thine eye of love.

2 Oft-times, in sad, unquiet thoughts I lan-
  guish,   [care,
Oppressed with sin and sorrow, strife and
Bowed down in spirit with a bitter anguish,
And fearful even to cry out in prayer.

3 But then if to thy throne of mercy turning,
I look to thee from life's o'er-darken'd ways
Thou givest me the oil of joy for mourning,
And for my heaviness the voice of praise.

4 The silent, shadowy hours move onward
  slowly,
But a sweet sense of joy abides with me;
One thought alone makes the night watches
  holy,   [thee!
The blessed thought that I am still with

5 And morning cometh! soon these watch-
  ings ended,
Soon all these earthly nights and vigils o'er,
On the freed soul shall break the radiance
  splendid
Of perfect day upon the sinless shore.

6 Oh, there shall be no more of restless
  sighing,
No more of sorrow and of blighting care;
For in that glorious home of bliss undying,
No shadow falleth and no night is there.
James B. Durand.

MISCELLANEOUS.

TALMAR. 8s. & 7s.

1. One there is, above all others, Well deserves the name of Friend;
His is love beyond a brother's, Costly, free, and knows no end!

619

2 Which of all our friends, to save us,
Could, or would, have shed his blood?
But our Jesus died to have us
Reconciled, in him, to God.

3 When he lived on earth abased,
Friend of sinners was his name;
Now, above all glory raised,
He rejoices in the same.

4 O for grace our hearts to soften!
Teach us, Lord, at length to love,
We, alas, forget too often
What a Friend we have above. Newton.

OLIVE. 7s.   PETER RITTER, J. J.   Arr. by P. G. L.

1. O the pow'r of love divine! Who its heights and depths can tell—
Tell Jehovah's grand design, To redeem our souls from hell.

620 (274) 1 John 2: 1; 4: 10.

1 O THE power of love divine!
Who its heights and depths can tell—
Tell Jehovah's grand design,
To redeem our souls from hell.

2 Mystery of redemption this—
All my sins on Christ were laid;
My offense was reckoned his:
He the great atonement made!

3 Fully I am justified;
Free from sin, and more than free:
Guiltless, since for me he died;
Righteous, since he lived for me.

4 Jesus, now to thee I bow:
Let thy praise my tongue employ.
Saved unto the utmost now,
Who can speak my heartfelt joy!
Bradford.

MISCELLANEOUS.

LOVE. C. M. D.

621

3 My sorrows past, and I, at last,
 Have heavenly comforts found;
My heart with Jesus and His saints
 In sweetest union bound.
4 If fellowship with saints below,
 Is to our souls so sweet,
What heavenly rapture shall we know
When round the throne we meet?

5 While here we sit and sing his love
 With raptures so divine,
Our joys are more like their's above,
 While in their songs we join.
6 Our hearts are filled with holy zeal,
 We long to see the King;
We long to see those heavenly hills,
 Where saints and angels sing.

SILVER STREET. S. M.

622 Psa. 95.
2 He formed the deeps unknown,
 He gave the seas their bound;
The watery worlds are all his own,
 And all the solid ground.
3 Come worship at his throne,
 Come bow before the Lord;

We are his works, and not our own—
 He formed us by his word.
4 To-day attend his voice,
 Nor dare provoke his rod;
Come, like the people of his choice,
 And own your gracious God.   Watts.

254 MISCELLANEOUS.

AMERICA. S. M.
WETMORE.

623
2 When he descends to show
  The wonders of his heart,
  His presence lays proud nature low,
  And guilty fears depart.

3 Rich mercy he proclaims
  To sinners in distress;
  And, by the most endearing names,
  Reveals to them his grace.

BALCOME. S. M.

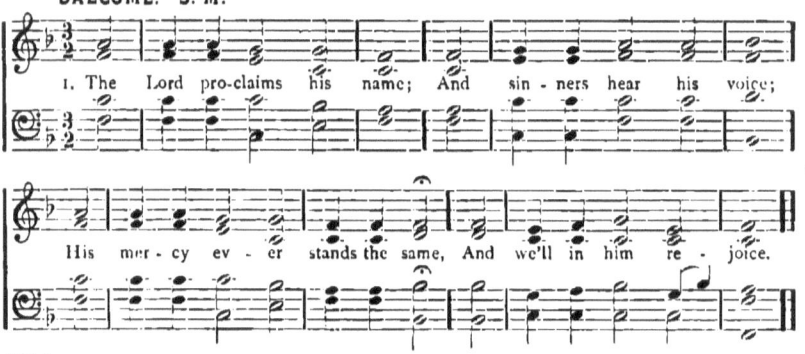

624 Exod. 33: 19.
2 His name is gracious still,
  And freely he bestows
  The bounty of his sovereign will,
  On all who feel their woes.

3 His patience long endures,
  And saved sinners know,
  A God, long-suffering, still restores
  Their joy and peace below.

4 The thousands whom he loves
  He pardons and forgives,
  Their persons he in Christ approves,
  And will while Jesus lives.

5 Lord, help us to believe,
  And make thy name our choice;
  Thy mercy freely to us give,
  And we'll in thee rejoice.

MISCELLANEOUS. **255**

HORTON. 7s.   X. S. VON WARTENSEE. 1786-1868.

1. Songs of praise the an-gels sang, Heav'n with hal-le-lu-jahs rang, When Je-ho-vah's work be-gun, When he spake, and it was done.

625

1 Songs of praise the angels sang,
Heaven with hallelujahs rang,
When Jehovah's work begun,
When he spake, and it was done.

2 Songs of praise awoke the morn
When the Prince of peace was born;
Songs of praise arose when he
Captive led captivity.

3 Saints below, with heart and voice,
Still in songs of praise rejoice;
Learning here, by faith and love,
Songs of praise to sing above.

4 Borne upon their latest breath,
Songs of praise shall conquer death;
Then, amidst eternal joy,
Songs of praise their powers employ.
James Montgomery. 1825.

626   7s.

1 Cast thy burden on the Lord;
Lean thou only on his word:
Ever will he be thy stay,
Though the heavens shall melt away.

2 Ever in the raging storm,
Thou shalt see his cheering form,
Hear his pledge of coming aid:
"It is I; be not afraid."

3 Cast thy burden at his feet;
Linger near his mercy-seat:
He will lead thee by the hand
Gently to the better land.

4 He will gird thee by his power,
In thy weary, fainting hour;
Lean, then, loving on his word;
Cast thy burden on the Lord.
George Rawson.

627   S. M.

1 My Father! cheering name!
  Oh, may I call thee mine!
Give me with humble hope to claim
  A portion so divine.

2 This can my fears control,
  And bid my sorrows fly;
What real harm can reach my soul
  Beneath my Father's eye?

3 Whate'er thy will denies,
  I calmly would resign;

For thou art just, and good, and wise:
  Oh, bend my will to thine!

4 Whate'er thy will ordains,
  Oh, give me strength to bear;
Still let me know a Father reigns,
  And trust a Father's care.

5 Thy ways are little known
  To my weak, erring sight;
Yet shall my soul, believing, own
  That all thy ways are right.
Steele.

MISCELLANEOUS.

SENTENCE.—FATHER, WE'LL REST IN THY LOVE. By per. R. M McIntosh.

ALPHABETICAL LIST OF TUNES.

		PAGE.			PAGE.
ALEXANDER	7, 6.	82	Dennis	S. M.	29
All Saints	L. M.	119	Desire	L. M.	143
Amazing Grace	C. M.	68, 87	Detroit	C. M.	148
Amboy	7, D.	131	Devizes	C. M.	89
America	6, 4.	155	Devotion	L. M.	49
America	S. M.	254	Disciple	8, 7, D.	139
Antioch	C. M.	21	Downs	C. M.	128
Ariel	C. P. M.	160	Dravo	C. M.	220
Arlington	C. M.	5, 198	Duane Street	L. M. D.	11, 51
Athens	C. M. D.	211	Duke Street	L. M.	64, 175
Autumn	8, 7, D.	138	Dunbar	S. M.	169
Avon	C. M.	66, 195	Dundee	C. M.	107
Aylsbury	S. M.	104	Dunlap	C. M.	17, 164
			Durand	C. M.	92
BALCOME	S. M.	254			
Balerma	C. M.	78, 201	ELIZABETHTOWN	C. M.	95
Baptism	C. M.	188	Eltham	7, D.	131
Barby	C. M.	88	Ernan	L. M.	77
Bartimeus	8, 7.	18	Evan	C. M.	12, 134
Bavaria	8. 7, D.	99	Evening	S. M.	100
Bealoth	S. M. D.	235	Evening Hymn	L. M.	76
Belief	C. M. D.	246	Evening Shade	S. M.	144
Believer	C. M.	151	Eventide	10.	243
Beloved	11, 8.	159	Exhortation	C. M.	218
Bethany	6, 4.	247			
Beverly	C. M.	169			
Blissful Home	S. M.	152	FAIRFIELD	C. M.	94
Boyleston	S. M.	190	Faithful Soldier	7, 6.	236
Bray		45	Father, we'll rest		256
Bridgewater	L. M.	48	Federal Street	L. M.	217
Brown	C. M.	83, 110	Ferguson	S. M.	73
			Forest	L. M.	142, 166
CADDO	C. M.	225	Foster	8.	199
Cambridge	C. M.	43	Foundation	11.	124
Chimes	C. M.	54	Fountain	C. M.	37
China	C. M.	209	Frederick	11.	227
Clarington	8, D.	81, 172	Fredericksburg	H. M.	56
Coleshill	C. M.	210			
Communion	C. M.	94	GANGES	C. P. M.	182
Complainer	7, 6.	216	Garden	C. P. M.	84
Condescension	C. M.	116	Geneva	7, 6, D.	239
Conflict	L. M.	171	Georgia	S. M.	104
Consolation	C. M.	123	Gerar	S. M.	15
Cook	7.	173	Give	C. M.	96
Coronation	C. M.	46	Golden Hill	S. M.	170
Cowper	C. M.	42	Goshen	11.	39
Cypress	C. M.	215	Gratitude	L. M.	35, 228
			Green	C. M.	158
DAYTON	S. M.	61	Greenville	8, 7, D.	233
De Fleury	8, D.	58, 93	Grinnell	L. M.	10
Denfield	C. M.	37	Guide	7.	98

ALPHABETICAL LIST OF TUNES.

		PAGE.			PAGE.
HADDAM	H. M.	174	NAOMI	C. M.	106
Hall	S. M.	126	New Britain	C. M.	75, 179
Hamburg	L. M.	102	Nettleton	8, 7, D.	156
Harwell	8, 7, D.	63	New Concord	6, 6, 9.	112
Harwich	H. M.	57	New Hope	S. M.	28
Hassell	C. M.	45	Ninety Fifth	C. M.	165
Hebron	L. M.	200, 229	Northfield	C. M.	22
Hedding	C. P. M.	98	Nottinghill	C. M.	47
He Lives	L. M.	230			
Hendon	7.	120	O, LAND OF REST	C. M.	135
Hiding-place	L. M.	72	Old Hundred	L. M.	198
Hillside	L. M.	25, 67	Oliphant	8, 7, 4.	214
Home	C. M. D.	69	Olive	7.	252
Horton	7.	255	Olmutz	S. M.	238
House of the Lord	12.	226	Ortonville	C. M.	71, 196
How calm	8, 6, 8.	250			
Hubert	C. M.	36, 150	PALESTRINA	C. M.	180
Hursley	L. M.	146, 193	Parting Hand	L. M. D.	136
			Peterborough	C. M.	7, 54
I DO BELIEVE	C. M.	122, 246	Pilgrim	8, 7, D.	233
Idumea	S. M.	177	Pisgah	C. M.	113
I'll lay my armor down	C. M.	134	Pleasant Hill	C. M. D.	219
Imandra	11.	222	Plenary	C. M. D.	6
Indian's Farewell	7, (6 l.)	137	Pleyel	7.	147
Indian's Lament	L. M.	64	Portugal	L. M.	197
Invitation	8, 7, 4.	33	Portuguese Hymn	11.	19
It is I	12, 8.	246	Prayer	7.	137
			Prospect	L. M.	40
JERUSALEM	C. M.	204			
Judah	8, 7.	108	RAPTURE	L. M. D.	130
Judkins	C. M.	20	Redemption	11.	222
			Refuge	L. M.	38
KEENE	8, 11.	213	Rest	L. M.	207
Kentucky	S. M.	202	Restoration	8, 7.	186
Kentucky	8, 11.	213	Retreat	L. M.	90, 231
King of Peace	7.	127	Ripley	8, 7, D.	138
Kingwood	C. P. M.	203	Rissah	C. M.	168
			Rochester	C. M.	70
LABAN	S. M.	61	Rockingham	L. M.	31, 162
Leander	C. M. D.	86	Russia	L. M.	206
Lebanon	S. M. D.	50			
Lenox	H M.	16	SABBATH	S. M.	9
Little Marlborough	S. M.	212	Salvation	C. M.	189
Liverpool	C. M.	141	Samantha	11.	74
Love	C. M. D.	97, 253	Seabury	7.	241
Loving Kindness	L. M.	2	Selborne		237
Luton	L. M.	103	Selggur	C. M.	13, 117
Lynn	L. M.	60	Sessions	L. M.	3, 160, 163
Lyons	10, 11.	80	Shawmut	S. M.	153
Lyra	C. M.	26	Sheldon	C. M.	55
			Sherburne	C. M.	23
MAITLAND	C. M.	62	Shirland	S. M.	191
Manoah	C. M.	36, 205	Siberia	8, 7, 4.	153
Marlow	C. M.	181	Sicilian Hymn	8, 7, 4.	33, 199
Martyn	7, D.	176	Siloam	C. M.	59
Mear	C. M.	140, 194	Silver Street	S. M.	157, 253
Melody	C. M.	4, 59	Smithfield	S. M.	73
Mendon	L. M.	65	Social Band	L. M. D.	85
Merlin	7, D.	154	Southampton	8.	129
Meribah	C. P. M.	27	Spanish Hymn	7, D.	178
Middleton	8, 7, D.	44	Spring	C. M.	249
Missionary Hymn	7, 6.	242	Star in the East	11.	24
Montgomery	7.	241	Star of Bethlehem	L. M.	185

ALPHABETICAL LIST OF TUNES.

		PAGE			PAGE
State Street	S. M.	145	Ward	L. M.	118
St. Martyns	C. M.	149	Ware	L. M.	132, 167
St. Petersburg	L. M. (6 l.)	243	Warwick	C. M.	161
St. Thomas	S. M.	8	Watchman	7, D.	176
Summer	11.	227	Watchman	8, 7.	156
Sweet Home	11.	240	Watchman, tell us	7, D.	232
			Waverly	L. M.	115
Talmar	8, 7.	252	Webb	7, 6.	111, 237
Tappan	P. M.	183	Wells	L. M.	14
Thatcher	S. M.	50	Wilmot	7,	34
The Bower of Prayer	11.	125	Windham	L. M.	187, 192
The Lone Pilgrim	11, 8.	238	Withers	L. M.	79
The Rock	11, 12.	245	Wondrous Love	1st, 2nd.	244
Theron	L. M.	30, 121	Woodbury	L. M.	41
Toplady	7. (6 l.)	52	Woodbury	S. M. D.	234
This World is Poor		183	Woodland	C. M. P.	53, 97
Union	8.	101	Woodside	C. M.	105, 223
Uxbridge	L. M.	1, 184	Woodstock	C. M.	224
			Woodworth	L. M.	114, 133
Varina	C. M. D.	208			
Vernon	L. M. (6 l.)	108	Zephyr	L. M.	132
Vigils	C. M.	221	Zella	H. M.	32
Vox Angelica	11, 10.	251	Zion	8, 7, 4.	91

METRICAL INDEX.

L. M.	PAGE.
ALL SAINTS	119
Bridgewater	48
Conflict	171
Desire	143
Devotion	49
Duane Street, D.	11, 51
Duke Street	64, 175
Eruan	77
Evening Hymn	76
Federal Street	217
Forest	142, 166
Gratitude	35, 228
Grinnell	10
Hamburg	102
Hebron	200, 229
He Lives	230
Hiding-place	72
Hillside	25, 67
Hursley	146, 193
Indian's Lament	64
Loving-kindness	2
Luton	103
Lynn	60
Mendon	65
Old Hundred	198
Parting Hand, D.	136
Portugal	197
Prospect	40
Rapture, D.	130
Refuge	38
Rest	207
Retreat	90, 231
Rockingham	31, 162
Russia	206
Sessions	3, 160, 163
Social Band, D.	85
Star of Bethlehem	185
St. Petersburg, (6 l.)	243
Theron	30, 121
Uxbridge	1, 184
Vernon, (6 l.)	108
Ward	118
Ware	132, 167
Waverly	115
Wells	14
Windham	187, 192
Withers	79
Woodbury	41
Woodworth	114, 133
Zephyr	132

C. M.	PAGE.
AMAZING GRACE	68, 87
Antioch	21
Arlington	5, 198
Athens, D.	211
Avon	66, 195
Balerma	78, 201
Baptism	188
Barby	88
Belief, D.	248
Believer	151
Beverly	169
Bray	45
Brown	83, 110
Caddo	225
Cambridge	43
Chimes	54
China	209
Coleshill	210
Communion	94
Condescension	116
Consolation	123
Coronation	46
Cowper	42
Cypress	215
Denfield	37
Detroit	148
Devizes	89
Downs	128
Dravo	220
Dundee	107
Dunlap	17, 161
Durand	92
Elizabethtown	95
Evan	12, 134
Exhortation	218
Fairfield	94
Fountain	37
Give	96
Green	158
Hassell	45
Home, D.	69
Hubert	36, 150
I do believe	122, 246
I'll lay my armor down	134
Jerusalem	204
Judkins	20
Leander, D.	86
Liverpool	141
Love, D.	97, 253
Lyra	26

	PAGE.
Maitland	62
Manoah	36, 205
Marlow	181
Mear	140, 194
Melody	4, 59
Naomi	106
New Britain	75, 179
Ninety Fifth	165
Northfield	22
Nottinghill	47
O Land of Rest	135
Ortonville	71, 196
Palestrina	180
Peterborough	7, 54
Pisgah	113
Pleasant Hill, D.	219
Plenary, D.	6
Rissah	168
Rochester	70
Salvation, D.	189
Selggur	13, 117
Sheldon	55
Sherburne	23
Siloam	59
Spring	249
St. Martyns	149
Varina, D.	208
Vigils	221
Warwick	161
Woodland	53
Woodside	105, 223
Woodstock	224

S. M.	
AMERICA	254
Aylsbury	104
Balcome	254
Bealoth, D.	235
Blissful Home	152
Boylston	190
Dayton	61
Dennis	29
Dunbar	109
Evening	100
Evening Shade	144
Ferguson	73
Gerar	15
Georgia	104
Golden Hill	170
Hall	126
Idumea	177

METRICAL INDEX.

	PAGE
Kentucky	202
Laban	61
Lebanon, D.	50
Little Marlborough	212
New Hope	28
Olmutz	238
Sabbath	9
Shawmut	153
Shirland	191
Silver Street	157, 253
Smithfield	73
State Street	145
St. Thomas	8
Thatcher	50
Woodbury, D	234

C P. M.

	PAGE
Ariel	160
Gauges	182
Garden	84
Hedding	98
Kingwood	203
Meribah	27
Woodland	97

H M.

	PAGE
Fredericksburg	56
Haddam	174
Harwich	57
Lenox	10
Zella	32

7s.

	PAGE
Amboy, D	131
Cook	173
Eltham, D.	131
Guide	98
Hendon	120
Horton	255
Indian's Farewell (6 l.)	137
King of Peace	127
Martyn, D	176
Merdin, D	154
Montgomery	241
Olive	252
Pleyel	147
Prayer	137
Seabury	241
Spanish Hymn, D	178
Toplady (6 l.)	52

	PAGE
Watchman, D	176
Watchman, tell us	232
Wilmot, D.	34

7s, 6s.

	PAGE
Alexander, D.	82
Complainer	216
Faithful Soldier	236
Geneva, D.	239
Missionary Hymn	242
Selborne	237
Webb, D.	111, 237

8s.

	PAGE
Clarington, D.	81, 172
De Fleury, D.	58, 93
Foster	199
Southampton	129
Union,	101

8s, 7s.

	PAGE
Autumn, D.	138
Bartimeus	18
Bavaria, D.	99
Disciple, D.	139
Greenville, D.	233
Harwell, D.	63
Judah	108
Middletown, D.	44
Nettleton, D.	156
Pilgrim, D.	233
Restoration	186
Ripley, D.	138
Talmar	252
Watchman,	156

8s, 7s, 4s

	PAGE
Invitation	33
Oliphant	214
Siberia	153
Sicilian Hymn	33, 199
Zion	91

8s, 6s, 8s.

	PAGE
How calm	250

8s, 11s.

	PAGE
Keene	213
Kentucky	213

6s, 6s, 9s.

	PAGE
New Concord	112

6s, 4s.

	PAGE
America	155
Bethany	247

10s.

	PAGE
Eventide	243

10s, 11s.

	PAGE
Lyons	80

11s, 10s.

	PAGE
Vox Angelica	251

11s.

	PAGE
Foundation	124
Frederick	227
Goshen	39
Imandra	223
Portuguese Hymn	19
Redemption	222
Star in the East	24
Summer	227
Sweet Home	240
The bower of prayer	125

11s, 12s.

	PAGE
The House of the Lord	226
The Rock	245

11s, 8s

	PAGE
Beloved	159
Samantha	74
The lone pilgrim	238

12s, 8s.

	PAGE
It is I	246

P M. or C. M.

	PAGE
Tappan	183
This world is poor	183
Wondrous Love, 1st, 2nd	244

SENTENCE.

	PAGE
Father, we'll rest	256

INDEX OF SCRIPTURE TEXTS.

Genesis.
CH. V.	HYMN
5 : 24,	560
12 : 11,	191
17 : 18,	227
22 : 6,	297
24 : 56,	469
32 : 26,	363

Exodus.
28 : 29,	133
33 : 19,	624

Numbers.
23 : 23,	386

Deuteronomy.
8 : 2,	572
33 : 25,	302

1st Samuel.
7 : 12,	286

2d Samuel.
16 : 17,	95

1st Kings.
3 : 5,	364
10 : 1–13,	570
17 : 16,	307

Nehemiah.
8 : 10,	274

Job.
7 : 16,	571
17 : 9,	591
19 : 25–27,	524
23 : 3, 4,	592
20 : 2,	417
40 : 4,	256

Psalms.
3 : 1–3,	317
3 : 3–6,	321
4 : 6,	280
6 : 4,	361
13.	411
17,	404
22 : 5–7,	366
24 : 7,	156
27,	373
27 : 4,	226
31,	377
31 : 15,	83
34 : 1,	83
35 : 3,	166
42.	260
43 : 3–5,	225
45,	170
46 : 4,	164
46 : 10,	294
46,	352
48,	350, 356
52 : 1,	508
57,	25
64 : 2,	428, 606
62 : 1,	382
66 : 16,	438
73 : 23–28,	216
73 : 25,	229, 411
77,	569
84,	139, 351, 353
85 : 9,	588
87 : 3,	310

CH. V.	HYMN
87 : 7,	110
89 : 1.	49
89 : 15,	34
89 : 28–34,	318
92.	331
95.	140, 516
104 : 34,	531
110 : 4,	102
115 : 1,	497
116 : 12,	391
119 : 32,	470
122,	358
133 : 1,	244
148 : 13,	384
119 : 1,	257

Canticles.
1 : 3,	608
1 : 15,	355
2 : 16,	316
3 : 11,	111
4 : 12,	249
4 : 16,	480
5 : 10–16,	610

Isaiah.
3 : 10,	71
8 : 20,	251
9 : 2,	107
12,	383
12 : 2,	196
32 : 2,	176
33 : 20, 21,	310
35 : 10,	381
45 : 19,	360
52 : 7,	37
56 : 5–11,	300
57 : 15,	214
60 : 18–20,	341
61 : 10,	92, 109
64 : 1,	415
66 : 13,	599

Jeremiah.
21 : 3,	440
31 : 3,	180
31 : 11,	498

Lamentations.
1 : 16,	395
3 : 24,	215
3 : 25,	197

Ezekiel.
11 : 19,	415

Micah.
5 : 5,	99
6 : 6–8,	163

Zechariah.
6 : 15,	132
13 : 1,	90

Matthew.
1 : 23,	84
5 : 2–12,	577
5 : 3,	253
6 : 10,	293
6 : 21,	327
6 : 28–30,	573
8 : 2, 3,	179
11 : 28,	325, 329
11 : 29,	463
12 : 20,	130

CH. V.	HYMN
14 : 27,	292
15 : 27,	367
24 : 45,	534
26 : 41,	371

Mark.
4 : 39,	208
9 : 24,	194
10 : 14, 15,	599

Luke.
2 : 25,	106
11 : 31,	579
12 : 32,	175, 381, 543
15 : 32,	581
23 : 42,	161
24 : 31,	592
21 : 51, 53,	149
29 : 10,	589

John.
3 : 7,	204
3 : 16,	118
4 : 8,	10
6 : 16–21,	427
10 : 16,	76
13 : 13–16,	502, 586
1* : 32,	143
14 : 10,	120
14 : 16, 17,	188
14 : 17–23,	485
14 : 21,	477
16 : 16,	479
19 : 30,	98
20 : 13,	213
21 : 15,	283
21 : 16,	315, 430
21 : 17,	230

Acts.
2 : 38,	460
4 : 12,	121
5 : 31,	311
11 : 22,	416
16 : 31,	198
22 : 16,	460

Romans.
3 : 19–22,	104
5 : 21,	66
7 : 19,	423
7 : 21,	2 6, 122
8 : 11,	540
8 : 29,	75
8 : 30,	76
8 : 33,	73
13 : 11,	552

1st Corinthians.
2 : 9, 10,	134
6 : 11,	153
6 : 17,	69
10 : 4,	126
10 : 16, 17,	476
11 : 23,	478
13 : 9,	110
13 : 12,	530
16 : 13,	280

2d Corinthians.
5 : 1, 5–8,	526
5 : 7,	193
5 : 17,	118
12 : 7 10,	282
12 : 9,	441
13 : 14,	501

Galatians.
CH. V.	HYMN
5 : 17,	394
6 : 11,	480

Ephesians.
1 : 4,	80
2 : 5–8,	169, 178
3 : 16,	492
4 : 15, 16,	113
6 : 14, 15,	490
6 : 13–17..	412

Philippians.
1 : 6,	79
1 : 21,	528
2 : 8,	101
3 : 3,	63
3 : 7–9,	281
4 : 4,	137

Colossians.
1 : 5, 6,	327
3 : 2,	81
3 : 11,	402

1st Timothy.
1 : 11,	129
1 : 15,	48

2d Timothy.
1 : 9,	74, 162, 584
1 : 12,	279

Titus.
2 : 10–13,	459, 527

Hebrews.
4 : 16,	365, 376
6 : 17–19,	78, 221
7 : 22,	382
10 : 19,	105
11	190
11 : 13,	413
12 : 2,	93
12 : 7,	262
13 : 20, 21,	500

James.
1 : 12,	431

1st Peter.
1 : 3–5,	151
1 : 6, 7,	429
1 : 18,	97
2 : 6,	198
2 : 7,	112, 252, 445

2d Peter.
1 : 4,	310

1st John.
1 : 7,	96
2 : 1, 4, 10,	620
3 : 1–3,	72
5 : 6,	475

Jude.
24, 25,	359

Revelation.
5 : 12,	102
5 : 11, 13,	392
21 : 22,	134
22 : 20,	442

INDEX OF FIRST LINES.

	HYMN.		HYMN.
Abide with me, fast falls the eventide	602	Behold the spouse oppressed with fears	296
A child of Jehovah, a subject of grace	559	Behold the throne of grace	376
A crumb of mercy, Lord, I crave	367	Behold, what wondrous grace	72
A debtor to mercy alone	199	Beneath the sacred throne of God	172
A few more days on earth to spend	511		
Afflicted saint, to Christ draw near	302	Blessed are the humble souls that see	577
Affliction is a stormy deep	421	Blessed are the sons of peace	270
A Friend there is, your voices join	308	Blessed are the souls that hear and know	31
A garden fenced from common earth	347	Blessed be the dear uniting love	65
Ah! I shall soon be dying	544	Blessed be the everlasting God	151
Ah, when with saints where Jesus reigns	553	Blessed be the tie that binds	245
Alas! and did my Saviour bleed	209	Blessed Jesus, Source of grace divine	405
Alas! what hourly dangers rise	371	Blessed Jesus, when my soaring thoughts	235
All hail the power of Jesus' name	111	Blow ye the trumpet, blow	40
All the elected train	80	Breathe from the gentle south, O Lord	372
Almighty King, whose wondrous hand	177	Brief life is here our portion	600
Although my Lord is now enthroned	512	Buried beneath the yielding wave	468
Amazing Grace! how sweet the sound	169	By faith in Christ I walk with God	195
Am I a soldier of the cross	280	By the poor widow's oil and meal	307
Amidst these various scenes of ills	425	By various maxims, forms and rules	93
Amid the splendors of thy state	10		
Among the princes, earthly gods	15	Cast thy burden on the Lord	626
And can my heart aspire so high	262	Cheer up, ye trembling souls	313
And did the Holy and the Just	101	Children of the heavenly King	381
And have I, Christ, no love to thee	232	Christ and his cross are all our theme	33
And is the gospel peace and love	540	Christ bears the names of all his saints	131
And must it, Lord, be so	431	Christ exalted is our song	382
And must this body die	533	Christians, dismiss your fears	592
Approach, my soul, the mercy-seat	366	Christians, if your hearts be warm	461
Arise, my soul, my joyful powers	407	Christ is mine and I am his	316
As branches from the vine	70	Christ is my all, my sure defense	402
Asleep in Jesus, blessed sleep	520	Christ the Lord is risen to-day	598
As on the cross the Saviour hung	161	Christ, whose glory fills the skies	128
A Sovereign Protector I have	321	Come, all ye sons of grace, and view	462
As the sun's enlivening eye	339	Come, and behold the place	473
As when the weary traveler gains	286	Come, blessed Spirit, source of light	187
At anchor laid, remote from home	186	Come, brethren, ye who love the Lord	503
At thy command, our dearest Lord	482	Come, Christian brethren, ere we part	337
Awake and sing the song	389	Come, dearest Lord, descend and dwell	492
Awake, awake, arise	41	Come, happy souls, approach your God	54
Awake, awake the sacred song	51	Come hither, all ye weary souls	329
Awaked by Sinai's awful sound	204	Come, Holy Spirit, Dove divine	464
Awake, my heart, arise, my tongue	109	Come, Holy Spirit, Heavenly Dove	183
Awake, my soul, in joyful lays	2	Come, let us join our cheerful songs	392
Awake, ye saints, and raise your eyes	552	Come, Lord, and warm each languid heart	549
Begin, my tongue, some heavenly theme	159	Come, my soul, thy suit prepare	364
Begone, unbelief, my Saviour is near	196	Come, raise your thankful voice	81
Begone, ye gilded vanities	290	Come, sound his praise abroad	622
Behold the leprous jew	179	Come, thou Almighty King	385
Behold the lilies, how they grow	573	Come, thou Fount of every blessing	386

INDEX OF FIRST LINES

	HYMN.		HYMN.
Come, thou long-expected Jesus	106	Glorious things of thee are spoken	340
Come, we that love the Lord	271	Glory to God on high	384
Come, ye that fear the Lord	438	Glory to thee, my God, this night	575
Come, ye that love the Saviour's name	116	God of my childhood and my youth	514
Compared with Christ, in all beside	64	God is the refuge of his saints	352
Constrained by their Lord to embark	427	God moves in a mysterious way	28
Convinced as a sinner, to Jesus I come	606	God, my supporter and my hope	216
Courage, my soul, behold the prize	306	God shall alone the refuge be	16
		God with us! O glorious name	84
DEAREST Saviour, we adore thee	47	Grace, like a fountain, ever flows	444
Dear Lord, and shall thy Spirit rest	188	Grace, 'tis a charming sound	178
Dear Lord, to us assembled here	365	Great Former of this various frame	6
Dear Lord, why should I doubt thy love	289	Great God, before thy throne	508
Dear Refuge of my weary soul	420	Great God, from thee there's naught	105
Dear Saviour, we are thine	69	Great God, how infinite art thou	17
Dear Saviour, when my thoughts recall	212	Great God, I own thy sentence just	524
Dear Shepherd of thy people here	369	Great God of Providence, thy ways	29
Death cannot make our souls afraid	523	Great God, we in thy name appear	463
Death may dissolve my body now	529	Great is the Lord, his works of might	14
Death is no more a frightful foe	528	Great Rock, for weary travelers made	330
Deep in the everlasting mind	75	Great Source of all eternal grace	86
Descend from heaven, immortal Dove	185	Great was the day, the joy was great	36
Did Christ the great example lead	506	Guide me, O thou great Jehovah	538
Dismiss us with thy blessing, Lord	496		
Does the gospel word proclaim	325	HAIL, mighty Jesus! how divine	170
Do not I love thee, O my Lord	233	Hail, sovereign grace, that first began	176
Down to the sacred wave	472	Hail, the blest morn, when the great	59
		Hail, thou once despised Jesus	46
ENCOMPASSED with clouds of distress	428	Happy the birth where grace presides	174
Enslaved by sin and bound in chains	97	Happy the heart where graces reign	228
Eternal God, enthroned on high	516	Hark! the blood-bought hosts above	66
Eternal Power, whose high abode	1	Hark! my soul, it is the Lord	315
Exceeding precious is my Lord	445	Hark! ten thousand harps and voices	152
Expand, my soul, arise and sing	74	Hark! the glad sound, the Saviour comes	55
		Hear what God the Lord hath spoken	341
FAITH is the brightest evidence	190	He dies! the Friend of sinners, dies	155
Far as thy name is known	356	Hence from my soul, sad thoughts, begone	273
Far from my thoughts, vain world, begone	400	His Master taken from his head	305
Far from these narrow scenes of night	555	Holy and reverend is the name	7
Far from the world, O Lord, I flee	272	Hosannah to the Prince of light	150
Father, I sing thy wondrous grace	103	How amiable, how fair	139
Father of heaven, Almighty King	484	How beauteous are their feet	37
Father, we'll rest in thy love	628	How calm and beautiful the morn	615
Father, whate'er of earthly bliss	264	How can I sink with such a prop	218
Firm as the earth thy gospel stands	44	How charming is the place	357
Fix my heart and eyes on thine	277	How did my heart rejoice to hear	343
Forever with the Lord	585	How firm a foundation, ye saints of the	310
For mercies countless as the sands	391	How great, how solemn is the work	470
For us the dear Redeemer died	318	How happy are the souls above	556
For weary saints a rest remains	328	How high a privilege 'tis to know	89
Free grace to every heaven-born soul	171	How long, O Lord, shall I complain	414
From all that dwell below the skies	158	How lost was my condition	590
From deep distress and troubled thought	85	How lovely, how divinely sweet	353
From east to west let others roam	334	How oft, alas, this wretched heart	210
From every stormy wind that blows	579	How oft have sin and Satan strove	78
From thee, my God, my joys shall rise	551	How pleasant, how divinely fair	351
From whence doth this union arise	248	How sore a plague is sin	422
		How strange is the course that a Christian	394
GIVE me the wings of faith to rise	219	How sweet and awful is the place	485
Give me thy Spirit, O my God	504	How sweet, how heavenly is the sight	236
Give to our God immortal praise	26	How sweetly flowed the gospel sound	35
Glad was my heart to hear	358	How sweet the name of Jesus sounds	608

INDEX OF FIRST LINES.

HYMN.	
How tedious and tasteless the hours	229
How vain are all things here below	568
How wondrous are the works of God	96
Humble souls, who seek salvation	460
Hungry, and faint, and poor	379
I AM a stranger here below	424
I asked the Lord that I might grow	416
If God is mine then present things	288
If I must sing, I'll sing of grace	173
If thou, dear Jesus, art my Lord	502
If to Jesus for relief	200
I know that my Redeemer lives	578
I love the Lord, he heard my cries	397
I love the sons of grace	216
I love the windows of thy grace	408
I love thy kingdom, Lord	586
I love to steal awhile away	563
I'm in a world of hopes and fears	189
I'm not ashamed to own my Lord	279
In all my Lord's appointed ways	469
In all my troubles and distress	399
In all the acts of sovereign grace	165
Indulgent God, to thee I raise	164
In heaven my choicest treasure lies	327
In hope of life eternal given	519
In my sorrow I cried unto God with my	569
In seasons of grief to my God I'll repair	605
In Sharon's lovely rose	122
In songs of sublime adoration and praise	180
In thee, O Lord, I trust	577
Into thine hand, O God of truth	398
In union with the Lamb	68
In vain the sealed cave	147
Is there ambition in my heart	250
I think of thee, my God, by night	564
I thirst, but not as once I did	401
It is not death to die	555
It shall be well, let Zion know	320
I waited patient for the Lord	449
I would but cannot sing	423
I would not live alway	571
I will praise thee every day	385
JEHOVAH is our shepherd's name	117
Jerusalem, my happy home	601
Jesus, and shall it ever be	283
Jesus, at thy command	432
Jesus, before thy face I fall	251
Jesus, behold thy children here	465
Jesus, by heavenly hosts adored	505
Jesus commands his saints	476
Jesus draws the chosen race	440
Jesus heals the broken-hearted	108
Jesus, I love thy charming name	112
Jesus is gone above the skies	479
Jesus, I sing thy wondrous grace	113
Jesus is our great salvation	584
Jesus is precious, saith the Word	252
Jesus, Lord, we look to thee	241
Jesus, lover of my soul	436
Jesus, merciful and mild	597
Jesus, my all, to heaven is gone	125

HYMN.	
Jesus, my Lord, how rich thy grace	238
Jesus, my love, my chief delight	118
Jesus, O name divinely sweet	486
Jesus, our soul's delightful choice	194
Jesus, source of our salvation	244
Jesus, the glorious head of grace	293
Jesus, the great, the mighty God	258
Jesus, the spring of joys divine	121
Jesus, the very thought of thee	614
Jesus, thou great exalted King	507
Jesus, thy blood and righteousness	92
Jesus, thy boundless love to me	250
Jesus, while our hearts are bleeding	269
Joy is a fruit that will not grow	274
Joy to the world, the Lord is come	52
KEEP silence, all created things	8
Kind are the words that Jesus speaks	287
Kindred in Christ, for his dear sake	354
LAMB of God, we fall before thee	243
Let all our tongues be one	475
Let me but hear my Saviour say	282
Let me, thou sovereign Lord of all	294
Let others boast how strong they be	30
Let others boast their ancient line	616
Let the little children come	599
Let those who inhabit the Rock	322
Let thy kingdom, blessed Saviour	342
Let us love, and sing, and wonder	153
Let worldly minds the world pursue	203
Let Zion and her sons rejoice	346
Let Zion in her songs record	451
Light of those whose dreary dwelling	107
Lo! what a glorious sight appears	56
Lo! what an entertaining sight	231
Lord, at thy table I behold	488
Lord, didst thou die, but not for me	284
Lord, dismiss us with thy blessing	500
Lord, fill thy servant's heart to-day	490
Lord, forever at thy side	326
Lord, help us on thy word to feed	498
Lord, how many are my foes	317
Lord, I am thine, but thou wilt prove	404
Lord, I believe; thy power I own	611
Lord, I cannot let thee go	363
Lord, let me see thy beauteous face	370
Lord, unto whom should sinners go	576
Lord, we adore thy vast designs	27
Lord, we are blind, we mortals, blind	5
Lord, what is man, poor feeble man	510
Lord, when my thoughts with wonder roll	145
Lord, when thou didst ascend on high	154
Lord, with a grieved and aching heart	208
Loud let the tuneful trumpet sound	34
Love is the fountain whence	247
MAY the grace of Christ, the Saviour	501
Meekly in Jordan's swelling stream	467
'Mid scenes of confusion and creature	596
My business lies at wisdom's gate	368
My Captain sounds the alarm of war	412

INDEX OF FIRST LINES.

First Line	HYMN
My dearest friends in bonds of love	335
My Father, cheering name	627
My gracious Redeemer I love	230
My God, in whom are all the springs	25
My God, my Father, blissful name	267
My God, my keeper, thou dost never	618
My God, my portion, and my love	411
My God, the spring of all my joys	406
My God, what endless pleasures dwell	348
My God, what silken cords are thine	184
My never-ceasing song shall show	13
My Saviour, let me hear thy voice	88
My Shepherd will supply my need	115
My soul, come meditate the day	530
My soul lies cleaving to the dust	419
My soul, repeat his praise	19
My soul, take courage from the Lord	360
My soul, this curious house of clay	541
My soul, with joy attend	22
My spirit looks to God alone	285
My time of sorrow and of joy	263
NEARER, my God, to thee	609
No, I'll repine at death no more	521
No more, my God, I boast no more	281
Nor eye hath seen, nor ear hath heard	134
Not unto us, but thee alone	497
Now be my heart inspired to sing	141
Now, dearest Lord, to praise thy name	110
Now for a theme of thankful praise	149
Now let our cheerful eyes survey	133
Now let our souls on wings sublime	518
Now let the Lord, my Saviour, smile	403
Now let us raise our cheerful strains	157
Now, Lord, inspire the preacher's heart	375
Now, Lord, thy saving power display	493
Now may the Lord reveal his face	168
Now to the power of God supreme	162
Now to thy praise, Eternal King	418
O BLESS the Lord, my soul	18
O Christ, he is the Fountain	589
O come, let us sing to the Lord	140
O could I speak the matchless worth	395
Of all the gifts thine hand bestows	192
Of God's great love ere time began	77
O for a closer walk with God	560
O for a glance of heavenly day	415
O for a heart to praise my God	561
O for a heart to seek my God	295
O for a thousand tongues to sing	390
O God, my sun, thy blissful rays	222
O God of love, how infinite and holy	617
O God of mercy hear my call	211
O happy day when saints shall meet	336
O happy souls who safely passed	532
O happy time long waited for	621
Oh, could I find some peaceful bower	255
O how happy are they	278
O how melodious was that voice	567
Oh, that I knew the secret place	562
Oh, that my soul as heretofore	456

First Line	HYMN
O land of rest for thee I sigh	333
O Lord, how lovely is thy name	448
O Lord, how vile am I	256
O Lord, I would delight in thee	226
O Lord, my best desires fulfill	261
O Lord, our heavenly King	20
O Love Divine, how sweet thou art	242
O my distrustful heart	79
O my soul, what means this sadness	225
Once more we come before our God	489
One there is above all others	619
One thing with all my soul's desire	373
On Jordan's stormy banks I stand	548
On Sion, his most holy mount	32
On the mountain's top appearing	224
On Zion's glorious summit stood	433
On Zion's sacred mount I saw	91
O that the Lord would guide my ways	443
O the delights, the heavenly joys	557
O the power of love divine	620
O thou in whose presence my soul takes	393
Our days, alas, our mortal days	513
Our God, how firm his promise stands	309
Our Jesus is the Christian's hope	215
Our Lord is risen from the dead	156
Our sins, alas! how strong they be	565
Our spirits join to adore the Lamb	483
Out of the depths of woe	437
O what a sad and doleful night	142
O when shall I see Jesus	588
O where shall rest be found	587
O Zion afflicted with wave upon wave	94
PEACE by his cross hath Jesus made	99
Pensive, doubting, fearful heart	300
People of the living God	441
Permit me, Lord, to seek thy face	234
Pilgrims we are, and heavenward bound	413
Plunged in a gulf of dark despair	100
Poor, weak, and worthless though I am	95
Praise God from whom all blessings flow	495
Prayer is the saints sincere desire	566
Prepare a thankful song	388
Prepare me, gracious God	534
QUIET, Lord, my froward heart	127
RAISE your triumphant song	30
Regard, great God, my mournful prayer	361
Rejoice, believer, in the Lord	63
Rejoice, the Lord is King	137
Rejoice, the Saviour reigns	138
Rise, my soul, and stretch thy wings	594
Rock of Ages, cleft for me	126
SAINTS, at your heavenly Father's word	297
Salvation! O melodious sound	166
Salvation! O the joyful sound	160
Salvation! what a glorious plan	167
Saviour, visit thy plantation	380
See a poor sinner, gracious Lord	254
Servant of God, well done	595

… INDEX OF FIRST LINES. 267

First Line	Hymn
Shepherds, rejoice! lift up your eyes	50
Show pity, Lord, O Lord, forgive	206
Sin enslaved me many years	201
Sing to the Lord, ye distant lands	53
So let our lips and lives express	459
Sometimes a light surprises	275
Songs of praise the angels sang	625
Sons of God by blessed adoption	539
Sons we are through God's election	82
Sovereign Ruler of the skies	83
Sprinkled with reconciling blood	362
Stand up, my soul, shake off thy fears	323
Submission to thy will, my God	265
Sweet is the memory of thy grace	12
Sweet is the work, my God, my King	331
Sweet was the time when first I felt	447
Teach me the measure of my days	515
Tell me no more of earthly toys	205
The billows swell, the waves are high	298
The church of God is fair	355
The cross of Christ inspires my heart	487
The day is past and gone	509
The glorious gospel of our God	43
The good old way that leads to God	124
The gospel brings tidings to each wounded	48
The hope set before us	312
The King of saints his table spreads	481
The Lamb is exalted repentance to give	311
The law by Moses came	38
The Lord, how wondrous are his ways	3
The Lord is on our side	439
The Lord my Shepherd is	123
The Lord of glory is my light	344
The Lord proclaims his name	624
The Lord, the Sovereign King	21
The Lord will happiness divine	211
The mighty God will not despise	581
The moon gives but a borrowed light	136
There is fountain filled with blood	90
There is a friend that sticketh fast	67
There is a house not made with hands	526
There is a land mine eye hath seen	545
There is a land of pure delight	522
There is an honr of peaceful rest	454
There is a period known to God	76
There is a place of hallowed peace	550
There is a world of perfect bliss	554
The saints Emmanuel's portion are	491
The saints should never be dismayed	191
The Saviour calls his people sheep	117
The Saviour! O what endless charms	114
The sinner that truly believes	198
The sinner who, by precious faith	558
The Spirit breathes upon the word	135
The spirits of the just	537
The table now is spread	477
The true Messiah now appears	57
This world is poor, from shore to shore	453
This God is the God we adore	499
Thou dear Redeemer, dying Lamb	102
Thou fountain of bliss, thy smile I entreat	197

First Line	Hymn
Thou great incarnate God	474
Thou lovely source of true delight	237
Thou only Sovereign of my heart	434
Through all the downward tracks of time	266
Through all the various shifting scenes	24
Thus far my God hath led me on	572
Thus far the Lord hath led me on	574
Thus was the great Redeemer plunged	466
Thy mercy, Lord, we praise	387
Thy mercy, my God, is the theme of my	49
Thy names, how infinite they be	11
Thy way, O God, is in the sea	410
Thy ways, O Lord, with wise design	23
Time is winging us away	593
Time, what an empty vapor 'tis	512
'Tis a point I long to know	430
'Tis by the faith of joys to come	193
'Tis finished! so the Saviour cried	98
'Tis hard, when we are sick and poor	268
'Tis midnight! and on Olive's brow	146
'Tis Jesus I sing, and salvation by grace	181
'Tis my happiness below	429
'Tis religion that can give	276
'Tis the gospel's joyful tidings	45
'Tis to his spouse that Jesus speaks	304
'Tis winter in my soul, my sin	612
To all eternity our Priest	132
To Christ the Lord, let every tongue	610
To God, the only wise	359
To thee, my Shepherd and my Lord	240
'Twas in the night when troubles came	446
'Twas on that dark, that doleful night	478
'Twas when the sea with horrid roar	319
'Twas with an everlasting love	62
'Twixt Jesus and the chosen race	60
Vain are the hopes the sons of men	104
Wait, my soul, upon the Lord	299
Wait, O my soul, thy Maker's will	4
Watchman, tell us of the night	582
We are a garden walled around	249
Welcome, sweet day of rest	148
We seek a rest beyond the skies	217
We travel through a barren land	221
What cheering words are these	71
What hath God wrought might Israel say	396
What jarring natures dwell within	455
What poor, despised company	471
What shall I render to my God	345
What think ye of Christ? is the test	141
What wisdom, majesty and grace	129
What wondrous love is this	664
When darkness long has veiled my mind	301
When from the precepts to the cross	450
When gathering clouds around I view	603
When God from sin's captivity	435
When God proclaims his name	623
When God revealed his precious name	202
When I can read my title clear	409
When in the clouds with colors fair	87
When I survey the wondrous cross	480

INDEX OF FIRST LINES.

	HYMN.		HYMN
When Jesus, with his matchless love	227	Why should a son, redeemed with blood	426
When languor and disease invade	531	Why should our mourning thoughts	540
When marshalled on the nightly plain	457	Why should the children of a King	182
When overwhelmed with doubts and fears	119	Why should the saints be filled with dread	61
When overwhelmed with grief	378	Why should we shrink at death's cold	527
When saint to saint, in days of old	349	Why should we start and fear to die	517
When shall all my sorrows end	442	Why sinks my weak, desponding mind	223
When shall we all meet again	338	With Christ in God our life is hid	324
When sins and fears prevailing rise	120	With earnest longings of the mind	260
When storms and tempests loudly howl	292	With eyes of faith and wings of love	239
When the Queen of the south heard of	570	With joy let each afflicted saint	291
When the storm in its fury on Galilee	607	With joy we meditate the grace	130
When thou, my righteous Judge shall	452	With melting heart and weeping eyes	207
When Zion's sons, great God, appear	494	With transport, Lord, thy saints proclaim	546
Where must a weary sinner go	332	With what delight faith lifts her eyes	547
Wherewith, O Lord, shall I draw near	163		
While in the vale of vision dead	42	Ye humble souls, approach your God	9
While shepherds watched their flocks by	58	Ye humble souls, complain no more	253
While sorrows encompass me round	536	Ye humble souls, rejoice	257
While winter's gloom was o'er me spread	613	Ye little flock, whom Jesus feeds	175
Whilst thee I seek, protecting Power	374	Ye pilgrims of Zion and chosen of God	591
Whither goest thou, pilgrim stranger	583	Yes, I shall soon be landed	543
Who is this trembling sinner? who	303	Ye trembling souls, dismiss your fears	320
Who shall the Lord's elect condemn	73	Yonder amazing sight I see	143
Why do we mourn departing friends	525	Your harps, ye trembling saints	314
Why is my heart so far from thee	417		
Why, mourning souls, why flow these	458		
Why, O my soul, why weepest thou	213	Zion's a city God hath blessed	356

www.ingramcontent.com/pod-product-compliance
Lightning Source LLC
Chambersburg PA
CBHW031950230426
43672CB00010B/2110